Lecture Notes in Computer Science 11841

More information about this series at http://www.springer.com/series/7409

Michael A. Herzog · Zuzana Kubincová ·
Peng Han · Marco Temperini (Eds.)

Advances in Web-Based Learning – ICWL 2019

18th International Conference
Magdeburg, Germany, September 23–25, 2019
Proceedings

Springer

Editors
Michael A. Herzog
Magdeburg-Stendal University of Applied Sciences
Magdeburg, Germany

Zuzana Kubincová
Comenius University in Bratislava
Bratislava, Slovakia

Peng Han
Chongqing Academy of Science and Technology
Chongqing, China

Marco Temperini
Sapienza University
Rome, Italy

ISSN 0302-9743 ISSN 1611-3349 (electronic)
Lecture Notes in Computer Science
ISBN 978-3-030-35757-3 ISBN 978-3-030-35758-0 (eBook)
https://doi.org/10.1007/978-3-030-35758-0

LNCS Sublibrary: SL3 – Information Systems and Applications, incl. Internet/Web, and HCI

This Springer imprint is published by the registered company Springer Nature Switzerland AG
The registered company address is: Gewerbestrasse 11, 6330 Cham, Switzerland

Preface

This volume presents the contributions of the 18th edition of the annual International Conference on Web-based Learning (ICWL). The first edition of ICWL was held in Hong Kong in 2002. Since then, it has been held 16 more times, on 3 continents: Australia (2003), China (2004, 2008, 2010), Hong Kong (2005, 2011, 2015), Malaysia (2006), UK (2007), Germany (2009), Romania (2012), Taiwan (2013), Estonia (2014), Italy (2016), South Africa (2017), and Thailand (2018).

In 2019, ICWL was organized by the Magdeburg-Stendal University of Applied Sciences. The first courses at the university started back in 1991. Within a short time, this place of research, teaching, and learning gained an outstanding reputation, not only for its well-rounded academic education program but also for the motivated student body. The university offers a diverse range of around 50 study programs, including unique opportunities that cannot be found anywhere else. Being divided into two campuses – one campus in Magdeburg and another one in Stendal – the university and students get the chance to interact in highly focused departments. Three departments are located at the Herrenkrug Campus in Magdeburg with approximately 4,000 students, and another two departments are situated in Stendal with about 2,000 students. Both campuses are well known for their beautiful green grounds, which create an inviting ambiance.

The topics proposed in the ICWL Call for Papers included several relevant issues, ranging from Semantic Web for E-Learning, through Learning Analytics, Computer-Supported Collaborative Learning, Assessment, Pedagogical Issues, E-learning Platforms, and Tools, to Mobile Learning.

We received 68 submitted contributions. Three contributions were withdrawn at an early stage. Six submissions were not sufficiently completed to go further in the review process. All of the submitted papers were assigned to three members of the Program Committee (PC) for double-blind peer review. All reviews were checked and discussed by the PC chairs, and additional reviews or meta-reviews were elicited if necessary.

Finally, we accepted 15 full papers, with an acceptance rate of 25%. We also included additional contributions as short papers (15) and poster papers (7) in the proceedings.

ICWL 2019 featured two distinguished keynote presentations, by renowned scholars: Irwin King, (Chinese University of Hong Kong, Hong Kong, China) on "Machine Learning for Online Education" and Sabine Graf (Athabasca University, Canada) on "Academic Analytics – Analysis and Mining of Educational Data to Support Teaching."

Furthermore, the conference continued the traditional initiative, started by ICWL 2016, of holding the 4th International Symposium on Emerging Technologies for Education (SETE) at the same location. SETE collected the traditional workshop activities managed by ICWL in the past years and additionally featured an organization in tracks. Workshops and tracks added new and hot topics on technology-enhanced learning, providing a better overall conference experience to the ICWL and SETE attendees.

Many contributions made the conference possible and successful. First of all, we would like to thank all the authors who considered ICWL for their submission. We thank the PC members, and the additional reviewers, for their evaluations, which made the selection of the accepted papers possible. Additional thanks go to the publicity chair Ivana Marenzi.

For the organization, the hosting SPiRIT research group under the direction of Michael A. Herzog served in multiple functions: local organization chairs Veronika Weiß and Leonore Franz, and Veronika Weiß, also as web chair. Their strong and continuous commitment made it a remarkable conference event with excellent design, smooth orientation, personal service, and warm hospitality. We also thank all the other members of the SPiRIT team for their excellent work and engagement: the student volunteers Oliver Friedl, Swantje van de Ven, Max O'Dell, Simon Gustavs, Anika Fuchs, Jan Sprigade, Merle Fabry, Amelie Ries, Janet Ahlers, Joe Einicke, Simon Krebs, and the scientists Elke Mählitz-Galler, Victoria Batz, and Klaus Magarin. In particular, we thank the president of Magdeburg-Stendal University Anne Lequy on behalf of the hosting institution for the excellent support of the ICWL 2019 conference edition.

We also thank the sponsor Springer, for the enlightened and much appreciated support that helped to dedicate the Best Paper Awards.

We hope that the reader of this volume will be pleased by the relevance of the topics and contents of the papers, and thus be enticed to contribute to the next editions of ICWL.

September 2019

Michael A. Herzog
Zuzana Kubincová
Peng Han
Marco Temperini

Organization

Conference Co-chairs

Michael A. Herzog	Magdeburg-Stendal University of Applied Sciences, Germany
Han Peng	Chongqing Academy of Science and Technology, China

Technical Program Committee Co-chairs

Zuzana Kubincová	Comenius University in Bratislava, Slovakia
Marco Temperini	Sapienza Università di Roma, Italy

Steering Committee Representatives

Ralf Klamma	RWTH Aachen University, Germany
Qing Li	The Hong Kong Polytechnic University, Hong Kong, China

Web Chair

Veronika Weiß	Magdeburg-Stendal University of Applied Sciences, Germany

Publicity Chair

Ivana Marenzi	Leibniz Universität, Hannover, Germany

Local Organization Chairs

Leonore Franz	Magdeburg-Stendal University of Applied Sciences, Germany
Veronika Weiß	Magdeburg-Stendal University of Applied Sciences, Germany

Program Committee

Marie-Helene Abel	HEUDIASYC, Université de Technologie de Compiègne, France
Dimitra Anastasiou	Luxembourg Institute of Science and Technology, Luxembourg
Maria Bielikova	Slovak University of Technology, Bratislava, Slovakia
Adriana Botha	University of Pretoria, South Africa
Maiga Chang	Athabasca University, Canada
Wei Chen	Chinese Academy of Agricultural Sciences, China
Dickson K. W. Chiu	The University of Hong Kong, Hong Kong, China
Maria-Iuliana Dascalu	Politehnica University of Bucharest, Romania
Maria De Marsico	Sapienza Università di Roma, Italy
Giuliana Dettori	CNR, Istituto di Tecnologie Didattiche, Italy
Tania Di Mascio	University of L'Aquila, Italy
Damiano Distante	Università degli Studi di Roma Unitelma Sapienza, Italy
Giovanni Fulantelli	National Research Council of Italy, Italy
Ed Gehringer	North Carolina State University, USA
Rosella Gennari	Free U. of Bozen-Bolzano, Italy
Denis Gillet	Swiss Federal Institute of Technology in Lausanne (EPFL), Switzerland
Sabine Graf	Athabasca University, Canada
Christian Gütl	Graz University of Technology, Austria
Preben Hansen	Stockholm University, Sweden
Tianyong Hao	South China Normal University, China
Andreas Harrer	University of Applied Sciences and Arts Dortmund, Germany
Eelco Herder	Radboud University, The Netherlands
Michael A. Herzog	Magdeburg-Stendal University of Applied Sciences, Germany
Mirjana Ivanovic	University of Novi Sad, Serbia
Elisabeth Katzlinger	Johannes Kepler Universität Linz, Austria
Ioannis Kazanidis	Eastern Macedonia and Thrace Institute of Technology, Greece
Michael Kickmeier-Rust	Graz University of Technology, Austria
Ralf Klamma	RWTH Aachen University, Germany
Tomaž Klobučar	Jozef Stefan Institute, Slovenia
Line Kolås	Nord University, Norway
Milos Kravcik	DFKI GmbH, Germany
Zuzana Kubincová	Comenius University, Bratislava, Slovakia
Amruth Kumar	Ramapo College of New Jersey, USA
Mart Laanpere	Tallinn University, Estonia
Luigi Laura	Sapienza Università di Roma, Italy
Elise Lavoué	LIRIS, Université Jean Moulin Lyon 3, France
Howard Leung	City University of Hong Kong, Hong Kong, China

Frederick Li	University of Durham, UK
Carla Limongelli	Università Roma Tre, Italy
Matteo Lombardi	Griffith University, Australia
George Magoulas	University of London, UK
Katherine Maillet	Institut Mines-Télécom, Télécom Ecole de Management, France
Ivana Marenzi	L3S Research Center, Germany
Alke Martens	University of Rostock, Germany
Harald Mayer	Joanneum Research, Austria
Tanja Mitrovic	Intelligent Computer Tutoring Group, University of Canterbury, Christchurch, New Zealand
Wolfgang Mueller	University of Education Weingarten, Germany
Umberto Nanni	Sapienza Università di Roma, Italy
Wolfgang Nejdl	L3S and University of Hannover, Germany
Kyparissia Papanikolaou	School of Pedagogical and Technological Education, Greece
Kai Pata	Tallinn University, Estonia
Elvira Popescu	University of Craiova, Romania
Francesca Pozzi	CNR, Istituto Tecnologie Didattiche, Italy
Hans Põldoja	Tallinn University, Estonia
Marco Ronchetti	University of Trento, Italy
Vasile Rus	The University of Memphis, USA
Marián Šimko	Slovak University of Technology, Bratislava, Slovakia
Demetrios Sampson	Curtin University, Australia
Olga C. Santos	aDeNu Research Group, UNED, Spain
Flippo Sciarrone	Open Informatica, Italy
Marcus Specht	Delft University of Technology and Open University of the Netherlands, The Netherlands
Andrea Sterbini	Sapienza Università di Roma, Italy
Davide Taibi	Italian National Research Council, Italy
Marco Temperini	Sapienza Università di Roma, Italy
Lorna Uden	Staffordshire University, UK
Carlos Vaz de Carvalho	GILT, College of Engineering (ISEP), Portugal
Pierpaolo Vittorini	University of L'Aquila, Italy
Riina Vuorikari	Institute for Prospective Technological Studies, Spain
Philips Fu Lee Wang	The Open University of Hong Kong, Hong Kong, China
Veronika Weiß	Magdeburg-Stendal University of Applied Sciences, Germany
Michal Winczer	Comenius University in Bratislava, Slovakia
Tak-Lam Wong	Douglas College, Canada
Charoenchai Wongwatkit	Mae Fah Luang University, Thailand
Zhenguo Yang	City University of Hong Kong, Hong Kong, China
Sergej Zerr	L3S Research Center, Germany
Yunhui Zhuang	City University of Hong Kong, Hong Kong, China
Di Zou	The Education University of Hong Kong, Hong Kong, China

Additional Reviewers

Anwar, Muhammad
Bernard, Jason
Ez-Zaouia, Mohamed
Hallifax, Stuart
Khuhro, Sarmast
Prenkaj, Bardh
Shaltev, Miroslav
Stabauer, Martin
Vlasov, Roman
Zhang, Ruofei

Contents

E-learning Platforms and Tools

Mobile Learning

Semantic Web for E-learning

Timing the Adaptive Learning Process with Events Ontology

Martin Homola(✉), Ján Kl'uka, Zuzana Kubincová, Patrícia Marmanová, and Milan Cifra

Faculty of Mathematics, Physics, and Informatics, Comenius University in Bratislava, Mlynská dolina, 842 48 Bratislava, Slovakia
{martin.homola,jan.kluka,zuzana.kubincova, patricia.marmanova,milan.cifra}@uniba.sk

Abstract. A number of studies in personalized adaptive learning have focused on generating suitable learning paths based on user's model, considering the current level of knowledge of the user, preferred learning styles and a model of the subject domain. These factors are sufficient in many e-learning applications, where users consume the learning content at their own pace. In other applications, such as within organized curricula there are other factors to be considered too. At the university, we deliver courses featuring project work and examination which the students have to deliver based on a schedule of deadlines. This time axis, therefore, presents a significant factor in recommending the most suitable learning objects at the given time of the term. To tackle this issue we have designed a courseware platform where time is one of the key factors determining the learner's context. In this paper, we focus especially on modelling the time access using an ontology and we show some preliminary results that are implied by this approach.

Keywords: Courseware · Personalization · Leaner's context · Time · Ontology

1 Introduction

The aim of personalized adaptive learning is to provide a tailored learning experience for each user according to their own needs. For example, recommender systems may be employed to help users to choose the most suitable and relevant learning materials that meet their individual learning needs [20,26]. Many of the existing e-learning recommender systems rely on techniques such as collaborative filtering, content-based, demographic-based, utility-based, and knowledge-based techniques which basically develop a rating system expressing the recommendation relation between users and the learning content [26].

However, a more current approach in personalized adaptive learning notes the importance to consider the learner's specific demands and requirements more explicitly [17]. Different learners have different background knowledge, learning

M. A. Herzog et al. (Eds.): ICWL 2019, LNCS 11841, pp. 3–14, 2019.
https://doi.org/10.1007/978-3-030-35758-0_1

history, competence level, preferred learning styles, etc. [7] which are not taken into consideration in conventional recommender systems like collaborative filtering and content-based recommenders [26]. This drawback may be overcome by integrating knowledge structures representing complex models of all aspects that are relevant to the learning process. In recent years, ontologies gained importance for representation of such models in e-learning systems.

Ontologies serve as formal definitions of concepts and their relations in some domain of interest of human expertise [11,24,25]. They are crafted with the purpose of making the conceptualization unambiguous and explicit. This goal is best achieved by writing ontologies in a formal and unambiguous language that supports reasoning. Currently, the most popular languages include RDFS [5] and OWL [10] (cf. [1,2]). Ontologies can then be used within information systems to provide schemas for data, to assure data interoperability, enable data reuse, etc. [25].

In personalized adaptive learning, ontologies are employed especially to describe (a) the abstract domain of learning objects, their different types and properties, (b) particular domains of topics of interests which are the subject of learning, (c) pedagogical properties of learning processes, (d) user models, including user's existing knowledge, skills, and preferred learning styles.

User's experience may then be tailored based on the available data from these domains, especially by recommending the most suitable learning objects or even generating personalized learning paths, consisting of sequences of learning objects.

While such knowledge structures may be sufficient in many application scenarios of e-learning, especially in self-directed learning, there are other factors relevant in learning processes. *Context*, i.e., "the circumstances in which the learning process occurs" becomes relevant as well [3]. While many earlier works stemming from adaptive hypermedia mostly explore context in the form of platform and device adaptation issues, a broader and more general sense of context is becoming increasingly relevant in this area [6].

In this work, we focus on the user's context within an organized education setting. There are possibly different contextual issues to be considered. We narrow our aim towards the temporal context imposed by the courses being scheduled in form of a series of events such as lectures and lab sessions occurring during a fixed time period framed by school years or terms. While lectures and lab sessions may often be scheduled equally for all course attendants and hence may not require personalization, other events such as assignments and examination sessions may be, e.g., subscription-based and hence different students may have different schedules. In addition, even if some events, such as lectures, are fixed, it is useful to include and consider them in the overall personalization framework uniformly together with the other events and other personalization aspects.

We start by a brief review of related works in Sect. 2. Then in Sect. 3 we focus on the organized education setting and discuss how learning content adaptation in such a setting must consider also the past or upcoming events, e.g., by considering learning materials associated with current lectures or labs, or recommended w.r.t. upcoming coursework deadlines and examination dates. In Sect. 4, we present our proposed LMS platform that is based on multiple ontologies, including a time-frame ontology, which we focus on in detail in Sect. 5. In Sect. 6 we discuss how users of our platform would benefit from this approach: as our very first result, we show how tracking the course of events during a course run using the time-frame ontology enables us to present the learning content in concise timeline automatically generated from the time-related metadata associated with the remaining content. We then conclude and discuss future possibilities in Sect. 7.

2 Related Works

While most of the studies addressing the recommendation of learning resources and personalization in e-learning environments using ontologies make only use of domain ontology [18,21] there were also ontology-based recommenders developed using more domain ontologies or other types of ontology [4,8,27].

Cobos et al. [8] developed an ontology-based hybrid recommender system (RSPP) which allows lecturers to define their best teaching strategies for use in the context of a specific class. To construct the RSPP, a reference ontology representing the pedagogical patterns and their interaction with the fundamentals of the educational process was defined.

Bahmani [4] presents a recommendation algorithm for personalization of course and curriculum content for individual students considering various kinds of context such as the academic background, interests, computing environment of the student, and also past recommendations made to students with similar profiles. Context modelling is based on a combination of a generic and a domain ontology.

The Protus tutoring system for Java programming [27] automatically guides the learner's activities and recommends relevant links and actions. It provides (a) content adaptation – recommending optimal resources and pathways based on the domain model and information about learning styles of the current learner; and (b) learner interface adaptation – adjusting the appearance and/or availability of learning resources on a course web page based on recommendations respective to different learners. Each system component is represented by its own ontology, thus domain ontology, task ontology, learner model ontology, teaching strategies ontology and interface ontology are incorporated.

Saleena and Srivatsa [22] propose an adaptive e-Learning system, which generates user-specific e-Learning content by comparing the concepts using similarity measures. A cross ontology measure is defined over a fuzzy domain ontology as the primary ontology and a domain ontology as the secondary ontology for the comparison process.

Yu et al. [28] make recommendations by exploiting the user context of a learner, knowledge about learning content, and knowledge about the learning domain. They consider two kinds of contexts: the learner's prior knowledge and her learning goal. They rely on three ontologies: learner ontology, learning content ontology, and domain ontology.

Schmidt and Winterhalter [23] present an integrative, ontology-based approach in which the ontology is divided into several sub-ontologies, such as: organizational ontology (roles, departments); process ontology (workflow representations); task ontology; knowledge area ontology. Each is organized in layers so that the upper layers can be shared with other entities and the lower layers can still be extended in a domain-specific way. This enables them to propose recommendations w.r.t. learner's context which is described (at a general level) in terms of organizational structure, the current task at hand and given workflow that is being followed, etc.

Jovanović et al. [16] introduced Learning Object Context – a collection of LO metadata capturing all the information that characterizes the specific situations (contexts) in which certain LO has been used. They also developed a corresponding ontology framework (LOCO) consisting of (a) learning object content structure ontology, (b) learning design ontology, and (c) learning object context ontology. The proposed framework was implemented in TANGRAM, a Web-based application for personalized learning in the area of Intelligent information systems.

The granularity of recommended learning objects varies, including courses and curricula [4], learning patterns [8], relevant learning links and actions [27], learning paths and content [15], various types of learning objects, etc.

3 The Organized Education Setting

Unlike many existing works reviewed above, we aim to apply adaptive learning in organized university education where other factors besides for those typically studied determine the learner's context.

The content of a typical university course is delivered in the form of learning sessions such as lectures or practicals that happen in precise points of time, typically within a regular sequence. However, the sessions may possibly be grouped either based on time intervals, such as weeks, or either based on related topics.

Besides learning sessions, there are other relevant events that the learners need to track and take part in, especially related to coursework and examination.

Modern university education often favours the *learning by doing strategy*. Thus learners are required to submit coursework and possibly even take part in formative peer review processes which generate a number of deadlines that they have to watch and prepare for.

Thus the learner's context is not determined only by their current level of knowledge and preferred learning styles, but also by current time instance in the course of events generated by the current development of the course.

As an example let us consider a Master's level web design course delivered at our university. In this course, the students work in teams on a term-long project assignment. The assignment is delivered in four consecutive rounds (specification, prototype, application, content) which are preceded by team formation phase. In each round, the learners first deliver an *initial submission*. Consecutively they *peer-review* these submissions, and based on the peer-feedback they deliver an *improved submission*, which is then graded by course instructors. Finally, learners rate the teamwork within their teams during the *team review* period. Together with midterm and final test, and the oral exam, learners have to track and deliver results respective to 20 consecutive deadlines. For more details on these assignment workflows please refer to our previous works [13, 14].

Our past experience shows that tracking all the deadlines is challenging for the students. Some of them deliver poor results simply because they missed some deadlines or did not prepare properly ahead of the deadlines. Therefore we are determined to explore the options not only to be able to notify the learner before the approaching deadline but also to be able to recommend the most suitable learning materials to prepare for the coming deadlines.

4 Proposed LMS Design Overview

We are currently developing a novel LMS system that will pay increased attention to learner's context. It consists of several modules centred around the system's core. The overall design is depicted in Fig. 1. The *core* manages common data and provides common services and user interface (UI) components. These include components presenting the users with a unified view of some of the data managed by other modules. A module typically manages a specific kind of learning objects or tasks and provides UI components to display the data and control the management. Data of one module can be interlinked with data of other modules and a module can embed another one's UI components into its own to manage the linked data.

In particular, the *Assignments* module manages the kind of peer-reviewed assignments described above in Sect. 3. Instructors can specify an assignment's task and which deliverables of various kinds (text, programming code, media, links) the learners are expected to submit. They also choose which follow-up tasks (peer review, improved submission, team review) the learners will perform after their initial submission and set their parameters (e.g., time periods, review rubrics). The module then enables the learners to submit the deliverables and fill in the assigned reviews. The instructors can see all the artefacts thus produced, provide feedback, and evaluate.

The *Quizzes* module supports learning by formulating questions and administration of quizzes and tests. The instructors can task the students with formulating questions of various kinds (open, simple answer, single choice, etc.) covering given topics. Instructors can also create questions, and task the learners with taking a quiz, manually or automatically created from already existing questions.

The *Documents* module manages internal and external documents and multimedia, used chiefly as learning materials, but also as assignment specifications and deliverables submitted by learners. The *Results* module manages evaluation results, awarded to learners by the instructors for learning tasks carried out both within the LMS or externally. In the former case, the result is linked with the respective task.

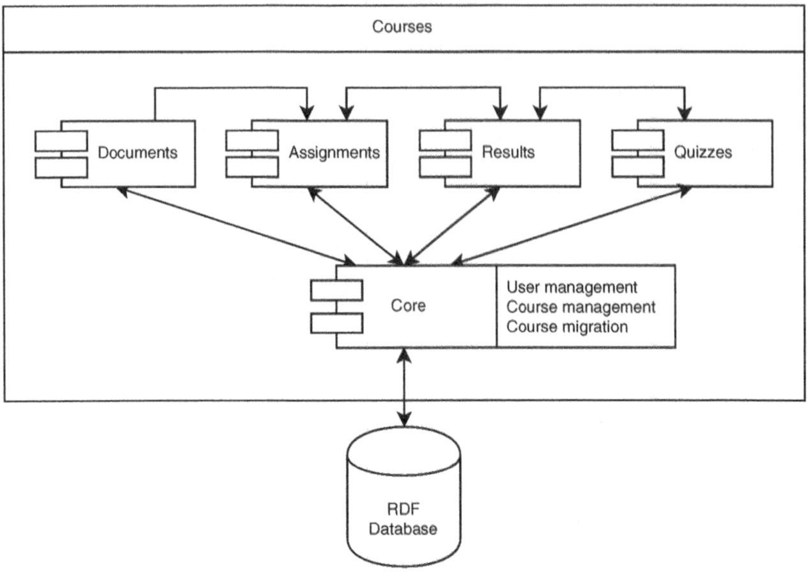

Fig. 1. System design overview

5 The Time-Frame Ontology

The LMS aims at contextual support of the learners' work during learning activities and their access to relevant learning objects. There are also secondary goals such as easy reuse of data among the modules and the core. Storing the data in an RDF database, with a system of interrelated OWL ontologies as its schema, is especially useful to achieve these goals, which is also apparent from the related work. In addition to usual ontologies that model learning objects and processes, and domain ontologies that model the topics which represent the subjects of learner's studies, we also integrate an ontology that covers the *time frame* of the learning activities. As noted in Sect. 3, time is an important component of learner's context in organized university education.

The time-frame ontology is depicted in Fig. 2 in a modified VOWL notation [19]. The classes in this ontology (solid-line ovals) are subclasses of the *Event* class and they represent the time frame of various learning activities (represented by classes depicted by dotted-line ovals, as they are external to the time-frame ontology).

A *CourseInstance*, a particular run of the course in an academic year or semester, is itself an Event. The time frames of all activities within this instance

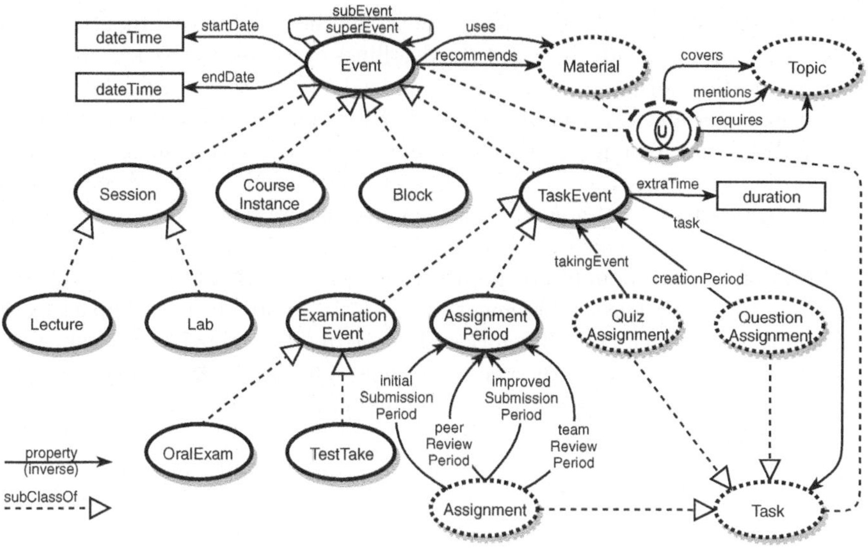

Fig. 2. Time-frame ontology

are its *subEvents*.[1] Time-based groups of activities are represented as *Blocks*. In the academic setting, one week is usually considered to be one block, but it is up to instructors to set up these blocks. A block may, e.g., span several consecutive weeks devoted to the study of one topic.

Blocks typically contain *Sessions* – classroom activities involving face-to-face interaction of instructors and students. Sessions are usually regularly scheduled and specialized to lectures and labs, which are represented by the respective subclasses of Session.

Activities which require learners to complete some task either within a longer time frame or only once or a few times during a course instance are modelled as *TaskEvents*. Examples of the latter kind are *ExaminationEvents* – midterm and final tests or oral examinations. The former kind has three special cases related via the property *task* to a learning activity (*Task*) administered by the Assignments and Quizzes modules. We discuss these three kinds of events in the next two paragraphs.

The learners' work on an *Assignment* managed by the Assignments module is coordinated as a sequence of time periods during which initial submission, peer review, improved submission, and team review have to occur. These time periods are represented as instances of the *AssignmentPeriod* class, a subclass

[1] Note the difference between subevent and subclass. The latter stands for a logical relation between two classes, one being more specific than the other (expressed by OWL subClassOf axiom). The former is an aggregative relation between two instances of events of different granularity a lecture happening during a course run (expressed by OWL object properties subEvent and superEvent).

of TaskEvent, related to their Assignment by the respective properties. The *endDates* of these periods represent the deadlines of the respective sub-activities.

The question formulation activity managed by the Quizzes module task is represented as a *QuizQuestionAssignment*. The value of its property *creationPeriod*, a TaskEvent instance, represents the time period within which it should be carried out. When instructors ask learners to take a quiz, a *QuizAssignment* is created, which has a *takingEvent*, another instance of TaskEvent, representing the time span within which the learners should take the quiz.

Tasks often have nominal deadlines which are advertised, but they are not strict because their strict enforcement by the LMS could adversely impact learners having minor technical difficulties. The *extraTime* property of TaskEvents thus allows the instructors to specify for how long the LMS should allow the learners to complete the task past its nominal endDate. We typically set extraTime to 45 min.

An Event, especially a Session, often *uses* some learning materials. A *Material* (also external to the time-frame ontology, thus depicted by a dotted-line oval) represents a hypertext document (e.g., lecture slides, labs exercises) or a multimedia file stored within the LMS or linked from external sources. For some Events, instructors can also *recommend* studying some materials beforehand (reading before a lecture, exercises before a test) or afterwards (reading with more details on a lecture's topic). Moreover, Events, Materials, and Tasks are related to *Topics* from the topics-of-interest (i.e., domain) ontology in several ways. They can *cover* or just *mention* a topic, or they may *require* the knowledge of a topic in order to complete the task or to understand the content discussed during the event or within the material.

Although learning activities are managed by different modules, their time frames are all derived from the Event class. This allows the LMS's core to integrate the data and to produce a unified presentation of the events, their related learning activities and objects, as discussed in Sect. 6. The core can also notify the learners on these events, suggest reviewing learning objects directly related to the event by the uses and recommends properties, or even derive related learning objects and previous or upcoming activities based on Topics related to the event or its activity.

The Event and CourseInstance classes, as well as the startDate, endDate, subEvent, and superEvent properties can be directly mapped to the respective types and properties in the Schema.org vocabulary [12]. Schema.org also specifies other properties (e.g., the *location* of an Event, the *instructor* of a CourseInstance), which may prove useful in the future development of the LMS. The start- and endDates can also be mapped to *Instants* and Events can be associated with *Intervals* of the Time Ontology [9]. However, we do not plan to do so in the time-frame ontology. Events and time intervals are different entities, as time spans of multiple events can be equal to a one time interval. Moreover, the level of detail of modelling temporal entities provided by the Time Ontology is not required, simple data values suffice.

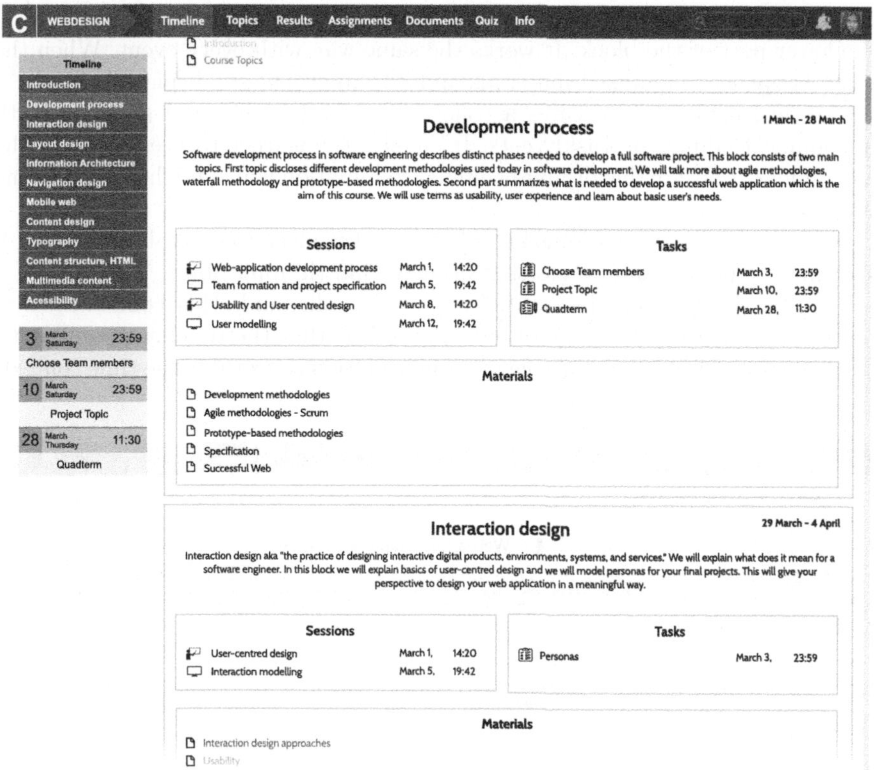

Fig. 3. Prototype of the timeline interface

6 Timeline Interface Generated from the Ontology

Tight integration of the time ontology with the remaining data enables us to visualize the course timeline in an automatically generated timeline interface. A prototype of this interface is depicted in Fig. 3.

The timeline puts all consecutive events in order and visualizes events of different specific types in a specific manner. It is generated from events as follows: All Blocks from the given course are taken and sorted by their startDate. They are displayed as larger boxes wrapping up other events occurring during their timespan. Subsequently, all events of type Session within each block are selected, sorted by their startDate and displayed to the learner as a schedule for the block. Similarly, all TaskEvents that will be due in the given block based on their *deadline* (mostly the endDate, but startDate in the case of ExaminationEvents) are selected, sorted by the deadline, and displayed as a kind of to-do list for the given block. Different types of sessions and tasks are distinguished by different icons. Notice, e.g., the *Development process* block in Fig. 3.

All materials linked to every event falling within the block are displayed in the lower part of the block. It works the same way with every event. When the event is opened, the linked materials and its sub-events are displayed.

Vertical navigation features a concise list of all Blocks and a section with upcoming deadlines of TaskEvents. It enables the learner to keep track of the assignments that are due or an upcoming examination which might require some preparation.

Clicking on an event zooms in and the event is visualized, as shown in Fig. 4, showing the details and events that occur within (if applicable).

Similar timelines can be created in, e.g., Moodle, and other courseware systems, however, the advantage of our approach is that the timeline is automatically generated from the available meta-information concerning the time context.

Fig. 4. Prototype of the zoomed-in lecture event interface

7 Conclusions and Future Work

We have argued that when applied in organized education, adaptive learning systems must also consider the context of the organized learning activity which is above all the time context given by a series of events constituting a typical course run. To that end, we have designed a time-frame ontology and described its role within a proposed LMS platform that we are currently developing. We have shown how interlinking the learning content with time metadata immediately enables to produce an automatically generated timeline, that helps users to orientate in the large pile of learning materials and deadlines associated with the course run *at any given time.*

Of course, using the ontology to keep track of all (even fine-grained) events associated with a course run in a uniformed way would bring many other benefits to our system and to its users. For example, as we explained above applying collaborative learning strategies including team assignments and peer-review of submitted coursework generates a number of deadlines. The previous version of our system used hardcoded notifications to call the students' attention to these deadlines. Modelling the assignments (together with all other events) in the ontology using task-events and their sub-events (such as e.g. initial submission, peer-review period, final submission, team-review period) and even dependencies such as peer-review period being a prerequisite of final submission enables us e.g. to base the notifications on the type of event (a lecture or lab session may be notified one day ahead, the midterm test may be notified three days ahead, and some other events may not be notified at all).

In addition, combining the time-related data based on the time-frame ontology with the other semantic information may be used to provide even more fine-grained and more narrowly directed suggestions regarding the recommended next learning actions. For example, the examination events will also be linked with concepts from domain ontologies representing the topics that the examination will cover. Together with topics linked to materials and other learning objects and together with data about the learners current level of knowledge and preferred learning styles this may be used to produce the recommended learning actions to take before the examination takes place. Exploring this direction is part of our ongoing work.

Acknowledgments. This work was supported from the Slovak national VEGA project no. 1/0797/18 and from APVV grant no. SK-TW-2017-0006.

References

1. Allemang, D., Hendler, J.: Semantic Web for the Working Ontologist: Effective Modeling in RDFS and OWL. Elsevier, Oxford (2011)
2. Antoniou, G., Van Harmelen, F.: A Semantic Web Primer. MIT Press, Cambridge (2004)
3. Aroyo, L., et al.: Interoperability in personalized adaptive learning. J. Educ. Technol. Soc. **9**(2), 4–18 (2006)
4. Bahmani, A., Sedigh, S., Hurson, A.: Ontology-Based Recommendation Algorithms for Personalized Education. In: Liddle, S.W., Schewe, K.-D., Tjoa, A.M., Zhou, X. (eds.) DEXA 2012. LNCS, vol. 7447, pp. 111–120. Springer, Heidelberg (2012). https://doi.org/10.1007/978-3-642-32597-7_10
5. Brickley, D., Guha, R.V. (eds.): RDF Schema 1.1. Recommendation, W3C, 25 February 2014
6. Brusilovsky, P.: From adaptive hypermedia to the adaptive web. In: Szwillus, G., Ziegler, J. (eds.) Mensch & Computer 2003, pp. 21–24. Springer, Heidelberg (2003). https://doi.org/10.1007/978-3-322-80058-9_3
7. Buder, J., Schwind, C.: Learning with personalized recommender systems: a psychological view. Comput. Hum. Behav. **28**(1), 207–216 (2012)
8. Cobos, C., et al.: A hybrid system of pedagogical pattern recommendations based on singular value decomposition and variable data attributes. Inf. Process. Manag. **49**(3), 607–625 (2013)
9. Cox, S., Little, C. (eds.): Time Ontology in OWL. Recommendation, W3C, 19 October 2017
10. Grau, B.C., Horrocks, I., Motik, B., Parsia, B., Patel-Schneider, P., Sattler, U.: Owl 2: the next step for owl. Web Semant.: Sci. Serv. Agents World Wide Web **6**(4), 309–322 (2008)

11. Gruber, T.R.: A translation approach to portable ontology specifications. Knowl. Acquisition **5**(2), 199–220 (1993)
12. Guha, R.V., Brickley, D., Macbeth, S.: Schema.org: evolution of structured data on the web. Commun. ACM **59**(2), 44–51 (2016). https://doi.org/10.1145/2844544
13. Homola, M., Kubincová, Z., Čulík, J., Trungel, T.: Peer review support in a virtual learning environment. In: Li, Y., et al. (eds.) State-of-the-Art and Future Directions of Smart Learning. LNET, pp. 351–355. Springer, Heidelberg (2016). https://doi.org/10.1007/978-981-287-868-7_43
14. Homola, M., Kubincová, Z., Kľuka, J., Švolík, M., Darjanin, M., Zapalač, P.: Team workflow and peer review in a virtual learning environment. In: 2017 16th International Conference on Information Technology Based Higher Education and Training, pp. 1–6. IEEE (2017)
15. Huang, C., Liu, L., Tang, Y., Lu, L.: Semantic web enabled personalized recommendation for learning paths and experiences. In: Zhu, M. (ed.) ICCIC 2011. CCIS, vol. 235, pp. 258–267. Springer, Heidelberg (2011). https://doi.org/10.1007/978-3-642-24022-5_43
16. Jovanović, J., Gašević, D., Knight, C., Richards, G.: Ontologies for effective use of context in e-learning settings. J. Educ. Technol. Soc. **10**(3), 47–59 (2007)
17. Klašnja-Milićević, A., Vesin, B., Ivanović, M., Budimac, Z.: E-learning personalization based on hybrid recommendation strategy and learning style identification. Comput. Educ. **56**(3), 885–899 (2011)
18. Lau, R.Y., Song, D., Li, Y., Cheung, T.C., Hao, J.X.: Toward a fuzzy domain ontology extraction method for adaptive e-learning. IEEE Trans. Knowl. Data Eng. **21**(6), 800–813 (2008)
19. Lohmann, S., Negru, S., Haag, F., Ertl, T.: Visualizing ontologies with VOWL. Semantic Web **7**(4), 399–419 (2016). https://doi.org/10.3233/SW-150200
20. Manouselis, N., Drachsler, H., Vuorikari, R., Hummel, H., Koper, R.: Recommender systems in technology enhanced learning. In: Ricci, F., Rokach, L., Shapira, B., Kantor, P.B. (eds.) Recommender Systems Handbook. CCIS, pp. 387–415. Springer, Boston (2011). https://doi.org/10.1007/978-0-387-85820-3_12
21. Robin, C., Uma, G.: An ontology driven e-learning agent for software risk management. Int. J. Acad. Res. **3**(2) (2011)
22. Saleena, B., Srivatsa, S.K.: Using concept similarity in cross ontology for adaptive e-learning systems. J. King Saud Univ.-Comput. Inf. Sci. **27**(1), 1–12 (2015)
23. Schmidt, A., Winterhalter, C.: User context aware delivery of e-learning material: approach and architecture. J. Univ. Comput. Sci. **10**(1), 28–36 (2004)
24. Sowa, J.F.: Knowledge Representation: Logical, Philosophical, and Computational Foundations. Brooks Cole Publishing (2000)
25. Staab, S., Studer, R. (eds.): Handbook on Ontologies. IHIS. Springer, Heidelberg (2009). https://doi.org/10.1007/978-3-540-92673-3
26. Tarus, J.K., Niu, Z., Mustafa, G.: Knowledge-based recommendation: a review of ontology-based recommender systems for e-learning. Artif. Intell. Rev. **50**(1), 21–48 (2018)
27. Vesin, B., Ivanović, M., Klašnja-Milićević, A., Budimac, Z.: Protus 2.0: ontology-based semantic recommendation in programming tutoring system. Expert Syst. Appl. **39**(15), 12229–12246 (2012)
28. Yu, Z., Nakamura, Y., Jang, S., Kajita, S., Mase, K.: Ontology-based semantic recommendation for context-aware e-learning. In: Indulska, J., Ma, J., Yang, L.T., Ungerer, T., Cao, J. (eds.) UIC 2007. LNCS, vol. 4611, pp. 898–907. Springer, Heidelberg (2007). https://doi.org/10.1007/978-3-540-73549-6_88

Ontology-Based Modelling for Cyber Security E-Learning and Training

Menelaos Katsantonis(✉) and Ioannis Mavridis

University of Macedonia, 156 Egnatia str., 54636 Thessaloniki, Greece
mkatsantonis@uom.gr

Abstract. The Conceptual Framework for e-Learning and Training (COFELET) constitutes a design standard for the enhancement of cyber security education by guiding the development of effective game-based approaches (e.g., serious games). The COFELET framework envisages cyber security serious games as highly organized and parameterized learning environments which monitor learner's actions, evaluate their efforts and adapt to their needs. To this end, the COFELET framework employs well known cyber security standards (e.g., MITRE's CAPEC, Lockheed Martin's Cyber Kill Chain model or CKC) as a vehicle for organizing educational environments which model learners' actions and strategies. In this light, the COFELET ontology is proposed aiming at providing a foundation for the development of a universal knowledge base for modeling such environments. The COFELET ontology provides an analytical description of the key elements of COFELET's compliant serious games along with the appropriate classes and their properties. These elements include the cyber security domain elements that model the actions attackers perform to unleash cyber security attacks (i.e., the tasks) and the strategies they employ to achieve their malicious objectives (e.g., CAPEC's attack patterns, the CKC model). The cyber security domain elements are associated with the educational elements (e.g., hints, utilized knowledge, exercised skills) that provide the means to infuse the didactics in the COFELET compliant approaches. A set of instances is presented to provide a better appreciation of the COFELET ontology rational, usage and usefulness. The proposed ontology is a cause and effect of the design and development process of a prototype COFELET compliant game.

Keywords: Cyber security · Serious games · Ontology · eLearning and training · COFELET framework

1 Introduction

While cyber security education becomes more important, new learning and training approaches need to be developed and validated. Cyber security game-based learning is a new field, promising to improve the effectiveness of cyber security education. However, there is a lack of design standards and methodologies aiding in the development of such approaches. In this light, the Conceptual Framework for e-Learning and Training (COFELET) has been proposed [1], which envisages cyber security serious games that adapt to the learners' needs and characteristics; dynamically assess and scaffold learners' efforts; and implement modern learning theories and innovative

M. A. Herzog et al. (Eds.): ICWL 2019, LNCS 11841, pp. 15–27, 2019.
https://doi.org/10.1007/978-3-030-35758-0_2

teaching approaches to ensure the effectiveness of cyber security game-based approaches. To support these features, the COFELET compliant serious games (COFELET games) form highly organized and parameterized learning and training environments, which keep in store the sequence of tasks (i.e., actions directed at the unleash of cyber-attacks) learners have to follow to achieve the game goals, along with the tasks' prerequisites. In such a way, COFELET games can track learners' tasks and evaluate their performance and adapt to learner's efforts. Moreover, the COFELET framework consider games in which instructors define scenarios containing the goals learners have to fulfill, the occurring conditions and the gaming contexts (i.e., game properties regarding scores, time limits, visualizations presented to the learners, coordinates of avatars etc.) and the games' narratives.

COFELET games seamlessly employ standard cyber security methodologies and models generally used in threat analysis and modeling approaches, such as the MITRE's CAPEC [2], the Lockheed Martin's Cyber Kill Chain [3], and the National Cybersecurity Workforce Framework (NCWF) of National Initiative for Cybersecurity Education of National Institute of Science and Technology (NIST) [4]. CAPEC is used for the analysis and modeling of the methods and techniques (i.e., attack patterns) attackers employ to accomplish their malicious goals. More specifically, CAPEC is used as the main reference for the definition of COFELET's primary elements [1] such as the goals and the tasks of the attackers, the attack's prerequisites (i.e., the conditions), the defense mechanisms and the attack patterns (APs) that are relevant to a specific attack. CKC can be used as a pilot for the definition of complex missions such as the unleash of advanced persistent threat (APT) attacks, whereas NCWF can form the basis for the definition of COFELET games learning objectives and the organization of the teaching content.

The main research question of the presented study is how the COFELET games will seamlessly integrate the aforementioned cyber security standards. To this end, the COFELET ontology is proposed, an ontology that constitutes a universal knowledge model for cyber security e-learning and training. The COFELET ontology provides an analytical description of the key concepts of cyber security learning environments (e.g., the COFELET games) and their relationships. Moreover, the proposed ontology is presented along with the methodology and the approach we employed to develop it.

For the development of the COFELET ontology, which is compliant with the 'Ontology Development 101' guide [5], we employed a middle-out process. According to the middle-out process we defined a set of middle-level concepts that we generalized and specialized to produce a set of high-level concepts and low-level concepts. In the first stage, we leveraged CAPEC's attack patterns and we identified the operationalizable APs that could be modeled as COFELET game's primary elements. Subsequently, we defined scenario execution flow (SEF) elements as realizations of CAPEC's APs. SEFs are composite elements that constitute generic representations of attacks describing the sequences of tasks attackers perform to unleash an attack along with the relevant information (e.g., prerequisites). Thus, we specified SEFs in terms of COFELET's primary elements (i.e., tasks, goals and conditions) and we generalized these elements to specify the primary element class. We also associated SEFs with the knowledge, skills, abilities (KSAs) and attitudes the learners have to utilize to apply them; and with the hints that can be presented to the learners to scaffold their efforts towards the achievement of the games' goals. In the subsequent stage of the COFELET ontology process, we specialized the defined elements to form the COFELET ontology.

In the remainder of the paper, the COFELET ontology is presented in Sect. 2. Due to the complexity of the subject, the COFELET ontology is presented at different levels that evolve in complexity and detail. Subsequently, in Sect. 3 an illustrative set of COFELET instances is presented and the paper concludes in Sect. 4 by providing an overall discussion of the presented work.

2 The COFELET Ontology

2.1 The Domain and Scope

The scope of the COFELET ontology is highly organized and parameterized cyber security learning environments (such as the COFELET games) and especially the facets describing the realization of attacks as assets. Specifically, we envisaged a COFELET game aiming at teaching cyber security fundamentals, methods and techniques (domain) to professionals working at law enforcement agencies, organizations and companies. According the NCWF, cyber security professions are assigned to job profiles corresponding to the roles, the tasks and the KSAs defined in the NCWF framework. Due to the numerous roles defined in the NCWF framework, we limited the scope of the presented ontology to a COFELET game focusing on training of vulnerability assessment analysts and target network analysts. Additionally, due to the numerous KSAs the NCWF framework assignes to the vulnerability assessment analyst and the target network analyst workforce roles, only a set of KSAs were utilized for the definition of the learning objectives. These KSAs refer to the networks' operation (e.g., protocols, addressing), the stages of cyber-attacks and the utilization of cyber security tools (e.g., network analysis tools).

2.2 The Key Concepts

Primary Elements. They are represented by objects (the Primary Objects) denoting that an agent acts on an entity or an entity has a property. Specifically, the primary objects are interpreted as statements of the form <subject, verb, object> or <entity, property, property_value> that are called triples (e.g., <Player, provides, host scanner discovery command>). The expression of such statements as triples is widely used in various frameworks and methodologies such as the Resource Description Framework (RDF) [7] and the ADL's Training & Learning Architecture (TLA) [8]. For brevity and simplicity, we adapted an extension of this approach based on quintuple statements in the form of <entity, property, property_value, source, destination> that can be effortlessly translated to the corresponding triples. For example, the quintuple <Port scanner, sends, ICMP type 8 packets, from player host, to destination network> can be transformed to the triples <Port scanner, sends, ICMP type 8 packets>, <ICMP type 8 packets, has source, player host>, <ICMP type 8 packets, directed to, destination network>.

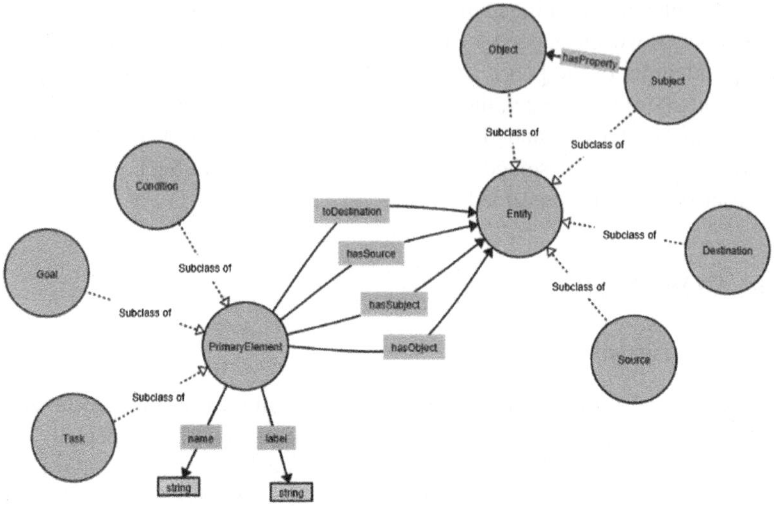

Fig. 1. COFELET primary elements (figure adopted by WebVOWL tool [9])

The Primary Objects instantiate the Task, the Condition and the Goal classes (primary classes) that are subclasses of the PrimaryElement class (Fig. 1). The primary classes inherit the hasSubject, the hasObject, the hasProperty, the hasSource and the toDestination object properties and the name and label data properties. The ranges of these properties are the subclasses of the Entity class that are the Subject, the Object, the Source and the Destination classes representing in-game entities such as players, hosts and networks. The Subject and Object classes are related by the 'hasProperty' object property. The 'hasProperty' is an object property with several sub-properties that represent the actions subject entities perform on object entities. These actions represent the tasks performed by agents (learners and non-playable characters such as mentors, teammates, adversaries) directed at the unleash of cyber-attacks such as entering commands, connecting to hosts, searching information and routing packets. The actions also represent the tasks performed by non-agent subjects (e.g., a tool that crafts and sends a packet, a firewall that drops a packet). Finally, the name and the label data properties represent the name and the human readable name of a primary object.

PrimaryElement objects are expressed in first-order predicate logic as follows:

$$\begin{gathered} \forall\, pe : PE \rightarrow \\ \exists\, subj, obj, src, dst : Entity \;\wedge\; \mathrm{hasSubject(pe, subj)} \wedge \mathrm{hasObject(pe, obj)} \wedge \\ hasSource(pe, src) \wedge toDestination(pe, dst) \wedge\; \exists hasProperty(subj, obj) \end{gathered} \tag{1}$$

Moreover, a PrimaryElement object can be an instance of either of its subclasses (i.e., Task class, Condition class, Goal class), whereas an object of the aforementioned classes cannot be an instance of more than one of these three classes (i.e., class disjointness):

$$\forall x(PE(x) \rightarrow Task(x) \vee Condition(x) \vee Goal(x) \quad (2)$$

$$\forall x\Big(Task(x) \bigwedge Condition(x) \bigwedge Goal(x) \rightarrow \bot\Big) \quad (3)$$

Entities. Entities in the COFELET ontology are represented by the Entity class. The Entity class is a top-level class with several middle-level classes (Fig. 2) that represent the most important concepts in the context of a COFELET game. For example, the middle-level Tool class is important as it represents the in-game tools used by the learners. The middle-level classes have numerous subclasses that represent various types and attributes. The Tool class is furtherly sub-classed to represent various types of in-game tools along with the tools' roles and characteristics. For example, a Tool object representing the 'ls' Linux tool (i.e., list directory contents) is an instance of DirNavigator class, whereas the 'msfvenom' Linux tool is an instance of PayloadGenerator class. The Command class represents the commands entered by learners to perform tasks (e.g., the command 'nmap -sS 192.168.1.0'). The Facade subclass stands for the different roles that the system plays (e.g., the instructor that manages the hints, the narrator that presents the narrations), whereas the Agent class represents the roles of game's characters (e.g., the learner, non-playable characters, host users).

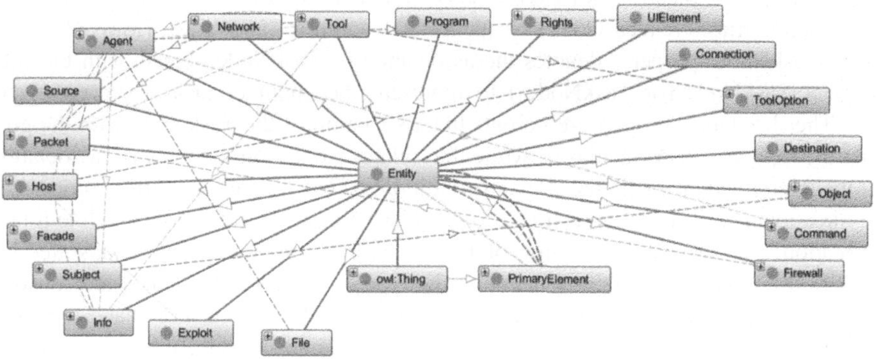

Fig. 2. COFELET middle-level entity classes (adopted from Protégé ontology editor tool [10])

Properties. Apart from the higher-level properties presented in the 'Primary Elements' section (e.g., hasSubject, hasObject), the COFELET ontology contains several properties defining the relations of Subjects to Objects and describing various actions occurring in the COFELET games. These properties are sub-properties of the hasProperty property a set of which is listed in Table 1 along with the corresponding Domains and Ranges and an example of usage.

Table 1. Sub-properties of the 'hasProperty' relating subjects to objects.

Domain	Properties	Range	Example
Agent	enters	Command	The learner enters "ping '*target*'"
Tool	crafts	Packet	Ping crafts ICMP type 8 packet
Tool	sends	Packet	Ping sends ICMP type 8 packet
Tool	solicits	Packet	Ping solicits ICMP type 0 packet
Agent	finds	Information	Learner finds the address of a host
Agent	hasAccess	Tool	Learner has access to use nmap tool
Firewall	accepts	Packet	Firewall accepts ICMP packets
Agent	knows	Information	Agent knows a vulnerable service
Host	establishes	Connection	A connection is established to the target
Agent	creates	File	Learner creates a weaponized file
Host	executes	Program	Payload is executed in the target host
HostUser	hasRights	Administrator	The user of the in-game host has administrator rights

Scenario Execution Flows. The primary elements are combined to form the Scenario Execution Flow (SEF) elements representing APs. The SEF elements are represented by the ScenarioExecutionFlow class (Fig. 3). The ScenarioExecutionFlow class includes a Goal object property, sequences of TaskNodes and sequences of Conditions. The TaskNode class is a composite task class. Apart from the properties that the TaskNode class inherits from the Task class (referring to the name, the label, hasSubject, hasObject, hasProperty, hasSource and toDestination), it contains the object properties: 'relates Goal', 'sequenceOf Condition' and 'next TaskNode'. The 'next TaskNode' property denotes the association of TaskNode objects with the subsequent TaskNode (or TaskNodes) to represent the chain of tasks representing an AP. The 'has Goal' property represents the association of the TaskNode with the goal that the represented AP achieves, while the 'relates Condition' denotes the association of the interpreted task with the relevant condition(s). The 'relates Condition' property is bi-directional as a condition can be a prerequisite for an executable task, while a task execution can activate a condition or it can cease its influence. The TaskNode also defines the 'type' data property denoting the type of the element such as the console-command task, the gui-event task and the auto-task. The console-command task designates a command that a learner enters to an in-game console; the gui-event task stands for a task that a learner performs in the game's graphical user interface; and the auto-task represents the tasks performed by the game's engine (e.g., packet sending and crafting). Finally, the TaskNode contains the 'interval' property denoting the time period that a task requires to execute.

The ScenarioExecutionFlow class also defines the 'relates KnowledgeSkillAbility' object property representing the knowledge and the competencies associated with the corresponding AP and the 'sequenceOf Hint' object property representing the list of hints presented to the learner. The 'defensiveMechanism' data property is a description of the AP countermeasures, the 'CAPEC_Name' data property holds the name of the CAPEC's attack pattern and the 'description' stores a description of the AP.

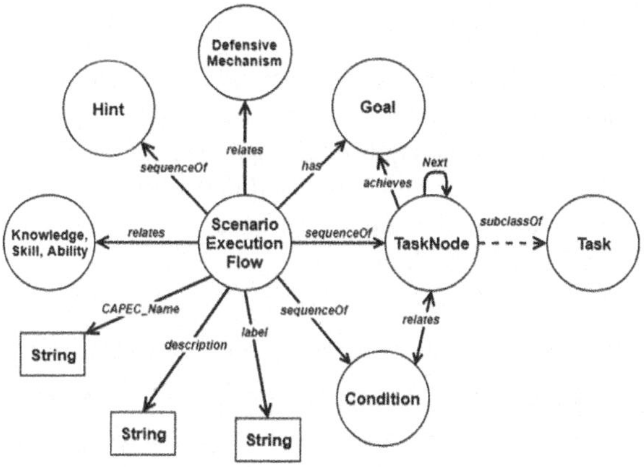

Fig. 3. COFELET scenario execution flow

The ScenarioExecutionFlow objects are grouped according to their goals. During the playtime, learners envisage an attack and they select a single scenario execution flow from a group of SEFs to fulfill a specific SEF's goal. For example, the CAPEC's APs 'ICMP Echo Request Ping', 'TCP SYN Ping' and 'TCP ACK Ping' are represented by SEF objects that share the goal "learner finds network's hosts". The learner can apply any of the aforementioned SEFs to achieve the host discovery goal.

Scenarios. The COFELET ontology foresees the utilization of the primary elements for the creation of game scenarios. A game scenario contains the necessary information for the setup of a game session. This information includes the specification of the games' conditions, the goals that learners have to achieve and the narrations of each scenario. The specified set of conditions forms the gaming context (i.e., the game's environment) in which learners operate. A scenario consists of a sequence of consecutive steps corresponding to the stages of multi-stage missions. Each step contains the goals that have to be fulfilled, a set of pre-conditions and a set of post-conditions. In complex missions a stage can correspond to several steps, providing the learners the opportunity to choose from a set of subsequent steps.

3 Excerpt of COFELET Knowledge Base

In the final step of the development of the COFELET ontology the individual instances of the presented classes were created. The defined instances correspond to COFELET games that retain a good repertoire of scenarios, foreseeing missions that vary in complexity and challenging levels. In the remainder of this section, an excerpt of the instances corresponds to complex missions requiring the learner to unleash an APT attack by applying the CKC model is presented.

3.1 Goals

The instances of the goal classes created correspond to scenarios of varying complexity from simple missions (e.g., a capture the flag mission from a vulnerable target) to complex missions (e.g., a mission requiring the appliance of the CKC model) (Table 2). The rational of a set of instantiated goals is listed in the following table (along with the matching stage in the CKC model and a goal code), whereas the definitions of some instantiated goals are listed in Table 3.

Table 2. A list of goals along with their description and the matching stage in the CKC model.

CKC stage	Code	Goal description
Reconnaissance	G1	Learner finds the alive hosts in the target network
	G2	Learner finds open ports on the target hosts
	G3	Learner finds clues on open ports by prompting the open ports with a remote console tool
Weaponization	G4	The learner finds exploits matching the vulnerable software running on open ports by searching an exploit database
	G5	Learner creates a payload file or weapon by using a payload generation program (e.g., msfvenom)
Delivery	G6	Learner delivers the weapon to the target host
Exploitation, Installation, C2	G7	A reverse tcp connection is established from the target host to the player's host
Actions on objectives	G8	Learner creates a new user by using the appropriate tool for remote access (e.g., the meterpreter)
	G9	Learner copies a flag file from the target host

Table 3. A list of goal instances

Subject	Property	Object	Source	Destination
Learner agent	finds	Target host information	Learner host	Target network
Learner agent	finds	Vulnerable service info	–	Target host
Learner agent	creates	Payload file	–	–
Payload	establishes	Connection	Target host	Learner host
Learner agent	solicits	Flag file	Target host	Learner host

3.2 Conditions

The instances of the condition classes represent the prerequisites needed to make the tasks doable. A list of condition instances is presented in the Table 4 below:

Table 4. A list of instantiated conditions

ID	Subject	Property	Object	Source	Destination
C1	Learner agent	knows	Target IP information	–	–
C2	Learner's network	routes	Packet	Learner's host	Target's host
C3	Learner agent	hasAccess	Host scanner tool	–	–
C4	Firewall	accepts	ICMP type 8 packet	Learner's host	Target's host
C5	Learner agent	has	Admin rights	–	–
C6	Firewall	accepts	TCP SYN, ACK & RST packets	Learner's host	Target's host
C7	Firewall	drops	ICMP type 8 packet	Learner's host	Target's host
C8	Firewall	drops	TCP SYN, ACK & RST packets	Learner's host	Target's host

3.3 Tasks and SEFs

A COFELET game foresees the implementation of a sustainable lifecycle of obtaining new KSAs and updating and reinforcing acquired KSAs. Moreover, a COFELET game needs to dynamically adjust its context to scaffold learners' efforts towards the achievement of the learning objectives with respect to the learners' profile [1]. For this reason, COFELET games provide scenarios of varying difficulty and challenge to the learners. To support these qualities COFELET games contain numerous SEF instances providing the instructors the ability to form educational sessions of varying characteristics. For example, a session aiming at teaching new KSAs to learners will present original scenarios with genuine goals that will require learners to apply new SEFs and have new experiences. On the contrary, a session, aiming at reinforcing or updating KSAs, will present scenarios with formerly achieved goals in diverse contexts in which learners will have to re-apply their strategy with diverse tasks and SEFs. Under this prism, COFELET approaches define sibling SEF instances that have the same parent classes; they are associated with the same goals; but they are achievable under different conditions or they consume different amount of resources (e.g., time). Such SEF instances are the 'ICMP Echo Request Ping', the 'TCP SYN Ping' and the 'TCP ACK Ping' that instantiate the HostDiscovery class (i.e., a subclass of the SEF class) related to the G1 goal instance. In the remainder of this subsection the rational of the host discovery SEF instances (not in full detail for brevity) along with, the related conditions and the corresponding sequence of tasks is presented.

Host Discovery Class. In host discovery attack patterns, the attacker (i.e., the learner) sends a probe to an IP address to determine if the host is alive (goal G1). To perform the AP, the learner needs to know the address of the target (condition C1) and to have logical access to the target (corresponds to the condition C2). The learner will have to perform a task of entering the appropriate host discovery command. Thus, she needs access to the appropriate host scanning tool (condition C3).

ICMP Echo Request Ping Instance. The learner' host sends an ICMP Type 8 'Echo Request' datagram and the target host responds with an ICMP Type 0 Echo Reply datagram. The firewall has to accept the ICMP Type 8 datagrams (condition C4).

TCP SYN Ping SEF Instance. The learner sends a TCP SYN packet to the target host. If a target port is open the target host responds with SYN/ACK packet (i.e., the second stage of the 'three-way handshake'), otherwise responds with a reset (RST) packet. The learner needs administrator rights to use a tool that crafts TCP SYN packets (condition C5) and the firewall has to accept the SYN packets and RST packets (condition C6).

TCP ACK Ping Instance. The learner' host sends a TCP ACK packet to the target host which responds with a RST packet, as the ACK packet in the TCP ACK ping is not part of an existing connection. The attack pattern has the same prerequisites with the 'TCP SYN Ping' (conditions C5 and C6).

The defensive mechanism of the above host discovery attack patterns is to use a firewall and properly configure it to block the type of packets associated with the aforementioned SEFs. For example, a firewall can be configured to block ICMP Type 8 (condition C7) to make the ICMP Echo Request Ping unachievable.

The TaskNode instances of the 'ICMP Echo Request Ping' and the 'TCP SYN Ping' SEF instances are listed in the Table 5 and the Table 6 respectively. Each table lists TaskNodes information including an identifier of the TaskNode (label ID), the TaskNodes' parent tasks (label Task) in the form of 'entity, property, property_value, source, destination', the ID of the properties that point to the next TaskNode (label Next), the type of the TaskNode (label Type), the interval of the task (label Interv.), the related conditions (label Cond.) and the associated goal (label G.). The TaskNode type of the presented instances is either a manual console-command (denoted with 'cmd') or a task performed by the game's engine (denoted with 'auto').

Table 5. 'ICMP Echo Request Ping' SEF instance TaskNodes

ID	Task	Next	Type	Interv.	Cond.	G.
1	Learner agent, enters, ICMP Echo Request Ping host discovery command	2	cmd	1	C1 C3	–
2	Host scanner tool, crafts, ICMP Type 8 packet	3	auto	1	–	–
3	Host scanner tool, sends, ICMP Type 8 packet, from Learner host, to Target network	4 or 5	auto	1	C2	–
4	Host scanner tool, solicits, ICMP Type 0 packet, from Target host, to Learner host	–	auto	3	C4	G1
5	Host scanner tool, solicits, null packet	–	auto	5	C7	–

Table 6. 'TCP SYN Ping' SEF instance TaskNodes

ID	Task	Next	Type	Interv.	Cond.	G.
1	Learner agent, enters, TCP SYN Ping host discovery command	2	cmd	1	C1 C3	–
2	Host scanner tool, crafts, TCP SYN flag packet	3	auto	1	C5	–
3	Host scanner tool, sends, TCP SYN flag packet, from Learner host, to Target network	4 or 5 or 6	auto	1	C2	–
4	Host scanner tool, solicits, TCP RST flag packet, from Target host, to Learner host	–	auto	3	C6	G1
5	Host scanner tool, solicits, null packet	–	auto	5	C8	–
6	Host scanner tool, solicits, TCP SYN/ACK flag packet, from Target host, to Learner host	–	auto	3	C6	G1

3.4 Knowledge, Skills and Abilities (KSAs)

The instances of the KSA classes correspond to the knowledge, the skills and the abilities defined in the NCWF framework for the vulnerability assessment analyst and the target network analyst workforce roles [4]. The adopted KSAs are listed below along with their NCWF identifier in the form of a letter followed by a number (the letter denotes the type of KSA: 'K' for knowledge, 'S' for skill and 'A' for ability):

- K0177: Knowledge of cyber-attack stages (e.g., reconnaissance, scanning, enumeration, gaining access, escalation of privileges, maintaining access, network exploitation, covering tracks).
- K0471: Knowledge of Internet network addressing (IP addresses, classless inter-domain routing, TCP/UDP port numbering).
- K0487: Knowledge of network security (e.g., encryption, firewalls, authentication).
- S0081: Skill in using network analysis tools to identify vulnerabilities (e.g., nmap).
- S0293: Skill in using tools, techniques, and procedures to remotely exploit and establish persistence on a target.
- A0106: Ability to think critically.

Thus, the demonstration of the manner that CAPEC, CKC and NCWF are infused in COFELET compliant games is completed.

4 Conclusion

In this work, the COFELET ontology is proposed, an ontology for modeling cyber security learning and training environments, and especially cyber security serious games. The proposed ontology provides an analytical description of the key elements the COFELET games need to comprise to represent cyber security attacks of varying complexities. To this end, the COFELET ontology describes the primary elements (i.e., the high-level elements such as tasks, conditions and goals) and the manner that these primary elements can be combined to form the scenario execution flow elements (SEFs). The SEFs represent attacks that virtually happen in COFELET scenarios and they are described in analogy to CAPEC attack patterns.

The COFELET ontology is a step towards the implementation of solutions that respond to the challenge of developing COFELET compliant serious games that dynamically adapt to learners' characteristics and the educational environment; and integrate cyber security standards generally used in threat analysis and modeling approaches (e.g., CAPEC, Cyber Kill Chain, National Cyber Security Workforce Framework). As a result, a formal description of the knowledge required in the design and development of a prototype COFELET compliant serious game is provided. The presented elements (e.g., SEFs associated with KSAs, hints and the defensive mechanisms) are independent from game genres and underlying platforms and technologies. Nevertheless, the presented set of individual instances aims at the formation of a shared knowledge base that will be extended and utilized in cyber security learning and training approaches that assimilate hacking activities. Through the utilization of the proposed ontology in the development of a prototype COFELET compliant game its usefulness has been verified and it will be furtherly examined under the prism of forming an improved extended version.

Acknowledgement. This research is funded by the University of Macedonia Greece Research Committee as part of the "Principle Research 2019" funding program.

References

1. Katsantonis, M.N., Kotini, I., Fouliras, P., Mavridis, I.: Conceptual framework for developing cyber security serious games. In: 2019 IEEE Global Engineering Education Conference (EDUCON) Proceedings, pp. 872–881. IEEE, Dubai (2019)
2. Common Attack Pattern Enumeration and Classification (CAPEC). https://capec.mitre.org. Accessed 30 May 2019
3. Martin, L.: Cyber Kill Chain. http://cyber.lockheedmartin.com/hubfs/Gaining_the_Advantage_Cyber_Kill_Chain.pdf. Accessed 30 May 2019
4. Newhouse, W., Keith, S., Scribner, B., Witte, G.: National Initiative for Cybersecurity Education (NICE) - Cybersecurity Workforce Framework. National Institute of Standards and Technology (NIST) Special Publication, 800, 181, April 2017
5. Noy, N.,F., McGuinness, D.L.: Ontology development 101: a guide to creating your first ontology (2001)
6. Uschold, M., Gruninger, M.: Ontologies: principles, methods and applications. Knowl. Eng. Rev. **11**(2), 93–136 (1996)
7. Fallon, C., Brown, S.: E-Learning Standards A Guide to Purchasing, Developing, and Deploying Standards-Conformant E-Learning. CRC Press LLC (2016)
8. Poltrack, J.: ADL Training & Learning Architecture (TLA). http://www.adlnet.gov/wp-content/uploads/2014/07/ADL-Training-and-LearningArchitecture-1.pdf. Accessed 30 May 2019

9. Lohmann, S., Link, V., Marbach, E., Negru, S.: WebVOWL: web-based visualization of ontologies. In: Lambrix, P., et al. (eds.) EKAW 2014. LNCS, vol. 8982, pp. 154–158. Springer, Cham (2015). https://doi.org/10.1007/978-3-319-17966-7_21
10. Protégé Stanford. http://protege.stanford.edu. Accessed 30 June 2019
11. Obrst, L., Chase, P., Markeloff, R.: Developing an ontology of the cyber security domain. In: STIDS, pp. 49–56 (2012)
12. Zhu, Y.: Attack pattern ontology: a common language for attack information sharing between organizations (2015)

Retrieval of Educational Resources from the Web: A Comparison Between Google and Online Educational Repositories

Carlo De Medio[1], Carla Limongelli[1](✉), Alessandro Marani[2], and Davide Taibi[3]

[1] Engineering Department, Roma Tre University, Rome, Italy
carlo.demedio@uniroma3.it, limongel@ing.uniroma3.it
[2] School of Information and Communication Technology, Griffith University, Brisbane, Australia
alessandro.marani@alumni.griffithuni.edu.au
[3] Italian National Research Council, Institute for Educational Technologies, Palermo, Italy
davide.taibi@itd.cnr.it

Abstract. The retrieval and composition of educational material are topics that attract many studies from the field of Information Retrieval and Artificial Intelligence. The Web is gradually gaining popularity among teachers and students as a source of learning resources. This transition is, however, facing skepticism from some scholars in the field of education. The main concern is about the quality and reliability of the teaching on the Web. While online educational repositories are explicitly built for educational purposes by competent teachers, web pages are designed and created for offering different services, not only education. In this study, we analyse if the Internet is a good source of teaching material compared to the currently available repositories in education. Using a collection of 50 queries related to educational topics, we compare how many useful learning resources a teacher can retrieve in Google and three popular learning object repositories. The results are very insightful and in favour of Google supported by the t-tests. For most of the queries, Google retrieves a larger number of useful web pages than the repositories ($p < .01$), and no queries resulted in zero useful items. Instead, the repositories struggle to find even one relevant material for many queries. This study is clear evidence that even though the repositories offer a richer description of the learning resources through metadata, it is time to undertake more research towards the retrieval of web pages for educational applications.

Keywords: Web search · Information retrieval for education · Technology Enhanced Learning

M. A. Herzog et al. (Eds.): ICWL 2019, LNCS 11841, pp. 28–38, 2019.
https://doi.org/10.1007/978-3-030-35758-0_3

1 Introduction

The Internet is today recognised as a reliable source of information and services in different domains. The significant improvement of Information Retrieval (IR) methods certainly played a role in this revolution, also in combination with the advance of other technologies and research areas [2]. When web retrieval methods became more efficient and effective, the Internet significantly and quickly gained trust from users. With a focus on the education field, the Web hosts plenty of platforms that offer online learning services like Learning Management Systems (LMS), Massive Open Online Courses (MOOCs) and dedicated channels in YouTube to name a few. While LMS and MOOCs are ready-to-learn courses, many other web pages from different sources include teaching content that might be useful for both teachers and students in their educational tasks. However, most of the research of IR in Technology Enhanced Learning (TEL) focuses on Learning Objects (LO) and Learning Object Repositories (LOR) [6]. LO is the most powerful solution for the sharing and retrieval of online teaching resources. The main reasons are that these resources are undoubtedly appropriate for education and have some educational metadata for facilitating any retrieval function. Nevertheless, the issue of low completeness of such metadata in popular repositories is not a new finding [17,18]. Bseides, web users started to rely more on the Web than LORs when seeking teaching resources [14], but the research trend is still mostly based on LORs with a considerable gap in addressing web IR for TEL applications [9,11].

For these reasons, this study wants to address the dilemma of either limiting IR to LORs or starting to look at the Web. Web users in education can already benefit from present search engines to find educational resources [14]. It is indeed more challenging to expand the search of educational material to the Web. In existing repositories, LOs are a safe zone as (i) they are educational resources, (ii) they theoretically come with educational metadata and (iii) the number of resources is minimal compared to the web. At the same time, these positive points hide some significant limits, especially in terms of diversity of the resources and domains coverage. These reasons are behind the IR studies in TEL which suggest embracing the Web in this research field [9,10]. In 2013, a study found out that teachers relied more on Google than LORs when searching for educational material in the medical field [14]. We can say that if teachers find web pages reliable enough to teach medical content, we should start considering the web as a source of educational material. Despite all this, to the best of our knowledge, we find that most of the new proposals are still based on LO [6,9].

This study presents a comparison between Google and popular LORs when searching for educational material in the Information and Communication Technology field (ICT). We chose this field not only because it is where us and the readers can easily relate to, but also because it contains a considerable number of topics which easily overlap with other domains (e.g. Mathematics, Physics, etc.). In particular, the research question we investigated in this study was: how many useful learning resources can a teacher find by searching on LORs and Google? This study evaluates the number of relevant resources, as determined by teachers, that Google and LORs can suggest; we do not further investigate their quality. On one side, this constitutes a limitation of this study, since it can be argued that resources retrieved in LORs can be more relevant even when they are less in number. However, our study proves that for many queries the searches performed in the repositories end up with no suitable material, according to teachers' evaluation.

2 Online Repositories of Educational Resources

We have detailed definitions for LOs: (i) "A LO is any entity, digital or non-digital, that may be used for learning, education or training" [7]. (ii) "A LO is any digital resource that can be reused to support learning" [21]. (iii) "A LO is a digital self-contained and reusable entity, with a clear educational purpose, with at least three internal and editable components: content, learning activities and elements of context. LOs must have an external structure of information to facilitate their identification, storage and retrieval: the metadata" [19]. Moreover, a LO is a small learning unit, typically ranging from 2 min to 15 min. It is self-contained (each LO can be taken independently), and it is reusable (a single LO may be used in multiple contexts for multiple purposes).

The benefits of using LOs for IR reside in the metadata. The most popular metadata standard is IEEE LOM [1], which provides descriptive information of the content of the LO. Such information describes the LO under many perspectives, not only educational. Unfortunately, LOM shows some semantic issues that complicate the information processing of the metadata [5,22], and authors of LO rarely annotate the metadata thoroughly and accurately [17,18]. Hence, many studies of IR in TEL edit LOM to have a different kind of information that better matches their specific retrieval or recommendation purposes [3,5,6].

Some research already addresses the drawbacks in using LORs for IR. Although the efforts to standardize the LOs into either federated or specialized repositories, the retrieval from LORs still finds many challenges [4]. These challenges are because some LORs: (i) do not physically host the resources but only metadata; (ii) have heterogeneous search interfaces (iii) use different ranking mechanisms.

So, we have collected a set of 50 queries, and we have used them to query some significant LORs and Google. A group of teachers has judged the suitability of the retrieved LOs.

After an analysis of LORs which are primarily used and studied for IR in TEL [6,13,14], we have excluded repositories such as iLumina[1], the MACE platform[2], ELENA[3], LRE-MELT[4], or ARIADNE[5]. These repositories are the result of European projects, and we do not have the certainty they are still maintained.

[1] http://digitalcollections.uncw.edu/digital/collection/ilumina/search/.
[2] https://www.fit.fraunhofer.de/en/fb/cscw/projects/mace.html.
[3] http://old.isn-oldenburg.de/projects/SINN/sinn03/proceedings/dolog.html.
[4] http://info.melt-project.eu/ww/en/pub/melt_project/welcome.htm.
[5] http://www.ariadne-eu.org.

For example, we know that ARIADNE, the largest project, retrieves many broken links [13]. We also have excluded digital libraries like OER Commons[6] or PROLEARN[7] which can contain a very different type of learning materials, not necessarily LOs as defined above, and they go beyond the scope of our investigation.

So, we compare Google with the following three most popular repositories [6, 14]. MERLOT[8]: it offers over 82.000 LOs, 22.000 bookmark collections, and 884 courses (we concentrate on LOs only).

Open Stax CNX - Connexions[9]: it allows to explore more than 2.000 books and more than 32.000 small knowledge chunks in different subject areas (Arts, Business, Humanities, Mathematics and Statistics, Science and Technology, Social Science). We will not consider books.

WISC-ONLINE[10]: it hosts over 2,500 LOs, mainly interactive flash files.

3 Data Collection

To compare Google and LORs, we need a set of queries and the relevance of the retrieved resources. The purpose of the data collection phase, implemented via an online survey, is to have a set of queries that teachers would use in real teaching scenario. With these queries, we interrogate both Google and LORs to compare the accuracy of their recommendations. Since Google does not necessarily refer to teaching materials, we asked the participants to evaluate the suitability of retrieved web-pages for teaching in a specific context. After the quality control of the annotations, the dataset consists of 50 queries, where, for each query, we have 10 web-pages with a score from 1 to 5 for expressing the suitability of the item for teaching in the particular educational context. The questionnaire is about the validation of our teaching context that shall elicit teaching aspects essential for the retrieval of web resources for education. It is composed of three blocks. The first one collects some general information about the sample such as age and teaching experience. The second block extracts from respondent instructors their current attitudes when using online systems for seeking educational resources. The last block is related to the perceived usefulness of the attributes of the proposed teaching context.

To complete the survey in a reasonable time-frame for the participants, teachers assess the usefulness of the results presented by Google only. For a reliable evaluation of the usefulness of a web-page, external assessors shall rate items with the highest level of knowledge and awareness of the purpose of the web-search [15]. We developed an online system where assessors could connect to retrieve web pages for a teaching scenario defined by course title, education level, difficulty, and a concept map of the course.

[6] https://www.oercommons.org/.
[7] http://www.prolearn-academy.org/.
[8] http://www.merlot.org.
[9] https://cnx.org.
[10] https://www.wisc-online.com/.

To make sure teachers were fully aware of the purpose and context of the query [15], we allowed them to define the teaching scenario, and then interrogate Google[11] with a query that they believed to best reflect the searching criteria. The survey presented, for each query, the top-10 items in a plain user interface so that teachers could not know that Google was elaborating their queries.

Also, the items were reported in a random order to avoid any bias due to the presentation order. The teachers evaluated the items using 5 points Likert scale. Given the rating scale, we consider useful those web-pages with a score of at least 3.

3.1 Participants

Since neither professional nor personal aspects of the participants can affect the evaluation process, instructors of any age, expertise, and teaching experience have been invited to the survey. We only restricted the invitations to teachers with teaching experience in machine learning or information systems subjects at the university level. 65 teachers participated in the questionnaire. Almost 80% of participants have more than 5 years of experience in teaching, and around 90% of participants' age is between 35 and 74. No participants in the age range 18 to 24 and 75+ have been recorded. Therefore, most of the participants in the questionnaire have been teaching for at least 6 years, suggesting a reliable sample. More details about the experiment can be found in [16].

3.2 Quality Control

When external assessors are invited to rate web-pages, we can expect that some of them randomly rate the items to conclude the survey quickly. For example, we experienced that some users assigned ratings from 4 to 5 to all the items without inspecting any of them, though it was clear that some documents were even off topic. This behaviour leads to misleading data for our experiments. We programmed our system to automatically perform quality control of the annotations by removing annotations of participants who did not inspect at least 50% of the rated web-pages. The ratings gathered for these web-pages are reliable and useful for our analysis.

3.3 Data Annotation

During the survey, the system records the response time of Google for producing the results set, the user's query, and the order of the items proposed by Google. About the educational data, we record the concept of the search as well as the teaching context data. For quality control of the assessments, the system tracks whether or not the assessor inspected the rated web-pages. It sets a flag to 1

[11] Google is queried by using the Google Custom Search service expanded to the entire web.

when the assessor clicks on the link to the web-page. After the online annotation of Google's results, we queried the subject LORs with the same 50 users' queries collected from the online survey. Since LORs host learning resources only, there is no need to determine whether or not a suggested item is for teaching purposes. So, the resources from the educational repositories only require an assessment of the relevance to the query. Because of our expertise in the field of machine learning and information systems subjects, and no professional or academic involvement in any of the systems under analysis, our evaluation is enough [20]. We, the authors, evaluated the items found by the subject LORs with a binary value (relevant or not relevant). A LO is labelled as relevant when it fully covers the query and concept object of the search. In the case of web-pages returned by Googles, teachers have labelled the usefulness of the retrieved web-pages.

4 Google vs LORs

This section presents the analysis of the quality of the results shown by the subject systems. This study aims to determine whether or not Google, a generic search engine, is an effective retrieval system of resources for education, representing a valid alternative to LORs. Figure 1 depicts the number of relevant items retrieved by the subject systems for each of the 50 queries. The more external is the line, the more relevant items the systems retrieves for a query. Google (the green line) is the system with predominantly better performance than the subject LORs. In just a few cases, some of the repositories found more relevant results than Google. In particular, MERLOT was better for 2 queries, CNX for 3 queries while WISC never found more relevant results than Google.

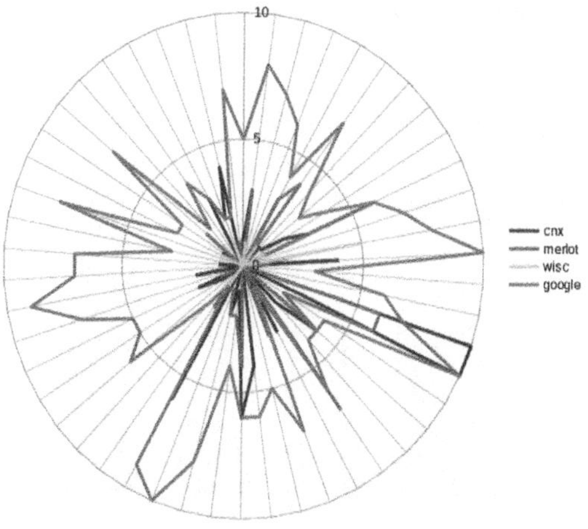

Fig. 1. The number of relevant items retrieved by the subject systems for each of the 50 queries. (Color figure online)

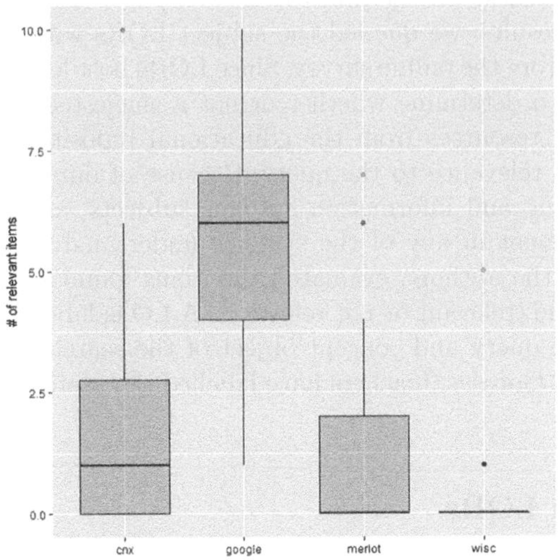

Fig. 2. The number of resources retrieved, on average, by Google, MERLOT, CNX and WISC for the 50 queries.

Table 1. Summary of the number of relevant items retrieved by Google, MERLOT, CNX and WISC.

System	Mean	Std. dev.	Min.	Max.
GOOGLE	5.44	2.392	1	10
MERLOT	1.28	1.917	0	7
CNX	1.66	2.37	0	10
WISC	0.22	0.764	0	5

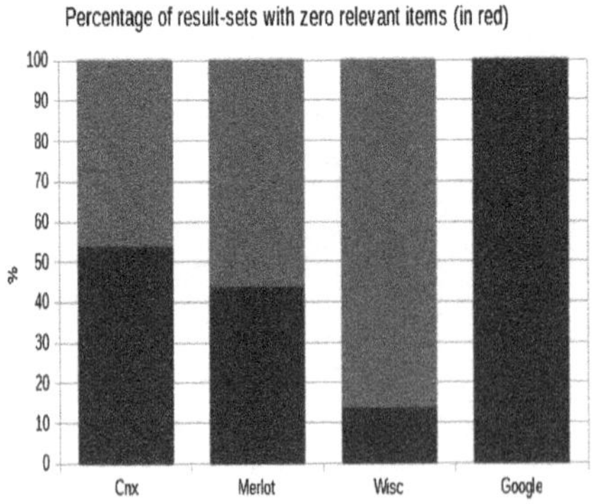

Fig. 3. The percentage of queries which resulted in zero relevant items (red) and in at least one relevant item (blue). (Color figure online)

Figure 2 and Table 1 dive us into the finding of this analysis: Google returned, on average, many more relevant resources than any of the three LORs. We can see that Google shows a nice and relevant distribution where the variance of the sample is not too large compared to the mean value. Instead, the three repositories report a significantly high deviation of the sample. Also, Google always presented at least one relevant item, while the repositories did not even retrieve one appropriate item for a considerable number of queries. Figure 3 highlights such result, where MERLOT did not find any relevant item for 28 queries (56% of the queries), CNX for 23 queries (46%) and WISC for 43 queries (83%). Another interesting outcome is that the educational repositories presented a set of less than 10 items for most of the queries, and sometimes even none. Google always retrieved more than 10 web pages per query.

For a generalisation of the results, we compute one-tailed two samples Students' t-tests to explore the statistical significance of the better performance of Google compared to the repositories. We use the t-tests to analyse if there is a significant difference in the performance of Google with each of the three subject repositories. The research hypothesis we investigate here is that Google retrieves more relevant items than MERLOT, CNX and WISC. Before to proceed with the computations, we further investigate the homogeneity of variances between the samples under comparison. To this aim, we run the F test of the samples of data from the subject systems with the sample of Google. The results indicate a similar variance of the data from Google with the samples of MERLOT and WISC. Instead, the sample of Google and WISC present a different variance, so, for this last case, we compute the Welch two-sample t-test. We use the default functions of the statistical software R for the F tests and t-tests. Table 2 reports the outcomes of the t-tests, strongly confirming and supporting the superior performance of Google.

Table 2. Results of the t-tests of the number of relevant items retrieved by Google compared with MERLOT, CNX and WISC.

Google VS	*t-value*	Degree of freedom	95% Conf. interval of mean diff.	*p-value*
MERLOT	9.596	98	3.440	4.55e−16
CNX	7.938	98	2.989	1.719e−12
WISC	14.701	58.889	4.627	<2.2e−16

All the t-tests retain our research hypothesis ($p < .01$), leaving no doubt of the statistical significance of the findings of our experiment. Reading the confidence intervals of the mean differences in Table 2, we can also assert that Google is likely to find at least 3 more relevant items than LORs. Finally, on average, Google presents at least 5 relevant items, while the repositories reported a mean value of just over 1 relevant item per query.

5 Conclusions and Future Works

In this work, we find evidence that searching educational material with Google is more effective than using LORs. The strong positive points of LORs is that they host educational materials with instructional metadata. On the other way, the web dimension, besides being a challenge, is also an excellent opportunity. Google accesses to a higher number of items than LORs; the problem is whether or not such items can be useful for education.

When researching in IR in TEL, some recent research is starting to transfer the IR research from LORs to the Web [8–10]. However, most of the research still uses LORs as the primary source of educational material [6,9]. This study helps to underline the potential of the Web for education, so that future research can further investigate in this direction. We compare the number of relevant items that teachers can find when searching with Google compared to three popular LORs: MERLOT, CNX and WISC. After collecting the ratings of web pages retrieved by Google for 50 queries, we examine if the LORs can return an equivalent number of relevant resources for those queries. The difference is evident and remarkable: on average, Google presents many more relevant items than LORs, and no queries resulted in an empty set of relevant items. We find that CNX is the repository that performed the best among the three subject LORs. On average, CNX returns 1.66 relevant items per query, which is significantly lower than 5.44 relevant items experienced with Google. Also, CNX did not find any relevant items for 46% of the queries, while Google presents at least one relevant item for all the queries. The other two repositories have a worse outcome than CNX. Finally, the *t*-tests do not reject our research hypothesis ($p < .01$) of a higher likelihood of finding more relevant items with Google than with LORs.

This study encourages to expand the IR methods in TEL to the web rather than LORs only. Some studies also show benefits of semantic approaches to improve the educational description of web pages [12], so further analysis of the benefits of such technologies would provide an additional insight of what direction the research on IR in TEL should take.

References

1. Learning object metadata, IEEE-LTSC. https://www.ieeeltsc.org/working-groups/wg12LOM/lomDescription/. Accessed 14 Feb 2019
2. Allan, J., Croft, B., Moffat, A., Sanderson, M.: Frontiers, challenges, and opportunities for information retrieval: report from swirl 2012 the second strategic workshop on information retrieval in Lorne. SIGIR Forum **46**(1), 2–32 (2012)
3. Bozo, J., Alarcón, R., Iribarra, S.: Recommending learning objects according to a teachers' contex model. In: Wolpers, M., Kirschner, P.A., Scheffel, M., Lindstaedt, S., Dimitrova, V. (eds.) EC-TEL 2010. LNCS, vol. 6383, pp. 470–475. Springer, Heidelberg (2010). https://doi.org/10.1007/978-3-642-16020-2_39
4. Curlango-Rosas, C., Ponce, G.A., Lopez-Morteo, G.A.: A specialized search assistant for learning objects. ACM Trans. Web **5**(4), 21:1–21:29 (2011)

5. Dietze, S., Yu, H.Q., Giordano, D., Kaldoudi, E., Dovrolis, N., Taibi, D.: Linked education: interlinking educational resources and the web of data. In: Proceedings of the 27th Annual ACM Symposium on Applied Computing, pp. 366–371. ACM (2012)
6. Drachsler, H., Verbert, K., Santos, O.C., Manouselis, N.: Panorama of recommender systems to support learning. In: Ricci, F., Rokach, L., Shapira, B. (eds.) Recommender Systems Handbook, pp. 421–451. Springer, Boston, MA (2015). https://doi.org/10.1007/978-1-4899-7637-6_12
7. Learning Technology Standards Committee: IEEE standard for learning object metadata. IEEE standard, **1484**(1), 2007-04 (2002)
8. Estivill-Castro, V., Limongelli, C., Lombardi, M., Marani, A.: DAJEE: a dataset of joint educational entities for information retrieval in technology enhanced learning. In: Proceedings of the 39th International ACM SIGIR Conference on Research and Development in Information Retrieval, pp. 681–684. ACM (2016)
9. Estivill-Castro, V., Lombardi, M., Marani, A.: Improving binary classification of web pages using an ensemble of feature selection algorithms. In: Proceedings of the Australasian Computer Science Week Multiconference, p. 17. ACM (2018)
10. Krieger, K.: Creating learning material from web resources. In: Gandon, F., Sabou, M., Sack, H., d'Amato, C., Cudré-Mauroux, P., Zimmermann, A. (eds.) ESWC 2015. LNCS, vol. 9088, pp. 721–730. Springer, Cham (2015). https://doi.org/10.1007/978-3-319-18818-8_45
11. Limongelli, C., Lombardi, M., Marani, A.: Towards the recommendation of resources in coursera. In: Intelligent Tutoring Systems: 13th International Conference, ITS 2016, 7–10 June 2016, Zagreb, Croatia, Proceedings, vol. 9684, p. 461. Springer, Heidelberg (2016)
12. Limongelli, C., Lombardi, M., Marani, A., Taibi, D.: Enrichment of the dataset of joint educational entities with the web of data. In: 2017 IEEE 17th International Conference on Advanced Learning Technologies (ICALT), pp. 528–529. IEEE (2017)
13. Lombardi, M., Marani, A.: A comparative framework to evaluate recommender systems in technology enhanced learning: a case study. In: Lagunas, O.P., Alcántara, O.H., Figueroa, G.A. (eds.) MICAI 2015. LNCS (LNAI), vol. 9414, pp. 155–170. Springer, Cham (2015). https://doi.org/10.1007/978-3-319-27101-9_11
14. Maloney, S., Moss, A., Keating, J., Kotsanas, G., Morgan, P.: Sharing teaching and learning resources: perceptions of a university's faculty members. Med. Educ. **47**(8), 811–819 (2013)
15. Mao, J., et al.: When does relevance mean usefulness and user satisfaction in web search? In: Proceedings of the 39th International ACM SIGIR Conference on Research and Development in Information Retrieval, SIGIR 2016, pp. 463–472. ACM, New York (2016)
16. Marani, A.: WebEduRank: an educational ranking principle of web pages for teaching. Ph.D. thesis, School of Information and Communication Technology, Griffith University (2018)
17. Ochoa, X., Klerkx, J., Vandeputte, B., Duval, E.: On the use of learning object metadata: the GLOBE experience. In: Kloos, C.D., Gillet, D., Crespo García, R.M., Wild, F., Wolpers, M. (eds.) EC-TEL 2011. LNCS, vol. 6964, pp. 271–284. Springer, Heidelberg (2011). https://doi.org/10.1007/978-3-642-23985-4_22
18. Palavitsinis, N., Manouselis, N., Sanchez-Alonso, S.: Metadata quality in learning object repositories: a case study. Electron. Libr. **32**(1), 62–82 (2014)
19. Rehak, D., Mason, R.: Engaging with the Learning Object Economy, pp. 22–30 (2003)

20. Tumer, D., Shah, M.A., Bitirim, Y.: An empirical evaluation on semantic search performance of keyword-based and semantic search engines: Google, Yahoo, Msn and Hakia. In: Fourth International Conference on Internet Monitoring and Protection, 2009. ICIMP 2009, pp. 51–55. IEEE (2009)
21. Wiley, D.: Connecting learning objects to instructional design theory: a definition, a metaphor, and a taxonomy. Learn. Technol. **2830**, 1–35 (2001)
22. Yu, H.Q., et al.: A linked data-driven & service-oriented architecture for sharing educational resources. In: Linked Learning 2011: the 1st International Workshop on eLearning Approaches for the Linked Data Age. ESCWC 2011 (2011). http://oro.open.ac.uk/28856/

Designing a User-Friendly Educational Game for Older Adults

Louise Sauvé[1(✉)], David Kaufman[2(✉)], and Patrick Plante[1(✉)]

[1] TÉLUQ University/SAVIE, Quebec G1K9H6, Canada
louisesauve25@gmail.com, pplante@teluq.ca
[2] Simon Fraser University, Burnaby, BC V5A 1S6, Canada
dkaufman@sfu.ca

Abstract. Given the importance of a well-constructed educational gaming interface and the costs involved in its development, it is important to identify the ergonomic requirements to be considered during the design process to ensure that the game be adapted to the characteristics of seniors. In a study of seniors aged 55 and older, we created and tested an educational game, "In Anticipation of Death", in order to measure usability in the sense of determining the intuitive capacity of the game (user-friendliness). This paper presents the variables of the study, the way we adapted the game Solitaire for seniors and the results of an experiment done with 42 older players. The latter showed a high degree of satisfaction with game navigation, the display mode and gameplay equipment. Recommendations are presented to guide the development of online educational games for seniors.

Keywords: Educational games · Ergonomics · Older adults · Validation · User-friendliness

1 Introduction

Researchers have pointed out that the effectiveness of educational games depends on players' needs and individual characteristics and that we need to develop systems that can adapt to the demands of their target audiences [1–4]. An inappropriate design can discourage seniors' use of online educational games [4].

In this article, we first define what we mean by user-friendliness in an educational game. Then, we describe how we have adapted the user-friendliness aspect of a well-known game, Solitaire, for seniors. We briefly present the results of a field test of the educational game, "In Anticipation of Death", made available online for testing with 42 seniors to determine their degree of satisfaction with the game's user-friendliness. Finally, we offer recommendations to guide the development of effective educational games for older adults.

2 User-Friendliness in the Game

Our game development approach is rooted in a User-Centered Design (UCD) methodology, which integrates an ergonomic approach into product development. This approach is based on criteria of usability. Usability refers to the ability of the game to

M. A. Herzog et al. (Eds.): ICWL 2019, LNCS 11841, pp. 39–46, 2019.
https://doi.org/10.1007/978-3-030-35758-0_4

adapt to the characteristics of the target user (user-centered design) and to be intuitive (user-friendly). User-friendliness refers to the qualities of a digital game that make it easy and pleasant to use and understand, even for someone with little computer knowledge. The role of the game's environment is to help the player focus on what is important.

The objective of the study was to evaluate the user-friendliness of the educational game for seniors. In order to meet the objective of the study, the interface of the Solitaire game was adapted to allow us to introduce educational content in the form of quizzes.

3 Choosing the Type of Game and Its Educational Content

We initially relied on a survey of 931 seniors from Quebec and British Columbia, as part of the project "Aging Well: Can Digital Games Help?" (2012–2016), in which the game of Solitaire was identified as one of the favourites of older adults [5].

3.1 Solitaire

Solitaire is a single-user game that is played with a deck of 52 cards. The first 28 cards are arranged into seven columns of increasing size, which form the Board. Only the last card of each column on the Board is placed face up. The 24 remaining (face down) cards make up the Stock pile, also called the Deck. Cards from the Stock pile are discarded, according to the player's choice, one or three at a time. Finally, the game ends when all the cards are placed into four piles for each suit and sorted in ascending order (from Ace to King), or when a player declares forfeit because they cannot move any more cards. In the latter case, the player can start a new game. For this study, the Solitaire interface is coupled with a questionnaire game.

To create the online educational game "In Anticipation of Death", we used the UCD process, which consists of testing the product (an educational game) at different stages of its development with its future users (in our case, 24 older adults) and making any modifications needed.

3.2 Learning Content

For the game's questionnaire, we interviewed 167 seniors aged 55 and over in a second study, "Promoting Social Connectedness through Playing Together - Digital Social Games for Learning and Entertainment" (2015–2020). These participants were interested in the actions to be taken upon the death of their spouse; more than 72% expressed a lack of knowledge about arranging the affairs of their spouse. The objectives of the game are to empower seniors to recover amounts owed to their spouse, to pay any outstanding debts, and to fulfill their spouse's wishes concerning the disposition of their body [6].

To integrate learning content into the game without creating cognitive overload for seniors, information should be broken up into small units (one or two lines) or simple questions (true/false or multiple choice with one or more answers or objects to be matched). Repeating content elements allows seniors to recognize them and consider them useful for their progress in the game [2, 9, 10].

For experimental purposes, we split the learning content into small units, which resulted in 70 closed questions (true/false or multiple choice with one or more answers), divided into three levels of difficulty (22 easy, 24 medium and 24 difficult) identified by one, two or three stars. This division ensures that the questions repeat at least once during a game with the goal of completing the four piles.

4 Navigation in the Game's Environment

To make a game environment intuitive for seniors, designers should ensure that players can easily access all components (cards, navigation buttons, instructions/tutorials and score) needed for the game to run smoothly [7, 8, 10]. To facilitate players' movement in the game, it is very important to make sure that the game and its components display without overflowing the screen and without blocking some game elements [4, 11]. For a comfortable gameplay experience, the design should use a predetermined frame or a responsive web design to maintain a standard display layout across screens. The game board and accessories for playing should cover most of the screen, and scroll bars in page displays should be avoided. In the game "In Anticipation of Death", we divided the game interface into three areas (see Fig. 1) to make it easier to navigate.

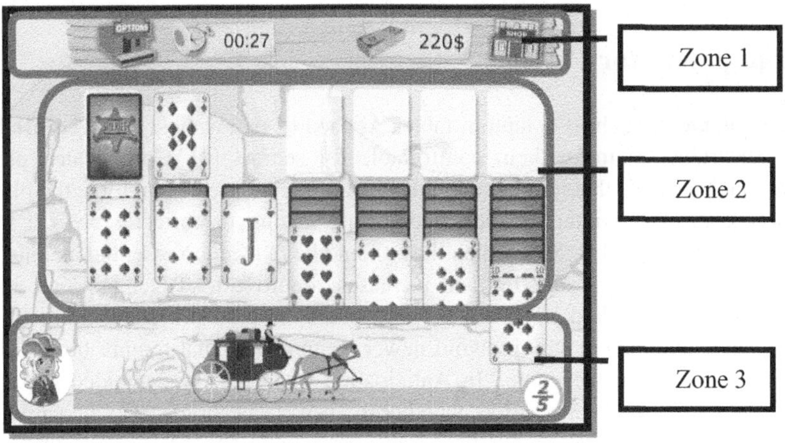

Fig. 1. Game environment

Zone 1 (Information) contains all the information needed to understand how the game unfolds: the options menu, the timer, the number of accumulated credits and the access icon for the privilege store. Zone 2 (The game board) includes all the playing elements of the game: the Stock pile, the seven columns and the four stacks of cards. Zone 3 (Apprenticeship) refers to the educational aspect of the game: a tutorial accessible at all times and a progression line that allows you to display a question to be answered after every five movements of the cards in the game.

To facilitate navigation within the game, the game elements and question content should be limited to one screen page. This avoids long and tedious scrolling on the screen, which particularly demotivates seniors with short attention spans [4, 7, 8, 10]. In the game "In Anticipation of Death", we restricted the display format of the game board to the smallest configuration used by our target audience: 1024 × 768. This window is always visible independently of the other windows that are superimposed

It is also important to minimize the use of superimposed windows during the course of a game. Because some older users are less likely to notice page changes and can become confused, a clear notification of a change of screens should be displayed as, for example, when the player goes from the "game" page to a "Questions/Information" page) [12]. In the game "In Anticipation of Death", we limited the number of windows to only two. When the second window appears in the center of the screen, the game board becomes gray and inactive.

Similarly, if question content is integrated into the game, all relevant information must be available to the player through single clicks. In the game "In Anticipation of Death", we designed learning questions to include on the same page all relevant information (question statements, answers, degree of difficulty, feedback, credits earned or lost). The questions, answers, feedback, etc. are displayed in a second window superimposed on the game board. The size of this window is variable, but always smaller than the board.

5 Equipment for Playing

Game equipment, such as a laptop, tablet, keyboard, or joystick, must be used with some constraints to make them comfortable for seniors [4]. Complicated physical actions, such as those that require a double click of the mouse or that force the player to precisely control a pointer on the screen while having to correctly press a button, should be avoided [4, 11]. Mouse handling should be reduced to essential actions, since it requires hand-eye coordination and increases cognitive load [13]. Instead, use the arrow keys of a standard keyboard or a keyboard adapted to handle the game. For seniors, game equipment should avoid newer technologies that require high skills for effective use [11]. In the game "In Anticipation of Death", we avoided requiring a double click to perform any action, whether to answer questions, to move cards in the game, to open the tutorial, to purchase a privilege, or to choose gaming options.

If a game controller is used, we recommend a one-handed device such as a computer mouse or the Wii Remote. Tablets must have screen sizes that are large enough to clearly display needed information [13, 14]. For experimentation purposes, we opted for computers with a mouse, 15" touchscreen laptops, and 10" tablets that allow seniors to move the elements of the game with their finger or mouse. We also integrated buttons with words and symbols to make it easier for seniors who were not born in the digital age.

6 The Methodology

6.1 Demographic Data

It is very difficult to find objective definitions for the terms “senior” or “elder.” “There is no current consensus on new definitions proposed by experts.” [15, p. 8]. These authors [15] identify two types of seniors: those who are currently 65, the threshold that defines the elderly according to Statistics Canada, and those considered to be the next generation of seniors, adults aged 55 to 64.

Among the 42 participants in the Solitaire Quiz experiment, there were 19 women and 23 men. The sample included 20 participants aged 55 to 60 years (48%) and 22 subjects aged 61 and over (52%). Among the sample, nine players said that they did not have the skills to use digital games, while 18 players identified themselves as “beginners” and 15 as “intermediate” participants. Of the 42 participants, 90.5% played the game at least five times for an average duration of 7.3 min, and 42.9% played between six and nine times for the duration of the experiment.

6.2 Technology

In order to assess the design of the educational game as adapted for seniors 55 and older, we tested the game with 42 older adults using a mouse, 15” touchscreen laptops, and Android and iPad tablets.

6.3 Experiment

The experiment took place over the course of two months. Participants were invited to play the game at least five times. This experiment was approved by the university’s ethics committee. Each participant was made aware of the research purpose and signed a paper or online consent form.

6.4 Measuring Instruments

Before the experiment, we administered a questionnaire on socio-demographic data and seniors’ habits (12 items). After the experiment, a self-administered questionnaire was given online on user-friendliness relating to navigation in the game’s environment (six statements), equipment for playing (three statements) and players’ interest in the game Solitaire Quiz (three statements). The items were operationalized by a Likert scale of five levels (from strongly agree to strongly disagree and the option does not apply). The questionnaire also included a section to collect written comments from respondents.

7 Results

For player perceptions concerning the user-friendliness aspect of the game (navigation in the game’s environment and equipment for playing), all the items had positive outcomes in that average ratings were above the favourable perception threshold (in agreement) of 4.00 (Table 1).

In addition, the standard deviations show a low dispersion of responses. In other words, the respondents' opinions were generally grouped around the average. The standard deviations of all items were below 1.00.

Table 1. Participants' perceptions about navigation and the playing equipment

Criteria	Items	Mean	SD
Navigation in the game's environment	Access: the three areas of the game interface	4.63	0.53
	Screen size and information displayed	4.63	0.61
	Representativeness of the icons	4.51	0.68
	Superimposition of windows	4.57	0.63
	Loading time of the pages	4.40	0.59
	Grouping actions in one page	4.74	0.50
Equipment for playing	Number of clicks	4.35	0.59
	Tactile screen	4.63	0.67
	Mouse	4.57	0.59

Finally, the vast majority (92.86%) of participants liked to play Solitaire enhanced with a Quiz and 90.48% of the players wished they could try a new quiz. All participants would recommend the game to others.

8 Recommendations

Although the perceptions observed in this study relate to a specific game (Solitaire Quiz), the results can be applied to different types of games. Some recommendations can be made to educational game designers:

- Avoid player confusion, organize gameplay information into zones and reduce as much as possible the number of controls necessary to accomplish a task.
- Reduce the number of windows and clicks needed to access and play the game. This speeds up the pace of the game and promotes player motivation.
- Design the game board components to minimize the game's download time.
- Group gameplay actions on one page without a superimposed window.
- Facilitate the movement of objects on the game board by using a touch screen (for tablet and touch-screen users) or a mouse (for PC and Apple users) by enlarging the surface object to move.
- Avoid actions that require a double click of the mouse. This double action is not easily performed by seniors and some of them regularly forget to do so, which creates a frustration and demotivation.

9 Conclusions

Our study shows that the design of an educational game must take into account its target audience. To make the game easier for seniors to use, it is important to make sure that the components of the game are visible within the screen, that the grouping of player actions accelerates the game and keeps up players' motivation, that the use of the mouse or the touch screen makes actions easy to perform in the game and requires little manual dexterity. In addition, our participants showed general interest in this educational game.

While obtaining positive results on the three dimensions of the study, our results are limited by the limited number of respondents (n = 42) and the experimentation time (2 months). Further studies will be needed to address these limitations and to examine the impact that the online educational game has had on seniors.

Acknowledgements. These two research studies were funded in part by grants from the Social Sciences and Humanities Research Council of Canada and from AGE-WELL NCE, Inc., a member of the Networks of Centres of Excellence of Canada. We would like to thank Curt Ian Wright for the translation, and Alice Ireland for editing.

References

1. Diaz-Orueta, U., Facal, D., Herman Nap, H., Ranga, M.-M.: What is the key for older people to show interest in playing digital learning games? Initial qualitative findings from the LEAGE Project on a Multicultural European Sample. Games Health **1**(2), 115–123 (2012)
2. Astell, A.J.: Technology and fun for a happy old age. In: Sixsmith A., Gutman, G. (eds.) Technologies for Active Aging. International Perspectives on Aging, vol. 9, pp. 169–187. Springer, Heidelberg (2013). https://doi.org/10.1007/978-1-4419-8348-0_10
3. Marston, H.R.: Design recommendations for digital game design within an ageing society. Educ. Gerontol. **39**(2), 103–118 (2013). https://doi.org/10.1080/03601277.2012.689936
4. Sauvé, L. Online educational games: guidelines for intergenerational use. In: Romero, M., Sawchuk, K., Blat, J., Sayago, S., Ouellet, H. (eds.) Game-Based Learning Across the Lifespan. Advances in Game-Based Learning, pp. 29–45. Springer, Cham (2017). https://doi.org/10.1007/978-3-319-41797-4_3
5. Kaufman, D., Sauvé, L., Renaud, L., Duplàa, E.: Enquête auprès des aînés canadiens sur les bénéfiques que les jeux numériques ou non leur apportent [Survey of Canadian seniors to determine the benefits derived from digital games]. Research report, TELUQ, UQAM, Quebec, Simon Fraser University, Vancouver (BC), University of Ottawa, Ottawa (2014)
6. Sauvé, L., Plante, P., Mendoza, G.A.A., Parent, E., Kaufman, D.: Validation de l'ergonomie du jeu Solitaire Quiz: une approche centrée sur l'utilisateur [Validation of the Ergonomics of the Game Solitaire Quiz: A User-Centered Approach]. Research Report, TÉLUQ, Quebec, Simon Fraser University, Vancouver (BC) (2017)
7. Barnard, Y., Bradley, M.D., Hodgson, F., Lloyd, A.D.: Learning to use new technologies by older adults: perceived difficulties, experimentation behaviour and usability. Comput. Hum. Behav. **29**(4), 1715–1724 (2013)
8. Ogomori, K., Nagamachi, M., Ishihara, K., Ishihara, S., Kohchi, M.: Requirements for a cognitive training game for elderly or disabled people. In: International Conference on Biometrics and Kansei Engineering (ICBAKE), October, pp. 150–154. IEEE (2011). https://doi.org/10.1109/ICBAKE.2011.30

9. Sauvé, L., Renaud, L., Mendoza, G.A.A.: Expérimentation du jeu de Bingo «Pour bien vivre, vivons sainement!» [Experimenting with the Bingo Game "Live Well, Live Healthy!"]. Research Report. CRSH, TÉLUQ, UQAM & SAVIE, Québec, Canada (2016)
10. Wu, Q., Miao, C., Tao, X., Helander, M.G.: A curious companion for elderly gamers. In: Network of Ergonomics Societies Conference (SEANES), 2012 Southeast Asian, pp. 1–5. IEEE, Langkawi, July 2012. https://doi.org/10.1109/seanes.2012.6299597
11. López-Martínez, Á., Santiago-Ramajo, S., Caracuel, A., Valls-Serrano, C., Hornos, M.J., Rodríguez-Fórtiz, M.J.: Game of gifts purchase: computer-based training of executive functions for the elderly. In: 1st International Conference on Serious Games and Applications for Health (SeGAH), November, pp. 16–18. IEEE Computer Society, Washington (2011). https://doi.org/10.1109/segah.2011.6165448
12. Shneiderman, B., Plaisant, C., Cohen, M., Jacobs, S., Elmqvist, N., Diakopoulos, N.: Designing the User Interface: Strategies for Effective Human-Computer Interaction, 6th edn. Pearson, Boston (2016)
13. Al Mahmud, A., Shahid, S., Mubin, O.: Designing with and for older adults: experience from game design. In: Zacarias M., de Oliveira J.V. (eds), Human-Computer Interaction: The Agency Perspective, vol. 396, pp. 111–129. Springer, Heidelberg (2012). doi.org/ https://doi.org/10.1007/978-3-642-25691-2_5
14. Marin, J.A.G., Navarro, K.F., Lawrence, E.: Serious games to improve the physical health of the elderly: a categorization scheme. In: CENTRIC 2011: The Fourth International Conference on Advances in Human-oriented and Personalized Mechanisms, Technologies, and Services, October, Barcelone, Espagne, vol. 8547, pp. 64–71 (2011)
15. Turcotte, M., Schellenberg, G.: Un portrait des aînés au Canada [A portrait of seniors in Canada]. Statistiques Canada, Canada, 321 (2006)

Learning Analytics

Be Constructive: Learning Computational Thinking Using Scratch™ Online Community

Bushra Chowdhury[1], Aditya Johri[2(✉)], Dennis Kafura[1], and Vinod Lohani[1]

[1] Virginia Tech, Blacksburg, VA 24061, USA
bushrac@gmail.com, kafura@cs.vt.edu, vlohani@vt.edu
[2] George Mason University, Fairfax, VA 22030, USA
johri@gmu.edu

Abstract. Online learning communities are predicated on the assumption that social interaction among participants will lead to learning. Yet, research has shown that not all interactions result in learning and that there is a need to develop a more nuanced understanding of the nature of activities in online communities and their relationship with learning. We analyzed data from the Scratch™ online learning community, a platform designed to teach Computational Thinking (CT) through block-based activities, using the Differentiated Overt Learning Activities (DOLA) framework to assess learning. We found that users who engaged in constructive activities demonstrated higher learning, as illustrated by the complexity of their contributions, compared to users who were merely active on the platform. We compared users across two sub-communities within Scratch and found that participation and contributions across the two domains resulted in different learning outcomes, showcasing the effect of context on learning within online communities.

Keywords: Online community · Computational thinking · Informal learning · Collaborative learning · Scratch

1 Introduction

The use of online communities to foster learning is well-documented in the literature especially for computational concepts and programming [28, 31]. The context for this research is Scratch™, specifically its community-based platform where one can code games, animations, and stories using media-based programming language. In Scratch, one uses 'blocks', which are puzzle shaped pieces, to create code. The blocks connect to each other like a jigsaw puzzle, where each block represents a particular programming concepts (e.g., if, do-if, repeat, end). Within Scratch, users have the opportunity to see projects completed by others, use pre-existing code, comment on others' projects and seek assistance from others. Community based interaction in Scratch manifests as commenting, remixing, and sharing of projects [11]. Scratch has been used in AP courses and introductory programming courses at the college level [9, 10]. Scratch has been designed primarily to support the development of Computational thinking (CT) in primarily in young people (ages 8 to 16) [4–7] but has also found some adoption

M. A. Herzog et al. (Eds.): ICWL 2019, LNCS 11841, pp. 49–60, 2019.
https://doi.org/10.1007/978-3-030-35758-0_5

among adults [8]. CT as a concept articulates a set of problem-solving thought processes derived from computer science but applicable in any domain [29]. In its earlier incarnations CT was largely seen as "algorithmic thinking" and referred to using an ordered and precise sequence of steps to solve problems. Wing (2006) defined it as "solving problems, designing systems, and understanding human behavior, by drawing on the concepts fundamental to computer science" [30]. Overall, CT is a broad umbrella term that encompasses core computational science concepts as well as programming skills.

2 Prior Work and Research Objective

Several studies of the Scratch community have examined the relational aspect of user's social behavior. Researchers have used comments, number of projects created, remixing, favorites, love-its and friend requests as a way to characterize collaboration [11–13]. Sylvan [14] investigated social interactions in terms of project influence and social influence. Project influence was measured as the number of times a project has been downloaded and social influence in terms of betweenness centrality of friendship networks. Studies have also looked at number of times a user's project had been featured and gallery participation [14]. Similarly based on social factors and differences in projects created, Scaffidi and Chambers [21] categorized users as project leader, active user, peripheral user and remixer/passive user and Monroy-Hernández and Resnick [22] categorized users in terms as active consumer, passive producer active producer. These studies have focused on the overall community or the user themself but have not examined CT. On the other hand, researchers that have examined the use of computational concepts within Scratch [15–20] have not focused on the interaction among users. The exception is Dasgupta et al. who in their study focused on the association between remixing and learning CT [5]. They studied number of remixes, downloads made by the user, experience of the user, comments received on projects created by the user, and number of different blocks used by the user as predictors.

Overall, although studies have looked at social and collaborative aspects of Scratch and also at CT, there is limited understanding of how specific kinds of activities that users engage in can lead to CT learning. This study hypothesizes that difference in the nature of social interactions exhibited by a user can lead to difference in learning of CT. To examine directly the relationship between the nature of interactions and learning outcomes, this study leverages a framework advances within the cognitive sciences and uses data from the online community for Scratch™.

3 Analytical Framework

3.1 Differentiated Overt Learning Activities (DOLA) Framework

Few frameworks allow for differentiation of learner activities so that we might be able to tease out what activities actually lead to learning. Chi proposed a framework – Differential Overt Learning Activities or DOLA – which categorizes learner activities as being active, constructive or interactive [3]. An interactive activity involves higher cognitive process than constructive and constructive is higher cognitively than active learning. In contrast to any form of active learning, passive learning involves teacher-centered methods and is a form of learning applicable largely to formal educational contexts, and therefore, not applicable to our study [23].

An active activity can be noticed when a person takes an action, does something physically or verbally. A constructive activity is demonstrated when the output of the interaction goes beyond the information initially provided. An interactive activity is exhibited between partners when both parties are involved in collaboration contribute equally. Table 1 below provides brief definitions of active, constructive and interactive activities and the supposed cognitive processes associated with them.

Table 1. Chi's Differentiated Overt Learning Activities (DOLA) framework

	Active	Constructive	Interactive
Feature	Doing something physically	Producing outputs that contain ideas that go beyond the presented information	Dialoging substantively on the same topic, and not ignoring partner's contributions
Cognitive processes	*Attending Processes* Activate existing knowledge Assimilate, encode, or store new information Search existing knowledge	*Creating Processes* Infer new knowledge Integrate new information with existing knowledge Organize own knowledge for coherence Repair own faulty knowledge Restructure own knowledge	*Jointly Creating Processes* Creating processes that incorporate partner's contributions

Classroom studies [23, 24] using Chi's DOLA framework have characterized selecting, repeating, paraphrasing as active behavior. In terms of virtual learning environments, simply manipulating an existing scenario in simulation software was considered to be active. On the other hand, when a learner elaborately explains a problem, makes a connection to previous problems, generates a hypothesis, compare and contrasts, draws analogies the learner is considered to be constructive. An interactive activity in collaboration is revealed when both partner's debate each other's ideas, when an instructor provides feedback which leads to a more extended dialogue discussing the issue etc. Although Chi's framework looks at all activities, alone or in collaboration, it can be easily extended to study collaborative learning and studies using Chi's DOLA framework have been used to evaluated student's collaborative behavior in learning concepts in physics, mathematics, bridge design, evolutionary biology, human circulatory system, introductory materials science and engineering.

3.2 Operationalizing DOLA for Scratch

For the purposes of this study, we operationalize Scratch users' activities in terms of being active and constructive and investigate their relationship to CT learning. Within the context of Scratch online community most activities are collaborative in the sense that they involve either interacting with or using elements of others' project. In particular, we were interested in understanding these socially driven activities since they are a better indicator of collaboration.

We did not examine interactive activity since the inherent affordances of the platform restricted interaction to asynchronous and even if users interacted synchronously, we did not have the data for the analysis (there was no clickstream data, for instance). We also did not operationalize passive activity since the online platform data did not contain data of passive activity such as number of times a user played or watched a project.

This study defines collaborative activities of a user by counting the number of times the user initiates different types of interactions. For example: the total number of users a particular user follows, a number of times user favorites other projects, the number of times a user goes out and makes comment on other's projects, and the number of times a user remixes another user's project. In case of adapting Chi's DOLA framework the study further classifies these interactions into active and constructive. Table 2 provides definitions of active interactions. Interactions that do not modify or elaborate on the topic were considered active (e.g. follow, favorite).

Table 2. DOLA operationalized for scratch – active category

Active activities	Definition
Favorited	Total number of times a user favorites other projects
Follow	Total number of users a particular user follows
Active_Comment	Total number of times a user makes active comments on other projects word count less than 18 usually emojis, encouraging phrases/verbs/adjectives [1]
Active_Remix	Total number of projects created by a user that was a remix of another user's project where the number of different types of blocks uses is the same as the original project

To categorize comments as active and constructive, Velasquez et al. [11]'s findings have been applied. According to Velasquez et al. [11], comments with word count less than 18 (usually emojis, encouraging phrases, verbs and adjectives) were categorized as active and comments with word count more 18 as constructive. However, in order to better understand the constructive nature of the comments, comments with greater than 18 words were manually coded for our study. An interaction was characterized as constructive interaction when a user is assumed to modify and elaborate on a particular topic (e.g. modify a projects code). Table 3 provides definitions of constructive interactions.

Table 3. DOLA operationalized for scratch – constructive category

Constructive activities	Definition
Original_Projects	Total number of original projects created by a user
Constructive_Comment	Total number of times a user makes constructive comments on other projects Word count >18.320 and containing constructive praise or criticism [1]
Constructive_Remix	Total number of projects created by a user that was a remix of another user's project where the number of different types of blocks uses is the more than the original project

4 Data Description and Selection

The scratch community datasets from 2007 through 2012 are publicly available to researchers for analysis through MIT Media Lab. Scratch Research Data (available at: https://llk.media.mit.edu/scratch-dataset/). This study used the following data tables for analysis: comments, downloaders, favorites, friends, projects, project_blocks, and users.

To find a relevant dataset within the larger data corpus, we used pre-classified data from Gelman et al. [2]. Gelman et al. [2] in their study identified clusters of Scratch 8184 users who had more than 25 followers. Gelman et al. used OpenOrd layout in Gephi to identify different models of community growth over time to understand how scratch user's behavior and dynamics impact community participation. OpenOrd is a multi-level, force-directed layout and uses average-link clustering based on both edge weights and distance, where distance is determined using a force-directed algorithm [25]. Clusters of nodes were replaced by single nodes, and the clustering was repeated until a certain distance threshold between the nodes was reached. After the clustering was complete, the graph was expanded by replacing the individual nodes with the original graphs in each cluster. Using a text mining approach and by concatenating project titles, descriptions, and tags for all projects within each cluster, each cluster was represented as a document with a bag-of-words approach. For each term, the term frequency inverse document frequency (TFIDF) value was calculated resulting in five clusters: a cluster that heavily featured old Scratch users (number of users 278), a young cluster of game makers (number of users 1798), an comparatively mature game making user cluster (number of users 2710), a cluster of users focusing on art projects and another cluster which had a Variety of projects (number of users 2260). The reason for choosing TFIDF over Term Frequency (TF) was to determine the relevance of a particular term within a particular cluster versus its relevance across all clusters.

We sub-selected two of the pre-identified clusters by Gelman et al. [2], the cluster with comparatively mature game makers and the cluster with variety of projects. The Gaming cluster initially had 2710 users. However, only 2173 users only had at least 5 projects. Similarly, in the Variety cluster initially 1934 out of 2260 users were used for analysis. From now onwards in this paper we will identify these two clusters as game cluster and Variety cluster. The reason for selecting two completely diverse clusters was to illustrate difference in cluster behavior. The Gaming cluster would exemplify comparatively keen CT learners and the Variety cluster would provide more of a general user behavior in Scratch.

5 Data Analysis

5.1 Learner Initiated Computational Thinking

In this study, we aim to focus only on actions initiated by the user. It is important to investigate such self-initiated social behaviors because these interactions are self-motivated and self-regulated by the learner himself/herself. Thus, in order to assess a learner's overall experience in learning in an open online line platform it is necessary to focus on what s/he does as well as what s/he learns from the community.

Figure 1 illustrates different social interactions initiated by a user in the context of the Scratch community. For example, User A in Fig. 1 can leave a comment on a project, favorite projects created by other users, and follow other users in the Scratch community. User A can also create a project from scratch (original project) or remixing code from pre-existing projects (remixed project). All these interactions: comment, favorite, follow and creating/remixing are user initiated.

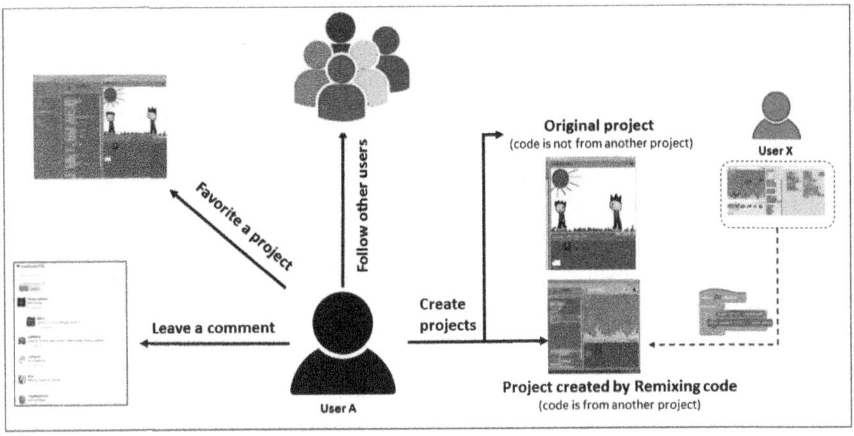

Fig. 1. Social interaction initiated by a user in scratch

5.2 Learning Analysis Using IDF

In this study, CT as a process has been evaluated as a combination of user's self-initiated social interactions and by evaluating the amount of CT learning skills the user is exhibiting with- in projects. One of the studies to directly examine learning within

Scratch is Yang et al. [15]. They used Inverse Document Frequency (IDF) to assess learning. IDF is a widely used statistical measure for assessing the importance of a word is in a document [26, 27]. Whereas, Term Frequency (TF) is simply the number of times a word appears in a document, IDF assigns more weight to key words that appear rarely than the ones that are more commonly used. Thus, IDF helps to better determine the breadth of use of different CT operators used with-in projects created by Scratch users. Yang et al.'s model assigned higher weight to computational blocks that were rarely used and lower weight to frequently used blocks. Based on the different types blocks used in original projects created by a user, Yang's model calculates a cumulative value of learning. We apply the same method to assess learning for all users in a cluster with at least 5 projects. The cumulative value was calculated based on all original projects created by a user. We further subcategorize learning across three parameters: loop learning, conditional learning and operator learning. Table 4 indicates the different blocks used to operationalize each sub learning categories. Studies evaluating CT in Scratch have similarly used blocks to assess the different categories CT learning [4, 5, 7].

Table 4. Categories of CT and corresponding blocks used for evaluation

Type of learning	Blocks used
Loop	forever, foreverIf, repeat, repeatUntil
Conditional	waitUntil, foreverIf, if, ifElse, repeatUntil, bounceOffEdge, turnAwayFromEdge, touching, touchingColor, colorSees, mousePressed, keyPressed, isLoud, sensor, sensorPressed, lessThan, equalTo, greaterThan, and, or, not, listContains
Operator	lessThan, equalTo, greaterThan, and, or, not, add, subtract, multiply, divide, pickRandomFromTo, concatenateWith, letterOf, stringLength, mod, round, abs, sqrt

6 Results and Discussion

In order to test the hypothesis proposed in this study we conduct three steps of analysis. For both clusters we first measure interactions of each user; second, we measure CT learning of each user; and third, we correlate interactions with CT learned. These three steps allow us to examine the one-to-one relationship between different types of social interactions and CT learning.

The summary statistics for measures of social interactions and learning of users of the Gaming and the Variety cluster are provided below in Table 5 (G: Gaming; V: Variety).

Table 5. Summary statistics for gaming and variety clusters

		M Median	x̄ Mean	Σ S.D	Range
Favorited	G	36	105	238.66	[0–4232]
	V	28	79.98	182.057	[0–3466]
Follow	G	43	90.92	152.9	[1–2061]
	V	44	95.94	177.350	[0–3070]
Active_Comment	G	276.95	414.95	491.908	[0–7400]
	V	206	352.39	456.456	[0–5882]
Active_Remix	G	8	16.67	27.27	[0–501]
	V	8	17.25	28.751	[0–429]
Original _Projects	G	44	71.89	93.04	[5–1841]
	V	38	70.22	117.350	[5–1903]
Constr_Comment		Very limited, disregarded this factor			
Constructive_Remix	G	7	14.31	25.93	[0–617]
	V	4	10.19	22.86	[0–565]
Total CT learning	G	101	99.15	36.65	[.8–318.54]
	V	72.07	73.60	43.03	[0–312.37]
Loop learning	G	4.19	3.66	.96	[0–4.19]
	V	3.13	2.97	1.39	[0–4.19]
Conditional learning	G	18.9	18.49	6.19	[0–31.48]
	V	15.25	14.34	7.47	[0–28.77]
Operator learning	G	12.47	12.43	6.11	[0–41.39]
	V	8.55	8.86	6.70	[0–41.39]

In terms of differences between clusters, values for favorites (Gaming cluster user's median favorited: 36, Variety cluster user's median favorited: 28) were higher in Gaming cluster than the Variety cluster. All other social interactions values were less in the same range for both the Gaming and Variety cluster.

In terms of learning, the Gaming cluster had higher values (user's median use of loop in a project: 4.19, conditional: 18.9 operator: 12.47) than the Variety cluster (loop: 3.13, conditional: 15.25, operator: 8.55). Before correlating social interactions with learning some factors (e.g. remix_active and constructive, follow, favorited) were log transformed to achieve normality. This was done because those particular data sets were highly skewed. Previous studies [5, 17] on Scratch data have also used log-transformed data sets for analysis. According to our model, the more challenging or rare and constructive is the nature of the task, the higher is the learning.

The findings of the study confirm the proposed hypothesis that in the context of Scratch users, difference in the type (active versus constructive) of activity exhibited by a user can lead to difference in learning of CT. For example, a user who had created more original projects and more remix projects with added features to the existing code learned more than a user who did less of either of these two constructive activities. Creating remixed projects and commenting on projects were also found to be active behavior that correlates to learning of CT.

In terms of separate CT concepts, including Loop, Conditions and Operators; Conditional learning correlated higher with constructive interactions than the Loop or Operator learning. For both clusters, learning from constructive interactions was found to be stronger than the relationship between CT learning and active interactions. In terms of difference between clusters and relationship between social interactions and learning CT, users of the Variety cluster learned more by creating original projects and extensively remixing (remix_constructive) projects than users of the Gaming clusters. However, when it came to active interactions, users of the Gaming cluster learned more by just following, commenting and simply remixing (remix_active) code than users of the Variety cluster (Table 6).

Table 6. Correlational analysis of activity and CT learning

		Total CT learn	Loop learn	Condition learn	Operator learn
Active Interactions					
log_follow	G	.077**	.067**	.072**	.070**
	V	.024	−.026	.002	.019
log_comment_active	G	.293**	.252**	.259**	.221**
	V	.351**	.278**	.297**	.282**
log_favorited	G	.228**	.199**	.228**	.191**
	V	.209**	.176**	.182**	.178**
log_remix_active	G	.378**	.268**	.347**	.363**
		.466**	.390**	.438**	.419**
Total_log_active	G	.321**	.261**	.293**	.261**
	V	.466**	.390**	.438**	.419**
Constructive Interactions					
log_original	G	.466**	.312**	.404**	.430**
	V	.545**	.450**	.507**	.483**
log_remix_constructive	G	.509**	.370**	.478**	.456**
	V	.636**	.533**	.603**	.588**
Total_log_constructive	G	.497**	.337**	.459**	.433**
	V	.636**	.533**	.602**	.588**

A stronger association of active interactions with the Gaming clusters and that of constructive interactions with the Variety clusters could be explained by the difference in the learning scores of the users in both clusters. Since users of the Gaming cluster scored higher compared to users of the Variety cluster, possibly users of the Gaming cluster learned more by casually investigating (favoriting/active_remix) projects, whereas the users of the Variety cluster needed to explore the project in depth (constructive_remix) to understand and use a computational concept. Users with higher prior knowledge found it easier to learn compared to a novice CT learner and a novice CT learner needs to do more constructive tasks to learn more.

7 Discussion and Conclusion

In this study, we evaluated social interactions initiated by users in the Scratch community using Chi's DOLA framework to characterize online behavior that suggests learning. The analysis revealed a relationship between active, constructive social interactions and learning of CT. Different clusters exhibited difference in learning based on the type of social interactions. Users of the Gaming cluster were able to learn at a higher rate while being socially active (active social interactions) whereas for users of the Variety cluster to be learning at higher rate they needed to be socially constructively. To put in simply, a seasoned CT learner (e.g. Gaming Cluster user) can gain knowledge by glancing at another project's code, whereas for a novice CT (e.g. Variety cluster users) learner needs to be hands-on constructively engaged to learn CT.

Overall, the findings from this study support prior work that shows a clear connection between the ability of online communities to support different forms collaborative activities and the affordances that provides for learning [28, 32–34]. This work also showcases the potential upside of using data mining and machine learning to analyze learning [35, 36]. In terms of practical application of this work, educators should design problems that foster active/constructive behavior in novice CT learners. Novice learners can start off by solving active problems such as examination of pre-written codes by experts, or making minor changes to pre-existing codes. Gradually, the learners should be encouraged to add new features to pre-written code (the constructive idea of remixing with added features) and keep on creating new computational projects.

8 Limitations

The primary limitation of this work is the lack of self-reported information (e.g., age, sex) of participants. We were unable to collect any data reported directly by the learner to assess learning. The dataset is relatively older but given the comprehensive nature of the data, it is still relevant for answering the research questions we have raised.

Acknowledgements. This work is supported in part by U.S. National Science Foundation Awards #142444, 1408674, & 1712129 (PI: Johri) and Award#1624320 (PI: Kafura). Any opinions, findings, and conclusions or recommendations expressed in this material are those of the authors and do not necessarily reflect the views of the funding agencies. We thank Ben Gelman for his support with the data collection and analysis.

References

1. Kreijns, K., Kirschner, P.A., Jochems, W.: Identifying the pitfalls for social interaction in computer-supported collaborative learning environments: a review of the research. Comput. Hum. Behav. **19**(3), 335–353 (2003)
2. Gelman, B., Beckley, C., Johri, A., Yang, S., Domeniconi, C.: Online urbanism: interest-based subcultures as drivers of informal learning in an online community. In: Proceedings of ACM Learning at Scale Conference 2016 (2016)

3. Chi, M.: Active-constructive-interactive: a conceptual framework for differentiating learning activities. Top. Cogn. Sci. **1**(1), 73–105 (2009)
4. Brennan, K., Resnick, M.: New frameworks for studying and assessing the development of computational thinking. Presented at annual meeting of the American Educational Research Association, Vancouver, Canada (2012)
5. Dasgupta, S., et al.: Remixing as a pathway to computational thinking. In: Proceedings of the 19th ACM Conference on Computer-Supported Cooperative Work & Social Computing (2016)
6. Robles, G., et al.: Software clones in scratch projects: on the presence of copy-and-paste in computational thinking learning. In: IEEE 11th International Workshop on Software Clones (IWSC) (2017)
7. Moreno-León, J., Robles, G., Román-González, M.: Scratch: automatic analysis of scratch projects to assess and foster computational thinking. RED Revista de Educación a Distancia **15**(46), 1–23 (2015). https://www.um.es/ead/red/46/moreno_robles.pdf
8. Resnick, M., et al.: Scratch: programming for all. Commun. ACM **52**(11), 60–67 (2009)
9. Ericson, B., Guzdial, M., Biggers, M.: Improving secondary CS education: progress and problems. In: ACM SIGCSE Bulletin. ACM (2007)
10. Bryant, R., et al.: Computational thinking: what is it, how is it relevant, who's doing what with it? J. Comput. Sci. Colleges **25**(1), 170–171 (2009)
11. Velasquez, N.F., et al.: Novice Programmers Talking about Projects: What Automated Text Analysis Reveals about Online Scratch Users' Comments (2014)
12. Scaffidi, C., Dahotre, A., Zhang, Y.: How well do online forums facilitate discussion and collaboration among novice animation programmers? In: Proceedings of the 43rd ACM technical symposium on Computer Science Education. ACM (2012)
13. Fields, D.A., Giang, M., Kafai, Y.: Understanding collaborative practices in the Scratch online community: Patterns of participation among youth designers. In: CSCL 2013 Conference Proceedings. International Society of the Learning Sciences (2013)
14. Sylvan, E.: Predicting influence in an online community of creators. In: Proceedings of the SIGCHI Conference on Human Factors in Computing Systems. ACM (2010)
15. Yang, S., Domeniconi, C., Revelle, M., Sweeney, M., Gelman, B., Beckley, C., Johri, C.: Uncovering trajectories of informal learning in large online communities of creators. In: Proceedings of ACM Learning at Scale (2015)
16. Manovich, L., Remixing and remixability. Retrieved on Jan, 2005. 10: p. (2008)
17. Hill, B.M., Monroy-Hernández, A.: The remixing dilemma the trade-off between generativity and originality. Am. Behav. Sci. **57**(5), 643–663 (2013)
18. Hermans, F., Aivaloglou, E.: Do code smells hamper novice programming? Delft University of Technology, Software Engineering Research Group (2016)
19. Matias, J.N., Dasgupta, S., Hill, B.M.: Skill progression in scratch revisited. In: Proceedings of the 2016 CHI Conference on Human Factors in Computing Systems. ACM (2016)
20. Ota, G., Morimoto, Y., Kato, H.: Ninja code village for scratch: Function samples/function analyser and automatic assessment of computational thinking concepts. In: Proceedings of 2016 IEEE Visual Languages and Human-Centric Computing (VL/HCC)
21. Scaffidi, C., Chambers, C.: Skill progression demonstrated by users in the Scratch animation environment. Int. J. Hum. Comput. Interact. **28**(6), 383–398 (2012)
22. Monroy-Hernández, A., Resnick, M.: Empowering kids to create and share programmable media. Interactions **15**, 50–53 (2008). ACM ID, 1340974
23. Menekse, M., et al.: Differentiated overt learning activities for effective instruction in engineering classrooms. J. Eng. Educ. **102**(3), 346–374 (2013)
24. Chi, M., Wylie, R.: The ICAP framework: linking cognitive engagement to active learning outcomes. Educ. Psychol. **49**(4), 219–243 (2014)

25. Martin, S., et al.: OpenOrd: an open-source toolbox for large graph layout. In: IS&T/SPIE Electronic Imaging. International Society for Optics and Photonics (2011)
26. Sparck Jones, K.: A statistical interpretation of term specificity and its application in retrieval. J. Documentation **28**(1), 11–21 (1972)
27. Manning, C.D., Raghavan, P., Schütze, H.: Introduction to Information Retrieval, vol. 1. Cambridge University Press, Cambridge (2008)
28. Bruckman, A.: Learning in online communities. In: Sawyer, R.K. (ed.) The Cambridge Handbook of the Learning Sciences, Cambridge University Press, New York, pp. 461–472 (2006)
29. Wing, J.M.: Computational thinking. Commun. ACM **49**(3), 33–35 (2006)
30. Yadav, A., Stephenson, C., Hong, H.: Computational thinking for teacher education. Commun. ACM **60**(4), 55–62 (2017)
31. Brandt, J., Guo, P., Lewenstein, J., Dontcheva, M., Klemmer, S.: Two studies of opportunistic programming: interleaving web foraging, learning, and writing code. In: Proceedings of CHI, Boston, MA, USA, pp. 1589–1598 (2009)
32. Johri, A., Yang, S.: Scaffolded help for informal learning: how experts support newcomers' productive participation in an online community. In: Proceedings of Communities and Technologies (C&T) (2017)
33. Almatrafi, O., Johri, A.: Showing and telling: response dynamics in an online community of makers. In: Proceedings of CSCL 2017 (2017)
34. Teo, H., Johri, A., Lohani, V.: Analytics and patterns of knowledge creation: experts at work in an online engineering community. Comput. Educ. **112**, 18–36 (2017)
35. Almatrafi, O., Johri, A., Rangwala, H.: Needle in a haystack: identifying learner posts that require urgent response in MOOC discussion forums. Comput. Educ. **118**, 1–9 (2018)
36. Lester, J., Klein, C., Rangwala, H., Johri, A.: Learning Analytics in Higher Education. ASHE Monograph Series, vol. 3, Issue 5 (2017). https://twitter.com/_CHINOSAUR/status/461864317415989248

What Can Interaction Sequences Tell Us About Collaboration Quality in Small Learning Groups?

Dorian Doberstein(✉), Tobias Hecking, and H. Ulrich Hoppe

COLLIDE Research Group, University of Duisburg-Essen, Lotharstr. 63, 47045 Duisburg, Germany
{doberstein,hecking,hoppe}@collide.info

Abstract. One advantage of small group collaboration in online courses is that it can enrich the students learning experience with regard to interactional and social dimensions. In this paper we apply a previously tested method of sequential analysis on group activity sequences. These activity sequences stem from an online course on computer mediated communication where the group tasks consisted of collaborative text production. Students activities in a group forum and a shared wiki were recorded and classified as coordination, monitoring, major/minor contribution. Analyses of clusters of similar sequences show, that there are characteristic patterns indicating productivity, fair work distribution, as well as satisfaction with the group work. Our findings are a step towards automatic diagnosis of collaboration problems in online group work to facilitate early interventions.

Keywords: Learning groups · Online courses · Sequence analysis · Collaboration patterns

1 Introduction

It is a well-known deficit of MOOCs (at least of xMOOCs) [3] and many online courses in general that they primarily address receptive learning behavior based on watching (videos), reading (instructional texts), and possibly filling-in quizzes. Adding more interactive and collaborative tasks is desirable for several reasons: First, it would increase the level of engagement on the part of the learners and thus enhance the learning experience. This assumption is backed by general pedagogical theories such as the ICAP framework proposed by Chi and Wylie [2]. Second, collaborative tasks such as small group writing assignments can be naturally combined with peer-to-peer feedback and peer assessment [9]. This would help to overcome the notorious shortage of individualized feedback in big online courses (due to a lack of human resources) [8, 11, 14]. Finally, these activities lead to producing learner-generated content that enriches the pre-defined set of learning materials in a way that incorporates and reflects the learner perspective.

Introducing productive small group activities to online courses can also create a feeling of being part of an active community, which can lead to reducing attrition rates

M. A. Herzog et al. (Eds.): ICWL 2019, LNCS 11841, pp. 61–71, 2019.
https://doi.org/10.1007/978-3-030-35758-0_6

[13]. Furthermore, the heterogeneity of background knowledge and point of views in a large audience can be exploited for different kinds of group compositions and to facilitate knowledge exchange and critical discourse between participants [14].

However, there is evidence that strategies for group composition, e.g. based on diversity, have to be combined with strategies for supporting group work. In pure online courses group work often takes place asynchronously and communication is mediated and constrained by technology. This requires additional coordination effort in collaborative task solving. This challenge is a central focus of the ongoing research project IKARion (see Sect. 2).

Our work aims at identifying success conditions for small group work in online courses based on indicators that rely on the analysis of action logs from collaborative writing activities. In our approach, human coding is used to categorize actions in the form of different contribution types (*coordination, monitoring, minor/major contribution*, and inactivity periods or "*gaps*"). Sequences of such action descriptors are then collected for portions of group work related to a given task. The technique of "sequence alignment", originally developed in bioinformatics to compare DNA sequences, is then used to calculate the similarity of such sequences. The ensuing similarity matrix forms the basis for a cluster analysis. The clusters show specific patterns especially regarding the distribution of inactivity and coordination, and they can also be compared in terms of group productivity, well-being and balancedness of the group work.

In previous studies using this approach [6, 7], we have been able to show that the clusters emerging from the sequence analysis capture important differences in the dependent variables related to the quality of group work. The most important finding was that not general inactivity (as one might expect) but a lack of coordination activities between the students in early phases was the most decisive negative indicator related to group work quality (including productivity and balancedness). I.e., the negative effects of a longer delay in starting co-productive work can be counterbalanced by early meta-level coordination.

This paper uses data from an environment in which different levels of group feedback were implemented to stimulate productive and balanced group work. So, in addition to the contingencies between clusters and quality of group work, we also address the potential of interventions that influence the group activities through feedback and scaffolds in the environment.

The remainder of this paper is organized as follows: Sect. 2 describes the IKARion project in more detail. Section 3 illustrates the analysis approach and Sect. 4 presents the results. The last Section discusses our findings and future work.

2 Background: IKARion Project

This paper emerged in the context of the IKARion Project[1] which is a joined project between the University of Applied Sciences Lübeck, University of Duisburg-Essen, and the Ruhr University Bochum. The aim of the project is the design of intelligent

[1] https://www.ikarion-projekt.de/.

support for small-group work in larger online courses. Part of the project is the analysis and diagnosis of interaction patterns in small-group work. Based on this and further analysis into problems of group work in online courses [12], an intervention system is being implemented and tested with the target of intelligent and customized feedback.

In the context of this project multiple studies are being conducted. In each study an online course is implemented, and different kinds of problems are investigated. Moodle was chosen as learning management system for all studies as it is already in use in all participating universities. The primary objective of the first study was to support groups during online group work with regard to a fair work distribution between group members and timely reactions to communication activities. The topic of the course was computer mediated communication. The course language was German, and a to receive credits, students had to actively participate in group work. Groups consisted of 4 students each and were randomly formed for 6 consecutive group tasks which were implemented throughout the duration of the course. For each task an introduction video, literature and a self-test quiz was offered as learning material. The duration for each group task was 2 weeks and the task was to collaboratively write a wiki article of at least 600 words. For the collaborative text production, the Moodle wiki plugin was utilized and communication between group members was supported by a separate Moodle group forum.

As the focus of this study was the support of the group work with regard to a fair work distribution and timely reactions to communication between the group members, interventions were offered to some groups. The groups were divided into 3 conditions: *Control*, *Mirroring*, *Mirroring&Guiding*. The *Control* groups received no form of interventions. In contrast to that, the *Mirroring* groups were shown visualizations of the current work distribution between group members (all texts written in the forum and wiki were considered) in form of a bar chart that showed how much each group member contributed to the group task. Furthermore, to address the problem of late answers to forum post a second visualization was offered to the *Mirroring* groups which showed the last three forum messages and the time that had passed since those activities occurred. The same visualizations were shown to the *Mirroring&Guiding* groups and additionally guiding messages were offered that based on previous activities in the group offered a short guiding message if an uneven work distribution between the group members was detected or if the time between reactions to forum posts were too long. The visualizations and guiding messages were integrated into the Moodle platform, so that they were apparent to the students while viewing the course material.

Given the relatively low sample size (29 groups are considered in the dataset that was analyzed for this paper) no significant differences between groups in different conditions with regard to the satisfaction with the group work or the distribution of participation within the group could be found. Therefore, the assumption that the feedback mechanisms work could not be made. While the main target of the first study was to support groups during online group work with regard to a fair work distribution and timely reactions to communication activities, and to investigate differences between groups with mirroring or guiding support, it was the aim of the second study to investigate differences between an automatized system assessment of student's behavior and a student self-assessment. One main question was if a system could asses the student's behavior based on action logs as well as students could assess their own actions with regard to the work distribution between group members. Due to a relatively small number of participants (27 students) no clear statement could be made if the system could capture student's behavior as well as the students could evaluate their own behavior. Thus, one aspect of a future study is to again compare system- and self-assessment with a larger sample size. Furthermore, the target of another study is to integrate "fake" inactive users into groups and investigate if the shaming of such inactive users could have a positive or negative impact on the group work. In all recent and following studies which are conducted in the context of the IKARion project the different support mechanisms are being improved with the aim to achieve a positive effect on groups that receive support by the system.

3 Approach

In this section we describe the analysis approach which was proposed in [6] and [7]. Prior to the sequence analysis, some preprocessing steps are necessary to construct the final activity sequences. Afterwards, pairwise distances are calculated which form the bases for a cluster analysis. To compare the clusters and assess the analysis process, multiple measures are described which are calculated based on the learner-generated artefacts (wiki articles) as well as results from surveys that the learners were given during and after each group task.

3.1 Dataset and Preprocessing

The dataset used in the following analysis process contains all for the group task relevant user activities for two group tasks from the first course described in Sect. 2 (topic: computer mediated communication). Overall, this dataset contains the activities of 29 groups (group task 1: 16 groups; group task 2: 13 groups). The topic for the first group task was "social presence" and the second topic was "brainstorming as a learning method". Relevant user activities in this context means, that only those activities appear in the activity sequence that are perceptible for other group members: posts to the forum and edits to the group wiki. Other activities such as views of forum post or views of the wiki are not included since these activities are not visible for the rest of the group and thus cannot affect actions of other group members. For each group, the relevant activities are collected and ordered based on temporal occurrence.

In the next step, all relevant activities in the sequences were classified according to the nature of the contribution, resulting in one encoded collaboration sequence per group. There were 4 possible classes: *major contribution*, *minor contribution*, *coordination*, *monitoring*. These classes are based on behavior categories for learner interaction during online collaboration proposed by Curtis and Lawson [4].

Contributions in the wiki were classified as either *major contributions* or *minor contributions*. *Major contributions* added a considerable amount of text (>110 words) and extended the semantic content of the text. These activities are typical for students who added their complete contribution to the group work in one activity instead of multiple additions of smaller amounts of texts.

Minor contributions were small improvements in spelling or smaller text modifications (<110 words). Those were contributions of users who either incrementally added their text and improved it over time or smaller additions and improvements for contributions of other group members. The threshold of 110 words was chosen as it distinguished quite well between contribution activities of users who prepared their part and only edited the wiki once and users who incrementally added text passages in multiple activities throughout the group task. For borderline cases, a closer look into the content of the contributions decided if a contribution was classified as *major* or *minor*.

Post to the forum were typically classified as either *coordination* or *monitoring*. Activities that were dedicated to organizing the group work were classified as *coordination*. Those messages had a prospective character such as distributing the work between group members or coordinating availability and work schedules.

In contrast to that, retrospective posts were classified as *monitoring*. Typically, those were reports regarding own contributions to the wiki or reflection on the progress. As it was done manually, the classification process was time consuming. If actions occurred that were not related to the group task (i.e. discussion of personal matters) these actions were deleted from the dataset.

The resulting encoded collaboration sequences only contained actions of the group members and therefore did not reflect phases of inactivity during which no group member was active in the forum or the wiki. Especially those inactive phases were of special interest since these can have a negative impact on the group work [5].

To also include these phases of inactivity, a new *gap* action was inserted into the collaboration sequence when all group members were inactive for 24 h. A *start* action was added as first item in each sequence with a timestamp that corresponds to the start time of the assignment. This was done, to identify inactive periods before the first activity of a group member took place. The final encoded collaboration sequences of the groups can be interpreted as a characteristic fingerprint of their collaborative activities. In the next step, a pair-wise comparison between the sequences is performed before similar sequences are clustered together.

3.2 Sequence Matching and Clustering

For the sequence matching, first the distance measure is calculated followed by similarity-based clustering on the basis of the ensuing distance matrix. A proper measure for the distance of two collaboration sequences can be derived from sequence alignment or optimal matching as used in bioinformatics. In the context of social studies, Abbot and Tsay [1] reviewed the application of similar techniques. The idea of optimal matching is the calculation of the minimal costs of transforming one sequence into another using insertion, substitution and deletion of elements (similar to the Levenshtein distance).

For this, different basic costs can be assigned to different operations. In this case, we defined the cost for insertion and deletion as 1 while the cost for substitution was 2 if a gap was involved and 1 in all other cases. Our reasoning is that we want to emphasize the difference between activity and inactivity. Hence, changing a gap into an action or an action into a gap should be more expensive since inactive periods can be an indicator for problematic group work. So, substituting inactivity with activity should be weighted accordingly.

The result of this step is a distance matrix which in the next step is used to group the sequences into clusters. The method partitioning around medoids (PAM) was used for the clustering [10]. Using PAM, the idea is to search for k representative instances (medoids) for each cluster. In the first step, the algorithm searches for a suitable set of representative instances (build phase) followed by a matching phase where other instances are assigned to their closest representative until no switch of objects between clusters improves the results. The clustering was performed with different number of clusters k, ranging from 2 to 4. Since for $k > 2$, clusters which contained only one activity sequence emerged, $k = 2$ was chosen as the aim of our analysis is to make more generalized predictions for the group work. Clusters containing only one sequence would not allow for such a generalized view.

3.3 Measures

To assess how well the clustering distinguishes between different kinds of groups, different measures are calculated for each group which describe the productivity (word count), the satisfaction with the group work and the work distribution between group members.

Word Count. The word count measure simply states the number of words in the final version of the produced wiki article. Therefore, it is based solely on the productivity of the group. As for all group tasks, the target was to write at least 600 words, taking just the word count for assessing the outcome produced by a group is of limited significance. It is however the case, that some groups exceeded this minimum by hundreds of words. For this reason, the word count can still be utilized to differentiate between groups that only achieved the minimum and groups that were more engaged in the group task.

Satisfaction. Following each group task, the individual students were given surveys. Included in this survey were questions regarding the satisfaction with the group work among group members. Two different statements were given and rated on a 5-point Likert scale. The first statement was that the learner was overall satisfied with the group work (*Satisfaction 1*). The second statement was that the learner would be willing to work with the same group members in future group tasks (*Satisfaction 2*). Since the sequential analysis approach presented in this paper aims at the investigation of groups and does not characterize learners on an individual level, for each group and each statement, a satisfaction level was defined as the mean of the satisfaction levels of all group members.

Work Distribution (Gini Index). The third property aims at the work distribution and measures how balanced the amount of text contributions between the group members are. First, the share of words that each group member has contributed to the group task was calculated. Both, text contributions to the forum and wiki were considered. Based on this, the Gini index for the contributed characters of the 4 group members was calculated. The Gini index is a measure of deviation of a distribution from an (ideal) uniform distribution and ranges between 0 and 1. For an even work distribution between group members, where everyone contributed the same amount the Gini index is 0 while for a most uneven work distribution where one did all the work it is 1.

4 Results

The clustering divided the 29 activity sequences into 2 clusters. The two clusters are depicted in Fig. 1. Cluster 1 contains 19 sequences and cluster 2 contains 10 sequences. Each sequence is arranged horizontally beginning with a start activity (red) which states the beginning of the task. Each action in the sequence is colored according to its class. Following the start activity, the other activities are ordered by temporal occurrence.

Table 1 describes the average number of activities, gaps, coordination activities and gaps and coordination activities during the first half of the task (first week) for each cluster. Table 2 shows the productivity (word count) the satisfaction with the group work based on survey results and the work imbalance between group members (Gini index) as described in Sect. 3.3.

Generally speaking, there are lots of phases of inactivity (gaps: 7.5–9.6) which is not surprising since the task was not too extensive and thus could be completed in one week and according to our experiences, groups tend to work more focused towards the deadline. Typically, inactive phases are in the beginning while longer periods of inactivity (48 h inactivity = 2 gaps) are rare in the later stages of the task, especially in cluster 2. The longest activity sequence can be found in cluster 2 and contains 35 user activities and 10 gaps. In contrast to that, the shortest sequence contains only 7 activities and 10 gaps (cluster 1). The sequences in cluster 1 are on average shorter (11.7 activities) than the sequences in cluster 2 (24.7 activities; gaps were ignored in this calculation).

Groups in cluster 2 showed more than three times as many coordination activities (11.5) than groups in cluster 1 (3.6). Likewise, groups in cluster 2 showed more than twice as many coordination activities during the first half of the task (3.3) than groups in cluster 1 (1.26). 70% of the groups in cluster 2 showed a coordination message within the first 3 days. In contrast to that, this is the case for only 47% of the groups in cluster 1. The difference increases if coordination attempts with responses are considered. Looking at the first 5 days of the task, 7 out of 10 groups (70%) in cluster 2 show 2 or more coordination activities. In contrast to that, only 4 out of 19 groups (21%) in cluster 1 performed 2 or more coordination activities within the first 5 days. With regard to longer periods of inactivity where none of the group members are active for a period of 5 days or more, this behavior can be found in 20% of the groups in cluster 2, while such inactive phases appeared in more than 3 out of 4 groups in cluster 1 (79%).

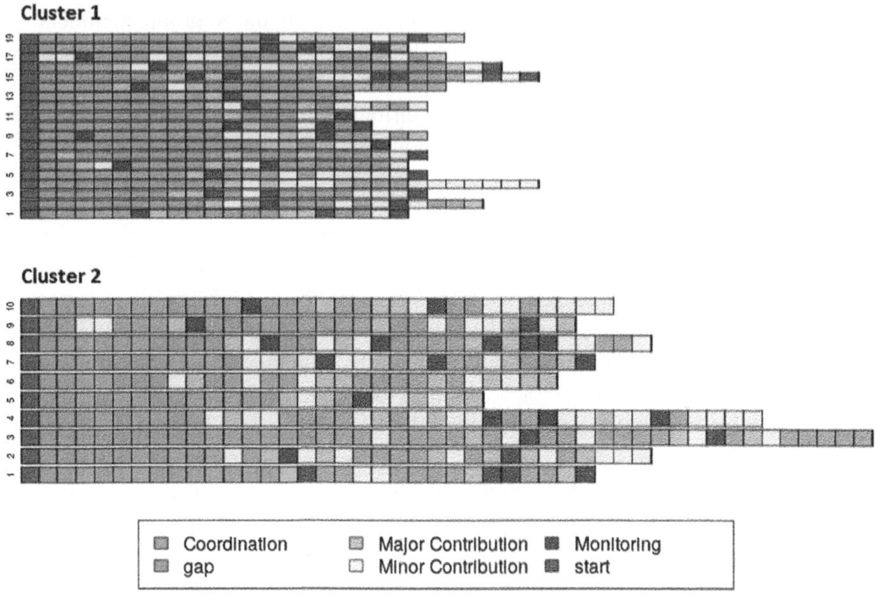

Fig. 1. Resulting clusters for the PAM clustering (k = 2). (Color figure online)

Since properties that are connected to the sequence representation (such as activity count, coordination count, gap count, …) have an impact on the distance calculation the large discrepancy between for example average activity count and coordination count between the clusters is not surprising. That said, we also compared the clusters in terms of productivity, satisfaction with the group work and work imbalance between the group members. These measures are not considered in the distance calculation, thus finding significant differences for those measures between the clusters would indicate that the sequential analysis approach presented in this paper can be utilized to differentiate between for example productive and non-productive group work. A significance test was conducted for these measures. Since the clusters are not equal in terms of number of sequences per cluster and with the small sample size a normality of the clusters cannot be guaranteed. Thus, a significance test based on ranks (Mann-Whitney U Test) was conducted to test for significance between the clusters.

Table 1. Average values for the number of activities, gaps (first half) and coordination (first half) for each cluster (best values in bold face).

Cluster	#Activities	#Gaps	#Coordination	#Gaps first half	#Coordination first half
1	11.7 (3.2)	9.6 (1.2)	3.6 (2.0)	5.8 (1.2)	1.3 (1.6)
2	**24.7** (5.3)	**7.5** (1.4)	**11.5** (5.3)	**5.0** (1.2)	**3.3** (2.2)

Table 2. Average values for word count, satisfaction and work imbalance for each cluster (best values in bold face). Significance levels: $p \leq 0.001^{***}$, 0.01^{**}, 0.05^{*}

Cluster	Word count***	Satisfaction 1**	Satisfaction 2*	Work imbalance (Gini index)*
1	823 (286)	2.97 (0.89)	2.66 (0.94)	0.53 (0.23)
2	**1222** (239)	**3.93** (0.55)	**3.61** (0.87)	**0.34** (0.15)

Notably is the significantly (p = .0009) higher productivity for the groups in cluster 2. On Average groups in this cluster produced 1222 words in their final wiki text, which is 399 words more than groups in the first cluster (823). Provided that a minimum for the text length of the wiki articles was specified (600 words), the groups in both clusters met the minimum requirements. The groups in cluster two however, exceeded this minimal value by more than twice the required amount, proving that these groups worked on the tasks more extensively. Moreover, the three groups that did not reach the specified minimum (word count: 401–566) all belong to cluster 1, while the three most productive groups (word count: 1414–1680) can be found in cluster 2.

With regard to the satisfaction with the group work it can be said that overall the learners in cluster 2 were more satisfied with the work inside the group (Satisfaction 1 for cluster 1: 2.97; cluster 2: 3.96; p = .0057). Likewise, learners in cluster 2 were more willing to work with the other group members in future tasks (Satisfaction 2 for cluster 1: 2.66; cluster 2: 3.61; p = .0107).

The last measure describes how evenly the work is distributed between the group members. Considering all activities that occurred during the group work, the work in cluster 2 was more evenly distributed (Gini index: 0.34) than in cluster 1 (Gini index: 0.53; p = .0162).

As described in Sect. 2 one goal of the study was to test the efficiency of the intervention mechanisms using different conditions for the groups. With regard to the cluster analysis, no significant connection between the cluster affiliation of a group and its condition could be found. This could mean, that either the intervention mechanisms were not effective enough to support the group work, or that the approach presented here is not suitable to distinguish between the activity sequences of groups for different conditions. Since no significant differences between the groups in different conditions could be found with regard to satisfaction with the group work and a fair work distribution between group members (see Sect. 2), the first option seems more likely.

Lastly, a spearman correlation analysis was conducted to find out if there is a connection between the satisfaction within the group and the work distribution. For this, the cluster affiliation was not considered, instead the correlation was calculated based on all 29 groups. The results showed, that the Gini index correlated with Satisfaction 1 (cor = −0.661, $p<0.001$) as well as Satisfaction 2 (cor = −0.662, $p < 0.001$). The negative correlation values are due to the fact that for the Satisfaction measure a Likert scale was used (higher = better) and for the Gini index a lower value means a more even work distribution. An obvious interpretation would be that group members are naturally more satisfied with the group work and willing to work together in the future if all members contribute equally. Another significant correlation could be found between the word count and the amount of coordination in the first half of the task (cor = 0.37, p = .046). This could mean that groups that coordinate in the beginning of the task have more time to write their wiki article and are therefore more thorough.

Furthermore, a correlation could be found between Satisfaction 2 (willingness to work together in the future) and the word count (cor = 0.39, p = .035). This could indicate that students prefer to work in groups that easily reach the minimum requirement for produced text.

5 Discussion

In this paper we explored the relationship between different collaboration patterns in online group learning tasks and the learners' level of satisfaction. The results add on to previous works, which report that early coordination is a good indicator for productivity and a fair distribution of work, in the sense that it could be shown these two productivity features go along with the stated satisfaction with the group work by the respective group members.

Learners who were associated with groups that had a good level of productivity and a more balanced work distribution were overall happier with the group work. This was shown by the high negative correlations between the satisfaction levels and the Gini index which measures the work imbalance, as well as a positive correlation between word count and the willingness to stay in the group.

Furthermore, there are characteristic collaboration patterns associated with the aforementioned variables. As in previous work, the importance of early coordination in the discussion forum has to be emphasized.

These finding have some implications on the design of scaffolding mechanisms for group work in online courses. On the one hand, no significant effect of the currently implemented mirroring and guiding mechanisms (see Sect. 2) could be found. However, on the other hand, desirable collaboration patterns could be identified that are positively related with effective group collaboration. Consequently, one hypothesis for future work is that the intervention mechanisms of a collaborative online learning platform should be advanced such that the learners are better guided to the desired mode of collaboration, i.e. early coordination of individual contributions and no unplanned phases of inactivity. This is a possible way to improve the overall level of satisfaction with distributed group learning and in conjunction therewith the individual learning experience.

However, in future work it will be important to investigate additional parameters for successful group work such as individual engagement of learners or different roles taken by group members. This would help to put the observation that early coordination indicates good group work in a broader context.

Acknowledgement. This study was conducted in the context of the IKARion Project and we want to thank the IKARion Project Team. The project was funded by the Federal Ministry of Education and Research (grant number: 16DHL1013).

References

1. Abbott, A., Tsay, A.: Sequence analysis and optimal matching methods in sociology: review and prospect. Sociol. Methods Res. **29**(1), 3–33 (2000). https://doi.org/10.1177/0049124100029001001
2. Chi, M.T.H., Wylie, R.: The ICAP framework: linking cognitive engagement to active learning outcomes. Educ. Psychol. **49**(4), 219–243 (2014). https://doi.org/10.1080/00461520.2014.965823
3. Clow, D.: MOOCs and the funnel of participation. Proc. Third Int. Conf. Learn. Anal. Knowl. - LAK '13. 185 (2013). https://doi.org/10.1145/2460296.2460332
4. Curtis, D.D., Lawson, M.J.: Exploring collaborative online learning. JALN - J. Asynchronous Learn. Netw. (presently OLC – Online Learn. Consortium) **5**(1), 21–34 (2001). https://doi.org/10.24059/olj.v5i1.1885
5. Davies, W.M.: Groupwork as a form of assessment: common problems and recommended solutions. High. Educ. **58**(4), 563–584 (2009). https://doi.org/10.1007/s10734-009-9216-y
6. Doberstein, D., et al.: Sequence patterns in small group work within a large online course. In: Gutwin, C., et al. (eds.) Collaboration and Technology, pp. 104–117 23rd International Conference on Collaboration and Technology (CRIWG), Saskatoon, SK, Canada (2017). https://doi.org/10.1007/978-3-319-63874-4
7. Doberstein, D., et al.: Using sequence analysis to characterize the efficiency of small groups in large online courses. In: Yang, J.C., et al. (eds.) Proceedings of the 26th International Conference on Computers in Education (ICCE 2018), pp. 247–256. Asia-Pacific Society for Computers in Education, Philippines (2018)
8. Ferschke, O., et al.: Fostering discussion across communication media in massive open online courses. In: Proceedings of the 11th International Conference on Computer-supported collaboration Learning (2015)
9. Gielen, M., De Wever, B.: Structuring the peer assessment process: a multilevel approach for the impact on product improvement and peer feedback quality. J. Comput. Assist. Learn. **31** (5), 435–449 (2015). https://doi.org/10.1111/jcal.12096
10. Kaufman, L., Rousseeuw, P.J.: Clustering by means of medoids. In: International Conference on Statistical Data Analysis Based on the L_1-norm and Related Methods, March, pp. 405–416 (1987)
11. Staubitz, T., et al.: Collaborative learning in a MOOC environment. In: Proceedings of the 8th International Conference of Education, Research and Innovation, Seville, Spain, pp. 8237–8246 (2015)
12. Strauß, S., et al.: Developing a library of typical problems for collaborative learning in online courses. In: Proceedings of the 13th International Conference of the Learning Sciences (ICLS), London, UK, pp. 1045–1048 (2018)
13. Tomar, G.S., et al.: Intelligent conversational agents as facilitators and coordinators for group work in distributed learning environments (MOOCs). In: AAAI Spring Symposium - Technical Report SS-16-01, pp. 298–302 (2016)
14. Wichmann, A., et al.: Group formation for small-group learning: are heterogeneous groups more productive? In: Proceedings of the 12th International Symposium on Open Collaboration, pp. 14:1–14:4 (2016). https://doi.org/10.1145/2957792.2965662

An Architecture and Data Model to Process Multimodal Evidence of Learning

Shashi Kant Shankar[1(✉)], Adolfo Ruiz-Calleja[2], Luis P. Prieto[1], María Jesús Rodríguez-Triana[1], and Pankaj Chejara[1]

[1] Tallinn University, Tallinn, Estonia
{shashik,lprisan,mjrt,pankajch}@tlu.ee
[2] GSIC-EMIC Group, University of Valladolid, Valladolid, Spain
adolfo@gsic.uva.es

Abstract. In learning situations that do not occur exclusively online, the analysis of multimodal evidence can help multiple stakeholders to better understand the learning process and the environment where it occurs. However, Multimodal Learning Analytics (MMLA) solutions are often not directly applicable outside the specific data gathering setup and conditions they were developed for. This paper focuses specifically on authentic situations where MMLA solutions are used by multiple stakeholders (e.g., teachers and researchers). In this paper, we propose an architecture to process multimodal evidence of learning taking into account the situation's contextual information. Our adapter-based architecture supports the preparation, organisation, and fusion of multimodal evidence, and is designed to be reusable in different learning situations. Moreover, to structure and organise such contextual information, a data model is proposed. Finally, to evaluate the architecture and the data model, we apply them to four authentic learning situations where multimodal learning data was collected collaboratively by teachers and researchers.

Keywords: MMLA · Architecture · Data model · Multimodal Learning Analytics

1 Introduction

There has been an explosive growth in the use of Learning Analytics (LA) to support evidence-based decision making in learning and teaching practice, targeting multiple stakeholders (e.g., teachers, students or researchers) [13]. To support such decision making, most LA solutions use learning evidence from the digital space, such as logs from Learning Management Systems (LMSs) [15]. Such emphasis on digital traces, however, provides only a partial view of the learning process and the environment where it occurs. To overcome this issue, Multimodal Learning Analytics (MMLA) [12] enables the data collection from digital as well as physical spaces, using multiple modalities [16] to understand the learning context (e.g., adding sensors or observations to the logs).

M. A. Herzog et al. (Eds.): ICWL 2019, LNCS 11841, pp. 72–83, 2019.
https://doi.org/10.1007/978-3-030-35758-0_7

Most current MMLA solutions target researchers, have been tested in rather controlled/lab settings, and are tailored for specific learning situations [14]. This directly clashes with the reality that teachers and students face in their everyday learning environments, which include a wide variety of learning situations and contexts, within the same day (or even the same lesson): collaborative learning in the morning, inquiry one hour later, focused individual work, etc. Moreover, MMLA solutions currently require researchers or other technical staff to be present for data collection. This makes them often unfeasible for use in authentic educational settings. In contrast, there is an increasing awareness in the field of LA about the need for involvement of end-users (e.g., teachers, students) to develop more relevant and reusable LA (and MMLA) solutions [1,3,6].

Additionally, MMLA solutions are inherently more complex and data-intensive (due to the multiplicity of data sources). Several pieces of contextual information about the enactment of the learning situation may play a crucial role in the processing of multimodal evidence [14]. For example, a five-minute delay in the start of the learning activities, or the fact that teacher instructions did not emphasize enough the identification codes that students need to use in questionnaires (to be aligned with log data), can make or break a multimodal analysis, unless timely noticed. While such contextual information is easily taken into account by researchers and technicians when performing the alignment of multiple data sources, it can become an insurmountable challenge for other actors in an authentic educational setting, if researchers are not present during multimodal data collection. However, structuring and organising such contextual information needed for data processing of the learning situation [5] is a complex task, not addressed so far in the (MM)LA literature, to the best of our knowledge.

Based on these two challenges (the lack of reusability and the need to take into account contextual information during data collection), this paper tries to provide answers to the following Research Questions (RQs):

RQ1. How to support reusability of MMLA solutions in different authentic learning scenarios where multiple stakeholders are involved?
RQ2. How to structure and organise the contextual information of a learning situation, in order to process multimodal evidence of learning?

We hypothesise that a technological infrastructure can be designed to address these questions. In this paper, we propose a Processing Architecture for Multimodal Evidence of Learning (PAMEL). As an initial evaluation of the reusability of the PAMEL (RQ1), an initial prototype implementation has been applied to four authentic learning situations. In these four case studies, PAMEL processed multimodal evidence of learning by taking into account the contextual information of the learning situation. To organise and structure such contextual information (RQ2), this paper also describes the PAMEL's data model[1].

The rest of the paper is organized as follows. Section 2 briefly summarises the state-of-the-art related to MMLA architectures. PAMEL and its data model are

[1] This is not an UML-based data model but it is a sample data model.

described in Sects. 3 and 4, respectively. Section 5 presents the initial validation of the PAMEL in four different authentic learning situations. The paper ends with Sect. 6, which lays out the implications and future work on this line of inquiry.

2 Related Work

Many Learning Analytics (LA) research projects consider only one modality within a learning situation: the interaction between learners and digital tools [8], represented by the tool's system logs. A modality is the communication channel available in a learning situation, which is used as a medium among the stakeholders and learning resources to progress learning [21]. Modalities thus represent the different ways in which data can paint a picture of a learning process. For example, a group of students may discuss an exercise and later submit it as an assignment in the school's LMS. This interaction between one learner in the group and the digital platform, is only one of the potential modalities reflecting the students' engagement with the learning activity. In addition to this, the teacher may look for other evidence about such group engagement, e.g., observing the group's behaviour in the physical space of the learning situation. Indeed, multiple modalities are usually available in the physical space (like observation, or video recordings), which can complement the digital evidence [11].

The availability of low-cost sensors and other Internet-of-Things (IoT) devices, provides opportunities to collect learning evidence from multiple modalities [12]. MMLA leverages this opportunity and enables certain improvements to provide a wider picture of the learning process, learning context and the learning environment [17]. To reach that goal, MMLA collects multimodal evidence of learning (i.e., covers multiple modalities). Such multimodal evidence is processed and analysed to provide a coherent view of a learning process, to support decision making of multiple stakeholders [20] like teachers, students and researchers.

In the last few years, several MMLA systems have been proposed for a variety of tasks, from the automated assessment of public speaking skills based on audio and video recordings [4], to the prediction of learning outcomes based on facial expressions and body gestures of the learners [7]. However, many of the proposed MMLA solutions share a common problem with these examples: they are tailored for the needs of very specific learning tasks. This poses two challenges for the MMLA community:

1. an increased development effort to carry out multimodal data analyses [5] (as a different system and analysis process needs to be built for each new kind of learning task to be supported); and
2. difficulties in the adoption of MMLA solutions in authentic learning situations [11] which are more complex than the lab/controlled studies that have dominated MMLA research so far.

Moreover, the contextual information of the authentic learning situation is complex to structure and organise. There is no space in current MMLA solutions to account for local peculiarities of the data gathering (e.g., students are using the digital platform which is hosted in a different timezone and thus the system logs need re-alignment with the observations teachers are providing *in situ*). Nor is there space for unexpected local modifications during activity enactment (e.g., two of the students getting sick and not being able to join the activities).

To avoid the limitations of current, ad-hoc MMLA solutions, the community has started to propose more general MMLA infrastructures. In a recent review [18], the authors analyse the state-of-the-art of the MMLA infrastructures through a conceptual lens of the Data Value Chain (DVC) [10]. This DVC (see Fig. 1) includes seven activities for the processing of raw data to support decision making. These seven activities can be grouped in three coarse areas: data discovery, fusion and exploitation.

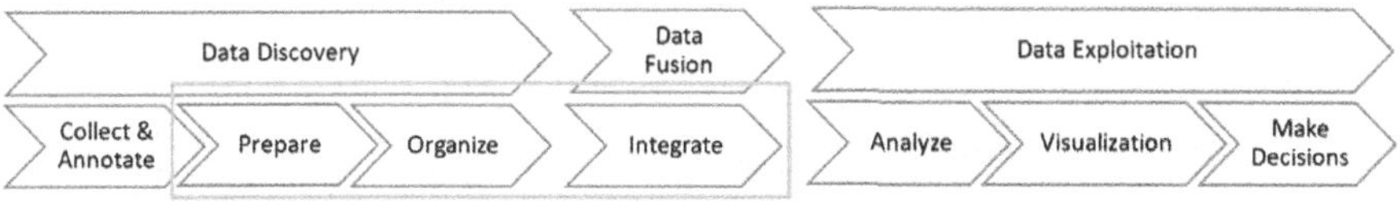

Fig. 1. Three key data processing activities of DVC for MMLA [10]

In the case of multimodal data processing, before data exploitation (i.e., analysis), the heterogeneous dataset needs to be prepared, organised and fused into a processed dataset on which usual machine learning or statistical analyses can be run. All together, to exploit the collected multimodal evidence with the contextual information of an authentic learning situation to support decision making of multiple stakeholders, we see the need of a software infrastructure which supports reusability and achieves data preparation, organisation and fusion activities taking into account the local variations of authentic educational settings. This includes also the need to structure and organise the contextual information that affects these three data processes.

3 PAMEL: Processing Architecture for Multimodal Evidence of Learning

To address our first research question on building a reusable infrastructure that can address a variety of authentic learning scenarios (RQ1), we propose a service-oriented architecture following the adapter-pattern. The service-oriented, adapters-based architectures [2] have two main advantages: being extensible to fetch data from additional physical and digital data sources (crucial to cope with current variety and future evolution of authentic settings); and supporting reusability in additional learning situations at a reduced development cost, as long as data is structured as per their specification.

The resulting Processing Architecture for Multimodal Evidence of Learning (PAMEL) (see Fig. 2) is a service-oriented architecture [9] following the *Adapter* pattern. PAMEL is designed to build MMLA solutions to support evidence-based decision making of multiple stakeholders like students, teachers and researchers, by taking the contextual information into account of the local (authentic) learning situation [17]. PAMEL carries out three data processing activities of the DVC: data preparation, organisation and fusion (see Sect. 2 above). The decisions which need to be taken in these three activities need the contextual information of the learning situation [5].

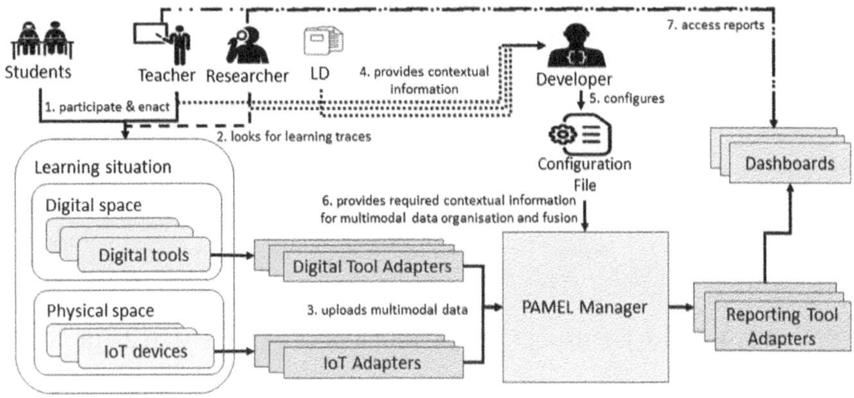

Fig. 2. PAMEL architecture

Such contextual information can be either fetched from learning orchestration related documents (like computer-interpretable learning designs) or provided by the multiple stakeholders acting in the learning situation. This fetched contextual information needs to be structured and organised. Thus, to address our second research question (RQ2), we propose a sample data model (see Sect. 4).

We followed the *Separation of Concerns* architectural design principle [19]: thus, we defined one architectural component to deal with each of those concerns.

In order to customize the MMLA solutions to the learning situation, and to adapt such solutions to serve the different stakeholders, teachers and researchers often need to collaborate [17]. To handle such learning situations, the proposed architecture includes three sets of adapters (two set of adapters are used for multimodal data preparation), a *PAMEL Manager* (the central component for multimodal data organisation and fusion), and a configuration file. The *Digital Tool Adapters* fetch system logs from the digital learning environments and feed them to the PAMEL Manager. Similarly, the *IoT Adapters* collect data from sensors and other devices placed in the physical learning environment, and send it to the PAMEL Manager. Additionally, these two sets of adapters translate the data into a common, often tabular, data format (e.g., a CSV). Then, the PAMEL Manager organizes and fuses the datasets. Finally, the *Reporting Tool Adapters* provide the fused learning evidence generated by PAMEL to the dashboards for later data analysis and visualisation.

In order to organise and fuse the multimodal evidence to present a coherent view of heterogeneous dataset, the PAMEL Manager requires contextual information of the learning situation. The contextual information changes along the learning activity and varies among/across learning situations. Moreover, pieces of the contextual information may be scattered over different learning orchestration related documents such as learning designs and teachers' notes. In some other cases, the contextual information is not documented at all, and only certain stakeholders are aware of it [5]. In any of those cases, the contextual information needed for the data processing has to be extracted, structured, and organised so that MMLA solutions can use them for multimodal evidence processing.

A configuration file is used to structure and organise this contextual information (see its proposed data model in Sect. 4). This file is currently assumed to be collaboratively defined by teachers, researchers and developers, not unlike existing proposals for multi-stakeholder involvement in LA projects [13]. For example, while teachers and researchers can provide details such as the number of participating students, or actual starting and ending time for the learning activities, developers (and researchers) can help with more technical aspects such as the correct timezone of each data source's timestamps. Please refer to Sect. 5 for further examples.

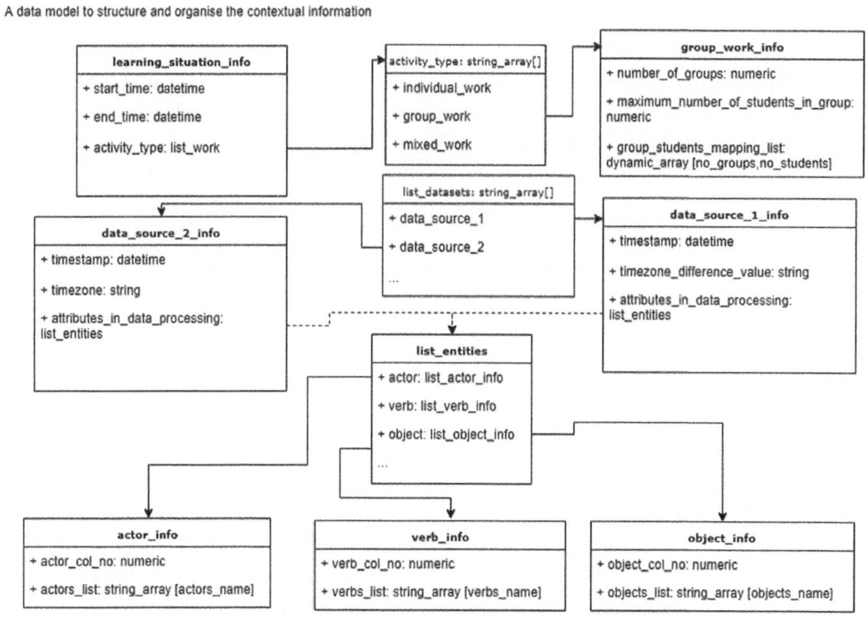

Fig. 3. A data model to structure and organise the required contextual information of a learning situation to exploit multimodal evidence of learning

4 A Data Model to Organise Contextual Information for Multimodal Data Processing

To answer RQ2 on how to organize the contextual information needed for the processing of multimodal data, we propose a data model (see Fig. 3). As in MMLA scenarios multiple heterogeneous datasets are exploited, the relationship among these datasets and their attributes need to be defined, to fuse them together. This includes selecting only those data points that are relevant (e.g., in the time window where the learning activities happened, or related to the participants in the learning activity). This requires either a list of relevant actors (be them individual learners or groups of them). The *'learning_situation_info'* class stores this information with three attributes; *'start_time'* and *'end_time'* to inform about the start and end time of the learning situation whereas *'activity_type'* informs whether the learning activity was individual, group-based or mixed. In the case of group or mixed work, the *'activity_type'* class stores information about the number of groups, maximum number of students in each group, and the mapping of individual students to groups.

The class *'list_modalities'* provides information about how many datasets are included. As per the number of datasets, it calls *'data_source_datasetNumber_info'* class. It is quite common that different tools and platforms use different timezones when storing their timestamps. Hence, the MMLA system should be aware of this information (stored in the *'timestamp'* and *'timezone'* attributes), to unify the timestamp attribute of different datasets. Moreover, another step of filtering for data fusion requires information about which actors, verbs and objects (which form the basis of each data point) should be taken into account for analysis. This is included in the class *'list_entities'*, which itself includes classes *'actor_info'*, *'verb_info'* and *'object_info'*.

5 Validating PAMEL and Its Data Model: Four Case Studies in Authentic Learning Situations

5.1 Research Methodology

The PAMEL described in this paper is being developed as part of a larger design-based research (DBR) aimed at developing MMLA infrastructures that are able to cater for the needs of multiple stakeholders (including teachers and researchers) in authentic educational settings. Against this backdrop, to provide a first evaluation of whether PAMEL and its data model represent valuable answers to our research questions about the reusability (RQ1) and contextual information (RQ2) of MMLA systems, we have developed a first prototype implementation of PAMEL. Then, we have evaluated its properties by applying it to four different authentic learning situations in which teachers and researchers collaborated in gathering data from multiple data sources, to answer questions leveraging MMLA. During such applications of the reference implementation, we have measured aspects such as the development time needed to develop an

MMLA solution that caters for the needs of the stakeholders, and looked at the contextual information and analysis decisions necessary to perform such analyses.

In this sense, the following sub-sections can be considered a very brief account of the multi-case study that represents a first iteration of the aforementioned DBR. The criteria for selection of the cases was that they had to be authentic learning situations involving multiple stakeholders (students, teachers, researchers and developers), whose enactment entailed activities across digital and physical spaces.

5.2 Context of the Studies

The four learning situations took place in Tallinn University, from October to December 2017. All of them were learning situations co-designed between teachers and researchers, in the context of open-doors events in which local schools visit the university to experience new learning and teaching methods during approximately four hours. In all cases the learning activities combined face-to-face and computer-mediated work, and had an emphasis on collaborative and/or inquiry learning, as well as subject integration. On the other hand, the topics and learning designs of each event varied widely (see Table 1). Students were aged 13 to 16 years old.

Table 1. Topics and stakeholders involved in the four authentic learning situations

Case	Topic	Students	Groups	Teachers	Researchers	Developers
Case study 1	Human body	22	10	4	3	2
Case study 2	Human body	18	4	2	3	2
Case study 3	Urban space	20	5	3	0	2
Case study 4	Stranded in an island	20	5	6	1	1

The multimodal data gathering and later pre-processing and analysis was rather similar in all four situations, stemming from the goals stated by teachers and researchers, respectively. For the teachers designing the scenarios, the resulting MMLA solution needed to answer the question: 'How was the engagement of the groups of students during the learning activities?'. Researchers, however, had the question: 'How to support teachers in answering pedagogically-rich questions by collecting multimodal evidence from digital and physical spaces, taking into account the available contextual information?'.

To answer these questions, teachers and researchers decided that the following kinds of data should be collected (see Table 2). Graasp (a digital learning platform designed to support inquiry-based learning) would be used to guide students along the learning activities; and its logs would provide digital evidence about the groups' engagement. Additionally, human observers (researchers and teachers) would make structured observations of each student's engagement every five minutes, using an observation sheet implemented through Google Forms[2].

To provide first answers to the aforementioned stakeholder questions and present a coherent view of student engagement, the MMLA solution would fuse this multimodal evidence. This would be done by taking five-minute windows (defined by the structured human observation), aggregating the group engagement in terms of each of the observed types of engagement (by averaging the observations available for the group members). These group-level features coming from the observation would be joined with a count of the logs/actions available for that group, during the same five-minute window. The solution should also take care of low-level data processing operations like aligning timestamps for both data sources (e.g., if they were in different timezones), and resolve actor identities across data sources (e.g., to match the observation about a certain student with the Graasp logs for the group in which such student was).

Table 2. Data sources, granularity, and multimodal evidence collected across spaces

Granularity of the data collection	Data source	Type of engagement
Individual	Observation (every 5 min, binary)	1. Totally disengaged
		2. Looking to others as they try to solve the task
		3. Talking with their group peers to solve the task
		4. Interacting with technology (e.g., phone, answer forms) to solve the task
		5. Interacting with other resources (e.g., paper, QRs, other physical objects) to solve the task
		6. Interacting with external people (observers, teachers, people in the street) to solve the task
Group	Graasp log (count)	1. Actions of type "Accessed"
		2. Actions of type "Create"
		3. Actions of type "Open"
		4. Actions of type "Update"

5.3 PAMEL Reference Implementation

A reference implementation[3] of the PAMEL was developed using .NET Framework 4.5, in C# language. Two adapters were created; one Digital Tool Adapter

[2] Observational form available at http://tiny.cc/adek5y.
[3] Reference implementation source code available at http://tiny.cc/7oek5y.

(see Fig. 2) to fetch Graasp logs[4]; and an IoT Adapter to fetch observations[5]. Both adapters would translate the original datasets into either CSV or XLS (Excel) format, passing them to the PAMEL manager. Meanwhile, configuration files[6] for each case were created according to the data model in Sect. 4. Furthermore, the PAMEL Manager would prepare, organise and fuse the two datasets as per the the logic above, specified in the previously-mentioned configuration file. A third set of adapters would fetch the resulting fused dataset from the PAMEL Manager (either in CSV or XLS format) for analysis and visualisation purposes. We have not implemented this adapter yet, as it belongs to the following DVC activities of data exploitation (i.e., out of the scope of the current paper).

5.4 Results

The reference implementation comprising a the first set of Digital Tool and IoT Adapters and the PAMEL Manager, was able to transform the datasets generated in all four authentic learning situations (see Table 1) and produce an output dataset fit for analyses of engagement aimed at teachers and researchers. The implementation of each additional scenario entailed a reduced development effort, from 180 to 20 min per scenario. Most of this development effort in adapting the reference implementation from one learning situation to the next, was spent in generating the configuration file. Moreover, to structure and organise the contextual information of the learning situation, the model proved to be expressive enough to guide the processing of multimodal evidence of learning as specified by stakeholders (see previous section).

6 Discussion

Coming back to our research questions (see Sect. 1), several lessons have emerged while creating and using an implementation of the PAMEL architecture and data model in four authentic learning scenarios. In terms of *reusability*, the code from the adapters and the PAMEL Manager were successfully reused. Given that most existing MMLA solutions are tailored to specific learning situations, our proposals could support the MMLA community in designing and implementing MMLA solutions applicable to different learning situations.

As already mentioned in previous research [17], this paper illustrates that involving multiple stakeholders in the design and implementation of MMLA solutions is not only feasible, but also beneficial in order to adapt the solutions to the specificities of local learning situations.

Despite these potential benefits, the present proposal exhibits a number of limitations. Both the architecture and the model have been tested in learning situations with similar profiles and following similar data collection structures.

[4] Example Graasp log available at http://tiny.cc/avek5y.
[5] Example observation data available at http://tiny.cc/1wek5y.
[6] A sample of the configuration file is available at http://tiny.cc/ead95y.

Further studies with more heterogeneous data sources and learning contexts should be carried out to ascertain the limits of applicability of the PAMEL.

Moreover, the configuration file so far has been generated by the PAMEL main developer by hand, using information gathered in conversations with the rest of the stakeholders. In the future, a more user-friendly solution should be provided to distribute this workload among stakeholders, and allow autonomous operation of PAMEL-based MMLA solutions without requiring the presence of a technical person. This will probably include a user interface to generate the configuration file, where the multiple stakeholders involved can input the pieces of the contextual information.

There are other limits to the proposal's applicability that need to be investigated. A key assumption of PAMEL is that contextual information about the learning situation (in terms of data collection setup or processing requirements) is known or accessible to the stakeholders. Thus, the feasibility of the required joint effort by stakeholders to provide such information, taking into account the tight constraints of authentic educational settings, still needs to be ascertained.

Acknowledgements. This research has been partially funded by the European Union via the European Regional Development Fund and in the context of CEITER and Next-Lab (Horizon 2020 Research and Innovation Programme, grant agreements no. 669074 and 731685).

References

1. Bano, M., Zowghi, D.: User involvement in software development and system success: a systematic literature review. In: Proceedings of the 17th International Conference on Evaluation and Assessment in Software Engineering, pp. 125–130. ACM (2013)
2. Buschmann, F., Henney, K., Schmidt, D.C.: Pattern-Oriented Software Architecture, on Patterns and Pattern Languages, vol. 5. Wiley, Hoboken (2007)
3. Chatti, M.A., et al.: Learning analytics: challenges and future research directions. eleed **10**(1) (2014)
4. Chen, L., Feng, G., Leong, C.W., Joe, J., Kitchen, C., Lee, C.M.: Designing an automated assessment of public speaking skills using multimodal cues. J. Learn. Anal. **3**(2), 261–281 (2016)
5. Di Mitri, D., Schneider, J., Klemke, R., Specht, M., Drachsler, H.: Read between the lines: an annotation tool for multimodal data for learning. In: Proceedings of the 9th International Conference on Learning Analytics & Knowledge, pp. 51–60. ACM (2019)
6. Farrell, T., Mikroyannidis, A., Alani, H.: "We're seeking relevance": qualitative perspectives on the impact of learning analytics on teaching and learning. In: Lavoué, É., Drachsler, H., Verbert, K., Broisin, J., Pérez-Sanagustín, M. (eds.) EC-TEL 2017. LNCS, vol. 10474, pp. 397–402. Springer, Cham (2017). https://doi.org/10.1007/978-3-319-66610-5_33
7. Grafsgaard, J., Wiggins, J., Boyer, K.E., Wiebe, E., Lester, J.: Predicting learning and affect from multimodal data streams in task-oriented tutorial dialogue. In: Proceedings of the 7th International Conference on Educational Data Mining. Citeseer (2014)

8. Hernández-García, Á., Conde, M.Á.: Dealing with complexity: educational data and tools for learning analytics. In: Proceedings of the Second International Conference on Technological Ecosystems for Enhancing Multiculturality, pp. 263–268. ACM (2014)
9. Krafzig, D., Banke, K., Slama, D.: Enterprise SOA: Service-Oriented Architecture Best Practices. Prentice Hall Professional, Upper Saddle River (2005)
10. Miller, H.G., Mork, P.: From data to decisions: a value chain for big data. IT Prof. **15**(1), 57–59 (2013). https://doi.org/10.1109/MITP.2013.11
11. Ochoa, X.: Multimodal learning analytics. In: Handbook of Learning Analytics, pp. 129–141 (2017)
12. Ochoa, X., Worsley, M.: Augmenting learning analytics with multimodal sensory data. J. Learn. Anal. **3**(2), 213–219 (2016)
13. Prieto, L.P., Rodríguez-Triana, M.J., Martínez-Maldonado, R., Dimitriadis, Y., Gašević, D.: Orchestrating learning analytics (OrLA): supporting inter-stakeholder communication about adoption of learning analytics at the classroom level. Australas. J. Educ. Technol. **4**(35) (2019). https://doi.org/10.14742/ajet.4314
14. Rodríguez-Triana, M.J., Prieto, L.P., Martínez-Monés, A., Asensio-Pérez, J.I., Dimitriadis, Y.: The teacher in the loop: customizing multimodal learning analytics for blended learning. In: Proceedings of the 8th International Conference on Learning Analytics and Knowledge, pp. 417–426. ACM (2018)
15. Rodriguez Triana, M.J., et al.: Monitoring, awareness and reflection in blended technology enhanced learning: a systematic review. Int. J. Technol. Enhanced Learn. **9**(2–3), 126–150 (2017)
16. Schneider, J., Börner, D., Van Rosmalen, P., Specht, M.: Augmenting the senses: a review on sensor-based learning support. Sensors **15**(2), 4097–4133 (2015)
17. Schneider, J., Di Mitri, D., Limbu, B., Drachsler, H.: Multimodal learning hub: a tool for capturing customizable multimodal learning experiences. In: Pammer-Schindler, V., Pérez-Sanagustín, M., Drachsler, H., Elferink, R., Scheffel, M. (eds.) EC-TEL 2018. LNCS, vol. 11082, pp. 45–58. Springer, Cham (2018). https://doi.org/10.1007/978-3-319-98572-5_4
18. Shankar, S.K., Prieto, L.P., Rodríguez-Triana, M.J., Ruiz-Calleja, A.: A review of multimodal learning analytics architectures. In: 2018 IEEE 18th International Conference on Advanced Learning Technologies (ICALT), pp. 212–214. IEEE (2018)
19. Tarr, P., Ossher, H., Harrison, W., Sutton, S.M.: N degrees of separation: multi-dimensional separation of concerns. In: Proceedings of the 1999 International Conference on Software Engineering (IEEE Cat. No. 99CB37002), pp. 107–119. IEEE (1999)
20. Worsley, M.: Multimodal learning analytics as a tool for bridging learning theory and complex learning behaviors. In: Proceedings of the 2014 ACM Workshop on Multimodal Learning Analytics Workshop and Grand Challenge, pp. 1–4. ACM (2014)
21. Worsley, M., Blikstein, P.: Leveraging multimodal learning analytics to differentiate student learning strategies. In: Proceedings of the Fifth International Conference on Learning Analytics and Knowledge, pp. 360–367. ACM (2015)

Cheating Detection Method Based on Improved Cognitive Diagnosis Model

Zhizhuang Li[1], Zhengzhou Zhu[1](✉), and Qiongyu Xie[2]

[1] School of Software and Microelectronics, Peking University, Beijing, China
zhuzz@pku.edu.cn
[2] Anhui Normal University, Wuhu, Anhui, China

Abstract. Cheating in examinations destroys the principles of fairness and justice in evaluation. Cheating detection is of great practical significance. Traditional cheating detection methods have many disadvantages, such as difficult to detect covert equipment cheating, multi-source cheating, difficult to distinguish plagiarists from plagiarists, difficult to distinguish plagiarists from victims, or plagiarism from coincidences. In this paper, the concept of knowledge point mastery Index is introduced to measure students' mastery of a certain knowledge point, and a test method of cheating based on improved cognitive diagnostic model is proposed. This method calculates the weight of each knowledge point in every examination question through linear regression and EM algorithm according to students' historical learning behavior, and then calculates students' mastering degree of knowledge point based on historical answers. Then calculate the mastering degree of knowledge point based on the examination results. Finally, we compare the mastering degree of knowledge point based on the examination results and the historical answers to detect students' cheating situation. The experiments show that the precision and recall rate of this method are significantly higher than those of the method based on the false-same rate, the method based on the false-same rate and the right-same rate and the method based on the Person-Fit index.

Keywords: Weight of knowledge point · Cheating detection · Mastering degree of knowledge point · Linear regression · Expectation maximization algorithm

1 Introduction

With the continuous development of science and technology, students have more and more means of cheating, and the phenomenon of cheating cannot be stopped. Although advanced anti-cheating devices such as signal jammer, monitor and alarm have great deterrence and restraint to prevent students from cheating at present, they cannot completely eliminate students' cheating. In addition, due to economic factors, these devices cannot be fully popularized at present and can only be used in important examinations. Therefore, the detection mechanism of students' cheating is still very important. At present, the main cheating detection methods are (1) the cheating detection method based on the similarity of test papers and (2) the cheating detection method based on person-fit index. However, the cheating detection method based on

M. A. Herzog et al. (Eds.): ICWL 2019, LNCS 11841, pp. 84–91, 2019.
https://doi.org/10.1007/978-3-030-35758-0_8

the similarity of test papers only aims at the content of the test, ignoring the evaluation of students' abilities in all aspects. It has the following limitations: (1) It is difficult to detect students who cheat using covert electronic devices. (2) It is difficult to detect multi-source plagiarism. (3) It is difficult to distinguish plagiarists from plagiarists. (4) It is difficult to distinguish plagiarism from coincidence. The traditional cheating detection method based on Person-Fit index has the disadvantage of limited precision ratio of students' modeling, because the existing theoretical model can only give students the discrete grasp degree of knowledge point (grasp or not grasp), so the ability is limited. Firstly, this paper introduces the concept of knowledge point weight, relying on linear regression and expectation maximization (EM for short) algorithm, through cognitive diagnosis, to judge whether students cheat or not. Experiments show that this method can overcome the shortcomings of traditional cheating detection methods based on test paper similarity and Person-Fit index.

The main contributions of this paper are as follows:

(1) The concept of the weight of knowledge point in the exercises is introduced, and a method of calculating knowledge point weight based on linear regression and EM algorithm is proposed. This method can calculate the weight of each knowledge point in exercise without manual labeling.
(2) The concept of knowledge point mastery index is put forward, and students' abilities are measured by knowledge point mastery index. Compared with the cognitive diagnosis model which can only give the students' discrete mastering degree of knowledge point, the model can give more accurate students' mastering degree of knowledge point, and has the advantages of simple logic and fast calculation speed.

2 Related Works

Many scholars at home and abroad have done a lot of research in the field of cheating detection. So far, cheating detection methods include cheating detection methods based on cheating detection equipment, cheating detection methods based on examinee's examination room behavior, cheating detection methods based on test paper similarity, and cheating detection methods based on Person-Fit index.

Cheating detection method based on the detection of cheating equipment can find out the cheating students by detecting whether the students carry or use the cheating equipment. Bajić can realize wireless communication detection and detect cheating devices with the method [1].

The cheating detection method based on the examinee's behavior in the examination room can catch the students' various behaviors in the examination room and find out the students with suspicious behaviors, so as to judge the cheating students. Yohannes et al. observed the physical behavior during the examination through video, so as to achieve the purpose of detecting cheating behavior in the examination room [2].

The cheating detection method based on the similarity of test papers judges the similarity of different students' test papers, thus identifying the students with higher similarity as cheaters. Zhu et al. introduced the concept of false-same rate, and determined that students whose false-same rate was significantly higher than the average level of the examination room were cheating candidates [3]. Liu et al. introduced the concept of right-same rate, and judged the examinees whose false-same rate and right-same rates were significantly higher than the average level of the examination room as cheating examinees [4].

The basic idea of cheating detection method based on Person-Fit index is to classify students' mastery level of each knowledge point (mastery or not mastery) through some theoretical models, and then predict students' performance. Finally, by comparing the students' predicted results with the actual test results, we can judge whether the students cheat or not. Karabatsos et al. proposed a variety of cheating detection methods based on Person-Fit index [5].

3 Method Design

This method first diagnoses each student's cognitive ability based on the students' historical answers record, and obtains the students' mastery of each knowledge point according to the students' history answer data. Then, according to the students' test answers data, cognitive diagnosis is made to the students, and the students' mastery of each knowledge point is calculated according to the test answers. Finally, we compare the same student's mastery of knowledge point calculated according to the test answers data and the history answer data, to judge whether the student is suspected of cheating.

3.1 Cognitive Diagnosis of Students Based on Their History of Doing Exercises

First, define the concept of knowledge point mastery Index. The concept of knowledge point mastery Index is used to measure a student's knowledge point mastery. Because the difficulty degree of each student's exercises is not exactly the same, the average score of all the exercises that the students have done can not be simply used as an index to measure a student's ability. In order to better measure each student's true mastery of each knowledge point, this paper defines knowledge point mastery Index as the degree of mastery of knowledge point b by student a. It is intuitively understood that the scoring rate of all exercises with knowledge point b by student a exceeds the average scoring rate of all exercises with knowledge point b by all students.

The formulas for calculating the mastery excellence of knowledge point are defined respectively when the weight of knowledge point is unknown or known.

The formula for calculating knowledge point mastery Index G_{ab} of knowledge point without assigning the weight of knowledge point is as follows:

$$G_{ab} = \frac{\sum_{i=1}^{n} (p_i - m_i)}{\sum_{i=1}^{n} t_i} \tag{1}$$

Among them, p_i is student a's score of the exercise which only contains knowledge point b, m_i is the average score of the exercise, and t_i is the total score of the subject.

The formulas for calculating knowledge point mastery Index G'_{ab} of knowledge point under the condition that the weight of knowledge point has been assigned are as follows:

$$G'_{ab} = \frac{\sum_{i=1}^{n}(s_i - m_i)k_i}{\sum_{i=1}^{n} t_i k_i} \tag{2}$$

Among them, s_i is the score of exercise i done by student a, m_i is the average score of the exercise, k_i is the weight of knowledge point b in the exercise, and t_i is the total score of the exercise.

The steps of cognitive diagnosis for students based on their history of answering exercises are as follows:

First, obtain the data of all students' history work. Using exercises with only a single knowledge point, use formula (1) to roughly calculate and store the knowledge point mastery Index of each student's all knowledge point based on the historical answer situation.

Linear regression model is used to calculate the weight of each knowledge point in each exercise contained in the history answer record of students. For a given topic, assuming that there are n knowledge point in the exercise, the predictive expression of the score of the ith student is as follows:

$$h_i = \sum_{j=1}^{n} k_j x_j + b$$

h_i is the predicted score of the assigned exercise for the ith student, x_j is the knowledge point mastery Index of the ith student for the jth knowledge point of this exercise, and k_j is the weight of x_j. The cost function of this model is as follows:

$$J(\theta) = \frac{1}{2}\sum_{i=1}^{n} (h_i - y_i)^2$$

$J(\theta)$ is the sum of the squared errors, and $\theta = (k_1, k_2, k_3, \ldots, k_n, b)$, is the function parameter, h_i is the predicted score of the designated exercise for the ith student, y_i is the actual score of the designated exercise for the ith student. The cost function of the model is minimized by training the model with the data of students' historical answer questions. At this time, each coefficient in the score prediction expression corresponding to this model is the weight of each knowledge point contained in this question.

Formula (2) is used to calculate the more accurate knowledge point mastery Index of each student for each knowledge point when the weight of each knowledge point is known.

Using the EM algorithm, the previously calculated value of knowledge point mastery Index, which is based on students' historical answer, is taken as the current value of students' knowledge point mastery Index. Each time, the current value of knowledge point mastery Index, which is based on students' historical answer, is used to calculate the weight of knowledge point in a new round of exercises by linear regression. Then, the weight of knowledge point in the new round of exercises is used to calculate the knowledge point mastery Index of the new round of students based on the historical answer situation through formula (2). After repeated iteration for 10 rounds, the final result of knowledge point mastery Index and the weight of knowledge point for students based on their history answers was obtained.

3.2 Cognitive Diagnosis of Students Based on Their Test Scores

Using the knowledge point mastery Index of each student's answer to each knowledge point based on the history of each knowledge point obtained above, the weight of each knowledge point in each examination question is calculated through the linear regression model. The calculation method of the weight of knowledge point in the examination questions is the same as that of the knowledge point in the students' history questions including exercises.

3.3 Students' Cheating Detection

For each student and each knowledge point, the difference between the knowledge point mastery Index of the knowledge point of a student based on the examination result and the knowledge point mastery Index of the knowledge point based on the historical answer is recorded as the difference of knowledge point mastery Index of the student for the knowledge point. The difference of knowledge point mastery Index reflects the difference between the student's normal performance and his/her performance on the test with the same knowledge point. Calculate the difference of knowledge point mastery Index of each student for each knowledge point.

For knowledge point j, the average value of the difference of knowledge point mastery Index of all students for knowledge point j was denoted as the average difference of knowledge point mastery Index, and it's sign was A_j.

Define dubious degree of knowledge point mastery, which is used to represent the possibility that the degree of knowledge point j mastered by the student I reflected in this exam is not true, denoted as D_{ij}, $D_{ij} = ReLU(d_{ij} - A)$.

Where, subscript i is the student ordinal number, subscript j is the knowledge point ordinal number, and the *ReLU* function is expressed as follows:

$$ReLU(x) = \begin{cases} x & if\ x > 0 \\ 0 & if\ x \leq 0 \end{cases}$$

The threshold of suspicious degree of knowledge point mastery degree is defined to define whether students are suspected of cheating on the test questions containing a certain knowledge point. For all students and all knowledge point, when a student's threshold of suspicious degree of knowledge point mastery degree of a certain knowledge point is greater than the threshold value, it is considered that the student is suspected of cheating on the test questions containing the knowledge point, and the knowledge point is called the doubtful knowledge point of the student.

Define the proportion threshold of doubtful knowledge point, which is used to define whether a student cheat or not. For all students, a student is judged to have cheated if the proportion of he's or she's proportion of doubtful knowledge point to the total knowledge point contained in the test paper is higher than this threshold.

4 Experiment

4.1 Experimental Environment

The data used in the experiment were data from three informal classroom tests of 124 students in a certain university and college and all the exercises data until the last classroom test. In this classroom test, the invigilator and the surveillance video manually marked the students suspected of major cheating. In order to cooperate with the experiment, the students' cheating behavior was not stopped. Classroom test data include student records of major suspected cheats and test answer data. Among them, the data of classroom examination includes student number, test number, score of this question, actual score, and test questions containing knowledge point. Normally, the data of doing exercises are collected through the online answer platform. Each data is the record of students' answers to each exercise, including student id, exercise number, score of the question, actual score, and knowledge point included in the exercise.

4.2 Experiment Process

In this experiment, the effectiveness of this method was verified by comparing the effect of using this method and traditional cheating detection method based on test paper similarity on cheating students. The evaluation index are precision ratio and recall ratio. The precision ratio was defined as the percentage of artificially labeled cheating suspects that were detected by cheating detection method. Recall ratio rate was defined as the proportion of artificially labeled cheating suspects that were detected by cheating detection method. The precision ratio indicates the percentage of suspected cheaters detected by cheating detection. The higher the precision ratio, the lower the proportion of students who are wronged. Recall ratios indicate the percentage of students who actually cheated who were detected, and a higher recall ratio indicates a higher percentage of students who were caught cheating. Therefore, it is reasonable to measure the precision ratio and recall ratio of a cheating detection method.

First, the students were given a cognitive diagnosis based on the historical answer records using the data of the historical answer questions, and then the students were given a cognitive diagnosis based on the test results using the data of this classroom test. Then, the suspicious degree of each student's mastery of each knowledge point was calculated, and the threshold of suspicious degree of knowledge point mastery and the threshold of proportion of suspicious knowledge point were set as 0.3/0.3, 0.3/0.5, 0.5/0.3, and 0.5/0.5, respectively, to screen out students with major cheating suspicion based on the combination of four thresholds.

Then using the traditional test paper similarity based cheating detection method: based on the error of right-same index of cheating detection method, based on the error of right-same index and right-same index of cheating detection method to the classroom test cheating detection, detection of a major suspected cheating students.

Finally, the precision ratio and recall ratio of these methods are compared.

4.3 Experiment Results

As shown in Table 1, this experiment statistics of the number of artificial markers to cheat in exam for the third time, and threshold value of dubious degree of knowledge point mastery and threshold value of percentage of doubtful knowledge point is set respectively for 0.3/0.3, 0.3/0.5, 0.5/0.3, 0.5/0.5 cases using this method (in order to facilitate, said in a table respectively to remember them for the threshold combination 1, threshold combination 2, 3 threshold combination, combination of threshold, 4) and use based on the rate of wrong with cheating detection method, based on the fault rate and right-same index of cheating detection method, used to DINA as a cognitive diagnosis model, lz college as individual fitting index based on Person-Fit index number detection method to detect the cheating students cheating, to detect the cheating students and artificial markers of intersection student Numbers. This experiment also calculated the knowledge point in the exam for the third time threshold value of dubious degree of knowledge point mastery and threshold value of percentage of doubtful knowledge point is set respectively for 0.3/0.3, 0.3/0.5, 0.5/0.3, 0.5/0.5 cases using this method and use based on the rate of wrong with cheating detection method, based on the fault with the rate and the rate of the same test method of cheating, cheating detection method based on individual fitting index of average precision and average recall rate.

Table 1. Test statistical table of cheating in exams

Round 1			Round 2			Round 3		
Methods	Precision	Recall	Methods	Precision	Recall	Methods	Precision	Recall
TSC1	62.5%	88.2%	TSC1	61.3%	86.4%	TSC1	66.7%	92.3%
TSC2	63.2%	70.6%	TSC2	54.2%	59.1%	TSC2	75.0%	69.2%
TSC3	86.7%	76.5%	TSC3	71.4%	68.2%	TSC3	84.6%	84.6%
TSC4	88.9%	47.1%	TSC4	92.3%	54.5%	TSC4	100%	61.5%
FSR	66.7%	47.1%	FSR	62.5%	45.5%	FSR	55.6%	38.5%
FSR&RSR	75.0%	35.3%	FSR&RSR	69.2%	40.9%	FSR&RSR	66.7%	30.8%
PFI	45.5%	58.8%	PFI	36.1%	59.1%	PFI	42.1%	61.5%

Remarks: TSC1 = This method based on Threshold combination 1; TSC2 = This method based on Threshold combination 2; TSC3 = This method based on Threshold combination 3; TSC4 = This method based on Threshold combination 4; FSR = The method based on false-same rate; RSR = The method based on false-same rate and right-same rate; PFI = The method based on Person-Fit index.

It can be seen from the experiment that increasing the threshold value of knowledge point to master the suspicious degree and the proportional threshold value of the suspicious knowledge point will improve the precision ratio and reduce the recall ratio. And reducing the threshold value of knowledge point to master the suspicious degree and the proportion threshold value of the suspicious knowledge point will reduce the precision ratio and improve the recall ratio. This is because increasing the knowledge point to grasp the threshold value of suspicious knowledge point and the threshold value of the proportion of suspicious knowledge point will make the criteria for judging a student to cheat stricter.

To sum up, in the case of simultaneously pursuing the precision ratio and recall ratio, the average precision ratio of this method is 31.3% higher than that based on the mismatching ratio, 23.9% higher than that based on the mismatching ratio and the matching ratio, and 96.2% higher than that based on the individual fitting index. The average recall ratio was 76.4%, 74.8% higher than the method based on the mismatching rate, 114.0% higher than the method based on the mismatching rate and the correct matching rate, and 27.8% higher than the method based on the Person-Fit index. In this method, the average accuracy is 52.1%, 38.6% and 127.3% higher than the other three methods. In the case of only pursuing the recall rate, the average recall rate was 103.7%, 149.3% and 48.8% higher than the other three methods respectively.

5 Conclusions

This paper proposes a collaborative learning grouping strategy with early warning function based on the degree of complementary mastery of knowledge points. Experimental results show that the grouping strategy proposed in this paper can effectively improve the learning effect of students. The average precision and average recall of LSTM based group early warning were 30.1% and 27.6% higher than that based on linear regression, respectively.

In the future, we will use the online learning platform to obtain the information of students' online learning behavior, and further explore various factors that may contribute to the improvement or decline of study groups' performance, so as to improve the accuracy of the group's early warning and propose more targeted intervention measures.

Acknowledgment. This paper was supported by National Key Research and Development Program of China (Grant No. 2017YFB1402400), Ministry of Education "Tiancheng Huizhi" Innovation Promotes Education Fund (Grant No. 2018B01004), National Natural Science Foundation of China (Grant No. 61402020, 61573356), and CERNET Innovation Project (Grant No. NGII20170501).

References

1. Bajić, J.: Universal wireless communication detector (UD-100) - preventing of high-tech cheating methods. In: Proceedings of the 35th International Convention on Information and Communication Technology, Electronics and Microelectronics, pp. 237–240 (2012)
2. Yohannes, Ayumi, V., Fanany, M.I.: Multimodal decomposable models by superpixel segmentation and point-in-time cheating detection. In: International Conference on Advanced Computer Science & Information Systems. IEEE (2017)
3. Zhu, J., Niu, Z., Guo, Y.: Research on software for detecting the misalignment rate of multiple choice questions in physician qualification examination. China High. Med. Educ. (1), 8–9 (2010)
4. Liu, S., Zhang, Q., He, J.: Research on cheating screening in an examination based on delphi platform. Chin. J. Soc. Med. **30**(5) (2013)
5. Karabatsos, G.: Comparing the aberrant response detection performance of thirty-six person-fit statistics. Appl. Meas. Educ. **16**(4), 277–298 (2003)

Measuring Students' Stress with Mood Sensors: First Findings

Henri Kajasilta(✉), Mikko-Ville Apiola, Erno Lokkila, Ashok Veerasamy, and Mikko-Jussi Laakso

Department of Future Technologies, University of Turku, Turku, Finland
henri.t.kajasilta@utu.fi

Abstract. Emotions and stress have considerable impact to wellbeing, growth and academic achievement. However, while devices with signal accuracy that is valid for clinical field research have become available, there is still a significant gap in knowledge about the relevance of such devices for digital learning. In this pilot study, a group of 17 university students of computing wore a moodmetrics smart ring device for one week. In addition, students kept short diaries about their study-related activities. Results from statistical analysis show a strong correlation between non-study and study-related stress level averages. Even when comparing the daily stress values, the correlation was strong and significant within the 95% confidence level. A total of 53 non-study and study average pairs were observed in the data. Our results reveal that stress of these students seemed not to vary between short-term study-events but it was found to be a more comprehensive issue. In the future, larger samples and more data are needed for more reliable research on individual study activities.

Keywords: Stress · Academic emotions · Stress measuring

1 Introduction

Emotions and stress have crucial importance in *wellbeing*, which reflects directly to success in almost all domains of life, including academic performance [4]. In a Finnish study, 33% of all students (32% male and 34% female) experienced considerable stress in 2016, and 25% of students hoped to receive help for stress management [16]. However, wellbeing and stress are currently not well researched areas in learning analytics in general, and particularly in computing education. Moreover, a large amount of the research in learning analytics has focused predominantly on factors, such as prior academic performance, demographics, and log data generated by learning management systems [10]. In computing, learning analytics has focused mostly on analysing simple log metrics [14].

This paper presents preliminary findings from our experiments with using a moodmetric device [15] in learning analytics. University students of computing

M. A. Herzog et al. (Eds.): ICWL 2019, LNCS 11841, pp. 92–99, 2019.
https://doi.org/10.1007/978-3-030-35758-0_9

wore the devices for one week and kept a diary about their study-related activities. The data from the sensors was subjected to quantitative and qualitative analyses. Also, practical issues and observations from the research setup were collected. This paper reports the findings from this experiment, and lays out a future research agenda. This research is a part of larger efforts in our research group to understand the role of sensors, social psychological and psychological aspects of learning in learning analytics (eg. [1]). The results may help in offering students more holistic support for growth and development in the future. The following three research questions were set for this study.

1. What is the relationship between study-related stress levels and non-study-related stress levels of students as measured by the moodmetric smart ring?
2. What other possibly interesting associations can be found in students' stress as measured by the moodmetric smart ring?
3. What usability or other practical issues arise in using the moodmetric smart devices in this research setup?

This research's purpose is also to help to understand educational psychology in digital learning, and to design related interventions and pedagogies to support the growth of both intellectual capacities, creativity, collaboration skills, soft skills and students' wellbeing in learning analytics.

2 Related Research

2.1 Emotions and Stress

There are seven inborn and "prewired" core emotions: *sadness*, *joy*, *anger*, *fear*, *disgust*, *excitement*, and *sexual excitement* [13, p. 5]. Emotions are survival programs that are preprogrammed in the brain and are not subject to conscious control. In the face of physical threat, fear is triggered automatically, while e.g. succeeding triggers emotions of joy and excitement [13, p. 5]. Emotions are crucial for survival. However, they also cause problems and the ability to block emotions by using defences is needed to succeed in society. But research shows that blocking emotions is detrimental to mental and physical health, and blocked emotions may lead to stress, anxiety and depression [13, p. 6]. The challenges of modern life, including pressure to succeed, pressure to fit in, desire to "keep up", and the "fear of missing out" may evoke combinations of conflicting emotions. Blocking core emotions may lead to detrimental types of stress [13, p. 6].

Stress is the human body's general reaction to external demands targeted towards it [8]. From an evolutionary perspective, the physiological stress response triggers increase of both physiological and mental functioning in order to meet imminent demands and to survive. Psychological stress is considered to occur in cases where environmental demands are perceived to exceed ones adaptive capability [6]. A stressed individual perceives external threats as unpredictable, uncontrollable, or both [5]. Research shows both positive and negative impacts of stress [5,6,8]. Stress can act as a motivator for proactive problem solving, and can increase cognitive performance by mechanisms, such as increasing brain processes and boosting memory [8]. *Stress-related-growth* refers to a process where stressful experiences enhance the development of mental toughness, heightened awareness, new perspectives, a sense of mastery, and other beneficial things [8].

On the other hand, a direct link has been established between stress—especially it's prolonged and chronic form—and a number of disastrous mental health and health issues [6]. Prolonged stress is linked to burnout [12]. In burnout, stress mounts, and psychological resources are increasingly diverted to combat its negative effects, until the resources are exhausted [12]. There is a direct link between stress, burnout and reduced job performance and job satisfaction, higher rates of accidents, increased withdrawal, and substance abuse [12]. Stress is important in various domains, including leadership [12].

Moreover, psychological stress and disease have clear links, particularly in regards of depression, cardiovascular diseases, and autoimmune diseases [6]. Links are emerging in other areas too, including upper respiratory tract infections, asthma, viral infections, and wound healing [6]. Behavioural changes may include increased smoking, decreased exercise and sleep, and poor adherence to medical regimens, which together establish a pathway between stress and poor health [6]. These fundamentally destructive effects of stress are linked especially to prolonged types of stress, while short-term stress is often linked with beneficial aspects that enhance health and performance [8]. These contradicting findings in relation to stress are sometimes called the *stress paradox* [8].

2.2 Academic Stress, Coping, and Mindset

Research shows that high stress in academic contexts is often associated with anxiety and depression and that academic burnout is a serious concern that may be related to "low sense of achievement", "depersonalisation", and "emotional exhaustion" [17]. In a Finnish study, 33% of all students (32% male and 34% female) experienced considerable stress in 2016, and 25% of students hoped to receive help for stress management [16]. The most frequent causes of stress were reported to be performing in public and difficulties in getting a grip on one's studies [16]. In Ireland, the quality of student–teacher interaction and peer relations were found to have a significant impact on stress levels of students [2].

2.3 Interventions for Stress

A number of interventions have been designed to combat stress. For example, stress-mindset-interventions have resulted in positive changes to mindsets and related decreased stress levels and increased academic achievement [20]. Mindfulness-interventions have also become increasingly popular, and research shows that interventions, such as Mindfulness-Based Stress Reduction Courses (MBSR) may reduce stress, anxiety, depression, and increase well-being [3]. Moreover, a review of 12 studies about the impact of mindfulness interventions in undergraduate medical students found evidence in favour of positive impacts of mindfulness-interventions to stress, depression and burnout [9]. Health applications, such as the moodmetrics application [15], contains exercises for decreasing the stress level. In the future, measurement scales and related interventions can be integrated into digital learning and learning analytics as standard features.

3 Research Design

3.1 Measuring Emotions and Stress

The moodmetric smart ring is a device for measuring electrodermal activity [15]. The signal accuracy of the device is reported to be comparable to laboratory devices, making the device valid for field research [19]. Electrodermal activity (EDA) is a well-known psychophysiological marker of the functioning of the autonomous nervous system. Applications of EDA measures include, among others, classifying arousal, classifying affect arousals in varying work-like or added-stress tasks in comparison to baseline cognitive load, and "biofeedback" for performance enhancement, with an affect-based music player as a recreational example [7]. In a project [11], a combination of heart rate and skin conductivity sensors were used to design a scarf that would change its colour according to the mood state of its user. Experiments show that by using the combination of heart rate, skin conductivity and skin temperature, it might be possible to detect basic emotions, such as happiness, sadness, angriness or neutral state [18]. However, much of the previous research on EDA has been limited to laboratory environments because of a lack of suitable wearable devices [15].

3.2 Context and Data

Students were recruited from two courses at the Department of Future Technologies in University of Turku. First course *Learning Analytics* is an advanced course, which gives students an overview of the state-of-the-art research in Learning Analytics. Second course is an intermediate-level course for computer science.

The moodmetric rings measure a person's emotional arousal on a scale from 0 to 100, which we refer here as a person's *stress level*. The users of the moodmetric device [15] first need to wear the devices for 12 hours for personalised calibration, which ensures that moodmetric values are comparable between two or more moodmetric devices. The ring provides other measurements also, but the moodmetric value is the most meaningful indicator, and the only indicator that was used in this research. A total of 17 students participated in the research.

The participants were given detailed instructions for the study. The students were instructed to wear the devices starting one day before the start of the week for calibration, and then to wear the device for one week, and record all their study related activities in a diary. The students were instructed to return both an excel sheet with exact times of studying-related events, as well as a free-form written diary about their study activities. Thus, the students had to fill the kind of study-activities they were doing, for example sitting in lectures or being at exercise sessions, or doing individual or collaborative studying at university premises, home, library or another place.

Data cleaning was done as follows. First, at night, stress levels normally come down when the body shifts to rest. This may balance the overall stress, which helps to manage higher stress levels at daytime. However, this means that night time measures can bias the results when comparing stress between study-related and non-study related activities. Detecting and separating sleep from active time for each person is not unambiguous. Without a better solution, a robust decision for removing all measurements between 11PM to 8AM was used. This method may have resulted in some bias.

Based on the data it is complex to tell, what actually counts for study-related activity. While studying, students may mentally process several things, which are not necessarily directly related to their present assignment. This processing may contribute to their high or low stress levels. To address this bias, all such days were removed from the data, where student had only had a maximum of 20 min of study-activities. The decision was based on the assumption that short study activities might be more vulnerable to stress impacts from previous or upcoming activities. In addition, in general, a relatively large variability in moodmetric values may have reduced the reliability for singular measures.

Second, the times of active study were cut out from the moodmetric data based on students' excel-diaries about their study activities. Therefore, any errors that students may have made in marking the beginning and end times in their study activities might have caused additional bias. However, there was no reason to suspect that this kind of bias actually materialised.

3.3 Methods

In many cases it is too hard to measure the value of a parameter of a population, but bootstrapping gives a simple and powerful way to obtain valuable information from our sample parameters. Bootstrapping relies on random sampling with replacement and allows to estimate e.g. a statistic's variance, standard error or confidence interval. If, for example, data is skewed, simple bootstrapping can be problematic. Because of this, in this research, a more advanced bootstrapping method called bias-corrected and acceleration (BC_a) bootstrapping [21] was used. This method requires calculating bias and acceleration constants, which are responsible for adjusting non-stable variance and taking care of possible skewness. Skewness can be assured in a multivariate case with Mardia's test, where a low probability indicates that the data is not normally distributed.

We report only confidence intervals instead of statistical significance and p-values, because confidence intervals are richer than a single p-value is, and also makes it also easier to observe the effect size as compared to presenting only a p-value. Confidence intervals are presented with the 95% confidence level.

We also tried to classify students' perceived stress based on their diaries. In the instructions for filling the diaries we asked students to describe their stress levels during various activities. Labelling students was done on scale of 1 (low stress), 2 (moderate stress) to 3 (high stress). There were 3 interpreters doing

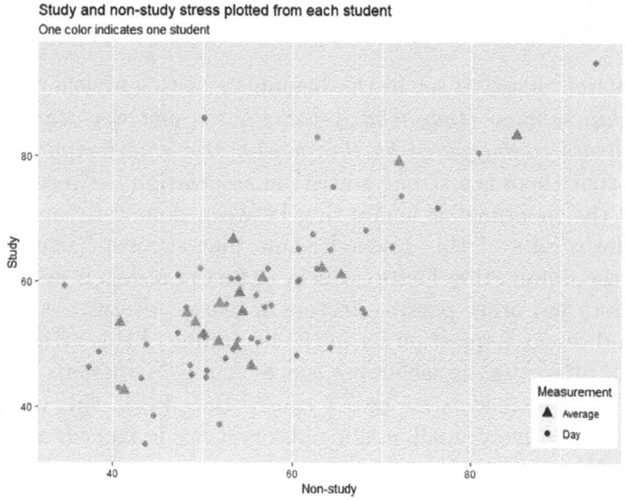

Fig. 1. The moodmetric-values for study-related activities versus non-study-related activities for each student. In addition, students' average moodmetric values from a whole measured week are plotted for comparison.

this analysis. We used percentage agreement and Krippendorff's alpha [22] to evaluate our labelling. For reliability considerations, α's value 0 indicates the absence of reliability whereas value 1 would be a perfect reliability. Even for tentative results we would like to have α's value close to .7, but results closer to 1 would be most desirable. No other common themes were found in the diaries.

4 Results

Figure 1 shows that stress levels in non-study and study activities have strong correlation in both when comparing students' average or daily moodmetric values. Calculated correlation values were as high as .68 for daily measurements and .85 for average values of all students. Figure 1 shows that most of the observations are centred close to the point (50,50), which is expected from individuals who are not overstressed or exceptionally calm. However, there are still values much higher than 50 and the data is skewed because of those higher measurements. This has been assured with Mardia's test, which gave us skewness = 18.41 with probability $p = .001$. For calculating a confidence interval to our data's correlation, the skewness is taken into account by using the BC_a bootstrap method, which ensures reliable results in this case. For these 53 observations from daily comparisons, we calculated a confidence interval of $(0.41, 0.84)$.

We did some research how different activities compared to each other, but found no clear patterns. Percentage agreement gave us only a result of 18.3% and Krippendorff's alpha .0472 when labelling students' stress levels, so no further examinations were done in regards of labelling students' stress either.

5 Discussions

The first research question set in the beginning of this article asked: *"What is the relationship between study-related stress levels and non-study-related stress levels of students as measured by the moodmetric smart ring?"* The analysis clearly show that there is a strong statistical association between stress levels as measured by the moodmetric smart ring between non-study and study-related activities. The results of this research show that students' overall stress level seems to be the dominating factor, which, in future research designs, should be considered first, and other possible factors or causes afterwards.

The second research question set in the beginning of this article asked: *"What other possibly interesting associations can be found in students stress measures as measured by the moodmetric smart ring?"* Because in this initial study the sample size was relatively small, making observations in regards of different types of study activities and their potential impact to stress levels felt unprofitable. More data in the future is needed to look into this issue with more depth.

It would have been also interesting to compare students' self-evaluation for their real moodmetric levels, but quite surprisingly our evaluations were nowhere close to each other and neither percentage agreement or Krippendorff's alpha ($\alpha \approx 0.05$) encouraged to use these evaluations. Based on such a low α -value there might have been some disagreements how to mark low, moderate and high stress levels. This is one interesting research avenue to explore further.

The third research question set in the beginning of this article asked: *"What usability or other practical issues arise in using the moodmetric smart devices in this research setup?"* Some students reported that the device is uncomfortable to wear, which is problematic, if measurements are required to be collected from longer periods. There were also some practical problems one device being mute and one student reported getting a rash from the device, which lead to excluding these cases from the data. Also some students have minor issues transferring the moodmetric data to research team. At overall, the device worked well.

References

1. Apiola, M., Laakso, M.-J.: The impact of self-theories to academic achievement and soft skills in undergraduate CS studies: first findings. In: Innovation and Technology in Computer Science Education (ITiCSE 2019). ACM (2019)
2. Banks, J., Smyth, E.: 'Your whole life depends on it': academic stress and high-stakes testing in Ireland. J. Youth Stud. **18**(5), 598–616 (2015)
3. Bennett, K., Dorjee, D.: The impact of a mindfulness-based stress reduction course (MBSR) on well-being and academic attainment of sixth-form students. Mindfulness **7**(1), 105–114 (2016)
4. Bonell, C., Humphrey, N., Fletcher, A., Moore, L., Anderson, R., Campbell, R.: Why schools should promote students' health and wellbeing. BMJ **348** (2014)
5. Cohen, S.: Aftereffects of stress on human performance and social behavior: a review of research and theory. Psychol. Bull. **88**(1), 82–108 (1980)
6. Cohen, S., Janicki-Deverts, D., Miller, G.E.: Psychological stress and disease. JAMA **298**(14), 1685–1687 (2007)

7. Cowley, B.U., Torniainen, J.: A short review and primer on electrodermal activity in human computer interaction applications. CoRR abs/1608.06986 (2016)
8. Crum, A.J., Salovey, P., Achor, S.: Rethinking stress: the role of mindsets in determining the stress response. J. Pers. Soc. Psychol. **104**(4), 716–733 (2013)
9. Daya, Z., Hearn, J.H.: Mindfulness interventions in medical education: a systematic review of their impact on medical student stress, depression, fatigue and burnout. Med. Teach. **40**(2), 146–153 (2018)
10. Gray, G., McGuinness, C., Owende, P., Carthy, A.: A review of psychometric data analysis and applications in modelling of academic achievement in tertiary education. J. Learn. Anal. **1**(1), 75–106 (2014)
11. Guo, C., Chen, Y.V., Qian, Z.C., Ma, Y., Dinh, H., Anasingaraju, S.: Designing a smart scarf to influence group members' emotions in ambience: design process and user experience. In: Antona, M., Stephanidis, C. (eds.) UAHCI 2016. LNCS, vol. 9738, pp. 392–402. Springer, Cham (2016). https://doi.org/10.1007/978-3-319-40244-4_38
12. Harms, P., Credé, M., Tynan, M., Leon, M., Jeung, W.: Leadership and stress: a meta-analytic review. Lead. Q. **28**(1), 178–194 (2017)
13. Hendel, H.J.: It's Not Always Depression: A New Theory of Listening to Your Body, Discovering Core Emotions and Reconnecting with Your Authentic Self. Penguin Random House, UK (2018)
14. Ihantola, P., et al.: Educational data mining and learning analytics in programming: literature review and case studies. In: Proceedings of the 2015 ITiCSE on Working Group Reports, pp. 41–63. ITICSE-WGR 2015. ACM, New York (2015)
15. Jussila, J., Venho, N., Salonius, H., Moilanen, J., Liukkonen, J., Rinnetmäki, M.: Towards ecosystem for research and development of electrodermal activity applications. In: Proceedings of the 22nd International Academic Mindtrek Conference, Mindtrek 2018, pp. 79–87. ACM, New York (2018)
16. Kunttu, K., Pesonen, T., Saari, J.: Student Health Survey 2016: A National Survey Among Finnish University Students. Finnish Student Heatlh Service (2017)
17. Lin, S.H., Huang, Y.C.: Life stress and academic burnout. Act. Learn. High Educ. **15**(1), 77–90 (2013)
18. Quazi, M.T., Mukhopadhyay, S.C., Suryadevara, N.K., Huang, Y.M.: Towards the smart sensors based human emotion recognition. In: 2012 IEEE International Instrumentation and Measurement Technology Conference Proceedings, pp. 2365–2370, May 2012
19. Torniainen, J., Cowley, B., Henelius, A., Lukander, K., Pakarinen, S.: Feasibility of an electrodermal activity ring prototype as a research tool. In: 37th Annual International Conference of the IEEE Engineering in Medicine and Biology Society (EMBC), pp. 6433–6436, August 2015
20. Yeager, D.S., Johnson, R., Spitzer, B.J., Trzesniewski, K.H., Powers, J., Dweck, C.S.: The far-reaching effects of believing people can change: Implicit theories of personality shape stress, health, and achievement during adolescence. J. Pers. Soc. Psychol. **106**(6), 867–884 (2014)
21. Efron, B.: Better bootstrap confidence intervals. J. Am. Stat. Assoc. **82**(397), 171–185 (1987)
22. Krippendorff, K.: Content Analysis An Introduction to Its Methodology, 2nd edn. Sage Publications, Thousand Oaks (2004). pp. 211–236

Measuring Similarity to Observe Learners' Syntactic Awareness in Web-Based Writing Environments

Min Kang[1(✉)], Koichi Kawamura[1], Shuai Shao[1], Harumi Kashiwagi[2], and Kazuhiro Ohtsuki[1]

[1] Graduate School of Intercultural Studies, Kobe University, Kobe 657-8501, Japan
kang@kobe-u.ac.jp
[2] Institute for Promotion of Higher Education, Kobe University, Kobe 657-8501, Japan

Abstract. Writing in a foreign language is a struggle for learners and revising their writings is time consuming for teachers as well. For this reason, writing support systems have been widely proposed and one of its main functions is to automatically detect and revise errors in learners' writings. However, the detection technologies are a work in progress and the effectiveness of error revision feedback is arguable. Meanwhile, numerous efforts have been made to enhance learners' writing proficiency and reduce errors. Reading is considered as one of the important strategies. However, few studies have reported the linguistic knowledge that learners pay attention to and how they use the knowledge of web-based learning in their writings. In this paper, we performed a reading-to-write experiment in a web-based writing environment and analyzed reading materials and learners' writings to explore how to observe learners' awareness of syntactic structures in materials. Sentence patterns, proposed in our previous studies, have been introduced to categorize sentences, and the syntactic similarities between reading materials and learners' writings have been calculated. The experimental results revealed that students showed higher comprehension of content but displayed poor attention towards syntactic structures in reading activities, if the structures were not significantly salient. It is assumed that the similarity measure is effective in observing students' awareness of syntactic structures in materials, and further studies are needed to automatically observe the awareness.

Keywords: Syntactic awareness · Reading-to-write · Similarity measure · Web-based EFL writing

1 Introduction

Writing in a foreign language is a struggle for learners. Besides organization and clarity in content, writing necessitates the accurate use of lexical and syntactic knowledge [1]. Hence, grammatical revision is an important process in foreign language writing. However, revising learners' writings is time consuming for teachers. For this reason, automatically detecting and revising errors in learners' writings is a popular research

M. A. Herzog et al. (Eds.): ICWL 2019, LNCS 11841, pp. 100–107, 2019.
https://doi.org/10.1007/978-3-030-35758-0_10

topic not only in the field of educational technology but also in natural language processing [2]. Writing support systems have been proposed [3–6]. Nevertheless, detection technologies for this purpose are still a work in progress and the effectiveness of error revision feedback is arguable [7–9].

On the other hand, considerable effort has been put in teaching writing to enhance learners' writing proficiency. This means that errors in learners' writings decrease as proficiency improves. Reading is regarded as one of the important strategies of enhancing writing proficiency. Reading and writing are interdependent and writers' linguistic skills, contextual awareness, and strategies, etc., are influenced by the information in source texts, in writers' prior experiences and learning etc. [10]. It has been stated that learners' writing skills concerning content, organization, vocabulary, and language use are associated with their reading skills [11]. Furthermore, the visual-syntactic text formatting technology that visualizes syntactic structures has been experimentally used on reading to enhance syntactic awareness. The experimental results clarified that the technology raised students' awareness of syntactic structures, and the written conventions and writing strategies of low-proficiency students were significantly influenced by the technology [12]. However, problems related to learners' awareness of linguistic knowledge in source texts and how the knowledge provides a scaffold of support to writing, emerged. We suggest that, in a web-based language learning environment, observing learners' attention towards linguistic knowledge in source texts is necessary as well. Based on the observation, a scaffold of support can be provided to writing at last.

In this paper, we aim to present an approach to automatically and quantitatively observe the correlation between the reading and writing activities. We focus the observation on learners' awareness of syntactic structures in reading materials. Although literature [12] has provided a technical method of raising syntactic awareness, it has not been reported how to automatically and quantitatively observe learners' awareness in a web-based language learning environment.

We consider that learners' awareness can be observed by measuring similarities between reading materials and learners' writings. Therefore, we aim to perform an experiment that includes reading-to-write tasks in a web-based writing environment and analyze reading materials and learners' writings. Sentence patterns, proposed in our previous studies, are introduced to categorize sentences, and the syntactic similarities between reading materials and writings are calculated [13]. In the next section, we explain the details of the experiment. We propose the method of similarity measure in Sect. 3, and then provide the experimental results and discussion in Sect. 4.

2 Experimenting with Reading-to-Write Tasks

2.1 Web-Based Writing Environment

Generally, there are two kinds of reading styles related to writing in classroom learning: reading-to-write and reading-to-integrate. We adopted the reading-to-write style in the experiment to investigate learners' awareness. Many studies have focused on the relationship between reading-to-write and writing. Most claimed that reading-to-write strongly influences writing [14]. Although it is evident that integrated reading improves learners' writing proficiency, it is a harder task to observe learners' awareness.

We developed a web-based writing system to perform the experiment. Two web-pages were designed to provide two reading-to-write tasks. Each page included a paragraph essay on the top followed by two related questions. The first question asks the participant if he/she has read the essay. The second asks to write a response essay in relation to the paragraph essay. An input space for writing is given below the second question. Meanwhile, in order to clarify if learners are sensitive to salient syntactic structures, we colored the present tense verbs in third person singular, which appear on the second page, red [15].

2.2 Reading Materials

As the study focuses on how to observe learners' awareness, easy-to-read materials were used to reduce comprehension difficulties and errors in writing. Two paragraphs were chosen from a text book for the freshmen of Kobe University. The essays consist of 156 words (13 sentences) and 152 words (15 sentences) with the topics focusing on bosses in offices and future jobs, respectively. Hence, the questions related to the response essays on the first page were as follows:

- Question 1: Have you read the paragraph before?
- Question 2: Please write a short essay on your boss.

2.3 Participants and Procedure

There are 12 participants consisting of second-year, third-year, and senior students of Kobe University, with a major in global culture. This makes the reading materials easy to read for them.

The students were required to log in to the web-based writing system, and then complete the two reading-to-write tasks without using a dictionary, in an orderly manner. To avoid losing participants' attention, the essays are limited to 5 sentences or 70 words so that the experiment takes around fifteen to twenty minutes.

3 Similarity Measure

Learners' awareness can be observed by measuring similarities between their writings and reading materials based on the hypothesis that a learner tends to imitate the syntactic structures he/she pays attention to during reading.

Numerous researches in the field of natural language processing have addressed the issue of similarity measures for semantic or syntactic analysis. Recently, Gali et al. proposed a framework for syntactic analysis [16]. Although we adopted the tree Levenshtein distance to measure syntactic similarities and failed to interpret the results, it is important to further investigate the similarity measures for analyzing learners' awareness.

In this paper, we measure syntactic similarities between documents by categorizing sentences according to sentence patterns and then calculating Euclidean distances.

3.1 Sentence Patterns

Table 1 gives the sentence patterns that learners are required to know at the start of English language learning [13]. In the column "Pattern description," we describe the features of the patterns. It is a common feature in patterns that a sentence is differentiated only by the subject or the verb of the sentence. In addition, each sentence pattern has four sub-classifications which are combinations of tense and polarity: (a) a present tense affirmative sentence pattern (pre_aff), (b) a present tense negative sentence pattern (pre_neg), (c) a past tense affirmative sentence pattern (past_aff), and (d) a past tense negative sentence pattern (past_neg). The pattern names will be used in the next section.

Table 1. Sentence patterns

Pattern names	Pattern description
P1	A subject is the first person "I"
P2	A predicate verb is am/is/are/be/have/has/exist/exists
P3	A predicate verb is think/believe/consider/guess/suppose/assume
P4	Can/be able to/am able to/is able to/are able to is included in a subject-verb phrase
P5	A subject-verb phrase is excluded from the above patterns

The subject-verb phrase of a sentence that starts with the subject and ends with the verb can be easily extracted by the use of a dependency parser. We used the Stanford Parser to extract subject-verb phrases of sentences [17].

3.2 Similarities Between Two Documents

We calculated the Euclidean distance of the two documents as similarities. For each document, all the sentences are categorized within the sentence patterns. The ratios of the patterns used in the document are calculated. Then, the Euclidean distance between the two documents is calculated by using the ratios, and is defined as the similarity. Understandably, the larger the value, the lower the similarity.

4 Results and Discussion

We collected 35 sentences and 34 sentences in the two reading-to-write tasks, respectively. There are 13 sentences in the first reading material (Reading_A) and 15 in the second reading material (Reading_B). Here, simple sentences, complex sentences, and complicated sentences are included.

First, we summarized students' writings. Then, we categorized all the sentences in each student's writings, Reading_A and Reading_B, and calculated the Euclidean distances of the writings and the materials.

4.1 Summary of Students' Writings

There are 11 students who answered "No" to Question 1 in the two tasks which indicated that it was the first time the students had read the materials. There were a few syntactic errors and spelling mistakes in their writings but all were easy to read. The writings showed high topic similarity as well. Therefore, the students had sufficient reading proficiency and writing proficiency concerning the reading-to-write tasks.

Conversely, it seems that students did not notice the display difference in the present tense verbs in third person between Reading_A and Reading_B, or they did not pay attention to the use of the present tense verbs in third person. There are 7 verbs ending in *–s* in Reading_A and 7 red verbs ending in *–s* in Reading_B. In the reading-to-write task related to Reading_A, 4 present tense sentences in third person singular were used in students' writings and one error was found. In the reading-to-write task related to Reading_B, there were 11 present tense sentences in third person singular while there were 5 verbs without *–s*. The error percentage in the second task is larger. It is thus believed that coloring does not raise students' awareness.

4.2 Observing Students' Awareness by Measuring Similarities

Table 2 shows the Euclidean distance values. The values related to Reading_A vary from 0.44 to 1.19, and the distances corresponding to Reading_B range from 0.21 to 0.90. Here, S1–S12 denote the 12 students, and the values are ordered by those in Reading_A. The syntactic structures in the writings of S1, S6, and S7 are very similar to that of Reading_A in comparison to S9's essay. The structures in S11's essay are most similar to Reading_B and those of S3 are far different.

Table 2. Euclidean distance values

Students	S1	S6	S7	S4	S8	S12
Reading_A	0.44	0.44	0.44	0.60	0.71	0.71
Reading_B	0.76	0.52	0.43	0.70	0.43	0.25
Students	S11	S3	S10	S5	S2	S9
Reading_A	0.74	0.83	0.85	0.88	1.05	1.19
Reading_B	0.21	0.90	0.52	0.52	0.56	0.38

We drew the distributions of sentence patterns used in the essays of S1, S6, and Reading_A in Fig. 1 and the distributions of S9 and Reading_A in Fig. 2. Here, the suffixes "Pre_Aff" and "Past_Aff" mean a present tense affirmative sentence pattern and a past tense affirmative sentence pattern, respectively, as mentioned in Sect. 3.1.

It can be observed in Fig. 1 that S1 and S6 tend to reuse sentence patterns appearing in Reading_A. Although the ratios of the patterns used in the students' writings are very different from the material, the sentence patterns are limited to those appearing in Reading_A. Students may be potentially or consciously influenced by syntactic structures in the material on reading.

However, Fig. 2 indicates that S9 did not refer to the patterns. There is no reuse of sentence patterns in Reading_A and the complete essay consists of past tense affirmative sentences with be verbs. Obviously, the student ignored the sentence patterns in Reading_A.

Because the results from the task for Reading_B were similarly inclined, as mentioned above, we omitted the figures corresponding to the second task.

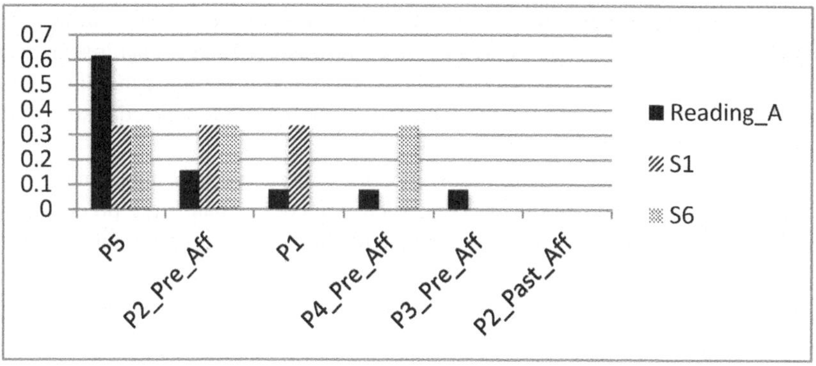

Fig. 1. The distribution of sentence patterns with high similarities

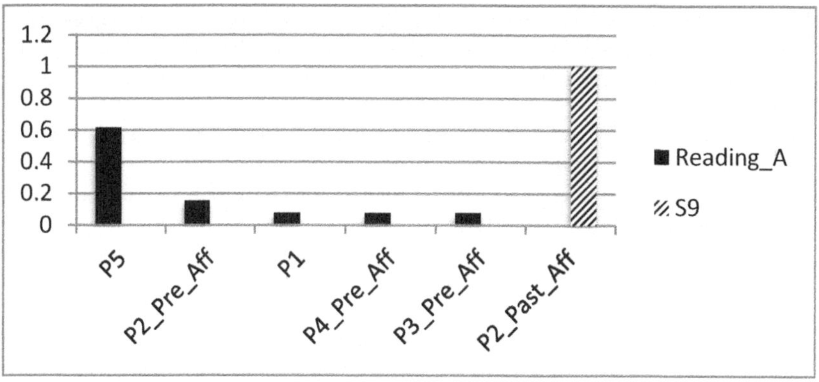

Fig. 2. The distribution of sentence patterns with low similarities

Therefore, it is noticed that a Euclidean distance value based on sentence patterns can prove if learners tend to reuse syntactic structures in reading materials. If the value is small, it means a learner may be aware of syntactic structures on reading. Furthermore, by verifying the distribution of the structures appearing in learner's writings, we may find which structure the learner tends to reuse on writing. The results claim that measuring similarity by categorizing sentences according to sentence patterns may be an effective approach to automatically observe learners' syntactic awareness.

5 Conclusion

In this paper, we performed a reading-to-write experiment in a web-based writing environment and analyzed reading materials and learners' writings. Sentence patterns that were proposed in our previous studies were introduced here to categorize sentences, and the syntactic similarities between reading materials and writings were calculated. The experimental results revealed that most of the students showed higher comprehension on topics but poor attention towards syntactic structures in reading activities, despite parts of the structures being colored. It is assumed that the similarity measure is effective in observing students' awareness of syntactic structures in materials.

On the other hand, the students involved in the experiment are limited and the essays are short. Therefore, we need to improve such points to enhance the precision of the approach. Further studies are still needed to automatically observe learners' awareness.

Acknowledgement. This work is supported by JSPS KAKENHI Grant Number JP17K01081.

References

1. Kimura, H., Kimura, T., Shiki, O.: Theory and practice in reading and writing: nurturing independent learning. Taishukan Publishing Co., Ltd., Tokyo (2010). (in Japanese)
2. Leacock, C., Chodorow, M., Gamon, M., Tetreault, J.: Automated Grammatical Error Detection for Language Learners, 2nd edn. Morgan & Claypool Publisher, San Rafael (2014)
3. Bowerman, C.: Writing and the computer: an intelligent tutoring systems solution. Comput. Educ. **18**(1–3), 77–83 (1992)
4. Yeh, S., Lo, J.: Using online annotations to support error correction and corrective feedback. Comput. Educ. **52**(4), 882–892 (2009)
5. Kunichika, H., Koga, T., Deyama, T., Murakami, T., Hirashima, T., Takeuchi, A.: Learning support for English composition with error visualization. Trans. Inf. Syst. (Jpn. Ed.) **91**(2), 210–219 (2008)
6. Wilson, J., Czik, A.: Automated essay evaluation software in English Language Arts classrooms: effects on teacher feedback, student motivation, and writing quality. Comput. Educ. **100**, 94–109 (2016)
7. Truscott, J.: The case against grammar correction in L2 writing classes. Lang. Learn. **46**(2), 327–369 (1996)
8. Chandler, J.: The efficacy of various kinds of error feedback for improvement in the accuracy and fluency of L2 student writing. J. Second Lang. Writ. **12**(3), 267–296 (2003)
9. Van der Kleij, F.M., Feskens, R.C.W., Eggen, T.J.H.M.: Effects of feedback in a computer-based learning environment on students' learning outcomes: a meta-analysis. Rev. Educ. Res. **85**(4), 475–511 (2015)

10. Ackerman, J.M.: Reading, writing, and knowing: the role of disciplinary knowledge in comprehension and composing. Res. Teach. Engl. **25**(2), 133–178 (1991)
11. Ito, F.: L2 reading–writing correlation in Japanese EFL high school students. Lang. Teach. **35**(5), 23–29 (2011)
12. Park, Y., Warschauer, M.: Syntactic enhancement and second language literacy: an experimental study. Lang. Learn. Technol. **20**(3), 180–199 (2016)
13. Kawamura, K., Kashiwagi, H., Kang, M.: An approach toward automatic error detection in learners' English writing based on the source language. In: 10th International Proceedings on Mobile, Hybrid, and On-Line Learning, pp. 62–65. IARIA, Roma (2018)
14. Delaney, Y.A.: Investigating the reading-to-write construct. J. Engl. Acad. Purp. **7**, 140–150 (2008)
15. Kuhbandner, C., Pekrun, R.: Joint effects of emotion and color on memory. Emotion **13**(2), 375–379 (2013)
16. Gali, N., Mariescu-Istodor, R., Hostettler, D., Fränti, P.: Framework for syntactic string similarity measures. Expert Syst. Appl. **129**, 169–185 (2019)
17. Klein, D., Manning, C.D.: Accurate unlexicalized parsing. In: Proceedings of the 41st Meeting of the Association for Computational Linguistics, pp. 423–430 (2003)

Cross-Cultural Reflections of Tertiary Students on ICT-Supported Innovations

Martina Maněnová and Dagmar El-Hmoudova(✉)

University of Hradec Kralove, Hradec Kralove, Czech Republic
{martina.manenova, dagmar.elhmoudova}@uhk.cz

Abstract. The paper focuses on the perception of innovations from the perspective of students. By innovations, in this case, we understand information and communication technologies. The aim of the research project is to compare the perception of innovations from the view of Czech and Asian students. We proceeded from Rogers' theory of diffusion of innovations (Rogers uses the words technology and innovation as synonyms), which defines five categories of adopters as classification of individual members of the social system, based on innovativeness. Diffusion is seen as a process, while innovations are passed on to other members of a particular social system during a certain time unit and through certain information channels. As a research tool, we used the Kankaarinta questionnaire. The research group consisted of Czech and Asian university students. Given the expansion and use of technology in Asian countries, we assumed that Asian students would be more inclined to innovate than the Czech ones. We worked with comparable groups (186 Czech students and 159 Asian students). Due to the fact that Czech students were from the Faculty of Education, female students prevailed in that group. Asian group of students was gender-balanced. In both groups, early majority prevailed, with a statistically significant difference between the two groups. Asian students seemed more innovative.

Keywords: Diffusion of innovations · Perception of ICT · Rogers's theory · Kankaarita questionnaire

1 Introduction

A characteristic feature of the society over the past decades is the general acceleration caused mainly by the penetration of information and communication technologies into all sectors of human activities [1]. This issue is closely related to the adoption of innovations, respectively the diffusion of innovations, by individual members in the society.

The issue of diffusion of innovation has been dealt with in many empirical researches and studies that were mainly focused on marketing [2]. For example, Gabriel Tarde, one of the founders of modern sociology and social psychology, focused on the research in the field of innovation penetration into society with his imitation theory [3]. One of the most important theorists of "diffusions" is Everett M. Rogers, who in 1962, based on his research on the spread of agricultural innovations among Iowa farmers, introduced the entire theory of diffusion of innovations [3].

M. A. Herzog et al. (Eds.): ICWL 2019, LNCS 11841, pp. 108–115, 2019.
https://doi.org/10.1007/978-3-030-35758-0_11

2 Theoretical Basis

Rogers' theory of diffusion of innovations is, according to Medlin [4], one of the most appropriate tools for researching the process of adopting technology in learning environment. We come across the synonyms of innovations and technology that Rogers uses. Rogers defines the concept of diffusion as a process by which innovation is communicated among members of a particular social system, namely during a certain time unit and through particular information channels [3]. The term communication is also, according to Rogers, a kind of process, in which participants create and share information with each other for a purpose of mutual understanding [3]. From the above we can conclude that the basic components of diffusion of innovation are:

- Innovation
- Communication channels
- Time
- Social system.

2.1 Innovation-Decision-Making Process

Based on the Rogers definition of diffusion of innovations, it is possible to identify the main factors affecting the uneven spread of innovation. It is about the nature of innovation, communication and the dynamics of the process that is influenced by the social framework. On the level of an individual, who decides to accept or reject innovation, we talk about the process. This process has several stages, and each of these stages causes some obstacles to a potential adopter. The phases are as follows:

- Knowledge - the individual knows about the existence of an innovative product and understands what it brings
- Persuasion - the attitude of the individual to innovation is either positive or negative
- Decision - the individual engages in activities that lead to acceptance or rejection of innovation
- Implementation - the individual starts using the innovation
- Confirmation - an individual evaluates the result of using innovation

2.2 Categories of Innovation Adopters

Rogers states in his publication that individuals, as members of a particular social system, do not adopt innovations in the same way. Each individual undergoes a particular decision making process of innovation accepting or rejecting, which happens over a period of time. This means that it is possible to divide the adopters on the basis of the time period, or the moment when they first applied the innovation [3].

Rogers defines categories of adopters as a classification of individual members of the social system based on innovativeness [3]. The subcategories are composed of enthusiastic innovators, visionary early adopters, pragmatic early majority, conservative late majority and skeptical laggards [5]:

- Innovators (enthusiasts) are people who enthusiastically share news with similarly targeted people. They try new things without fear of failure. Enthusiasts deal very well with the high degree of uncertainty at innovations, being often misunderstood. They can have a positive impact on the spread of innovations in their surroundings. According to Rogers, this is the smallest category represented only by 2.5% of the population.
- Early adopters (visionaries) are, in certain characteristics, similar to innovators. They are more restrained in accepting innovations, and most likely become the opinion leaders, whose example is worth following. They focus solely on their social group, which is how they differ from innovators. They approach innovation with greater caution. Rogers calculations determine 13.5% of these adopters in the population.
- The early majority (pragmatists) have not a leading role, and if so then rarely. Together with a group of early users, they can play the role of a mediator of a level of uncertainty in the process of spreading innovations. They undergo a much longer process than previous groups before they accept innovation - the period of their innovation-decision-making process is relatively long. According to Rogers, 34% of the population belong to this group.
- The late majority (conservatives) in Rogers' theory make up about one-third of all members of the social system (34%). They are very insecure, and careful in acquiring innovations. Adoption will take place only after pressure of peers, regulations or norms. If uncertainty prevails, they will not accept innovations.
- Laggards (skeptics) are the last to accept innovations. They follow traditional values and solutions, and are fixed with the past. Their relationship to innovations is distrustful and they associate with a specific social group. According to Rogers, 16% of the population belong to this group (see Fig. 1).

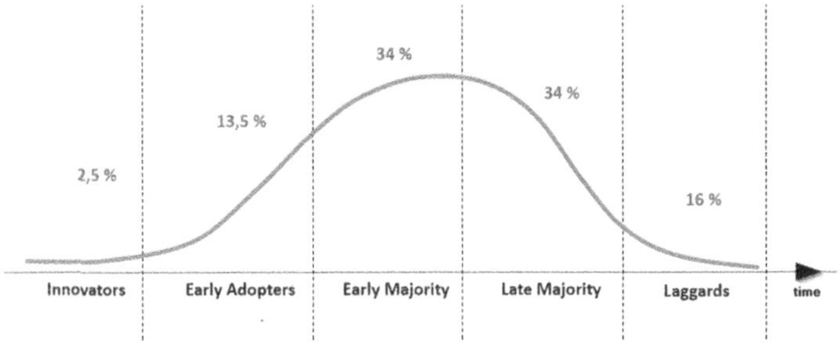

Fig. 1. Individual categories of adopters depending on their approach to innovation (Source: Rogers [3]).

In each of the aforementioned categories of adopters, individual members resemble each other's level of innovativeness, which Rogers defines as the degree of belief that an individual or other unit of adoption applies innovation relatively earlier than another individual member of the social system [3].

A different form of definition is presented by Braak [6], who describes innovativeness as a relatively stable, socially built and innovatively dependent characteristic that signals an individual's good will to alter their family practices [7]. Innovativeness is thus crucial for understanding the desired and essential behavior in the innovation-decision-making process [5].

3 Research Project

The main goal of the project was to find out the perception of innovations in relation with information and communication technologies in two groups of tertiary students with different ethnic background.

Sub-objectives:

- Describe the perception of innovation from the perspective of Czech students.
- Describe the perception of students from the perspective of Asian students.
- Verify whether the obtained distributions correspond to Rogers typology based on the theory of diffusion of innovations.
- Perform comparisons with researches focused on the view or perception of innovations.
- Based on the objectives, the following research questions were formulated:
- What is the attitude of Czech students to innovations in ICT?
- What is the attitude of Asian students to innovation in ICT?

3.1 Methodology

Based on research goals and questions, quantitative research was chosen. An exploratory research method was used and a questionnaire was chosen as the basic research technique. The original and the Czech version (for Czech students) of the Kankaanrinta questionnaire was used. The Czech version of the Kankaarinta questionnaire was already used by Černochová [7]. The questionnaire consisted of five pentads of claims (25 items), and respondents, using a scale from 1 to 5 (5 - agree, 4 - rather agree, 3 - no opinion, 2 - rather disagree, 1 - disagree), expressed the level of acceptance of the claims. Each set of claims was formulated to be as responsive and reflective as possible, so that the respondents could express their views according to the five groups of Rogers categories, i.e. innovator, early adopter, early majority, late majority, and laggard.

The research group consisted of 186 Czech students from the University of Hradec Králové and 142 students from Chinese (resp. Asian) universities. All of them were teacher-training students, who use the technology mainly for personal and educational purposes (PC, laptop, tablet, smartphone) and social networks. The characteristics of the research sample (selection) were as follows, see Table 1.

Table 1. Characteristics of research sample (selection).

	Czech students	Chinese students
Total number of students	186	142
Male	28	59
Female	158	83
Age (in average)	22.1	21.1
Standard deviation	2.4	1.3
Minimum	19	19
Maximum	36	24
Modus	22	21
Median	22	21

4 Research Results

Based on individual scores, we obtained a distribution of respondents in terms of their perspective and attitudes towards innovations in the field of information and communication technologies. The largest proportion of Czech students belongs to Early majority (60%), in contrast with early Adopters (4%), who were represented the least.

In the group of Chinese students dominated the Early majority (38%) as well, followed by Innovators (26%) and Laggards (5%) were represented the least, see Fig. 2.

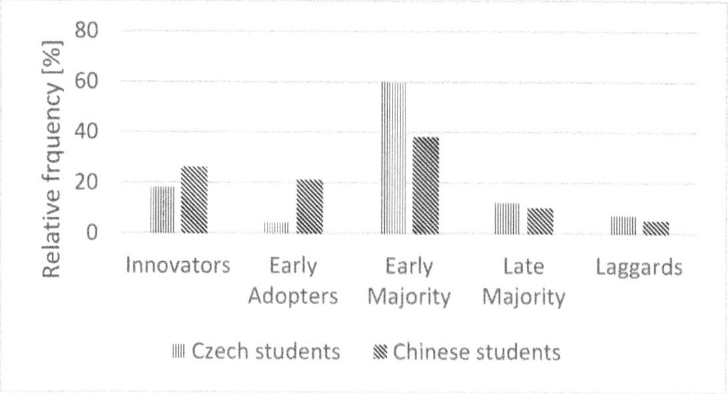

Fig. 2. Distribution of Czech and Chinese students.

Our further objective was to find out if the two groups of students differ significantly in terms of ICT innovations. For testing, we used due to the abnormal data distribution (based on the normality tests Kurtosis, Skewness and Omnibus, the normality cannot be rejected), Kolmogorov-Smirnov test and for verification the

Mann-Whitney test. The null hypothesis was not accepted at the significance level $\alpha = 0.05$ (Kolmogorov-Smirnov test $p = 0.020127$; Mann-Whitney test $p = 0.015282$). For the resulting box charts see Fig. 3.

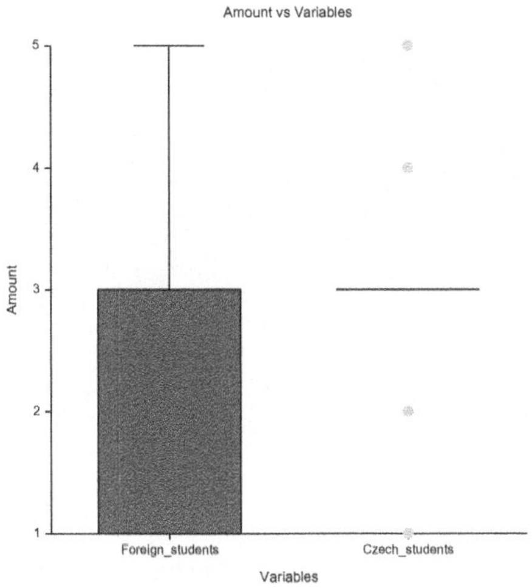

Fig. 3. Box charts of data distribution of both groups of students.

If we compare the obtained results with relevant researches (see Table 2), we can state that unlike Kankaarintas' [8] and Rogers' [3] results the group of Czech students corresponds most closely with the results of Zounek [4] and Cirus [9]. In all cases, they were teacher training students. The group of Chinese students seems relatively innovative (26%).

We can also observe a certain trend that there is a reduction in the proportion of displaced persons in favour of the Early majority or Early adopters or Innovators, which corresponds to innovative ICT trends [10, 11] (see Fig. 4).

Table 2. Relevant researches.

Category	Kankaanrinta [8]	Rogers [3]	Zounek [4]	Círus [9]	Czech students	Foreign students
Innovator	3	2,5	10	13,2	18	26
Early adopter	13	13,5	3	6,6	4	21
Early majority	34	34	66	69,2	60	38
Late majority	34	34	20	8,8	12	10
Laggard	16	16	1	2,2	7	5

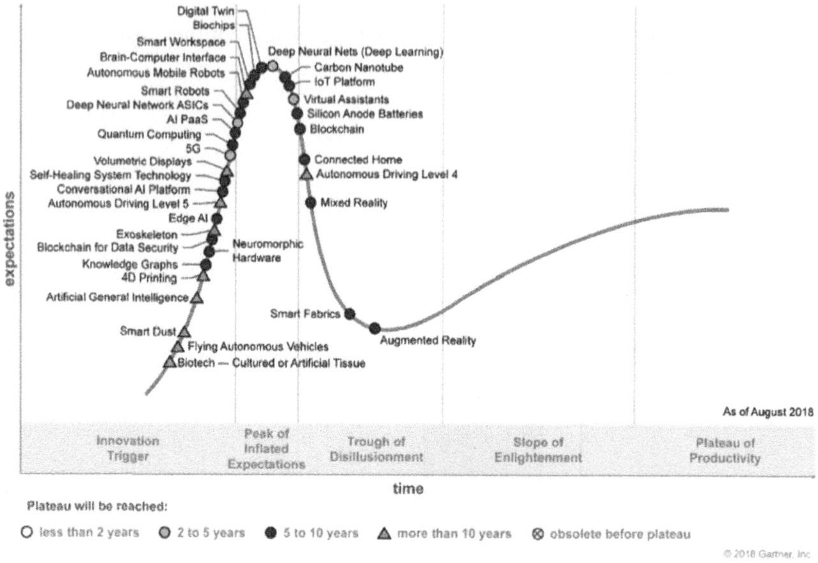

Fig. 4. Gartner Hype Curve of Emerging Technologies in 2018 (Source: Panetta [9]).

5 Conclusion

The described research detected the university students' attitudes to ICT innovations. The research was based on Rogers' theory of diffusion of innovations and its categorization. We took into account similar researches. The results of the research showed that the groups of students were different in terms of the perception or adoption of innovations in the field of ICT. Both selected groups of students were dominated by Early Majority, however, Chinese students, according to research, tend to be more inclined to progressive adoption of ICT innovations.

From the perspective of innovations in the development of technologies, we used the Rogers definition. The Gartner curve, see Fig. 4, depicts trends in technology and the understanding of technology cycles. The 2018 curve no longer shows the technologies commonly used by students. There you can find technologies focused on artificial intelligence, ecosystems, Do-It Yourself Biohacking, Transparent Immersive Experiences and Ubiquitous Infrastructure. From the development of the curve we can deduce that contrary to the results of Rogers [3] and Kankaarinta [8], the perception of technologies (PC, laptop, tablet, smartphone) and social networks is shifted to the categories of innovator, early adopter and early majority.

We are aware that our research is subject to potential limitations. First, there is insufficient sample size for statistical measurement and thus we cannot generalize in any way. Second limitation concerns conflict arising from cultural bias and other personal issues of the selected group of students, who come from different cultural backgrounds. The authors are also aware that triangulation of methods is necessary to obtain relevant data. There is also a certain limit in the theory of diffusion. We agree with the statement of Brdicka [12] that the theory of diffusion can only be applied (without any problems) to the technical side of technology implementation in teaching. Despite all the limits, we believe that information and communication technology is one of the fastest growing areas and teachers' as well as students' attitudes to innovations in this area are important for the further development of education.

References

1. Steffen, W., Broadgate, W., Deutsch, L., Gaffney, O., Ludwig, C.: The trajectory of the anthropocene: the great acceleration. Anthropocene Rev. **2**(1), 81–98 (2014). https://doi.org/10.1177/2053019614564785. http://journals.sagepub.com/doi/10.1177/2053019614564785. ISSN 2053-0196. [cit. 2.3.2017]
2. Meade, N., Islam, T.: Modelling and forecasting the diffusion of innovation–A 25-year review. Int. J. Forecast. **22**(3), 519–545 (2006)
3. Rogers, E.M.: Diffusion of innovations. Simon and Schuster, New York (2003)
4. Zounek, J., Sebera, M.: Budoucí učitelé a inovace v oblasti informačních a komunikačních technologií. Studia paedagogica **53**(10), 95–108 (2005)
5. Sahin, I.: Detailed review of Rogers' diffusion of innovations theory and educational technology-related studies based on Rogers' theory. Turkish Online J. Educ. Technol.-TOJET **5**(2), 14–23 (2006)
6. Van Braak, J.: Individual characteristics influencing teachers' class use of computers. J. Educ. Comput. Res. **25**(2), 141–157 (2001)
7. Černochová, M., Siňor, S., Kankaanrinta, I.K.: Jak přijímají budoucí učitelé novinky z oblasti informačních a komunikačních technologií? In: Nové možnosti vzdělávání a pedagogický výzkum: IX. celostátní konference ČAPV s mezinárodní účastí u příležitosti 10. výročí vzniku Ostravské university: sborník příspěvků: Ostrava 27, 28 June 2001. Ostravská univerzita, Pedagogická fakulta, Ostrava (2001). ISBN 80-7042-181-9
8. Kankaanrinta, I.K.: Finnish kindergarten student teachers' attitudes towards modern information and communication technologies. In: Media, Mediation, Time and Communication. Helsinki: University of Helsinki. Department of Teacher Education, 2000, pp. 147–170 (2000). ISBN 951-45-9350-2
9. Cirus, L.: The influence of the teacher on the formation of digital literacy of primary school pupils. Hradec Kralove: Pedagogical faculty of Univerzity of Hradec Kralove, dissertation work, 195 p. (2017)
10. Panetta, K.: Widespread artificial intelligence, biohacking, new platforms and immersive experiences dominate this year's Gartner Hype Cycle. Smarter Gartner (2018) https://www.gartner.com/smarterwithgartner/5-trends-emerge-in-gartner-hype-cycle-for-emerging-technologies-2018/. [cit. 2019-05-06]
11. Pikhart, M.: Technology enhanced learning experience in intercultural business communication course: a case study. In: Hao, T., Chen, W., Xie, H., Nadee, W., Lau, R. (eds.) SETE 2018. LNCS, vol. 11284, pp. 41–45. Springer, Cham (2018). https://doi.org/10.1007/978-3-030-03580-8_5
12. Brdicka, B.: Role internetu ve vzdělávání: studijní materiál pro učitele snažící se uplatnit moderní technologie ve výuce. Kladno: AISIS, 2003. 122 s (2003). ISBN 80-239-0106-0. [cit. 2019-14-04]. http://omicron.felk.cvut.cz/~bobr/role/

Computer Supported Collaborative Learning

The Characteristics of Tutor Blogging Predicting Student Reflection in Blogs

Karmen Kalk[1(✉)], Piret Luik[2], and Merle Taimalu[1]

[1] Institute of Education, University of Tartu, Salme 1A, 50103 Tartu, Estonia
karmen.kalk@ut.ee, merle.taimalu@ut.ee
[2] Institute of Computer Science, University of Tartu, J. Liivi 2, 50409 Tartu, Estonia
piret.luik@ut.ee

Abstract. During the learning process students need time, space and interaction with peers and tutors. One way to fulfil these conditions is to apply e-learning tools, for example blogs. An important part of teacher training is reflection, and it needs attention. The learning process is influenced by several factors and one is the participation of the tutor. Previous studies have indicated that tutor participation in the learning process can influence student reflection, but not all the activities by the tutor are effective. However, it is important to examine more specifically how tutors can support student reflection through interacting in the blog. The aim of this study is to find out what characteristics of tutor blogging predict the level of reflection in blog posts by student teachers and induction year teachers. The sample consisted of 207 student teachers and induction year teachers, and 29 tutors from two Estonian universities. All students had the opportunity to communicate with each other and with their tutor in the blog. Characteristics of tutor blogging and the level of student reflection were identified in blog posts using a quantitative content analysis. A stepwise multiple regression analysis indicated that five significant characteristics of the content of blog posts by tutors and one characteristic of how active their blogging was predicted reflection in the blog on the part of the students. These include communication with students, actively writing in the blog, blog posts about success, reflective blog posts, posts about the tutors' experience and posting questions in the blog.

Keywords: Teacher education · Reflection · Blog · Tutor

1 Introduction

It is important for teachers to analyse and reflect upon teaching experiences [17]. Reflection is a social process that facilitates learning from one's own experiences and those of others [21] and requires interaction with others to express and interpret the experience more clearly. Consequently, teacher educators have to decide which form, process and method are most useful for encouraging student teachers to reflect [27]. It is important to offer environments that give students more time for discussion and reflection outside the classroom [28]. For example, learning communities offer time and space where student teachers have learning relationships with peers, tutors or others

M. A. Herzog et al. (Eds.): ICWL 2019, LNCS 11841, pp. 119–129, 2019.
https://doi.org/10.1007/978-3-030-35758-0_12

from schools and universities [16]. To promote reflection, one way is to use a collective blog in teacher education, where student teachers and their tutors can publish posts in one blog and read and comment on each other's posts [3]. Previous studies [e.g. 4, 6, 24] and authors of this study [15] have focused on students' perspective, investigating the impact of the characteristics of student blogging on their reflection. Likewise, studies have pointed out that also tutor participation in online discussions is one of the key elements to effective learning [22, 25, 26], and current article is about characteristics of tutor blogging that predict students reflection in the blog.

1.1 Related Work

Tutor presence in a shared blog seems to be necessary for the professional development of student teachers including the recording of this process in the blog [11]. Simply because students and tutors are participating together does not mean that learners can reflect because the reflection process needs educational support [21]. The activity of the tutor should be to encourage deep learning [22], but the quality of the guidance is an essential part of student teaching through instruction and modelling [2]. The nature of the guidance influences student reflection, and therefore it is important to define the guidance specifically [20]. Tutors may play a minimalist background role or a highly engaged active role [9, 26], or student-centred or instructor-centered discussions or a combination of these [22] in the online environment. From one perspective, the tutor may support or respond to students, but does not participate in discussions, and from another perspective the tutor may participate in discussions and challenge students to discuss and think more deeply [9, 26]. Based on the previous studies [e.g. 3, 7, 13, 18], the activities of the tutor can be divided as follows: setting learning activities that encourage deeper thinking, modelling reflective behaviour, discussing positive and negative experiences, providing feedback and asking questions.

Earlier studies have shown that student teachers have considered it significant that the tutor presents contradictory opinions to promote reflective thinking, as well as summarizing discussions and making conclusions based on the concepts behind problems [18]. The level of reflection in students also improved in the online forum when: their tutor encouraged them to share their own reflections, ideas and comments [28], the tutor's modelled reflection encouraged the students to reflect upon the online discussions [13, 28], and using a reflective model, tutor supervision and real situations positively influenced the student teachers' reflective portfolios [23].

Discussions with a tutor to guide student teachers in linking theory and experience [13], and discussions with a tutor about experiences which come from the student teachers' blog posts [3] could promote reflection of student teachers. Experiences may contain successful and unsuccessful aspects. More is learned from problems, but sometimes learners do not want to discuss their problems [7]. It has also been important for the students that their tutor or supervisor is empathetic, positive and friendly in the online discussions [26]. Successful experiences give positive feelings and a willingness to analyse the positive situation [7].

Providing feedback [17, 18, 22, 26], focusing the discussion [18] and developing community are important activities for the tutor [22]. The student teachers perceived professional support in the tutor's comments as highly significant support in the individual blogs [3], and the comments by the tutor facilitate deeper reflection, but the tutor should also promote peer support rather than only share their own expert knowledge in the blog [5]. In addition, tutor's comments without offering the student teachers guidance in the blog contributed more to a social atmosphere than the reflection process [13]. Solving questions and problems, and posing questions is also an essential activity of the tutor [22], which creates collective sense in learning community. Asking higher order thinking questions [28] or posing questions [3, 5, 13] promotes student reflection in the online discussions.

Previous studies have also shown that periodic intervention in the discussion by the tutor [22], timely responding [26] and actively writing tutors [18, 26] are also important factors for the students, and may promote their reflection. The results indicated that active tutor in the online discussions keeps the students engaged in the learning process [22], and the number of tutor discussion board posts is positively related to the number of student posts [25]. Student teacher reflection improved when the tutor spent more time communicating and supporting them [20], and continuous communication between tutor and student teachers enabled constant learner reflection [1]. Inversely, students also felt comfortable if the tutor was passive in online discussions [12].

There is a lack of studies about which characteristics of the activities of tutors could promote learning in online discussions [22, 25, 26], and how tutors can best support student teacher reflection [2]. It is important to further investigate how the activities of the tutor in online learning during teaching practice changes the level of reflection [13]. Guidelines for tutors on how to encourage students in online discussions are also necessary [18, 25]. Accordingly, further exploration of the characteristics of the blogging activity of tutors and the content of their blog posts is important to promote reflection in online learning communities. The aim of the current study is to find out which characteristics of the blogging of tutors predict the level of student reflection in blog posts in teacher education. The following research questions were posed in this study:

1. Which characteristics of the content of blog posts by tutors predict the level of reflection in student blog posts during teacher education?
2. Which characteristics of the blogging activity of tutors predict the level of reflection in student blog posts during teacher education?

2 Method

2.1 Context

Student teachers during their teaching practice and newly qualified teachers during their induction year were investigated in the current study. The teaching practice took place in different schools and kindergartens. Each student had their own mentor in the school/kindergarten and also a tutor from the university. There was no difference between the practice tasks for school and kindergarten teachers. During the practice, the students had to observe the activities of teachers, and plan and carry out their own lessons/activities supervised by their mentor. Newly qualified teachers worked officially at the school or kindergarten as teachers and participated in an induction year program throughout the first school year. They had a mentor in the school/kindergarten, but no supervisor from the university. They participated in seminars in university during the induction year where they discussed situations and problems.

As there were only some student teachers in the same school during their practice and their schedules did not allow them to communicate, and the newcomers in schools were mostly alone, separated from other newly qualified teachers, we found that a blog could provide a suitable environment to discuss professional issues and successes and problems experienced during their practice and induction year. Each blog had one or more tutors included, whose task was to support communication and reflection in the blogs by asking questions and replying to students.

2.2 Participants

The current study included data collected from 207 students and induction year teachers from the University of Tartu and Tallinn University. The criterion for selection was the following: posted at least two posts in the blog and also filled the pre-questionnaire. There were 15 male (7%) and 192 female (93%) participants, 112 of them students in their teaching practice (54%) and 95 induction year teachers (46%). The average age was 25.3 (SD = 4.96) years. The participants were student teachers and newly qualified teachers from different subject areas. Seventy-nine respondents (38%) had reported in the pre-questionnaire that they had experience with blogging. In this paper we will refer to student teachers and induction year teachers uniformly as 'students.'

There were 29 tutors involved in these blogs, who encouraged communication between students, answered questions and supported reflection. The number of tutors in a blog varied from one to four tutors (in one blog). The background of the tutors varied – 15 were university teachers and 14 were in-service teachers. These tutors were related to the practice or the induction year. Three of these tutors were male and 26 female. The age of the tutors ranged between 26 and 60.

2.3 Instruments

In 27 collective blogs, 207 students have written altogether 1,858 posts (1,184 new posts and 672 comments), and tutors 547 posts (267 new posts and 280 comments).

As a dependent variable of this study we used the average level of student reflection in new posts. The level of the student reflection in new posts was determined on the basis of the Gibbs reflection model [10]. The model follows a hierarchy and presents six levels of reflection from description as the lowest to action plan as the highest. In this study, we added level 0 (Nothing = no reflection) to note posts with no descriptive level; for example, short answers (e.g. "Yes!"). The independent variables were as follows: characteristics of the blogging activity of tutors (see below) and characteristics of the content of the blog posts of tutors.

Characteristics of the Content of Tutors' Blog Posts

As the theoretical review revealed, several studies have discovered links between tutor's activities or the content of their writing and the reflection of their students [e.g. 3, 7, 13, 22, 28]. In this paper we used the following characteristics to describe the activities and content of blog posts by tutors:

- Percentage of posts about success and problems. The extent to which tutors posted about their own successful experiences was indicated by the percentage of posts about success. These posts included tutors writing about good, positive or happy feelings, success stories or happiness. The posts by the tutors about problems were indicated by the percentage of posts about problems. These posts involved writing about situations what the tutor had perceived as a problem or failure. Neutral posts were also included here – there was no success or problem described but the posts were about something.
- Average level of success and problems in posts. Average level of success and problems in posts was used as a characteristic where all three levels (posts about success, problems and neutral) were included.
- Average level of reflection in new posts by tutors. Average level of reflection in new posts by tutors was defined according to Gibbs' model (see above) on seven levels from the posts matching the 0 level without any reflection to those posts matching the 6th level that included an action plan.
- Different behaviours in the blog. Tutor behaviour in the blog was divided into eight different types: (1) sharing information – provides information on, for example, practice requirements, etc.; (2) sharing own experiences – descriptive posts about the tutor's own experiences; (3) giving instructions, suggestions, guidance – gives suggestions, or direct guidance, instructions; (4) proposing questions, problems – asking questions or giving problems for others to discuss; (5) answering questions and problems – answering different questions or responding to issues raised; (6) offering support – supporting, comforting, praising students, encouraging, etc.; (7) agreement with something in a student's post – agreement, accepting what the student has written; 8) contradiction with something in a student's post – arguing, opposing.
- Four levels of collectivity. the four levels of collectivity were used in our research to describe the extent to which tutors encouraged communication with each other in the blog. The first level was individual where the tutor only presented information in a self-centred way without no links to others posts or addressing others. At the second level, the perception of others occurred, at least in the title or at the end of the post, where the tutor used a phrase to turn to the students. However, there was no link to other posts, rather a self-centred sharing of information or experience. The third level shows real communication with others; for example, asking questions, answering other's questions or commenting on somebody's post. The final, fourth level is supporting the learning community, where calls were addressed to all or several blog members calling them to discuss some problems or the like.

Characteristics of the Blogging Activity of Tutors
Previous studies [e.g. 18, 20, 26] have found that student reflection is positively related to how actively tutors communicate with students. The blogging activity among tutors was indicated here on the basis of the number of comments and the total number of posts (the sum of new posts and comments). The length of the tutors' posts was shown by the average number of words in new posts and the average number of words in all posts.

2.4 Procedure

All students were divided into 27 collective blogs. Each blog group had an introductory seminar where the students were first introduced to the purpose and potential of using the blog during their teaching practice and induction year. Each participant was instructed to create an account on Blogger (http://www.blogger.com), and the first post was written to practice writing in the blog, as well as to introduce students to the technical options they can use in the blog. The participants were also told about the ethical aspects – that the blog is closed and only the members of this blog and of the research group can read the posts in the blog and write posts, that blogging is voluntary and not assessed as part of the practice or induction year. In addition, students were asked not to use the names of schools, teachers and students in their posts. Students also had the opportunity to use a pseudonym (or nickname) on the blog if they did not want to write under their own name.

A coding manual was developed to facilitate the quantitative content analysis. At the first stage the four researchers coded independently 20 randomly selected postings until the Kappa coefficient for agreement was 0.83. After that all researchers coded postings individually. Meantime we repeated the first stage and calculated again the Kappa coefficient. For a more detailed description of the data analysis see our previous papers [15, 19]. Descriptive statistics (counts, percentages, means, standard deviations) of the characteristics of blogging activity and post content were calculated for each tutor. The average level of student reflection in new posts was also found. We used IBM SPSS Statistics 25 for the data analysis. A stepwise multiple regression analysis was used to reveal which characteristics of the content of the tutors' blog posts and the activity of the tutors' blogging (independent variables mentioned above) predicted the average level of reflection by students in new posts (dependent variable) in the blog.

3 Results

At first, we present descriptive statistics about how active the tutors were. On average there were 4.5 new posts, 4.7 comments and 9.3 posts per tutor per blog. The average length of one post (new post + comment) was 56.8 words, and 64.6 words in new posts.

The minimum average level of reflection in the students' posts using Gibbs model on a 6-point scale was .5 and the maximum level was 4.5. The average level of reflection was 2.56 (standard deviation .909). The skewness was −.223 and kurtosis −.494 indicating that the data were fairly symmetrical. The average level of reflection among the students was mostly in the range 2–4 (see Fig. 1).

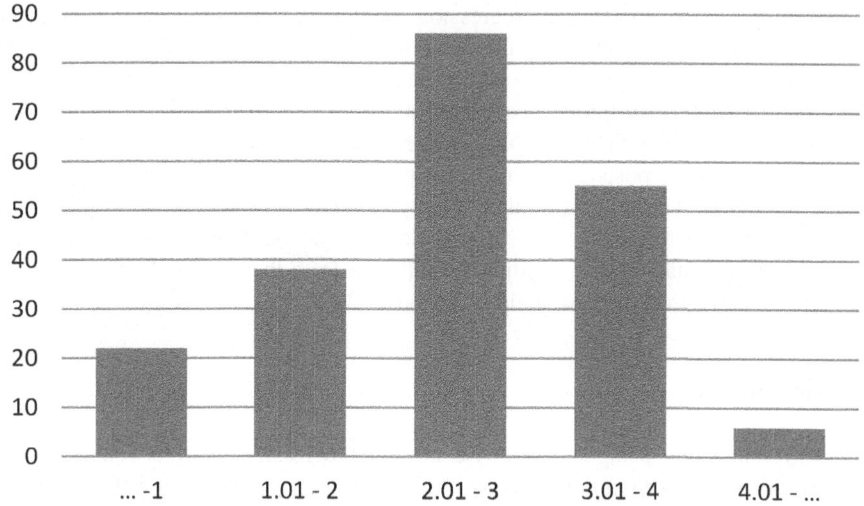

Fig. 1. Frequency of student posts with different levels of reflection according to Gibbs model

In terms of predicting the average level of reflection in student posts, the regression analysis result indicated significance (R2 = .435, F = 12.965 p < .001) in regard to seven variables. Because the VIF values for the variables 'Number of posts by tutor' and 'Number of comments by tutor' were above 10 (accordingly VIF = 14.322 and 13.832) and the tolerance values were below .10 (accordingly Tolerance = .070 and .072), the variable 'Number of comments by tutor' was removed from the regression analysis. The results of this multiple regression analysis are presented in Table 1. We arrived at a model with six variables explaining 40.8% of the total variance of the average level of reflection in student posts.

Table 1. Multiple regression analysis on average level of reflection in student posts

R^2	F	Model	β	T	Tol	VIF
.408	13.651	Percentage of tutor's posts with communication with others	−.819	−4.758**	.168	5.950
		Number of posts by tutor	.708	6.158**	.376	2.659
		Average level of success in tutor's posts	−.648	−5.300**	.333	3.004
		Average level of reflection in tutor's posts	.509	6.161**	.729	1.371
		Percentage of tutor's posts about his/her experience	−.359	−2.491*	.240	4.173
		Percentage of tutors' posts with questions	.289	2.586*	.399	2.505

*p < .05
** p < .01

According to the standardized regression coefficients, the significance of precursor variables on the positive factors influencing the average level of reflection in student posts are as follows: number of posts by tutor, average level of reflection in tutor's posts, and percentage of tutors' posts with questions. The percentage of tutors' posts with communication with others, the average level of success in tutor's posts, and percentage of tutor's posts about his/her experience were negative factors. The VIF values were well below 10 (or alternatively, tolerance values all well above 0.1) indicating no multicollinearity in the data Field [8]. The distribution of the standardized residuals was not statistically significantly different from the normal distribution (with the Kolmogorov-Smirnov Test statistic .045 $p = .200$).

4 Discussion

In the present study using the stepwise multiple regression analysis found that six characteristics of the blogging of tutors predicted the level of student reflection in the blog posts during teacher education.

To answer the first research question, we found that five characteristics of the content of tutors' blog posts predicted the level of reflection in student blog posts. The most significant negative predictor was the percentage of tutor's posts with communication with others. Accordingly, online discussions that included questions, answers or comments from the tutors reduced the level of reflection in the students' blog posts. By contrast, percentage of tutors' posts with questions was found to positively predict student reflection. The latter result is supported by previous studies [3, 5, 13]. In our study, percentage of tutors' posts with communication with others included not only questions, but also answering student questions and commenting on what the students had written. Therefore, the influence on reflection may depend on how the tutor communicates in online discussions. Furthermore, [13] tutor's comments without guidance in the blog was found to rather support a social atmosphere than learner reflection. Consequently, the tutors asking questions promotes student reflection and may cause students to think more carefully and deeply about how to respond, but just commenting or answering questions might even reduce reflection.

The level of student reflection in the blog posts was also negatively predicted by the average level of success in the tutor's blog posts. This result may be due to more is learned from problematic experiences as claims Ellis, Carette, Anseel, & Lievens [7]. Therefore, student reflection could be supported more via discussions with the tutor about problems than about successes. It is interesting to compare this with our previous results, in which student posts about success had the opposite effect, increasing the level of reflection, and blogging group posts about problems decreased the students' level of reflection in the blog [15]. Therefore, when communicating online in blogs, differences have been found in the impact of student and tutor activities on student reflection, where student posts about success can promote reflection, while conversations with tutors about success may decrease the level of reflection. This could be because students are willing to discuss their own successful experiences in depth, but tutors writing about their successes or the successes of others does not promote deeper thinking or reflection in the students.

In addition, the percentage of tutor's posts about his/her experience negatively predicted student reflection in the blog posts. This can also be explained on the basis of the results from the same previous study [15] that when tutors write more new blog posts, there is a decrease in the students' evaluations of their reflection. Therefore, many of the experiences that the tutors share may seem to the students to be presenting the correct way to communicate and share experiences, but do not necessarily support the students' level of reflection [14]. Our result confirms previous findings [3] that discussing learner experiences and not the tutors' own experiences is important for developing student reflection, although Dalgarno et al. [5] have stated that sharing expert opinions on the part of the tutors could also promote student reflection in online discussions. As previous studies [13, 28] have shown that tutor's modelling reflection promoted student teacher reflection in online learning, we have also found that the average level of reflection in tutor's posts positively predicted the students' level of reflection in blog posts.

To answer the second research question only one characteristic of the activity of tutor blogging, number of posts by the tutor, positively predicted the student level of reflection in blog posts. This is confirmed by previous studies [1, 20, 22]. Therefore, tutors might contribute one part of the learning process for the students by being visibly active through continuous posting in the blog. Students might feel comfortable to engage in a higher level of reflection if the tutor in the blog follows and thinks about the learning process with the students. It indicates that in collective blog students need communication with both tutors and peers as we found in our previous study [15].

5 Conclusion

In summary, when using online discussion tools such as blogs in the learning process, it is necessary to consider which factors promote student reflection. The current study confirmed earlier findings that one important factor in the process of student reflection is the tutor. Student reflection depends on how the tutor communicates in online discussions and students should be guided to share rather their own success stories and discuss their own experiences than their tutor's. Furthermore, the tutor should be active in the blog and write reflective posts as an example for the students. Students may feel more comfortable and confident if they feel that someone is following their learning process and guides them if necessary. Comparing the impact of student blogging characteristics and tutor blogging characteristics on student reflection in blog posts revealed that the blogging characteristics of peers and tutors are different, and this helps to predict the students' level of reflection in online discussions. It is essential to consider these findings when online discussion tools such as collective blogs are used to support student reflection in teacher training.

There is a lack of previous studies about the impact of the activity levels of tutors and the content of posts on student reflection in online learning communities. More specifically, the effect of the tutor when using a blog in teacher education has been studied little. Clarifying the role of the tutor in online discussions is essential to provide guidelines about what conditions contribute to student reflection. The current study helped fill this gap by studying tutors' posts in collective blogs. Web-based learning is relevant, and therefore the impact of the characteristics of students and tutors on learner reflection could be further explored in the future. This would provide a more comprehensive understanding of how to support student reflection in online learning. The limitations of this study included the fact that the sample is not representative, and little background information was collected about the tutors to obtain more in-depth results to support student reflection in teacher education. Subsequent studies could consider not only the characteristics of the tutors' blogging, but also the background and personal characteristics of the tutors.

References

1. Ali, M.F., Sukri, N.M., Tahir, L. M., Said, M.N.H.M.: Developing critical reflection skill among pre-service teacher through collaborative inquiry using social media. In: International Conference on Learning and Teaching in Computing and Engineering (LaTICE), pp. 43–48. IEEE, Hong Kong (2017). https://doi.org/10.1109/latice.2017.15
2. Bates, A.J., Ramirez, L., Drits, D.: Connecting university supervision and critical reflection: mentoring and modeling. Teacher Educ. **44**(2), 90–112 (2009). https://doi.org/10.1080/08878730902751993
3. Biberman-Shalev, L.: Personal blogs or communal blogs? Pre-service teachers' perceptions regarding the contribution of these two platforms to their professional development. Teach. Teach. Educ. **69**, 253–262 (2018). https://doi.org/10.1016/j.tate.2017.10.006
4. Chang, C.-C., Chen, C.-C., Chen, Y.-H.: Reflective behaviors Under a web-based portfolia assessment environment for high school students in a computer course. Comput. Educ. **58**(1), 459–469 (2012). https://doi.org/10.1016/j.compedu.2011.08.023
5. Dalgarno, B., Reupert, A., Bishop, A.: Blogging while on professional placement: explaining the diversity in student attitudes and engagement. Technol. Pedagogy Educ. **24**(2), 189–209 (2015). https://doi.org/10.1080/1475939X.2013.847481
6. Dos, B., Demir, S.: The analysis of the blogs created in a blended course through the reflective thinking perspective. Educ. Sci.: Theory Pract. **13**(2), 1335–1344 (2013)
7. Ellis, S., Carette, B., Anseel, F., Lievens, F.: Systematic reflection: implications for learning from failures and successes. Curr. Dir. Psychol. Sci. **23**(1), 67–72 (2014). https://doi.org/10.1177/0963721413504106
8. Field, A.P.: Discovering Statistics Using SPSS: (and Sex and Drugs and Rock'n roll), 3rd edn. Sage Publications, London (2009)
9. Gerber, S., Scott, L., Clements, D.H., Sarama, J.: Instructor influence on reasoned argument in discussion boards. Educ. Technol. Res. Dev. **53**(2), 25–39 (2005). https://doi.org/10.1007/bf02504864
10. Gibbs, G.: Learning by Doing: A Guide to Teaching and Learning Methods. Further Education Unit, London (1988)
11. Hramiak, A., Boulton, H., Irwin, B.: Trainee teachers' use of blogs as private reflections for professional development. Learn. Media Technol. **34**(3), 259–269 (2009). https://doi.org/10.1080/17439880903141521
12. Hurt, N.E., Moss, G.S., Bradley, C.L., Larson, L.R., Lovelace, M.; Prevost, L.B., Riley, N.: The 'Facebook' effect: college students' perceptions of online discussions in the age of social networking. Int. J. Scholarsh. Teach. Learn. **6**(2), 1–24 (2012). https://doi.org/10.20429/ijsotl.2012.060210

13. Jones, M., Ryan, J.: Learning in the practicum: engaging pre-service teachers in reflective practice in the online space. Asia-Pacific J. Teach. Educ. **42**(2), 132–146 (2014). https://doi.org/10.1080/1359866X.2014.892058
14. Kalk, K., Luik, P., Taimalu, M.: Blogging and self-evaluation on the use of reflection in teacher education. In: Mikk, J., Veisson, M., Luik, P. (eds.) Lifelong Learning and Teacher Development. Estonian Studies in Education, vol. 4. Peter Lang, Frankfurt (2012)
15. Kalk, K., Luik, P., Taimalu, M.: The characteristics of students, blog group and blogging that predict reflection in the blog during teaching practice and induction year. Teach. Teacher Educ. **86**, 102900 (2019). https://doi.org/10.1016/j.tate.2019.102900
16. Le Cornu, R., Ewing, R.: Reconceptualising professional experiences in pre-service teacher education…reconstructing the past to embrace the future. Teach. Teach. Educ. **24**(7), 1799–1812 (2008). https://doi.org/10.1016/j.tate.2008.02.008
17. Liakopoulou, M.: The role of field experience in the preparation of reflective teachers. Aust. J. Teach. Educ. **37**(6), 42–54 (2012). https://doi.org/10.14221/ajte.2012v37n6.4
18. Lim, C.P., Cheah, P.T.: The role of the tutor in asynchronous discussion boards: a case study of a pre-service teacher course. Educ. Media Int. **40**(1–2), 33–48 (2003). https://doi.org/10.1080/0952398032000092107
19. Luik, P., Taimalu, M.: Factors of participants and blogs that predict blogging activeness during teaching practice and induction year. Int. Rev. Res. Open Distrib. Learn. **17**(1), 180–194 (2016)
20. Mauri, T., Clarà, M., Colomina, R., Onrubia, J.: Educational assistance to improve reflective practice among student teachers. Electron. J. Res. Educ. Psychol. **14**(2), 287–309 (2016). https://doi.org/10.14204/ejrep.39.15070
21. Mauri, T., Clarà, M., Colomina, R., Onrubia, J.: Patterns of interaction in the processes of joint reflection by student teachers. J. Educ. Teach. **43**(4), 427–443 (2017). https://doi.org/10.1080/02607476.2017.1296542
22. Nandi, D., Hamilton, M., Harland, J.: Evaluating the quality of interaction in asynchronous discussion forums in fully online courses. Distance Educ. **33**(1), 5–30 (2012). https://doi.org/10.1080/01587919.2012.667957
23. Ogan-Bekiroglu, F.: Quality of preservice physics teachers' reflections in their teaching portfolios and their perceived reflections: do they intersect? Action Teach. Educ. **36**(2), 157–170 (2014). https://doi.org/10.1080/01626620.2014.901197
24. Ottenberg, A.L., Pasalic, D., Bui, G.T., Pawlina, W.: An analysis of reflective writing early in the medical curriculum: the relationship between reflective capacity and academic achievement. Med. Teach. **38**(7), 724–729 (2016). https://doi.org/10.3109/0142159X.2015.1112890
25. Ringler, I., Schubert, C., Deem, J., Flores, J., Friestad-Tate, J., Lockwood, R.: Improving the asynchronous online learning environment using discussion boards. J. Educ. Technol. **12**(1), 15–27 (2015)
26. Sheridan, K., Kelly, M.A.: The indicators of instructor presence that are important to students in online courses. MERLOT J. Online Learn. Teach. **6**, 767–779 (2010)
27. Shoffner, M.: Informal reflection in pre-service teacher education. Reflective Pract. **9**(2), 123–134 (2008). https://doi.org/10.1080/14623940802005392
28. Szabo, Z., Schwartz, J.: Learning methods for teacher education: the use of online discussions to improve critical thinking. Technol. Pedagogy Educ. **20**(1), 79–94 (2011). https://doi.org/10.1080/1475939X.2010.534866

A Collaborative Learning Grouping Strategy with Early Warning Function Based on Complementarity Degree

Zhizhuang Li[1], Zhengzhou Zhu[1](✉), and Qiongyu Xie[2]

[1] School of Software and Microelectronics, Peking University, Beijing, China
zhuzz@pku.edu.cn
[2] Anhui Normal University, Wuhu, Anhui, China

Abstract. Organizing groups is a critical process in implementing cooperative learning. The grouping strategy based on the degree of complementarity is a popular grouping strategy at present. However, the existing collaborative learning grouping strategy based on the degree of complementarity has disadvantages such as insufficient modeling accuracy for students' ability and lack of rationality for the reasons of regrouping. This paper proposes a collaborative learning grouping strategy with early warning function based on the degree of complementary mastery of knowledge points. First, we take knowledge points as the minimum unit, and use linear regression and expectation maximization algorithm to accurately model each student's mastery of each knowledge point. Then we use the inverse clustering algorithm based on knowledge points to classify students. Finally, we use LSTM neural network to predict the scores of each group in the next week, and early warning was given to the groups with significantly reduced predicted scores, and targeted suggestions were put forward for them according to the types of the warned groups. Experimental results show that the grouping strategy proposed in this paper can effectively improve the learning effect of students. The average precision and average recall of LSTM based group early warning were 30.1% and 27.6% higher than that based on linear regression, respectively.

Keywords: Cooperative learning · Grouping strategy · Learning early-warning · Cognitive diagnosis · LSTM · EM algorithm · Linear regression

1 Introduction

With the rapid development of educational information and the reform of teaching methods, both e-learning and classroom teaching tend to take collaborative learning as the dominant teaching method. B. Jong et al. have proved that collaborative learning plays a positive role in improving students' learning effect [1–3]. The collaborative learning process is mainly completed by organizing relevant group activities. In this sense, group learning is the basic organizational form of collaborative learning, and grouping strategy will have an important impact on the effect of collaborative learning. Over the years, many educational researchers have proposed a variety of different collaborative learning grouping strategies. H. m. Su et al. proposed a collaborative learning

M. A. Herzog et al. (Eds.): ICWL 2019, LNCS 11841, pp. 130–142, 2019.
https://doi.org/10.1007/978-3-030-35758-0_13

grouping strategy based on the degree of complementarity [4–9]. In order to solve the problem that students' mastery of knowledge will change dynamically after grouping for a period of time, Jong et al. proposed a dynamic collaborative learning grouping strategy based on the degree of complementarity, which can regroup the learning group or some members within the group whose complementarity has significantly decreased [10].

However, the existing collaborative learning grouping strategies based on complementarity have the following disadvantages:

1. The existing strategies take a chapter or a course as the minimum inspection unit to measure the degree of complementarity between students, which is not accurate enough.
2. The existing strategy can only give students the degree of discretization of the knowledge of a certain module, and the accuracy is insufficient.
3. As students can help each other with the knowledge they are good at, the gap between the two sides will be narrowed, so the degree of interaction between students in the group is positively correlated with the rate of decline of the degree of complementarity. Strong interactivity is conducive to this kind of group members to better learn new knowledge points. Therefore, it is unreasonable to judge whether the degree of complementarity has decreased significantly as the criterion of whether the group should be regrouped.

In order to solve the disadvantages of the existing collaborative learning grouping strategy based on complementarity, this paper proposes a collaborative learning grouping strategy with warning function. Firstly, the concept of weight of knowledge points is introduced. Relying on linear regression and EM algorithm, students' mastery of each knowledge point is calculated through cognitive diagnosis. Then, an inverse clustering algorithm based on the mastery of knowledge points is proposed to divide the students into groups. Finally, the LSTM neural network based learning group warning method is proposed, and targeted suggestions were put forward for the types of the warned groups. The test shows that the grouping strategy proposed in this paper can effectively improve the learning effect of students, and the accuracy and recall of the early-warning method proposed in this paper are both higher than the early-warning method based on linear regression.

The main contributions of this paper are as follows:

(1) a method that can accurately measure and calculate students' mastery of knowledge points is proposed. This method can give the continuous value of students' mastery of knowledge points.
(2) the degree of students' mastery of each knowledge point is taken as the minimum inspection unit to measure the degree of complementarity between students, and the degree of complementarity between students is measured according to the degree of students' mastery of each knowledge point, which has a high accuracy.
(3) An inverse clustering algorithm based on the mastery of knowledge points is proposed, which can divide students with strong complementary mastery of knowledge points into a group.
(4) A learning group early-warning method based on LSTM neural network is proposed. This method can predict the learning group's performance in the next week according to the learning group's performance in the previous weeks, and put forward specific Suggestions for the type of the warned group.

2 Related Works

2.1 Grouping Strategies in Collaborative Learning

The grouping strategy based on the degree of complementarity divides the students who have great differences in the knowledge of each module into a group, which is conducive to mutual guidance and help among students. Chan et al. proposed a grouping strategy based on evaluation concept map and thinking mode [4]. Wang et al. put forward a grouping strategy to divide students with high complementary abilities into a group to improve their English learning performance [5]. Wu et al. proposed a grouping strategy based on knowledge structure diagram and learning combination [6]. H. m. Su et al. considered the complementarity between learners' learning state and social networks, and adopted genetic algorithm to group students [7]. Tien et al. proposed a grouping strategy based on genetic algorithm to help teachers build heterogeneous collaborative learning groups that take into account multiple student characteristics [8, 9]. B. Jong et al. proposed a dynamic grouping strategy based on concept map [10].

2.2 Learning Early Warning

Learning warning can help identify students with hidden dangers and is an effective way to optimize teaching effect. Macfadyen et al. used Logistic model, AdaBoost, classification and regression tree (CART), Random Forest Algorithm and other methods to give early warning to students with poor predicted exam results [11–15]. D. Sansone combines machine learning with economic theory to predict which students will drop out of high school [15].

3 Method Design

As shown in Fig. 1, we first use linear regression and EM algorithm to calculate each student's mastery of each knowledge point. Then we use the inverse clustering algorithm based on knowledge point mastery to group the students, and divide the students with high similarity of knowledge point mastery into different groups as far as possible. We then used the LSTM neural network to predict the performance of each study group in the next week based on the data of each group's answers in the last 3 weeks. We identified all groups whose relative performance had dropped by more than five points, called them risk groups, and gave them early warning. Define the concept of the upper limit value of group knowledge point mastery index. We find out the students in each group who have the highest mastery level of the knowledge point, and define their mastery in the knowledge point as the upper limit value of group knowledge point mastery index. We calculate the upper limit value of each group's knowledge of each knowledge point. Finally, according to the average of the upper limit value of each group's knowledge of each knowledge point, we divided all risk groups into 2 categories and put forward specific Suggestions for them.

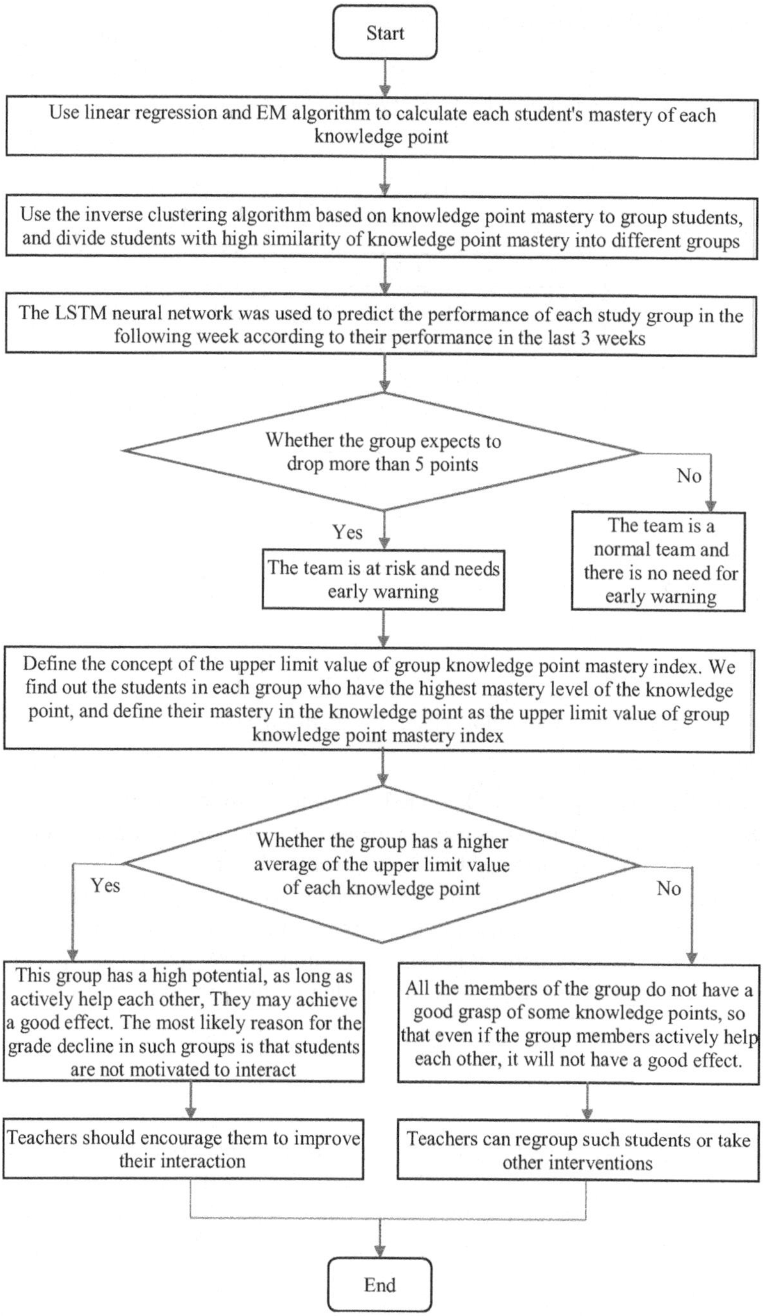

Fig. 1. Algorithm flow chart of collaborative learning grouping strategy with early warning function

3.1 Cognitive Diagnosis of Students

As shown in Fig. 2, we use linear regression and expectation maximization algorithm to accurately model each student's mastery of each knowledge point.

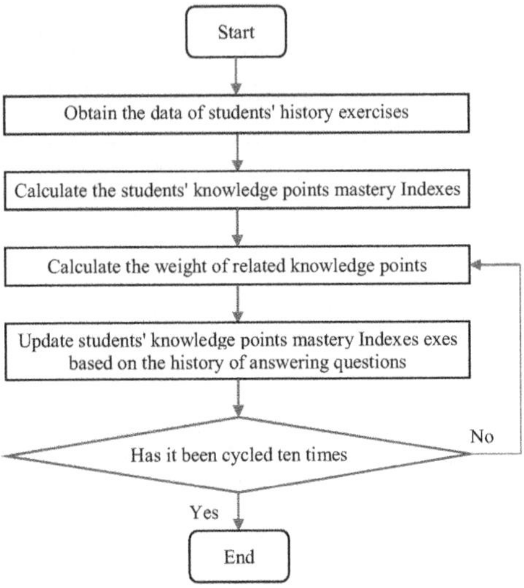

Fig. 2. Algorithm flow chart of cognitive diagnosis of students

First, define the concept of knowledge points mastery index. The concept of knowledge point mastery index is used to measure the degree of students' mastery of a certain knowledge point above or below the average level.

The formulas for calculating the knowledge points mastery index are defined respectively when the weight of knowledge point is unknown or known.

The formula for calculating knowledge point mastery Index G_{ab} of knowledge point without assigning the weight of knowledge point is as follows:

$$G_{ab} = \frac{\sum_{i=1}^{n}(p_i - m_i)}{\sum_{i=1}^{n} t_i} \tag{1}$$

Among them, p_i is student a's score of the exercise which only contains knowledge point b, m_i is the average score of the exercise, and t_i is the total score of the subject.

The formulas for calculating knowledge point mastery Index G'_{ab} of knowledge point under the condition that the weight of knowledge point has been assigned are as follows:

$$G'_{ab} = \frac{\sum_{i=1}^{n}(s_i - m_i)k_i}{\sum_{i=1}^{n} t_i k_i} \tag{2}$$

Among them, s_i is the score of exercise i done by student a, m_i is the average score of the exercise, k_i is the weight of knowledge point b in the exercise, and t_i is the total score of the exercise.

The steps of cognitive diagnosis for students based on their history of answering exercises are as follows:

First, obtain the data of all students' history work. Using exercises with only a single knowledge point, use formula (1) to roughly calculate and store the knowledge point mastery Index of each student's all knowledge point based on the historical answer situation.

We use the linear regression model to calculate the weight of each knowledge point in each exercise contained in the student's history answer record. We illustrate the use of the linear regression model with example exercise e and student s. We assume that there are n knowledge points in exercise e, student s's score prediction formula for exercise e is as follows:

$$h_i = \sum\nolimits_{j=1}^{n} k_j x_j + \mathrm{b}$$

h_i is the predicted score of exercise e for student s, x_j is the knowledge point mastery Index of the student s for the jth knowledge point of exercise e, and k_j is the weight of x_j. We use all the student history answer data to train the model, then we can get the weight of each knowledge point in each exercise.

We use formula (2) to calculate the more accurate knowledge point mastery Index of each student for each knowledge point when the weight of each knowledge point is known.

Using the EM algorithm, the previously calculated value of knowledge point mastery Index, which is based on students' historical answer, is taken as the current value of students' knowledge point mastery Index. Each time, the current value of knowledge point mastery Index, which is based on students' historical answer, is used to calculate the weight of knowledge point in a new round of exercises by linear regression. Then, the weight of knowledge point in the new round of exercises is used to calculate the knowledge point mastery Index of the new round of students based on the historical answer situation through formula (2). After repeated iteration for 10 rounds, the final result of knowledge point mastery Index and the weight of knowledge point for students based on their history answers was obtained.

3.2 Grouping of Students

First, we define the concept of knowledge point mastery level distance, recorded as d_{ab}, which indicates the level of overall difference between the two students' mastery of each knowledge point, and measures the complementarity of the two students. It is assumed that there are n knowledge points in total, mark student i's knowledge point mastery Index of knowledge point j as G_{ij}, then the formula for calculating the knowledge point mastery level distance between student a and student b is as follows:

$$G_{ab} = \frac{\sum_{i=1}^{n} |G_{ai} - G_{bi}|}{n} \tag{3}$$

Obviously, the value of G_{ab} is positively correlated with the degree of complementarity of student a and student b.

In this paper, inverse clustering algorithm based on knowledge points is used to group students, and the number of students in each group can be freely selected. Let's say there are m students, and we want to divide them into n groups. First, randomly select a student, s_1, and put and put him/her into group 1. Find out the student s_2, who has the smallest knowledge point mastery level distance from s_1, and put him/her into group 2. Find out the student s_3, who have the smallest average knowledge point mastery level distance form s_1 and s_2, and put him/her into group 3… Find the student s_n, who has the smallest average knowledge point mastery level distance form s_1, s_2,…, s_{n-1}, and put him/her into group 3 into group n. The purpose of this is to divide the students with similar mastery of various knowledge points into different groups so as to improve the complementarity of the students in the same group.

Each time a student who has not been grouped is randomly selected. Calculate his/her knowledge point mastery level distance with all the students who have been grouped, and then calculate the average distance of his knowledge points with all the students in each group. Select the group whose members have the largest average knowledge point mastery level distance with the student and put the student into the group. Until all students are grouped. The purpose of this is to group students with low levels of similarity in knowledge points (highly complementary) into one group.

Define the concept of the upper limit value of group knowledge point mastery Index. Assume that in group g, the student with the highest knowledge point mastery Index of knowledge point k is student s. Student s's knowledge point mastery Index of knowledge point k is defined as the upper limit value of group knowledge point mastery Index of the group g. The concept of the upper limit value of group knowledge point mastery Index is used to measure the maximum knowledge point mastery Index of all students in a group can be achieved together only by mutual tutoring among members of the group. Obviously, the greater the upper limit value of group knowledge point mastery Index of a group's knowledge points for a knowledge point, the higher the mastery level of the knowledge points that the group's students can theoretically achieve through mutual counseling.

The above grouping method was repeated for 10 times, and 10 grouping schemes were obtained. For each grouping scheme, the sum of the upper limit value of group knowledge point mastery Index for each knowledge point of each group was calculated in the case of using the scheme. Select the grouping scheme with the largest sum of the upper limit value of group knowledge point mastery Index of corresponding knowledge points as the final grouping scheme.

3.3 Group Early Warning

This method uses the data of each study group in the last 5 weeks to predict the group's performance in the next week.

Define the concept of group relative score, which is equal to the average score of the group minus the average score of all students. Because of the difficulty of each test, it is more convincing to measure the level of a group by its group relative score than by its average score.

Define the concept of the group knowledge point mastery level distance, the group knowledge point master level distance is equal to the average value of the knowledge point mastery level distance between all the students in the group. Define the concept of the average upper limit value of group knowledge point mastery Index. For a group, the average upper limit value of group knowledge point mastery Index is equal to the average value of the group's upper limit value of group knowledge point mastery Index for all the knowledge points.

The answer data of all students are given in weekly units, and the data of each week are taken as a group. Based on the weekly answer data, calculate the group relative score of each group (calculated on a scale of 100). Use the cognitive diagnosis method in 3.1 to calculate each student's mastery of each knowledge point based on the answer record of this week. Then calculate the group knowledge point mastery level distance of each group and the average upper limit value of group knowledge point mastery Index within this week of each group, and normalize all the data.

We use the Keras framework to establish the LSTM neural network model, set one hidden layer, 50 neurons in the hidden layer, the time step is set to 5, the activation function is sigmoid, the number of iterations is 1000, the batch size is 8, and the loss function is Mean square error. Each group's weekly group relative score, group knowledge point mastery level distance, average upper limit value of group knowledge point mastery Index as a characteristic value of the training sample, the same team for next week's group relative score as a forecast of the same training samples. All training samples were fed into the LSTM neural network model for training.

The trained LSTM neural network model can predict the group's group relative score in the next week based on group relative score, group knowledge point mastery level distance, average upper limit value of group knowledge point mastery Index of the students in the last 5 weeks.

According to the group relative scores of each group in this week and that of the group in next week predicted by this model, the rise or fall of the group relative scores of each group was calculated. Groups whose group relative scores fell by more than five points were called risk groups and given an early warning.

All groups that were alerted were divided into two groups. The first kind of group is the group with the higher average upper limit value of group knowledge point mastery Index. The second group is the group with the lower average upper limit value of group knowledge point mastery Index.

In the first group, the average upper limit value of group knowledge point mastery Index is relatively high, indicating that they have a high potential. As long as they actively help each other, they will have a chance to achieve good learning results. The most likely reason for this kind of group performance decline is that students are not active in interaction, so teachers should encourage them to improve their interactivity.

The most likely reason for the decline of the performance of the group in the second category is that all the members of the group do not have a good grasp of certain knowledge points, so that the interaction effect is poor. Teachers may consider regrouping such students or other interventions.

4 Experiment

4.1 Experimental Environment

To verify the grouping method proposed in this paper and the effect of group early warning, 140 undergraduates of Peking University were selected for a four-month experiment. The experiment was conducted on software engineering, a compulsory course for 140 students. This course includes 29 knowledge points. The course gives students two classroom quizzes a week and a final exam at the end.

4.2 Grouping Effect Experiment

The experiment divided the students into groups one month after the start of the course. Divide the students into two parts, 80 students in the first part and 60 students in the second part. For the students in the first part, cognitive diagnosis was conducted by using the answer data of the students in the first month's classroom test, and then the grouping strategy in this paper was adopted to divide them into 20 groups. In the second part, students were randomly divided into 15 groups.

As shown in Table 1, after the grouping completed, we calculate the initial average score, group knowledge point mastery level distance, average knowledge point mastery Index, average upper limit value of group knowledge point mastery Index. Then we calculated the mean values of the above indicators for the groups using the grouping strategy in this paper and those using the random grouping strategy.

Table 1. Initial state statistics table after grouping

Group type	Average score	Average group knowledge point mastery level distance	Average knowledge point mastery Index	Average upper limit value of group knowledge point mastery index
Use the grouping strategy in this article	76.13	0.31	−0.01	0.14
Use a random grouping strategy	77.54	0.13	0.01	0.08

As can be seen from Table 1, the average score and average knowledge point mastery Index of type 1 students are slightly lower than that of type 1 students, but the group average knowledge point mastery level distance and the upper limit value of group knowledge point mastery Index are significantly higher than that of type 2 students. It can be seen that the group adopting the grouping strategy in this paper has a significantly higher degree of complementarity than the group adopting the random grouping strategy.

The average score, average knowledge point mastery Index, group average knowledge point mastery level distance and the upper limit value of group knowledge point mastery Index of each group in each week were calculated according to the results of the classroom test. Record the average of the above indicators for each group, and calculate and record the same indicators based on the final exam. Figure 1 records the change trend of the average knowledge point mastery level distance of the two types of students with time. Figure 3 shows the trend of the average scores of the two types of students over time, and the results of the two types of students in the final exam are recorded in the last column.

As can be seen from Fig. 3, the average knowledge point mastery level distance of type 1 students and type 2 students both show a downward trend, while in the first month, the former declines faster obviously.

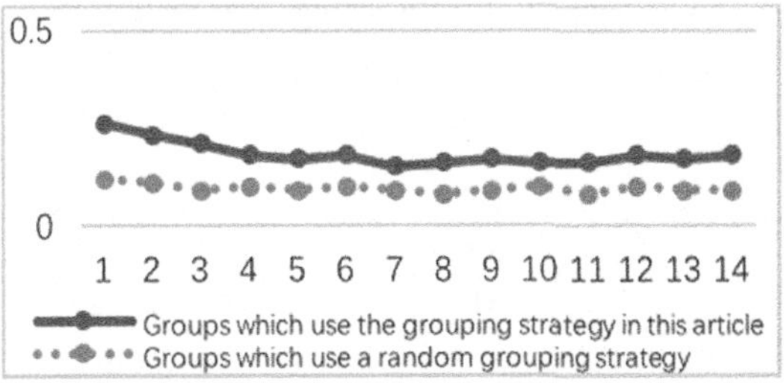

Fig. 3. Trend chart of average group knowledge point mastery level distance of the group

It can be seen from Fig. 4 that the class test scores and final exam scores of type 1 students are both better than that of type 1 students on the whole. Therefore, the grouping strategy proposed in this paper can effectively improve the learning effect of students. After the first month, the gap between the two decreased significantly, which may be the result of the significant decrease in the degree of complementarity of type 1 students after the first month.

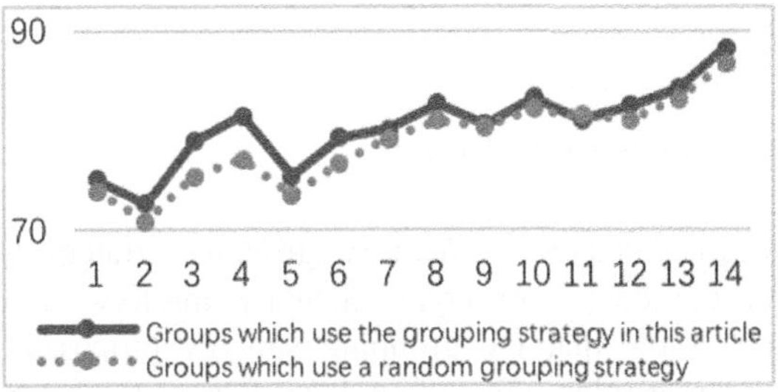

Fig. 4. Trend chart of the average score of the group

4.3 Early Warning Effect Experiment

As shown in Table 2, this experiment used the answer data of all students' classroom tests in the first two months as training data, and established the prediction model with the method in 3.3 of this paper. All the test data of 8 classroom tests in the last two months and the final exam were used as test data to test the accuracy of early warning. At the same time, the prediction method based on linear regression was used as the control group. In this experiment, the groups whose predicted group relative score have declined by more than 5 points are called risk groups. We separately counted the number of groups with a group relative score fell by more than 5 points in each exam, the number of groups that were predicted to be risk groups by the method based LSTM, the number of groups that were predicted to be risk groups by the method based linear regression, the number of groups that were predicted to be risk groups by the method based LSTM and the actual group relative scores fell by more than 5 points, the number of groups that were predicted to be risk groups by the method based linear regression and the actual group's group relative scores fell by more than 5 points.

Table 2. Early warning effect table

Methods	The number of groups actually regressed by more than 5 points	The number of groups that were predicted to be risk groups by the method	The number of groups that belong to the intersection of the previous two classes
LSTM	45	50	37
Linear regression	45	51	29

The accuracy rate was defined as the proportion of the group that was predicted to be a danger group and whose group relative score actually declined by more than 5 points in the group that was predicted to be a danger group. The recall rate was defined as the proportion of the group that was predicted to be a danger group and whose group relative score actually declined by more than 5 points in the group whose group relative score actually declined by more than 5 points. By calculation, the average accuracy of LSTM based group warning is 74.0%, which is 30.1% higher than the average accuracy of linear regression based group warning. The average accuracy of early warning in LSTM group was 82.2%, which was 27.6% higher than that of linear regression method.

5 Conclusions and Future Work

This paper proposes a collaborative learning grouping strategy with early warning function based on the degree of complementary mastery of knowledge points. Experimental results show that the grouping strategy proposed in this paper can effectively improve the learning effect of students. The average precision and average recall of LSTM based group early warning were 30.1% and 27.6% higher than that based on linear regression, respectively.

In the future, we will use the online learning platform to obtain the information of students' online learning behavior, and further explore various factors that may contribute to the improvement or decline of study groups' performance, so as to improve the accuracy of the group's early warning and propose more targeted intervention measures.

Acknowledgment. This paper was supported by National Key Research and Development Program of China (Grant No. 2017YFB1402400), Ministry of Education "Tiancheng Huizhi" Innovation Promotes Education Fund (Grant No. 2018B01004), National Natural Science Foundation of China (Grant No. 61402020, 61573356), and CERNET Innovation Project (Grant No. NGII20170501).

References

1. Webb, N.M., Troper, J.D., Fall, R.: Constructive activity and learning in collaborative small groups. J. Educ. Psychol. **87**(3), 406–423 (1995)
2. Jong, B., et al.: Effect of knowledge complementation grouping strategy for cooperative learning on online performance and learning achievement. Comput. Appl. Eng. Educ. **22**(3), 541–550 (2014)
3. Lai, C., et al.: The impact of peer interaction on group strategy in cooperative learning environment. https://www.scientific.net/AMR.271–273.1213
4. Chan, T.Y., et al.: Applying learning achievement and thinking styles to cooperative learning grouping. In: Frontiers in Education Conference-Global Engineering: Knowledge Without Borders. IEEE (2007)
5. Wang, Y., Li, Y., Liao, H.: Using a genetic algorithm to determine optimal complementary learning clusters for ESL in Taiwan. Expert Syst. Appl. **38**(12), 14832–14837 (2011)
6. Wu, Y.: Using complementary grouping strategy for cooperative learning. Int. J. Intell. Inf. Database Syst. **8**(1), 49–63 (2014)
7. Su, H.M., Shih, T.K., Chen, Y.H.: Grouping teammates based on complementary degree and social network analysis using genetic algorithm. In: International Conference on Ubi-Media Computing & Workshops. IEEE (2014)
8. Tien, H.-W., Lin, Y.-S., Chang, Y.-C., Chu, C.-P.: A genetic algorithm-based multiple characteristics grouping strategy for collaborative learning. In: Chiu, D.K.W., et al. (eds.) ICWL 2013. LNCS, vol. 8390, pp. 11–22. Springer, Heidelberg (2015). https://doi.org/10.1007/978-3-662-46315-4_2
9. Jong, B., Wu, Y., Chan, T.: Dynamic grouping strategies based on a conceptual graph for cooperative learning. IEEE Trans. Knowl. Data Eng. **18**(6), 738–747 (2006)
10. Macfadyen, L.P., Dawson, S.: Mining LMS data to develop an "early warning system" for educators: a proof of concept. Comput. Educ. **54**(2), 1–599 (2010)
11. He, W., Yen, C.J.: Using data mining for predicting relationships between online question theme and final grade. J. Educ. Technol. Soc. **15**(3), 77–88 (2012)
12. Hu, Y.H., Lo, C.L., Shih, S.P.: Developing early warning systems to predict students' online learning performance. Comput. Hum. Behav. **36**, 469–478 (2014)
13. Cheng, X., et al.: A novel learning early-warning model based on random forest algorithm. In: Nkambou, R., Azevedo, R., Vassileva, J. (eds.) ITS 2018. LNCS, vol. 10858, pp. 306–312. Springer, Cham (2018). https://doi.org/10.1007/978-3-319-91464-0_32

14. Liu, J., Yang, Z., Wang, X., Zhang, X., Feng, J.: An early-warning method on e-learning. In: Liu, S., Glowatz, M., Zappatore, M., Gao, H., Jia, B., Bucciero, A. (eds.) eLEOT 2018. LNICST, vol. 243, pp. 62–72. Springer, Cham (2018). https://doi.org/10.1007/978-3-319-93719-9_9
15. Sansone, D.: Beyond early warning indicators: high school dropout and machine learning. Oxford Bull. Econ. Stat. **81**(2), 456–485 (2019)

Does Group Size Affect Students' Inquiry and Collaboration in Using Computer-Based Asymmetric Collaborative Simulations?

Meeli Rannastu(✉), Leo Aleksander Siiman, Mario Mäeots, Margus Pedaste, and Äli Leijen

University of Tartu, Tartu, Estonia
meeli.rannastu@ut.ee

Abstract. This study investigated students' collaborative inquiry learning with 5th grade (N = 58, M_{age} = 11.3 years) and 6th grade (N = 74, M_{age} = 12.4 years) participants. Students were divided into two- and four-person groups to study whether group size affects their learning with asymmetric collaborative simulations. They worked in online digital learning spaces using tablet computers and communicated face-to-face. The Collaborative Rate of Photosynthesis Lab from the Go-Lab portal (golabz.eu) was used to establish the condition of asymmetric collaboration, and tasks related to it were developed to assess students' inquiry. To assess students' collaboration, we used an adapted self-assessed collaboration skills instrument to measure three dimensions: contribution, interaction with others and team learning. The results show that collaboration did not statistically significantly differ depending on group size in the 5th grade, but did in the 6th grade, with 2-person groups reporting better collaboration. Regarding students' inquiry, analysis of performance on the asymmetric collaborative tasks showed that there were no statistically significant differences between groups in either grade. However, the inquiry task scores were generally low (28% and 40% for 5th and 6th graders respectively), indicating that asymmetric collaborative inquiry is challenging for students in these grades.

Keywords: Collaboration skills · Asymmetric collaboration · Inquiry learning · Online labs · Smart devices

1 Introduction

Preparing young people for the future demands integrating 21st-century skills like collaboration and communication, problem-solving and critical thinking into the school curriculum. However, a challenge remains in determining effective ways of teaching these skills, as well as reliably assessing them [1]. Collaboration skills have received recent attention from international educational assessment initiatives like PISA and ATC21S, which have both attempted to measure students' collaborative problem-solving skills [2, 3]. In general, supporting and developing students' collaboration skills is among several important goals relevant to all educators. In science,

The original version of this chapter was revised: The original version of this chapter was previously published non-open access. It has now been changed to open access under a CC BY 4.0 license and the copyright holder has been updated to 'The Author(s).' The book has also been updated with this change. The correction to this chapter is available at https://doi.org/10.1007/978-3-030-35758-0_38

M. A. Herzog et al. (Eds.): ICWL 2019, LNCS 11841, pp. 143–154, 2019.
https://doi.org/10.1007/978-3-030-35758-0_14

collaboration is valued because research on the way scientists work in groups suggests that making successful discoveries is more likely when scientists distribute reasoning among several people, so as to better generate and evaluate alternative representations of a problem [4].

To identify situations as collaborative, Dillenbourg [5] identifies four features: peers at more or less the same level, able to perform the same actions, having a common goal and working together. To further characterize the first two features, he suggests that the degree of symmetry in a collaborative situation is a key factor, and although most collaborative situations are generally symmetrical, a slight degree of asymmetry may be desirable in triggering conflict, which in turn can facilitate learning through conflict resolution.

Technology-enhanced solutions to facilitate collaboration skills have demonstrated promising results. Chen et al. [6] synthesized 425 empirical studies in a meta-analysis and found that computer-supported collaboration had significant positive effects on knowledge gain (ES [effect size] = 0.42), skill acquisition (ES = 0.64), and student perceptions (ES = 0.38).

1.1 Effect of Group Size on Collaboration

Previous research suggests that the size of a collaborative group can affect individual learning outcomes and also group results. However, there is no consensus about what an optimal group size should be. Some studies suggest that pairs are best because then disruption of thought is minimized [7]. Slavin [8] found that learning outcomes were better for pairs compared to four or more member groups. At the same time, other studies suggest that larger groups (i.e., three or more students) give better opportunities to bring out multiple perspectives and form a better final result [9]. A meta-analysis by Sung et al. [10] analyzing different mobile computer-supported collaborative learning studies found that larger groups (i.e. four or more members) had better outcomes than smaller groups (i.e. two or three members).

1.2 Measuring Collaborative Skills in Educational Contexts

As the definition of collaborative learning has multiple views, the dimensions of collaboration skills connect to cultural, domain-specific and numerous other factors. Several self-assessment tools have been developed to measure different dimensions of collaboration skills. One of the difficulties in assessing collaboration skills is the absence of a well-validated and reliable instrument applicable to a variety of situations. For example, the team self-diagnostic learning framework measures only teamwork skills [11]. The Collaborative Self-Assessment Tool (CSAT) was developed as a general-purpose tool to help teachers model successful collaboration skills, and focused on both intrapersonal (motivation/participation; quality of work; time management; preparedness; reflection) and interpersonal (contribution; team support; team dynamics; interactions with others; role flexibility) skills [12]. Hinyard et al. [13] adapted CSAT to focus on student perceptions of collaboration skills and created an 11-item scale consisting of three dimensions of collaboration: information sharing, team learning, and team support.

1.3 Asymmetric Collaboration

One way of assessing students' collaborative problem-solving skills, developed by the Assessment and Teaching of 21st Century Skills (ATC21S) project, involved using computer-based tasks to distribute resources and information differently (i.e. asymmetrically) between two collaborators [2]. For example, in a computer simulation about balancing a beam, one student could place weights on only the left side of the balance, whereas another student, working remotely on another computer, could place weights on only the right side. Both students could see the effect of the weights on their individual computer screens, but neither could complete the task without depending on the other. Positive interdependence is mentioned by Johnson and Johnson [14] as one of five essential elements of cooperative learning. The authors define positive interdependence as the perception that team members are obliged to rely on one another in order to succeed.

Tasks involving asymmetric collaborative simulations bear a resemblance to the hidden profile task. The hidden profile task describes a condition where prior to a decision-making group beginning a discussion, information is asymmetrically distributed among group members, with some information being common to all members (shared information) and some information unique to individual members (unshared information); the shared information favoring a less optimal decision than when both shared and unshared information are considered together [15]. Research using the hidden profile task has found that groups rarely discover the optimal decision because they tend to focus on shared information at the expense of unshared information [15–17]. Improving performance on the hidden profile task generally requires getting group members to more thoroughly consider unshared information.

The effect of group size on the hidden profile task has been mixed [16]. Cruz et al. [18] found that small groups were better at solving the hidden profile task and suggested that social loafing in larger groups prevents a thorough discussion of unshared information. On the other hand, Stasser and Stewart [19] found that larger groups mentioned and repeated more unshared information than smaller groups, noting that the larger groups tended to have longer discussions. Mennecke [20] found that group size did not affect the proportion of shared or unshared information mentioned.

1.4 The Current Study

Asymmetric collaborative simulations offer a potentially promising way to extend inquiry learning with computer simulations to include a stronger emphasis on collaboration. However, it is not clear what the optimal group size should be for learning with asymmetric collaborative simulations to be most effective. The main research question addressed in this study is: To what extent does group size affect students' inquiry and collaboration in using computer-based asymmetric collaborative simulations?

2 Method

Two experiments, one with a 5th grade class and another with a 6th grade class of students at a public school in Tartu, Estonia were conducted. A total of 132 students participated. In the 5th grade experiment there were 58 students (28 girls, 30 boys, M = 11.3 years) and in the 6th grade experiment there were 74 students (43 girls, 31 boys, M = 12.4 years). The large size of these classes was due to the fact that this school applies an open classroom methodology for teaching science in grades 4 to 6, which can accommodate larger classes. The open classroom approach enables flexible use of space, furniture, equipment and digital technology to promote collaboration and group-based learning. In our study, students were divided into 2-person and 4-person groups. The groups worked on an inquiry learning activity using iPad tablet computers and communicated face-to-face. Students in 2-person groups had one iPad device per student, while students in 4-person groups had one iPad device per pair of students.

2.1 Materials

Asymmetric Collaborative Simulations

Two asymmetric collaborative simulations, available from the Go-Lab Portal (golabz.eu), were used in this study. The first one, the Collaborative Seesaw Lab (https://www.golabz.eu/lab/seesaw-lab; see Fig. 1 top), was used as a demonstrative example to familiarize students with the type of task associated with using an asymmetric collaborative simulation. It allowed students to place masses on a seesaw and share masses between each other. In one version of this simulation, a student could place masses only on the left side of the seesaw. In the other version, a student could place masses on only the right side. The effects of the masses on the seesaw were simultaneously seen by both students, but the location and weight of the masses of the collaborating partner were hidden (see Fig. 1 top). The task associated with this simulation required students to determine if it is possible to balance the seesaw using either two or three masses. The second simulation, the Collaborative Rate of Photosynthesis Lab (https://www.golabz.eu/lab/rate-of-photosynthesis-collaborative-lab; see Fig. 1 bottom), was used in the learning phase and the tasks associated with it were scored for the purposes of assessing students inquiry in this study. The Collaborative Rate of Photosynthesis Lab shows an aquatic plant immersed in a glass of water situated in a room with a desk lamp and a window. In one version of this simulation (labeled as Version A), a student can control the season of the year, whereas in the other version (labeled as Version B), a student can control the intensity of the desk lamp. The effects of both variables are seen simultaneously to both students. Furthermore, by clicking on the play button in the simulation, the aquatic plant begins to release bubbles due to the process of photosynthesis releasing oxygen gas. A time counter indicates the number of seconds that have elapsed and animation in the simulation, as well as text labeled "Number of bubbles", indicate how many bubbles have been emitted.

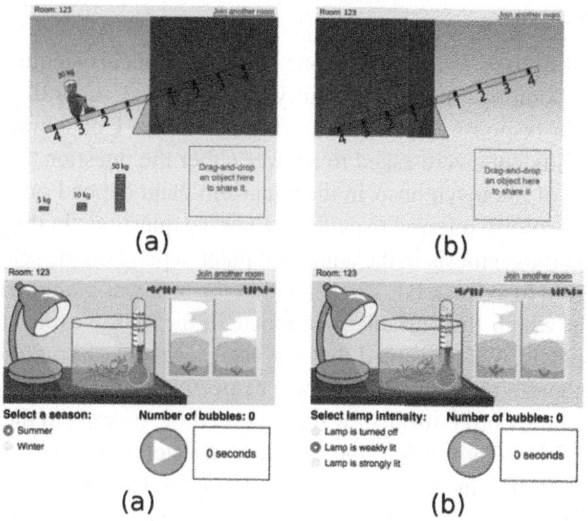

Fig. 1. (Top) The Collaborative Seesaw Lab simulation: (a) Version A allows a student to interact with only the left side of the seesaw, and (b) Version B allows a student to interact with only the right side of the seesaw. (Bottom) The Collaborative Rate of Photosynthesis Lab simulation: (a) Version A allows a student to control only the season of the year (indicated by seeing green foliage and blue sky through the window during summer and seeing snow during winter), whereas (b) Version B allows a student to control only the light intensity of the lamp.

Teacher Co-creation of Learning Materials

The lesson plan of how to instruct and use the asymmetric collaborative simulations with students was co-created with the teacher in whose classes the two experiments were conducted. The teacher gathered appropriate instructional material to introduce photosynthesis to his students and provided feedback on how to best implement the lesson in his classes. He had prior experience using iPads for group work in his classes and saw the benefits of enriching his 5th and 6th grade science classes with technology-enhanced learning materials.

Learning Environment

For the current study, two inquiry learning spaces (ILSs) were created in the Go-Lab authoring environment (https://graasp.eu/). The Go-Lab (Global Online Science Labs for Inquiry Learning at School) environment is an online open educational resource aimed at facilitating the use of online labs and digital resources by science teachers [21]. Inquiry learning spaces in Go-Lab can contain rich multimedia and educational resources that work well for in-class group work using smart devices [22]. The two spaces we created were identical except for the fact that they included different versions of the asymmetric collaborative simulations and had slightly different tasks, as explained below. Links to English translated versions of these ILSs (the actual ILSs used in the study were in Estonian) are available at https://graasp.eu/s/cw6fmu and https://graasp.eu/s/unlxjc and referred to as Version A and Version B respectively.

2.2 Measures

Two measures were used in this study, one to assess students' inquiry and another to assess their collaboration. Students' inquiry was assessed according to their performance on an open-response question requiring use of the Collaborative Rate of Photosynthesis Lab. Students were asked to answer either the question "In this simulation, how does the rate of photosynthesis in the aquarium plant depend on the light intensity of the lamp?" (henceforth referred to as Task A) or the question "In this simulation, how does the rate of photosynthesis in the aquarium plant depend on the season of the year?" (henceforth referred to as Task B). The version of the task was paired with the version of the simulation in which the variable mentioned in the task was *not* available for the student to manipulate. We presumed that this interdependency condition would oblige students to collaborate more in solving their respective tasks, since the variable being asked about could only be controlled by their partner(s). Answers to the task were coded according to the following rubric: 2 points for completely correct, 1 point for partially correct and 0 points for incorrect. The correct answer for Task A is that the rate of photosynthesis increases as light intensity increases. The correct answer for Task B is that the rate of photosynthesis does not depend on the season of the year. This apparently contradictory finding is because the aquatic plant was placed indoors, and the temperature of the water did not change as the season of the year changed. In the simulation, a thermometer paced in the glass of water showed that the water temperature remained constant. In any case, the task expects students to perform experiments, and base their conclusions on data obtained from experimental trials, which for the case of the season of the year variable indicates that the number of bubbles released over a predefined time interval remains constant. Interrater reliability of Tasks A and B showed very good agreement, Cohen's kappa of .76 and .84 respectively. The disagreements were discussed to reach consensus on assigning a final code.

To measure students' collaboration, the self-assessed collaboration skills questionnaire of Hinyard et al. [13] was adapted for use. It presumably measures three dimensions of collaboration: information sharing, team support and team learning. We selected 4 items, out of 11, related to these dimensions which were judged to be most relevant in a short-term intervention like the one in our study. Items related to collaboration over a longer period of time were excluded or rephrased in a way that students could interpret them in the context of the collaboration in this study. The adapted items we used were "I shared information easily with my partner", "I acknowledged my partners' efforts", "I supported my partner" and "I sought out different views than my own during the collaboration". The internal consistency reliability of these items was good (Cronbach's alphas equal to .80 and .83 for 5th and 6th grade students respectively). Since 4-member groups required a pair of students to share an iPad while working in Go-Lab, we decided not to integrate the questionnaire online, but instead printed it on paper. This enabled us to collect responses from all individuals involved in the study.

2.3 Procedure

Both experiments followed the same procedure. The total time of an experiment was 135 min. Figure 2 presents a flowchart of the lesson plan showing how the experiment was conducted. The structure of inquiry phases in the lesson plan was based on the inquiry-based learning framework of Pedaste et al. [23], in which learning is structured according to an inquiry cycle model. For completeness, all the phases and associated activities are mentioned in Fig. 2, but the main focus of this study was on students' inquiry as assessed on the asymmetric collaborative tasks found in phase 6, and students' collaboration as assessed in phase 7.

The first phase of the lesson involved the teacher forming 2-person and 4-person groups and distributing two iPads per group. This was followed by the second phase, in which the teacher introduced students to the Go-Lab learning environment and to an example task involving an asymmetric collaborative simulation. Next, in the third phase, students worked collaboratively to complete the example task. The fourth phase involved the teacher demonstrating to students the correct answers to the example task and highlighting the importance of sharing unique information in order to successfully solve such a task. The fifth phase began a new topic about photosynthesis and included background reading; quiz questions were used to ensure that students read the information found in the text. The sixth phase included Task A or Task B depending on which version of the ILS was used. The seventh phase involved students completing an adapted version of the self-assessed collaboration skills questionnaire. The remaining

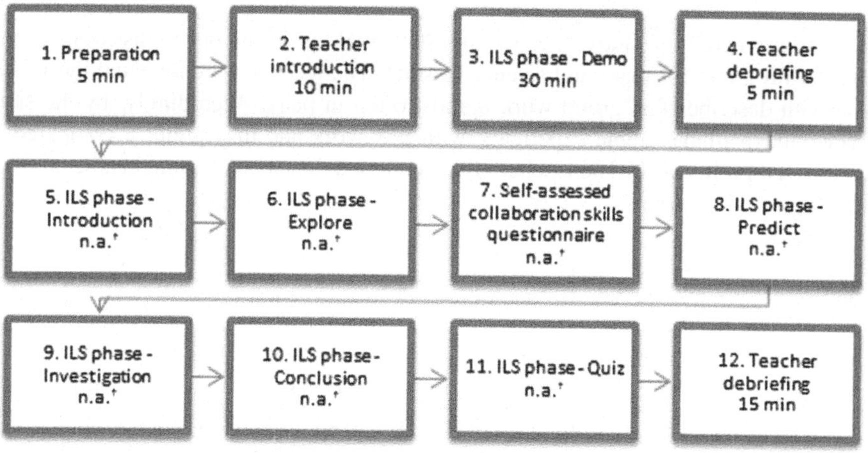

Fig. 2. Lesson plan of this study showing various inquiry phases, the approximate amount of time spent in a phase, learning activities and learning objectives. †The time for phases 5 to 11 was not separately determined since groups worked at their own pace, but altogether lasted about 70 min. See the ILS links https://graasp.eu/s/cw6fmu or https://graasp.eu/s/unlxjc for details regarding the exact content in an ILS phase.

phases involved generating a hypothesis, conducting experiments with another simulation about the effect of temperature on photosynthesis, making conclusions, answering a post-test quiz and a debriefing by the teacher. They were not the focus of this study and therefore not discussed further. The final debriefing by the teacher, phase 12, did include a review and demonstration of the correct responses to Tasks A and B.

3 Results and Discussion

The aim of this research was to study how group size affects students' inquiry and collaboration in using computer-based asymmetric inquiry tasks. Tasks A and B were used to assess students' inquiry and an adapted self-assessed collaboration skills questionnaire used to assess their collaboration.

Table 1 presents the inquiry scores for 5th and 6th grade groups. Although 2-person groups performed better than 4-person groups on the combined score of Tasks A and B, the results did not reach statistical significance. The highest score was obtained from 6th grade students working in pairs (61%) and the lowest score from 5th grade students working in 4-person groups (20%). Analysis of students' collaboration (Table 2), shows that group size did not statistically significantly differ in the dimensions of sharing, support or learning for 5th grade groups, but did for 6th grade groups. Students working in pairs in the 6th grade reported higher collaboration skills in all dimensions of collaboration compared to students working in 4-person groups.

One possible reason why 6th grade students reported better collaboration in 2-person groups is because they are more experienced working in such sized groups. At the school where they study, the students start working in the open classroom beginning in 4th grade for math and science lessons. The teacher we co-created the lesson plan with describes that group work is most often in pairs. Accordingly, by the sixth grade, students have ample experience with pair work and may prefer it compared to larger sized group work. The teacher also mentioned that social loafing can be an issue with larger sized groups.

Table 1. Inquiry scores for 5th and 6th grade groups. Tasks A and B were each scored out of a maximum of 2 points.

Grade	Inquiry task	2-person groups		4-person groups		Mann-Whitney U		
		N	M (SD)	N	M (SD)	U	Z	p
5	Task A	10	0.90 (0.88)	10	0.40 (0.70)	33.5	−1.384	.166
	Task B	10	0.20 (0.63)	10	0.40 (0.84)	45.0	−.610	.542
	Task A + B	10	1.10 (1.29)	10	0.80 (1.32)	40.5	−.776	.438
6	Task A	7	1.14 (0.90)	15	0.67 (0.72)	36.0	−1.244	.213
	Task B	7	1.29 (0.95)	15	0.87 (0.99)	40.5	−.938	.348
	Task A + B	7	2.43 (1.40)	15	1.53 (1.13)	31.0	−1.582	.114

Table 2. Self-assessed collaboration ratings of 5th and 6th grade individuals. Items were rated on a 7-point Likert scale ranging from completely disagree to completely agree.

Grade	Collaborative dimension	Individuals in 2-person groups		Individuals in 4-person groups		Mann-Whitney *U*		
		N	*M* (SD)	*N*	*M* (SD)	*U*	*Z*	*p*
5	Sharing	20	6.0 (1.4)	38	5.9 (1.6)	379.0	−0.18	.986
	Support	20	5.6 (1.6)	38	5.5 (1.6)	361.0	−.316	.752
	Learning	20	4.8 (1.7)	38	5.2 (1.9)	306.5	−1.235	.217
6	Sharing	14	6.9 (0.5)	60	5.4 (1.2)	130.5	−4.891	<.001
	Support	14	6.9 (0.2)	60	5.2 (1.4)	71.0	−4.891	<.001
	Learning	14	6.1 (0.9)	60	5.3 (1.3)	266.0	−2.226	.026

As previously mentioned, inquiry task scores were higher for 2-person groups but did not reach statistical significance. The inquiry scores were generally poor for all groups (see Table 1). To better understand why scores were low, we analyzed the types of errors students made in solving the inquiry tasks. Three types of errors were coded:

1. Syntax. These errors relate to students answering the open-ended questions ambiguously or using poor grammar, e.g. "bubbles coming", "then bubbles come faster", "In winter, the plant makes less nutrients."
2. Collaboration. These errors relate to a student not answering his or her task question but answering as if they had the same question as their partner.
3. Inquiry. These errors relate to students not thoroughly conducting experiments in the simulation, such as changing more than one variable at a time and thereby obtaining incorrect results, e.g., "Slowly in winter (every 10–30 s) but fast in summer (every 6 s)".

The error categories were independently coded by two raters and a good interrater reliability (kappa = .73) was obtained. Table 3 summarizes the results of the error analysis in terms of number of errors made by the different groups. Students working in 4-person groups made more errors and in the 5th grade the types of errors were mostly Syntax. In the 6th grade the errors were also mostly Syntax, but also several errors were made in the Inquiry type. In addition, 2-person groups in the 6th grade made the least amount of errors. Sixth grade students have the most practice working in 2-person groups, and therefore one may hypothesize that this might be the reason why they made fewer mistakes compared to the other groups. Task A students did not make Inquiry type errors. Only Task B students made these errors, indicating that it was easier to answer the question about how light intensity affects the rate of photosynthesis, perhaps relying on prior knowledge rather than conducting experiments, compared to answering the question about the influence of the season of the year variable.

Table 3. Number of errors made by grade 5 and grade 6 students on Tasks A and B.

Task	Error category	5th grade groups				6th grade groups			
		2-person		4-person		2-person		4-person	
		N	No. of errors	N	No. of errors	N	No. of errors	N	No. of errors
A	Syntax	10	3	10	6	7	0	15	5
	Collaboration	10	0	10	1	7	0	15	2
	Inquiry	10	0	10	0	7	0	15	0
B	Syntax	10	2	10	2	7	0	15	2
	Collaboration	10	3	10	2	7	2	15	1
	Inquiry	10	3	10	2	7	0	15	5
	Total		11		13		2		15

Similar to the poor performance on the hidden profile task, working on asymmetric collaborative inquiry tasks proved to be challenging for students. However, unlike the hidden profile task, the asymmetric collaborative inquiry activity in this study strongly suggested to students the need to unshared information in order to successfully solve the tasks (i.e., a demo activity with a practice asymmetric collaborative simulation explicitly highlighted the importance of relying on unshared information and the main task itself asked students to examine a variable that their version of the simulation did not even allow on to manipulate). Nevertheless, task performance was generally low for both 5th and 6th grade students (35% and 25% for 5th grade 2-person and 4-person groups, and 71% and 50% for 6th grade 2-person and 4-person groups respectively). Similarly, Chang et al. [24] studied asymmetric collaboration in the context of physics problem-solving and found that 6 out of 10 groups were unable to formulate plans that would have led them to successfully solve their problem. All in all, the results suggest that more guidance or practice may be necessary for students to perform better on asymmetric collaboration inquiry activities. Particularly interesting would be a longitudinal study to see whether practice with different asymmetric collaborative simulations, over several lessons, has an effect on students' inquiry and collaboration. In addition to the two simulations used in this study, the Go-Lab portal (golabz.eu) currently offers two other asymmetric collaborative simulations: the Collaborative Rabbit Genetics Lab (https://www.golabz.eu/lab/collaborative-rabbit-genetics-lab) and the Collaborative Dollhouse Electricity Lab (https://www.golabz.eu/lab/collaborative-dollhouse-electricity-lab).

4 Conclusion

As interest towards integrating collaboration skills with inquiry learning increases, we believe that asymmetric collaborative simulations offer a promising way to structure a beneficial learning experience. However, more research is needed to study the instructional conditions and support that can best utilize the potential of asymmetric collaboration for enhanced inquiry learning.

We also have to keep in mind that teachers play a crucial role in supporting students' collaborative learning. Van Leeuwen and Janssen [25], in a review of teacher guidance during collaborative learning, highlight that teachers can facilitate productive collaborative learning by giving feedback, prompting and questioning students, and guiding students to be self-directed learners. These general strategies are also promising for supporting collaborative inquiry learning.

In the future, a longitudinal study should be carried out with a larger sample size where students are more supported in asymmetric collaboration and with inquiry-tasks that cover a range of different subjects.

Acknowledgements. This work was partially funded by the European Union in the context of the Next-Lab innovation action (Grant Agreement 731685) under Research and Innovation H2020 Framework Programme. In addition, this study was partly sponsored by the Estonian Research Council (ERC) through the institutional research funding project "Smart technologies and digital literacy in promoting a change of learning" (Grant Agreement No. IUT34-6). This document does not represent the opinion of the European Union or ERC, and these organizations are not responsible for any use that might be made of its content.

References

1. National Research Council: Assessing 21st Century Skills: Summary of a Workshop. The National Academies, Washington, DC (2011)
2. Griffin, P., Care, E.: Assessment and Teaching of 21st Century Skills: Methods and Approach. Springer, Dordrecht (2015)
3. OECD: PISA 2015 Results (Volume V): Collaborative Problem Solving. PISA, OECD Publishing, Paris (2017)
4. Dunbar, K.: How scientists think: on-line creativity and conceptual change in science. In: Ward, T.B., Smith, S.M., Vaid, J. (eds.) Creative Thought: An Investigation of Conceptual Structures and Processes, pp. 461–493. American Psychological Association, Washington (1997)
5. Dillenbourg, P.: What do you mean by "collaborative learning"? In: Dillenbourg, P. (ed.) Collaborative Learning: Cognitive and Computational Approaches, pp. 1–16. Elsevier Science, Amsterdam (1999)
6. Chen, J., Wang, M., Kirschner, P.A., Tsai, C.-C.: The role of collaboration, computer use, learning environments, and supporting strategies in CSCL: a meta-analysis. Rev. Educ. Res. **88**(6), 799–843 (2018)
7. Lohman, M.C., Finkelstein, M.: Designing groups in problem-based learning to promote problem-solving skill and self-directedness. Instr. Sci. **28**(4), 291–307 (2000)
8. Slavin, R.E.: Ability grouping and student achievement in elementary schools: a best-evidence synthesis. Rev. Educ. Res. **57**(3), 293–336 (1987)
9. Wiley, J., Jensen, M.: When three heads are better than two. In Proceedings of the 28th Annual Conference of the Cognitive Science Society, pp. 2375–2380 (2006)
10. Sung, Y.T., Yang, J.M., Lee, H.Y.: The effects of mobile-computer-supported collaborative learning: meta-analysis and critical synthesis. Rev. Educ. Res. **87**(4), 768–805 (2017)
11. Koh, E., Shibani, A., Tan, J.P.-L., Hong, H.: A pedagogical framework for learning analytics in collaborative inquiry tasks: an example from a teamwork competency awareness program. In: Proceedings of the Sixth International Conference on Learning Analytics & Knowledge (LK 74–83). ACM, New York (2016)

12. Ofstedal, K., Dahlberg, K.: Collaboration in student teaching: introducing the collaboration self-assessment. J. Early Child. Teacher Educ. **30**(1), 37–48 (2009)
13. Hinyard, L., Toomey, E., Eliot, K., Breitbach, A.: Student perceptions of collaboration skills in an interprofessional context: development and initial validation of the self-assessed collaboration skills instrument. Eval. Health Prof. (2018). https://doi.org/10.1177/0163278717752438
14. Johnson, D.W., Johnson, R.T.: Making cooperative learning work. Theory Pract. **38**(2), 67–73 (1999)
15. Stasser, G., Titus, W.: Pooling of unshared information in group decision making: biased information sampling during discussion. J. Pers. Soc. Psychol. **48**(6), 1467 (1985)
16. Wittenbaum, G.M., Hollingshead, A.B., Botero, I.C.: From cooperative to motivated information sharing in groups: moving beyond the hidden profile paradigm. Commun. Monogr. **71**(3), 286–310 (2004)
17. Lu, L., Yuan, Y.C., McLeod, P.L.: Twenty-five years of hidden profiles in group decision making: a meta-analysis. Pers. Soc. Psychol. Rev. **16**(1), 54–75 (2012)
18. Cruz, M.G., Boster, F.J., Rodríguez, J.I.: The impact of group size and proportion of shared information on the exchange and integration of information in groups. Commun. Res. **24**(3), 291–313 (1997)
19. Stasser, G., Taylor, L.A., Hanna, C.: Information sampling in structured and unstructured discussions of three-and six-person groups. J. Pers. Soc. Psychol. **57**(1), 67 (1989)
20. Mennecke, B.E.: Using group support systems to discover hidden profiles: an examination of the influence of group size and meeting structures on information sharing and decision quality. Int. J. Hum Comput. Stud. **47**(3), 387–405 (1997)
21. de Jong, T., Sotiriou, S., Gillet, D.: Innovations in STEM education: the Go-Lab federation of online labs. Smart Learn. Environ. **1**(1), 3 (2014)
22. Siiman, Leo A., et al.: Design and evaluation of a smart device science lesson to improve students' inquiry skills. In: Xie, H., Popescu, E., Hancke, G., Fernández Manjón, B. (eds.) ICWL 2017. LNCS, vol. 10473, pp. 23–32. Springer, Cham (2017). https://doi.org/10.1007/978-3-319-66733-1_3
23. Pedaste, M., et al.: Phases of inquiry-based learning: definitions and the inquiry cycle. Educ. Res. Rev. **14**, 47–61 (2015)
24. Chang, C.J., et al.: An analysis of student collaborative problem solving activities mediated by collaborative simulations. Comput. Educ. **114**, 222–235 (2017)
25. van Leeuwen, A., Janssen, J.: A systematic review of teacher guidance during collaborative learning in primary and secondary education. Educ. Res. Rev. **27**, 71–89 (2019)

Towards the Design and Deployment of an Item Bank: An Analysis of the Requirements Elicited

Claudia-Melania Chituc(✉), Marisa Herrmann, Daniel Schiffner, and Marc Rittberger

Leibniz Institut Für Bildungsforschung Und Bildungsinformation, Frankfurt, Germany
{Chituc,Herrmann,Schiffner,Rittberger}@dipf.de

Abstract. Assessments are an important phase in the learning process. Information and communication technologies advancements determined the development of e-learning software tools which support e-learning activities, including e-assessment. The increasing usage of summative and formative e-assessments led to the challenge of managing items. The concept of an item bank is meant to support teachers and students alike, to provide an overview when taking assessments or creating exams. This article presents an on-going R&D project towards the design and deployment of an item bank for computer-based tests, and discusses its role within a service-oriented system architecture which enables the execution of activities related to e-assessment, ranging from item design and test creation, to the analysis of event logs generated by test-takers. The research methodology followed for the requirements elicitation and main findings are presented, and directions for future work are discussed.

Keywords: E-assessment · E-learning · Item bank · Requirement

1 Introduction

The use of computer technologies to enhance learning activities can be traced back to 1959 [1]. Advancements in information and communication technologies and the emergence of standards for educational technologies determined the development of e-learning software tools which support e-learning activities, including e-assessment. As emphasized in [2], e-assessment enhances the measurement of learners' outcome and allows the reception of immediate and direct feedback. Other advantages associated when using e-assessment include [3]: improvements in students' performance, reduction in time and effort for teachers, decrease cost for the institution. Although associated with numerous benefits, the increasing usage of summative and formative e-assessments leads to the challenge of managing items.

The concept of an item bank emerged, which reflects a structured collection of items, e.g., [4]. The notion of computerized item banking surfaced in the development of commercial and other large-scale tests [4]. Several studies exist that emphasize the benefits of item banking, e.g., [5, 6], and lay out basic guidelines towards developing

M. A. Herzog et al. (Eds.): ICWL 2019, LNCS 11841, pp. 155–162, 2019.
https://doi.org/10.1007/978-3-030-35758-0_15

an item bank, e.g., [7]. Although numerous studies focus on item banks, they center primarily on a specific domain, on test development and delivery. Design guidelines from a software engineering perspective are missing, and the integration of a newly developed item bank into an existing architecture is not analyzed. This work addresses this gap. We present in this article an on-going R&D project towards the design and deployment of an item bank for computer-based assessments and discuss its role within a service-oriented system architecture which enables the execution of activities related to e-assessment, ranging from item design and test creation, to the analysis of event logs generated by test-takers.

This work is organized as follows. Background information is introduced next. Section 3 refers to related work. The requirements elicitation approach and main findings towards the design and deployment of an item bank are presented in Sect. 4. The role of the item bank within a service-oriented system architecture which enables the execution of activities related to e-assessment is analyzed in Sect. 5. The paper concludes with a section addressing the need for further research.

2 Background

2.1 E-Assessment

E-assessment is increasingly becoming relevant in higher education. Formative e-assessment supports educators in determining what students have learned and it helps students to retain, reproduce, reconstruct and engage in learning [8]. E-assessment can enhance the learning experience by giving the opportunity to assess one's learning process through the feedback received [9]. Several tools exist to support e-assessment, such as: Moodle Quizzes and Assignments (moodle.org), Turnitin (turnitin.com), Exam-Online (www.intelligentassessment.com), SCHOLAR (scholar.hw.ac.uk), Hot Potatoes (hotpot.uvic.ca), Maple T.A. (www.maplesoft.com), TOIA (www.toia.ac.uk). E-assessment systems support activities such as [9–12]: monitor students' progress, immediate feedback, automatic marking, weighted-average grade calculation, flexible learning and adaptive learning, personalization of quizzes, monitor questions' quality using statistical analysis, randomize questions along with timers. Most of the existing e-assessment tools and systems very often provide only pre-determined, relatively simple types of questions [13, 14], which are sufficient to assess the students' knowledge level [15]. However, as noted in [16, 17]: different and more (complex) questions are required to assess skill levels. In order to address complex test questions, the concept of item emerged, which is briefly introduced next.

2.2 Item and Item Bank

An item represents a task that a test taker is asked to perform. It needs to include a stimulus, which can be a simple question, or a question followed by several alternative answers, and it may be part of a larger structure that consists of multiple stimuli [4]. The IMS QTI specifications (www.ims.org) refer to an item as the tiniest assessment object [18]. Accordingly, an item contains the question and the instructions to be presented, the response processing to be applied to the test taker response(s), and the feedback that might be presented. The IMS provides specifications for a class of objects for expressing items and assessments. The wide use of e-assessment led to a dramatic increase in item types. An item bank is useful when dealing with a large number of complex items. Two main functions are associated with an item bank in [4]: to author, and to organize items in the bank. The complexity of the items required nowadays to assess knowledge and skills requires a revision of the main functions of an item bank. This work addresses this topic; it discusses the main findings of the requirements elicitation process towards the design and deployment of an item bank.

3 Related Work

Different works exist that relate to the item bank concept. An item bank for computerized adaptive test measurement of pain is introduced in [19]. In [20], an item bank for computerized linear and adaptive testing in geography is illustrated. These studies focus on the design of the items and do not refer to the actual design and implementation of an item bank.

A learning architecture towards an interoperable learning ecosystem is advanced in [21]. A learning assistant tool, PKIP, for managing question items in item banks is presented in [22]. The evaluations results illustrate the accuracy and user satisfaction for the proposed solution. Although highly relevant, information on the approach or methodology followed towards the design of the tool or item bank is not referred.

Learning management systems may provide a basic organization tool for questions. Moodle Question Bank plugin (docs.moodle.org/37/en/Question_bank), for example, contains several options on how to organize elements, and it enables easy integration into courses for learning. TAO (www.taotesting.com) provides a QTI-authoring and test delivery open source solution. However, TAO requires the items to be part of the whole software process. The H5P initiative (h5p.org) is an open-source content collaboration framework that allows the creation, sharing and reuse of content in existing publishing platforms, including virtual learning environments, and tracking of user interactions using the xAPI specifications (xapi.com). Yet, the authoring of items is limited to the supported question types. These methods lack the ability to include external tools to allow for versioning or quality control when creating items. This work addresses this gap.

4 Requirements Elicitation

4.1 Approach

Considering the diversity of items and tests aimed to be represented in the item bank, the specificities of the diverse e-assessment projects (e.g., targeting the e-assessment of knowledge and skills in educational institutions and professional organizations) and the vision to integrate the item bank within an existing software architecture, a use case scenario approach was chosen for the requirements elicitation, to reflect all the tasks the stakeholders need to perform with the item bank. This was complemented with face-to-face interviews, where the stakeholders explained in more detail the functionalities they want the system to have and referred to specific projects.

The use case scenarios approach has been successfully used during the last years for requirements elicitation and modeling, e.g., [23, 24]. As noted in [25]: the goal of the use cases approach in requirements elicitation is to describe all the tasks the stakeholders will need to perform with the software system. A use case may consist of multiple scenarios that capture stakeholders' requirements by determining a sequence of interactions between the system and the stakeholders.

Although the use case approach is successfully used to elicit requirements, potential weaknesses are indicated in the literature (see: [26]), e.g., the use cases are written from the system's (and not stakeholders') point of view, the stakeholder names are inconsistent, the use case specifications are confusing, the use case does not correctly describe functional entitlement. To avoid such pitfalls, a well-documented template was designed following guidelines from relevant works (e.g., [27, 28]) and handed to all the stakeholders. In addition, face-to-face talks were held with the stakeholders. The information collected was clustered considering the main functionalities indicated, as illustrated in the next section.

4.2 Main Findings

The approach described allowed us to collect 64 scenarios from ten stakeholders, and identify the functional and non-functional requirements for an item bank, and the stakeholders' constraints for the technical solution. Figure 1 illustrates the UML use case representation of the item bank functionalities. The main stakeholders identified include: *item designer*, a person who designs the layouts of items and provides a concept to the item author; *item author*, a person who creates and edits items with the templates and requirements from didactic experts, and the guidelines from the item designer; *item bank administrator*, a person who is responsible for the management of user rights, e.g., adds and deletes users of the item bank; *item translator*, a person who translates the content of an item into another language, reviews and validates both the translated items and tests; *project manager*, a person who coordinates a project and needs to overlook all the activities concerning the items and test(s) that are relevant for the respective project and access relevant information (e.g., item metadata); *psychometrician*, a person who defines a test design and interprets the results to assess a person's skills or other psychological attributes.

A detailed description of the use cases illustrated in Fig. 1 is in [29]. The *Create Item* use case, for example, reflects that the item bank shall allow the creation of items (from scratch or from a template); the *Edit Item* use case concerns editing the content of an item (e.g., translate an item) and editing a set of items; the *Manage Quality Control* use case concerns quality assurance (e.g., revise and test items). Examples of non-functional requirements identified are: *availability* - the item bank shall be available during normal working hours; *reliability*; *security* - the data needs to be stored securely and adequate access rights need to be carefully assigned; *usability*, e.g., the item bank needs to be easy to use and support a user to fulfill tasks; *scalability* - the item bank shall support the increasing number of users, requests, data stored. The requirements elicited allowed us to sketch a system architecture, presented next.

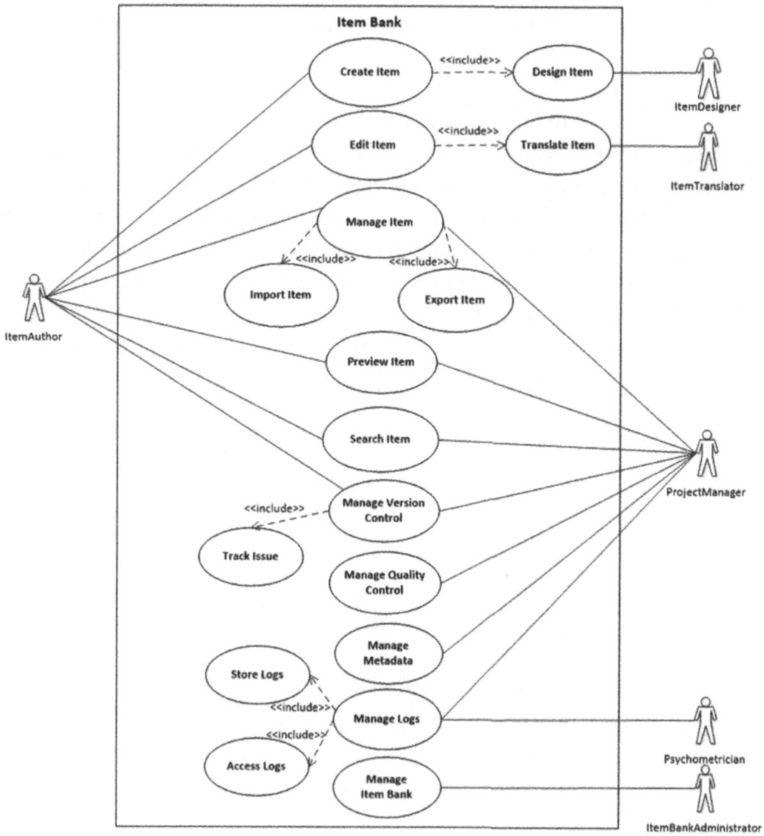

Fig. 1. Main actors for the item bank (UML)

5 Towards a Service-Oriented Item Bank Architecture

Figure 2 illustrates a simplified view of the service-oriented system architecture for the item bank, designed based on the requirements elicited. The *Create/Edit Item and Test* component receives as input the item design executed by the item designer, and allows the creation of an item from scratch or from a template, the editing of an item (e.g., translate the content of an item, change layout) and the creation of a test, by making use of item authoring tools such as: Moodle, H5P, TAO, ItemBuilder (itembuilderwiki.tba-hosting.de). The items are stored in the *Item Database*, the associated metadata is stored in the *Metadata Database*, and the logs (e.g., interaction patterns when using an item) in the *Logs Database*. The *Preview Engine* allows the visualization of items and tests. The *Search Engine* supports the execution of search commands. The *Quality*

Control Engine supports the execution of activities relevant to guarantee the quality control of items. The *Versioning Engine* provides the functionality of a version control of items (e.g., track changes, branching, retrieve previous versions of an item).

The item bank gives the necessary information for a *Sequencing Engine* by providing unique identifiers along with needed metadata, such as a version or titles. The *Sequencing Engine* connects to the other engines, e.g., *Preview Engine*, to provide a visual feedback while arranging and configuring an assessment. If a configuration is finalized, all the data (including parameters for a delivery and the used items) is stored to enable tracking of the created sequences. Note that this storage is separated from the core item bank. The unique identifier provided by the *Sequencing Engine* can be used to reconstruct an assessment. Furthermore, it enables access to data by a public API, which is used, for example, in combination with the *Logs Database*, *Metadata Database* and *Versioning Engine* to reconstruct a complete assessment at a given point in time. It serves as an abstraction layer for the following steps, such as the test taking or the log data generation. APIs are used for the communication be-tween the architecture components, which also allow binding mechanisms to be plugged in.

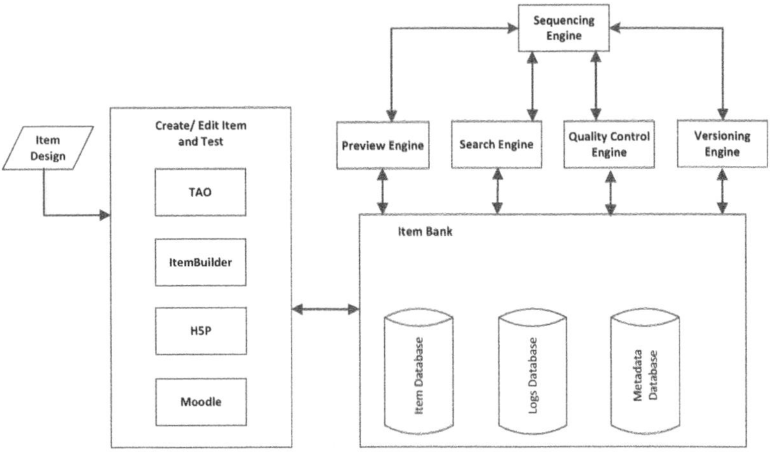

Fig. 2. System architecture

6 Conclusions and Future Work

Computer-based assessment is increasingly used nowadays in educational institutions and professional organizations to assess the knowledge and skills of students and professionals. The notion of item bank emerged, which supports educators, researchers and test takers in the assessment activities. Although numerous learning management systems exist, the authoring process of quizzes and items is rather limited, and they lack the ability to embed external tools to allow versioning or quality control functionalities. This work addresses this gap. We reported in this article on an on- going R&D project towards the design and deployment of an item bank for computer-based assessment and discuss its role within a service-oriented system architecture which enables the execution of activities related to e-assessment, ranging from item design and test creation, to the analysis of event logs by psychometricians, and the configuration of the assessment sequence. We describe the requirements elicitation approach and report the main findings (in Sect. 4). An initial architecture is designed based on the main findings of the requirements elicited (Fig. 2).

Future work will focus on the implementation of a software prototype following the architecture and specifications elaborated. We also want to address interoperability and integration issues (e.g., to allow the use and exchange of items from different vendors and with different versions), as well as adaptive testing challenges. Future work shall also focus on scalability challenges related to an increasing number of users and data stored. We will investigate the use of a private or hybrid cloud storage service. Cloud-based storage services would address elasticity concerns. The use of a private cloud overcomes end-to-end confidentiality and privacy concerns. However, a thorough technical and financial feasibility study needs to be performed to support the decision to use a private or hybrid cloud-based storage service.

References

1. Molnar, A.: Computers in education: a brief history. Technol. Horiz. Educ. **24**, 63–69 (1997)
2. Gilbert, L., Whitelock, W., Gale, V.: Synthesis report on assessment and feedback with technology enhancement (2011). https://eprints.soton.ac.uk/273221/
3. Alruwais, A.N., Wills, G., Wald, M.: Advantages and challenges of using e-assessment. Int. J. Inf. Educ. Technol. **8**(1), 34–37 (2018)
4. Vale, D.C.: Computerized Item Banking (Chap. 11). In: Downing, S.M., Haladyna, T.M. (eds.) Handbook of Test Development, pp. 261–285. Lawrence Erlbaum Associates, Publishers London, Mahwah (2006)
5. Umar, J.: Item banking. In: Masters, G.N., Keeves, J.P. (eds.) Advances in Measurement in Educational Research and Assessment. Pergamon, New York (1999)
6. Chapelle, C.A., Voss, E.: 20 years of technology and language assessment in language learning & technology. Lang. Learn. Technol. **20**(2), 116–128 (2016)
7. Ward, A.W., Murray-Ward, M.: Guidelines for the development of item banks. Educ. Meas.: Issues Pract. **13**(1), 34–39 (1994)
8. Biggs, J.: Aligning teaching and assessment to curriculum objectives, Imaginative Curriculum project, LTSN Generic Center (2003)
9. Hettiarachchi, E., Huertas, M.A., Mor, E.: E-assessment system for skill and knowledge assessment in computer engineering education. Int. J. Eng. Educ. **31**(2), 529–540 (2015)
10. Bull, J., Mckenna, C.: Blueprint for Computer-Assisted Assessment. Routledge, London (2003)
11. Tselonis, C., Sargeant, J.: Domain-specific formative feedback through domain-independent diagram matching. In: Khabdia F. (ed.) 11th International Computer Assisted Assessment Conference (CAA), 10–11 July 2007, pp. 403–420. Loughborough University, UK (2007)
12. Sitthiworachart, J., Joy, M., Sutinen, E.: Success factors for e-assessment in computer science education. In: Bonk C., et al. (eds.) Proceedings of E-Learn 2008 – World Conference on E-Learning in Corporate, Government, Healthcare, and Higher Education, Las Vegas, USA, pp. 2287–2293 (2008)

13. Marriott, P.: Students' evaluation of the use of online summative assessment on an undergraduate financial accounting module. Br. J. Educ. Technol. **40**(2), 237–254 (2009)
14. Daly, C., Pachler, N., Mor, Y., Meller, H.: Exploring formative e-assessment: using case stories and design patterns. Assess. Eval. High. Educ. **35**(5), 619–636 (2010)
15. Beevers, C., et al.: What can e-assessment do for learning and teaching? Part 1 of a draft of current and emerging practice review by the e-Assessment Association expert panel. Int. J. E-Assess. **1**(2) (2011)
16. Wellington, P., Thomas, I., Powell, I., Clarke, B.: Authentic assessment applied to engineering and business undergraduate consulting teams. Int. J. Eng. Educ. **18**(2), 168–179 (2002)
17. Millard, D., et al.: Mapping the e-learning assessment domain: concept maps for orientation and navigation, In: Richards, G. (ed.) Proceedings of e-Learn 2005 – World Conference on E-Learning in Corporate, Government, Healthcare, and Higher Education, pp. 2770–2775. AACE, Vancouver (2005)
18. IMS: IMS Question & Test Interoperability Assessment Test, Section and Item Information Model, v2.1, 31 August 2012 (2012)
19. Petersen, M.A., et al.: Development of an item bank for computerized adaptive test (CAT) measurement of pain. Qual. Life Res. **25**(1), 1–11 (2016)
20. Burrghof, K.L.: Assembling an item-bank for computerized linear and adaptive testing in geography. Int. Educ. J. **2**(4), 74–83 (2001)
21. Smith, B., Shane Gallagher, P., Schatz, S., Vogel-Walcutt, J.: Total learning architecture: moving into the future, I/ITSEC, paper no. 18224 (2018)
22. Nuntiyagul, A., Naruedomkul, K., Cercone, N., Wongsawang, D.: Adaptable learning assistant for item bank management. Comput. Educ. **50**(1), 357–370 (2008)
23. Jackson, M.: Software Requirements & Specifications: A Lexicon of Practice, Principles and Prejudices. Addison-Wesley Publishing Co., ACM Press, Boston, New York (1995)
24. Fricker, S.A., Grau, R., Zwingli, A.: Requirements engineering: best practice. In: Fricker, S., Thummler, C., Gavras, A. (eds.) Requirements Engineering for Digital Health, pp. 22–46. Springer, Cham (2015). https://doi.org/10.1007/978-3-319-09798-5_2
25. Wiegers, K.E.: Software Requirements, 2nd edn. Microsoft Press, Redmond (2003)
26. Lilly, S., Use case pitfalls: top 10 problems from real projects using use cases. In: Proceedings of Technology of Object-Oriented Languages and Systems - TOOLS 30, pp. 174–183, IEEE, Santa Barbara (1999)
27. Kotonya, G., Sommerville, I.: Requirements Engineering: Processes and Techniques, 1st edn. Wiley, Hoboken (1998)
28. Pohl, K.: Requirements Engineering: Fundamentals, Principles, and Techniques, 1st edn. Springer, Heidelberg (2010)
29. Chituc, C.-M., Herrmann, M.: Item bank: requirements elicitation and specification, DIPF Technical Report, DIPF (2019)

Assessment and Pedagogical Issues

Self-regulation Strategies of Students Enrolled in a Distance and Online University Education Program

Louise Sauvé(✉), Nicole Racette, Cathia Papi, Serge Gérin-Lajoie, Guillaume Desjardins, and Sophie Marineau

TÉLUQ University, Quebec, QC G1K9H6, Canada
louisesauve25@gmail.com, {nicole.racette, cpapi, serge.gerin-lajoie, Guillaume.Desjardins, sophie.marineau}@teluq.ca

Abstract. Mastering self-regulation strategies would seem to be essential in distance and online university studies since the workload is much greater and students need to be more independent and responsible for their own learning. By self-regulation strategies, we mean the student's mental activities aimed at creating favorable conditions for learning, including managing their concentration, motivation, time and tasks. With the aim of identifying self-regulation strategies used or not by students enrolled in distance and online learning, an initial study of 1,060 students was conducted. Various analyses were carried out. The results indicate that at least 29% of students have difficulty setting and adhering to a study schedule and trouble getting down to work. They also have difficulty focusing on their course and maintaining attention and concentration. They generally feel tense or under pressure during their studies and afraid or worried when performing learning activities in a course. When they need help, they find it difficult to turn to other students and communicate with them in order to support their learning process. In addition, three respondent profiles were identified. They stand out in relation to strategies for task management, concentration and asking for help: (1) living alone, single and under 25 years old, (2) living with a common-law partner and 25 to 34 years old and (3) living with a spouse and children, 35 to 44 years old.

Keywords: Self-regulation strategies · University studies · Online courses

1 Introduction

Drop-out rates range from 26.9% to 43.2% among students enrolled in a distance education university program, all years combined [1]. Several studies point to the lack of learning strategies, especially self-regulation strategies for students in the context of Distance and Online Learning (DOL). That is to say, an education (synchronous and asynchronous) where the teaching and learning activities are overall carried out using Web technologies [2].

The aim of our study is identifying the learning strategies that have the greatest impact on dropping out of an online course and a distance and online program. Several

M. A. Herzog et al. (Eds.): ICWL 2019, LNCS 11841, pp. 165–176, 2019.
https://doi.org/10.1007/978-3-030-35758-0_16

specific objectives derive from this goal, notably identifying self-regulation strategies with regard to certain sociodemographic and academic variables, which is the subject of Phase 1 of our study and of this report.

We will first present the studies that examined the sociodemographic and academic variables of students in a context of abandoning post-secondary education[1]. We will then discuss studies that identify the self-regulation strategies that have the greatest impact on dropping out of university studies. These strategies were the subject of a questionnaire that grouped them in seven categories. 1,060 students responded to the questionnaire. We will report the results obtained using three types of statistical analysis: descriptive, of variance and two-step cluster method. Finally, we will discuss the results and make some recommendations for future research.

2 Sociodemographic and Academic Variables

The profile of the student at risk of abandoning university studies is that of an older student with a spouse or children who no longer lives with his or her parents [3]. The authors find that the gender variable does not seem to have a significant impact on the drop-out rate.

Several studies note that as students grow older, participation in postsecondary studies and drop-out rates tend to increase [4]. The OECD [5] agrees with this in regard to participation in post-secondary studies, stating that, on average, 38% of people aged 25 to 34 in its member countries have higher education diplomas compared to 23% of people aged 55 to 64. The university drop-out rate is lower among students with a parent who has a post-secondary diploma (12%) than those whose parents have no post-secondary education (20%) [6].

In Quebec, 33% of students abandon their university studies when they are in a bachelor's program [7] and nearly half of these drop-outs occur during the first year of enrolment in a bachelor's program [8]. Finally, the reported studies do not link the drop-out rate to the type of university program in which the student enrolls: short program, certificate and bachelor's degree.

In our study, we took these variables into account for the variance and cluster (two-step method) analyses.

3 Self-regulation Strategies

As part of the phenomenological current of educational research that aims to understand the learning strategies of university students from their varying subjective perspectives, self-regulation strategies (or strategies for managing cognitive activity) are defined as self-regulating mental operations based on metacognitive knowledge, consisting mainly of planning, mobilizing and managing the external and internal resources required for the intended learning [9]. For external resources, we find management strategies for the

[1] In Quebec, post-secondary studies include college and university studies.

workspace and tasks as well as time. For internal resources, we find emotional strategies that affect the maintenance of motivation, concentration, confidence in ability to succeed in school, management of stress and asking for help.

Studies [10–13] have found that students do not seem to have clear ideas about the learning strategies they use. Since learning strategies can be innate as well as learned [14], learning and gaining knowledge about these strategies can lead students to better understand their behaviour toward studying. They will then be able to better adapt to different teaching situations, especially those offered in DOL.

The most important of the deficient self-regulation strategies that were identified among university students are: management strategies for external resources such as time and tasks [6, 9, 10] and the ability to manage emotions [4, 9, 15, 16]. The same difficulties are also noted among Quebec university students who have studied at distance [17–20].

Students who use learning strategies the least in their online learning are those who are most at risk of abandoning their studies after the first year [21]. Students who practice using learning strategies generally demonstrate better coping skills when the distance and online learning process is underway. If a strategy being used is not effective enough, students will have a more natural reflex to adapt and change their strategy [22] and thus persevere in their studies. Finally, these strategies are all the more essential in DOL because the workload is much greater, students are much more independent and they are therefore responsible for their learning [23].

In terms of external self-regulation strategies, research shows that students who abandon have difficulty planning and managing their tasks: they do not know how to avoid falling behind in handing in their work. Good planning has many benefits for supporting perseverance in studies: it facilitates starting and regulating actions, improves performance, reduces stress, and thus enhances a student's psychological well-being [6, 10, 24].

Other research finds that students who drop-out tend to attribute insufficient time to their studies [10, 25]. Students cannot manage their time effectively or estimate the time they need to spend on their studies. They wait until the last minute to study or to do their work. They lack discipline in setting study times during the week and feel incapable of estimating the time required to complete their work. The time management difficulties campus students experience are the same in DOL [19]. Finally, the time management strategies (designing an effective work plan, planning study times and staying organized throughout their studies) and motivation (continuing to learn even when the subject matter is of little interest) have an impact on students' ability to persevere or drop-out when they encounter difficulties during their studies [26].

In terms of internal self-regulation strategies, students do not control their stress well during exams, they would like to learn strategies to reduce their stress-related symptoms, and they also say they are overworked and regularly worried [27]. Students also tend to become discouraged when they experience difficulties in their courses, are unaware of their attitudes toward schooling and what motivates them to learn. Students must be able to control their emotions, diligence, rigor and motivation, especially in the DOL context which often puts them to the test [14, 21, 28, 29].

Moreover, students who drop-out do not have much confidence in their ability to succeed academically [30]. When they are in doubt, they do not know how to verify if the work they have done is appropriate. They wonder if limiting themselves to doing only the mandatory exercises is enough to succeed in their course. They question their ability to use effective study strategies and their ability to progress steadily in their studies. Students who drop-out also have trouble concentrating when they want to study. They think they have learning difficulties (slowness, lack of concentration) and they wait for inspiration before starting to work or study for an important exam [27].

Finally, the asking for help plays a central role in academic success and perseverance [31]. It is clear that during the process of asking for help, the student must go through several stages and use various skills [32]. However, to accomplish this, the student asking for help will have to self-regulate in order to take action. Other authors [33] find that a majority of students (campus, distance) do not use the necessary strategies for taking action and asking for help from students or using university resources even if they acknowledge that they have problems with their studies.

Taking into account the context of our research, distance and online university studies, we have retained the self-regulation strategies that seem to have the most influence on persevering or dropping out of studies.

4 Methodology

4.1 The Population

In establishing our sample, three elements were taken into account for the choice of courses. First, we made sure that the selected courses came from at least three different departments (language department, social sciences and administrative sciences). Second, we took into consideration the number of students per course. This number averages 312 annual registrations (based on 2017 data), but some courses have more than 900 registrations per year. Third, we took into account the variability of the courses in terms of the rates of failure, drop-outs and success. The 17 selected courses have failure variations ranging from 5.95% to 23.64% and drop-outs between 8.86% and 17.34%.

4.2 Data Collection Instruments

Students completed an online questionnaire during three sessions (Summer and Fall 2018, Winter 2019). The first part comprises 21 statements to identify socio-demographic and academic variables as well as financial variables. In the second part, 37 statements deal with self-regulation strategies grouped into 7 categories: task management (6 statements), time management (4 statements), concentration (3 statements), confidence in ability to succeed (7 statements), motivation (8 statements), stress (5 statements) and asking for help (4 statements).

4.3 Analytical Methods

The first step consists of a reliability analysis of the statements according to their respective category. To this end, an analysis of the Cronbach alpha (α) coefficient was performed. The results are in the acceptable range, varying between 0.584 and 0.72 depending on the category. This finding indicates that the results of the statements are sufficiently correlated without being redundant [34]. Subsequently, variances between the categories mentioned were analyzed with respect to the various socio-demographic factors observed among students: age group, civil status, number of semesters of study in DOL, type of program, parents' schooling. Following the ANOVA, a post-hoc test (Tukey) was carried out on the meaningful results.

5 Results

5.1 Sociodemographic and Academic Data

Of the 3,864 e-mail solicitations, 1,060 students (27%) responded to the questionnaire. 75.8% are women and 24.2% are men. As well, 44.7% of respondents are 25–34 years old, 29.3% are 35–44, 14.9% are over 45 and 11.1% are under 25. In addition, 67.1% of respondents live with a spouse and children and 32.9% live alone with or without children. In addition, 63.6% live with a partner (married or common-law), 32.9% are single and 3.4% are divorced.

On the academic level, 67.6% of respondents are enrolled in the first three semesters of university studies, 16.9% in the 4th to the 6th semester, 10.8% in the 7th to 9th semester and 4.7% in 10 semesters or more. Finally, 54.6% are enrolled in a certificate program (30 credits) and 32.8% in a bachelor's degree, 6.6% in a short program (between 9 and 15 credits) and 6.0% are independent students.

5.2 Self-regulation Strategies

As a first step, a descriptive analysis of the self-regulation strategies was carried out. The results indicate that no respondent used all of the self-regulation strategies during their studies. In order to identify the self-regulation strategies that are likely to have an influence on perseverance in DOL studies, we relied on the percentage of students who completed the courses that were selected for the study, i.e. 82.66%. Only 14 of the 37 strategies were used by students (Table 1). These are mostly strategies that affect the maintenance of confidence in the ability to succeed (5/7 statements) and motivation (7/8 statements) as well as task management (2/6 statements). More specifically, students are motivated because their choice of courses corresponds to their interests or professional requirements (96%) and they want to obtain a university diploma (95.1%). They feel able to successfully complete their exams and work (95.1%) and they put in place an enabling environment that facilitates their management of educational tasks (90%).

Table 1. Self-regulation strategies used by respondents (n = 1,060).

Categories	Self-regulation strategies	Used %	Not used %
Task management (2/6 statements)	I create an atmosphere that can facilitate my educational tasks (music, going to the library, setting up a workplace, etc.)	90.0	10.0
	When I'm dealing with a difficult task, I divide it into several small tasks	85.7	14.3
Confidence in ability to succeed (6/7 statements)	I feel able to pass my exams and do well in my assignments	95.1	4.9
	I take initiatives in my studies to make sure I succeed	94.3	5.7
	I feel able to make steady progress	91.7	8.3
	I have confidence in my ability to use effective learning strategies	91.1	8.9
	I call into question my work methods when my results are not up to my expectations	88.1	11.9
Motivation (7/8 statements)	My choice of courses corresponds to my interests or professional requirements	96.0	4
	I really feel like I'm wasting my time in university courses	6.8	93.2
	Having a university degree is very important to me	95.1	4.9
	I am usually satisfied with what I achieve in my courses	92.7	7.3
	I see the link between my courses and the professional practice being exercised or sought	92.0	8.0
	I am pleased with taking my course online	88.2	11.8

In order to identify the self-regulatory strategies that are likely to influence dropping out in DOL, we relied on the lowest percentage rate of university studies in DOL drop-outs in Canada, that of 26.9%. Table 2 indicates that 11 of the 37 strategies are not used by 29% or more of the respondents. It is mainly strategies for managing tasks (1/5 statements), time (3/3 statements), concentration (2/3 statements), confidence in Ability to Succeed (1/7 statements), stress (2/5 statements) and asking for help (2/4 statements) that are the least used by respondents. More specifically, students have trouble concentrating in their course. When they need help, they don't turn to other students and they don't communicate with their when they need support for learning. They don't know what to do when they feel tense or under pressure when they study. Finally, they don't can control their fear or worry when they do learning activities.

As a second step, an analysis of the variances between the categories was made with respect to the students' various socio-demographic factors. Table 3 shows the statistically significant results between the categories under study and the sociodemographic variables. The categories of Time Management, Task Management, Stress and Confidence in ability to succeed have no statistically significant difference.

Table 2. Self-regulation strategies not used by respondents (n = 1,060).

Categories	Self-regulation strategies	Used %	Not used %
Task management (1/6 statements)	I plan work periods based on when I'm most productive	69.7	30.3
Time management (3/4 statements)	I estimate how much time my work will take in order to avoid being late	68.6	31.4
	I can fix a study schedule and adhere to it	70.7	29.3
Concentration (2/3 statements)	I can maintain my attention and concentration adequately	68.7	29.3
	I can concentrate easily in this course	68.2	31.8
Confidence in ability to succeed (1/7 statements)	I can get down to work without any difficulty to speak of	68.2	31.8
Stress (2/5 statements)	I can normally manage stress and pressure when studying	52.6	47.4
	Normally, I can control my fear or worry when I do learning activities	61.0	39.0
Asking for help (2/4 statements)	When I need help, I turn to other students	37.2	62.8
	I communicate with other students when I need support for learning	33.0	67.0

Table 3. Convincing results from the factorial ANOVA.

Category	Variables[a]	F	*p*
Concentration	Age grouping	1.864	0.041
	Civil status	1.816	0.048
Motivation	Age grouping	1.681	0.026
Asking for help	Age grouping	2.394	0.002
	Type of program	2.122	0.006
	Civil status	1.976	0.012
	Family situation	1.8	0.027

N = 965 [a]The analyses are univariate. $p = 0.05$

While an ANOVA analysis (Table 3) can demonstrate if a variable has a statistical significance difference, it does not indicate which groups have theses relations, even less the direction of the relation. In order to do so, a post-hoc test must be realized. We use Tukey test to appreciate these differences between groups (p = 0.05). With regard to age variables, the 25-and-under group use on average fewer concentration (Tukey = 0.008) and motivation (Tukey = 0.007) strategies than those aged 45 and over. More specifically, those aged 25 and under use motivation strategies on average less than all other age groups. However, the age group of 25 and under indicates that they feel able to ask for help more easily than those over 45 (Tukey = 0.011). In terms of civil status, single students on average use fewer concentration strategies than students living with their common-law partner (Tukey = 0.048) and married students (Tukey = 0.005). On the other hand, single students on average use their help seeking strategies more than students living with common-law partners (Tukey = 0.001) and married students (Tukey = 0.021). These results are also consistent with the student's family situation: students living with both parents, on average, use more strategies asking for help compared to students living with their common-law partner (Tukey = 0.001) and students living with one or more children (Tukey = 0.001).

Thirdly, a cluster analysis (two-step cluster method) [35, 36] was carried out on socio-demographic data in order to highlight types of student profiles. Three profiles are put forward. Table 4 shows the sociodemographic variables characterizing these groups.

Table 4. Cluster analysis results.

Cluster	N (%)	Family situation	Civil status	Age grouping
1	315 (32.6%)	Lives alone	Single	Less than 25 years old
2	263 (27.3%)	Lives with spouse	Common-law partner	25–34 years old
3	387 (40.1%)	Lives with spouse and child(ren)	Common-law partner/married	35–44 years old

Subsequently, these three groups were used in factorial analyses to obtain a more general portrait of the student in relation to their use of self-regulation strategies. This analysis reveals three categories of strategies that vary significantly by group. For task management, group 2 on average uses these strategies more than group 3 ($F = 6.581$, $p = 0.001$). For the category concentration, group 3 on average uses these strategies less than group 1 ($F = 4.327$, $p = 0.014$). Finally, for the category asking for help, group 1 on average uses these strategies more than groups 2 and 3 ($F = 8.029$, $p = 0.001$).

6 Discussion

More than 60% of distance and online learning respondents do not seek help from other students when they need it or communicate with them to support their learning. These results are consistent with the authors' conclusions [32] who find that a large majority of university students have difficulty asking for help. Students who have difficulty making interesting contacts with other students are likely to abandon their studies [3]. This is also noted by others authors [37, 38].

More than 50% of students typically feel tense or under pressure during their distance and online studies, and they experience fear or worry when carrying out learning activities. This state of stress (anxiety) has been noted by several authors [e.g. 14, 21] who associate this stress with the very context of DOL which is considered more demanding for students. According to these authors, there should be intervention to enable students to increase their stress control and thus reduce the risk of dropping out of their studies.

30% or more of our respondents do not plan work periods based on the times when they are most productive, they do not evaluate the time needed to devote to their work and they do not set a work schedule which they follow. Some have difficulty concentrating and maintaining their attention. These management strategies for time, tasks and concentration were also identified by some authors [19, 26, 27] as drop-out indicators if no action is taken to help these students improve these strategies.

The academic variable, the number of sessions or academic year, does not seem to have a significant influence on the use or non-use of self-regulation strategies by DOL students. This observation allows us, like these authors [21], to hypothesize that if the strategies for the management of tasks, time, concentration, motivation, confidence in ability to succeed, stress and asking for help are not used by the respondents in their learning in DOL, they may abandon their studies, regardless of the progress they have made, and not only in first year studies.

The combination of variables (age, civil status and family situation) revealed three profiles of students who use fewer self-regulation strategies (time management, asking for help and concentration) in DOL. These profiles will enable us to implement targeted or personalized interventions so students can develop these strategies, which, when deficient, can influence dropping out [39]. Using a cluster model to identify three typical student profiles makes for a more encompassing and realistic analysis than a factorial analysis of variance. This is the case, for example, with strategies for task management which become statistically significant when analysis of age, civil status and family situation are combined. It is therefore possible to argue that certain self-regulation strategies should not be studied according to a single criterion, but rather by combining various socio-demographic aspects of a university student's typical situation.

7 Conclusion

A study of students enrolled in DOL was conducted, by means of an online questionnaire, to identify the self-regulation strategies they use the most and the least. Descriptive, univariate and multivariate analyses were performed. Various findings have been identified which will be used in the second phase of our study, namely to determine whether these strategies influence dropping out of a distance and online course.

It should be noted that the results of this study are limited in two respects. First, only 27% of people from our population responded to the survey. Second, our sample is made up of more women than men. A population analysis is underway to verify if the characteristics of our respondents reflect those of the population.

Acknowledgements. This research studies was funded by grants from Quebec Research Fund - Society and Culture and Ministry of Education and Higher Education. We would like to thank Curt Ian Wright for the translation, and Janet Coulombe for editing.

References

1. Powell, R.: Openness and Dropout: A Study of Four Open Distance Education Universities. Athabasca University, Athabasca, Canada (2006)
2. Conseil supérieur de l'éducation [CSE]: La formation à distance dans les universités québécoises: un potentiel à optimiser [Distance Education in Quebec Universities: A Potential to Optimize]. Avis au ministre de l'Éducation, de l'Enseignement Supérieur et de la Recherche [Advice to the Minister of Education, Higher Education and Research]. Conseil supérieur de l'éducation, Québec, QC, Canada (2015)
3. Fortin, A., Sauvé, L., Viger, C., Landry, F.: Nontraditional student withdrawal from undergraduate accounting programs: a holistic perpective. Acc. Edu.: Int. J. 1–42 (2016). http://dx.doi.org/10.1080/09639284.2016.1193034
4. Berger, J., Motte, A., Parkin, A.: Le prix du savoir. L'accès à l'éducation et la situation financière des étudiants au Canada. [The price of knowledge: Access and Student Finance in Canada], 4th edn. La Fondation canadienne des bourses d'études du millénaire. Montréal, Québec, Canada (2009)
5. Organisation for Economic Co-operation and Development [OECD]: Education at a Glance 2012 HIGHLIGHTS: OECD Indicators. Secretary-General of the OECD, Paris, France (2012). https://www.oecd.org/education/highlights.pdf
6. Shaienks, D., Gluszynski, T.: Participation aux études postsecondaires: diplômés, persévérants et décrocheurs, résultats de l'EJET, 4e cycle. [Participation in Postsecondary Education: Graduates, Continuers and Drop-outs, Results from YITS Cycle 4]. Statistiques Canada, Ottawa, Ontario, Canada, no. 81595MIF2007059 (2007)
7. Ministère de l'Éducation, du Loisir et du Sport [MELS]. Indicateurs de l'éducation – Édition 2012. [Education Indicators]. Gouvernement du Québec, Québec, Canada (2012). http://www.education.gouv.qc.ca/fileadmin/site_web/documents/PSG/statistiques_info_decisionnelle/Indicateurs_educ_2012_webP.pdf
8. Conseil supérieur de l'éducation [CSE]: Des acquis à préserver et des défis à relever pour les universités québécoises. Avis à la Ministre de l'éducation, du loisir et du sport. [Québec universities: Maintaining achievements and facing the challenges. Memorandum to the Minister of Education, Recreation and Sports]. Conseil supérieur de l'éducation, Quebec, QC, Canada (2008)
9. Ruph, F.: Guide de réflexion sur les stratégies d'apprentissage à l'université. [Guide to developing learning strategies in university], 2nd édn. Rouyn-Noranda, Presses de l'Université du Québec, Québec, Canada (2010)
10. Ferla, J., Valcke, M., Schuyten, G.: Relationships between student cognitions and their effects on study strategies. Learn. Individ. Differ. **18**(2), 271–278 (2008)
11. Al-Harthy, I.S., Was, C.A., Isaacson, R.M.: Goals, efficacy and metacognitive self-regulation: a path analysis. Int. J. Educ. **2**(1), 1–20 (2010)
12. Dawson, D.L., Meadows, K.N., Haffie, T.: The effect of performance feedback on student help-seeking and learning strategy use: do clickers make a difference? Can. J. Scholarsh. Teach. Learn. **1**(1), 1–20 (2010). Article 6
13. Sauvé, L., et al.: Les difficultés en lien avec les stratégies d'apprentissage, la mise à niveau en mathématiques et en français des étudiants ayant ou non des troubles d'apprentissage et de déficit d'attention en première année d'études au collège et à l'université et l'apport des outils d'aide pour résoudre ces difficultés. [Problems addressed by learning strategies and mathematics and French remediation for college or university freshmen with or without learning difficulties or attention deficits, and use of tools to help overcome these difficulties]. FQRSC, Québec, QC, Canada (2012)

14. Kizilcec, R.F., Pérez-Sanagustin, M., Maldonado, J.J.: Self-regulated learning strategies predict learner behavior and goal attainment in Massive Open Online Courses. Comput. Educ. **104**, 18–33 (2017)
15. Bartels, J., Jackson, S.: Approach-avoidance motivation and metacognitive self-regulation: the role of need for achievement and fear of failure. Learn. Individ. Diff. **19**, 459–463 (2009)
16. Kozanitis, A.: L'influence d'innovations pédagogiques sur le profil motivationnel et le choix de stratégies d'apprentissage d'étudiantes et d'étudiants d'une faculté d'ingénierie. [The influence of pedagogical innovations on the motivation profile and learning strategy choices of students in an engineering faculty]. Revue internationale de pédagogie de l'enseignement supérieur **26**, 1 (2010). https://ripes.revues.org/385
17. Sauvé, L., Debeurme, G., Martel, V., Wright, A., Hanca, G.: Soutenir les étudiants (distance et sur campus) présentant des difficultés susceptibles d'entraîner l'abandon des études universitaires lors de la première session: constats de recherche et pistes d'intervention. [Supporting Students (Distance and on Campus) Presents Difficulties that are Likely to Lead to the Abandonment of University Studies during the First Session: Research Findings and Lines of Intervention], Revue internationale de pédagogie universitaire **4**, 3, 58–72 (2007)
18. Audet, L.: Recherche sur les facteurs qui influencent la persévérance et la réussite scolaire en formation à distance. Recension des écrits. [Research on the Factors that Influence Perseverance and Academic Success in Distance Learning. Review of the Literature] REFAD, Montréal, QC, Canada (2008). http://bv.cdeacf.ca/record.php?record=192100241 24910382069
19. Racette, N.: La conception d'un programme motivationnel destiné aux cycles supérieurs en formation à distance. [Development of a motivational programme for higher education programmes in distance education]. Revue de l'Éducation à Distance **23**(2), 1–23 (2009). http://www.ijede.ca/index.php/jde/article/view/479/895
20. TELUQ (Télé-Université): Horizon 2015: L'université à distance de l'avenir (préambule et éléments de contexte) [Horizon 2015: The distance university of the future (preamble and background)]. Télé-Université, Québec, QC, Canada (2010)
21. Han, C.-W., Farruggia, S.P., Solomon, B.J.: Latent profiling university students' learning strategies use and effects on academic performance and retention. High. Educ. Res. Dev. 1–15 (2018). https://doi.org/10.1080/07294360.2018.1498460
22. Littlejohn, A., Hood, N., Milligan, C., Mustain, P.: Learning in MOOCs: motivations and self-regulated learning in MOOCs. Internet High. Educ. **29**, 40–48 (2016)
23. Tuckman, B.W., Kennedy, G.J.: Teaching learning strategies to increase success of first-term college students. J. Exp. Educ. **79**(4), 478–504 (2011)
24. Zusho, A., Edwards, K.: Self-regulation and achievement goals in the college classroom. New Dir. Teach. Learn. **126**, 21–31 (2011)
25. Ma, X., Frempong, G.: Raisons de l'inachèvement des études postsecondaires et profil des décrocheurs des études postsecondaires: Rapport. [Reasons for non-completion of postsecondary education and profile of postsecondary dropouts: Report]. No. SP-837-05-08F. Ressources Humaines et Développement Social Canada, Ottawa, Ontario, Canada (2008)
26. Broadbent, J.: Comparing online and blended learner's self-regulated learning strategies and academic performance. Internet High. Educ. **33**, 24–32 (2017)
27. Sauvé, L., Fortin, A., Viger, C., Landry, F.: Ineffective learning strategies: a significant barriers to post-secondary perseverance. J. Further High. Educ. 1–18 (2016). https://www.tandfonline.com/doi/full/10.1080/0309877X.2016.1224329
28. Wang, C.-H., Shannon, D.M., Ross, M.E.: Students' characteristics, self-regulated learning, technology self-efficacy, and course outcomes in online learning. Distance Educ. **34**(3), 302–323 (2013)

29. Gulnara, M., Monowar, M.: Personality, learning strategies, and academic performance: evidence from post-Soviet Kazakhstan. Educ. + Train. **56**(4), 343–359 (2014)
30. Fortin, A., Sauvé, L., Landry, F., Viger, C.: La persévérance et la réussite universitaires d'étudiants inscrits à des programmes de premier cycle en sciences comptables au Québec. [The Perseverance and Academic Success of Students Enrolled in Undergraduate Accounting Programs in Quebec]. Experimental Report. FODAR, Quebec, QC, Canada, January 2015
31. Karabenick, S.A.: Seeking help in large college classes: a person-centered approach. Contemp. Educ. Psychol. **28**(1), 37–58 (2003)
32. Karabenick, S.A., Newman, R.S.: Help Seeking in Academic Settings: Goals, Groups, and Contexts. Erlbaum, Mahwah (2006)
33. Debeurme, G., Caron, A., Sauvé, L.: Demander de l'aide ou non? Savoir faire les premiers pas. [Asking for Help or Not? Know How to Take the First Steps]. Unpublished article. Université de Sherbrooke, Sherbrooke, QC, Canada (2013). http://www.savie.ca/SAVIE/Publications/06-Debeurme_et_al_DemandeAide_25janvier2013.pdf
34. Cho, E., Kim, S.: Cronbach's coefficient alpha: well known but poorly understood. Organ. Res. Methods **18**(2), 207–230 (2015)
35. Chiu, T., Fang, D., Chen, J., Wang, Y., Jeris, C.: A robust and scalable clustering algorithm for mixed type attributes in large database environment. In: Lee, D., Schkolnich. M., Provost, F., Srikant, R. (eds.) Proceedings of the Seventh ACM SIGKDD International Conference on Knowledge Discovery and Data Mining, San Francisco, CA, USA, 26–29 August 2001, pp. 263–268 (2001)
36. Bacher, J., Wenzig, K., Vogler, M.: SPSS TwoStep Cluster-A first evaluation. Social Science Open Access Repository. Friedrich-Alexander-Universität Erlangen-Nürnberg, Lehrstuhl für Soziologie, Nürnberg (2004). https://www.researchgate.net/publication/234112237_SPSS_TwoStep_Clustering_-_A_First_Evaluation
37. Coffman, D., Gilligan, T.: Social, support, stress and self-efficacy: effects on student's satisfaction. J. Coll. Student Retent. **4**(1), 53–66 (2003)
38. Dussarps, C., Paquelin, D.: L'abandon en formation à distance: analyse socioaffective. [Abandonment in distance education: socioaffective analysis]. In: Journées Communication et Apprentissage Instrumentés en Réseau (JOCAIR), Paris, France, 25–27 June 2014. https://journals.openedition.org/dms/1039
39. Endrizzi, L.: Réussir l'entrée dans l'enseignement supérieur. [Successful entry into higher education]. Dossier d'actualité de la VST 59. École normale supérieure de Lyon, Institut français de l'éducation, Lyon, France (2010). https://www.researchgate.net/profile/Laure_Endrizzi/publication/264991736_Reussir_l%27entree_dans_l%27enseignement_superieur/links/58ee2167a6fdcc61cc122e33/Reussir-lentree-dans-lenseignement-superieur.pdf

Visualising and Re-using Innovative Pedagogical Scenarios

Marina Kurvits(✉), Mart Laanpere, Terje Väljataga, and Romil Robtsenkov

Tallinn University, Narva mnt., 25, Tallinn, Estonia
mkurvits@tlu.ee

Abstract. The paper takes a critical look at the existing approaches and online tools that are supposed to enhance the sharing and reusing of innovative pedagogical scenarios among teachers, such as IMS LD, LAMS, LessonPlanner, etc. We argue that there is a need for new ways of sharing pedagogical scenarios that would promote innovative approaches to learning and teaching, would be easy to use and would scale up the sharing and reusing of innovative pedagogical scenarios among teachers. As a potential solution to this challenge, the paper introduces a framework and online tool called LePlanner. We summarise the results of the first evaluation study, which engaged 20 teachers in actively using the tool over a period of 4 months.

Keywords: Pedagogical scenario · Authoring tool · Pedagogical innovation · Learning Design

1 Introduction

The main goal of the new national strategy for lifelong learning in Estonia is to change the approach to learning and teaching at all levels in all forms of education. More precisely, this change should lead towards more creative, collaborative, self-directed and personalised learning experiences. The 21st century teacher is no longer the only source of the knowledge and information acquired by students. The main task of the teachers today is to design learning opportunities and conditions in which the learner can be actively engaged in the knowledge creation process and can develop skills such as creativity, collaboration, an entrepreneurial mindset and self-regulation [26].

The modification of the existing teaching practices is one of the greatest pedagogical challenges today, and teachers need support in this process of changing their approach to teaching [13].

One possible way of encouraging the spread of pedagogical innovation is to use digital technology to support teachers in experimenting with new lesson scenarios that have been designed and tested by their innovative colleagues. While there is a range of frameworks and digital tools that exist for composing and sharing lesson plans among teachers (e.g. IMS LD, LAMS, LessonPlanner), they

M. A. Herzog et al. (Eds.): ICWL 2019, LNCS 11841, pp. 177–189, 2019.
https://doi.org/10.1007/978-3-030-35758-0_17

seem to be used only by a small number of teachers and their impact on upscaling the innovations in classrooms is low. Below, we argue that one of the reasons for this is the pedagogical neutrality of these pedagogical planning tools. We suggest that a digital tool for designing and sharing pedagogical scenarios should promote new learning theories so that it can help teachers gradually change their practices. This statement leads us to the following research questions:

1. What constitutes an innovative pedagogical scenario and how can it be represented? 2. What are the design requirements for a digital tool that supports changes in classroom practices through visualising and spreading innovative pedagogical scenarios among teachers?

The results of our design-based research are described in this paper as follows: firstly, the paper describes the concept of pedagogical innovation and takes a critical look at the existing approaches and online tools for creating, re-using and sharing pedagogical scenarios. Later, the framework and corresponding online tool called LePlanner, which is designed for supporting pedagogical innovation, is introduced. Finally, the results of the first trial and user evaluation of the LePlanner prototype are presented.

2 Pedagogical Innovation in the Digital Age: Key Concepts and Theoretical Considerations

Pedagogical innovation can be identified and supported on the three different levels: the micro level (classroom), meso level (school or local community) and the macro level (state or national entities) [16]. In this paper, we will focus on the micro level - changes in the pedagogical practices in classrooms that occur by supporting teachers in visualising and sharing innovative lesson scenarios.

According to the concept of "new pedagogy" suggested by Fullan [7], pedagogical innovation is defined through changing partnerships between teachers and students in which the learning process becomes a collaborative way of discovering, creating and using knowledge in a ubiquitous technological context. The main learning outcomes of new pedagogy are the student's ability to learn and develop continuously while persevering through the challenges that he/she comes across during real-life situations. Fullan argues that the learning process should be re-structured to replace mastery learning with collaborative knowledge creation processes, where digital tools and resources are used for enabling and accelerating the process of deep learning. Researchers from Finland have promoted a knowledge-creation metaphor and a trialogical approach to learning that describes pedagogical innovation in the 21st century [9]. Such an approach to learning focuses on the process of creating and collaboratively developing new knowledge objects in form of digital artefacts, which leads to conscious knowledge advancement through the use of new digital tools [10]. Students take a more active stance in their relationship and interaction with the (digital) learning resources, up to the point of assuming the role of a co-author. They are not only consumers of the learning resource and the knowledge embedded in it, but become creators and producers in the process of the co-construction of new knowledge [12,14,29].

Based on these new learning theories, we claim that innovative lessons should be designed so that students have the opportunity to discover, interact and create new knowledge in the form of digital artefacts (e.g. they build upon, enhance, adapt, remix or even create the digital learning resources from scratch), and not just consume pre-packaged learning content. This line of thinking led Väljataga and her colleagues (2015) to design a taxonomy called Levels of Co-Authorship (LoCA) that defines seven levels of engagement by learners in relation to the digital learning resources they use in their learning process:

0. Consume – the lowest and the most static way of interacting with content, e.g. viewing a video clip, listening to a podcast or just reading a text;
1. Annotate – the annotation of content with various types of metadata, e.g. highlighting, favouring, rating, tagging or commenting;
2. Manipulate – learners interaction with software that gives immediate personal feedback, e.g. self-testing;
3. Submit – learners are prompted to solve some problems or enter responses to questions, so that the teacher can collect their responses and give feedback;
4. Expand – students extend or enhance the given resource by adding some micro content to the original set of materials;
5. Remix – the original content is modified by adding, removing and/or changing parts of the resource;
6. Create – students create a new digital resource from scratch, using the same tools and formats as the authors of the original resource.

This taxonomy can be used for comparing digital textbooks and other learning resources regarding their affordances and their support of the trialogical learning approach. For instance, a learning resource in the form of a PDF file can only be used at Level 1 of the LoCA, while an iBook affords Level 3 (as the teacher cannot see the results of the learner's interaction with the content). In summary, we can say that pedagogical innovation at the micro level means the designing of learning activities in a way so that learners will discover, use, create and share new knowledge and apply it to real-world problems using digital tools. The teacher and the learners form a new kind of partnership in this knowledge creation process, where the teacher is not the sole source of the valid knowledge; rather, her role is to facilitate the self-directed, creative and collaborative learning of the students. However, it is a challenge to support teachers in the designing of pedagogical scenarios that will make such a change happen in their classroom. We will define the pedagogical scenario as a template for describing, sharing and re-using innovative teaching practices [17]. An innovative pedagogical scenario should promote the new learning theories and approaches by supporting the implementation of new practices and methods in the classroom. It should also reflect (in a visualised and easy-to-grasp manner) how a teacher facilitates learning through collaborative knowledge creation, engages the students in solving authentic problems, supports cooperation between the students, and supports the development of self-regulation using digital tools and resources. These were the initial design ideas for LePlanner – an experimental online tool that allows teachers to easily create, share and re-use innovative pedagogical scenarios. Prior to developing the new tool, we conducted a critical review of the existing tools in the same field.

3 Related Research

Describing the learning process in a formal and standardised way is not a trivial task, and is something that is still challenging for researchers and practitioners. In the next part, we briefly discuss the related work in this field. Our review of publications in the field of pedagogical scenarios revealed the dominance of the IMS Learning Design and its related tools [1,2,5,15,19,28]. The IMS LD is a technical standard that provides a formal meta-language for describing pedagogical scenarios in a machine readable and interoperable form. Koper [15] defined a few principles of Learning Design, one of which is the flexibility to express various pedagogies without assigning a preference to any specific one. As a result, the IMS LD is pedagogically neutral since it has no single preferred underlying pedagogy [25]. While the pedagogical neutrality of the IMS LD has usually been seen as a positive aspect [2,19], from our point of view it can become a disadvantage when seeking a clear preference for certain innovative pedagogical approaches at the expense of the more traditional alternatives. For the purpose of changing the approach to teaching, teachers should implement innovative pedagogical scenarios based on the new learning theories. These pedagogical scenarios require a fundamentally different role for teachers and for learners as well. The teachers also need instructional support in implementing innovative pedagogical practices that can support the learners' acquisition of learning skills, creativity and entrepreneurship with the use of ICT [3,13,23]. When representing the innovativeness of a pedagogical scenario, it is not enough to just define a linear sequence and the types of activities, related tasks and assessment formats for students.

The IMS LD has been criticised for its limitations and deficiencies, such as an insufficient flexibility in describing the learning scenarios [2], a low adoption among teachers due to the complexity of the specification [24], as well as its implementation difficulties for individual teachers [8]. However, the IMS LD has remained the dominant framework for developing the tools for creating and sharing pedagogical scenarios, such as Collage [11], ScenEdit [6] and the Reload LD editor [20].

One of the most popular tools for creating and sharing pedagogical scenarios seems to be the LAMS: Learning Activity Management System (see a more detailed analysis in [17]). LAMS provides educators with a visual environment for creating sequences of learning activities [1]. However, LAMS doesn't support the teachers in expressing the innovative characteristics of their teaching approach [1]. Another popular tool in this field is Learning Designer, which assists teachers in designing learning activities for their students [1]. Learning Designer differentiates between six types of learning activities and describes a mixture of these activities during a lesson. However, this tool doesn't visualise how the roles of the teacher and students change in a specific scenario and how actively or creatively the learners are engaged in the learning process. Probably the most common way the teachers use to describe their own practices is writing a narrative lesson plan in a structured manner, which is mostly used for administrative purposes (e.g. inspections, lesson observations, quality assurance). There are some software tools that include such lesson planning templates; for example Lesson Plans[1], Lesson Builder[2], and Scenario Development Environment[3].

Unfortunately, the pedagogical scenarios presented through these tools tend to become long, uninspiring texts and their structure looks the same for all pedagogical approaches. Therefore, it is difficult to imagine how this way of describing pedagogical scenarios could support other teachers in changing their approach to teaching (even if the original scenario was a truly innovative one when implemented in the classroom). When the students are involved in a self-directed inquiry or in a collaborative knowledge creation project, the teacher does not deliver the content in a linear manner, but instead provides an open-ended context and the conditions for creative learning. This can be quite challenging for teachers, because they are not aware of or struggle to implement alternative practices for structuring the pedagogical process and supporting their students [18].

4 Research Design

The empirical data collection and design was conducted in three iterations that took place during three consecutive years (2014, 2015 and 2016), as often happens with DBR studies. In each iteration, a different sample of respondents was involved in the participatory design sessions.

We dedicated two years to completing an iterative design-based research process, which eventually led us to the development of a fully functional prototype of LePlanner – a tool for visualising, sharing and re-using innovative pedagogical scenarios.

Multiple participatory design methods were combined in the process, including creating personas and usage scenarios, conducting participatory design sessions, concept mapping, writing user stories, creating paper prototypes and developing interactive, high-fidelity prototypes.

5 Results

In the first iteration (Fig. 1) we asked a group of Estonian teachers to describe a pedagogical scenario using paper stickers. During this activity, we tried to

[1] http://lessonplanspage.com/.
[2] http://thelessonbuilder.org/.
[3] http://www.itec-sde.net/en.

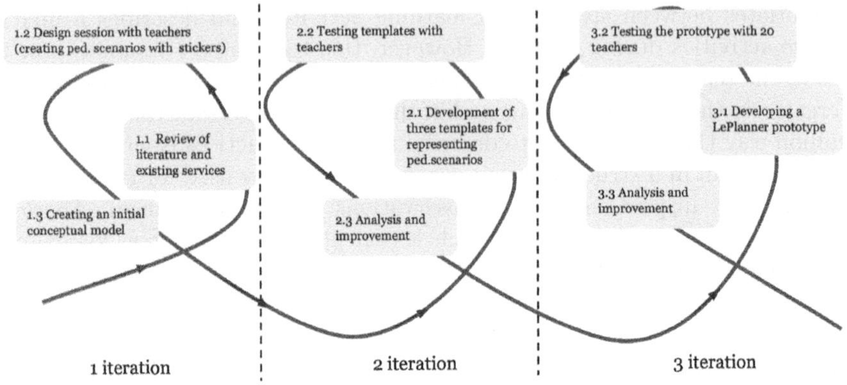

Fig. 1. Three iterations of research-based development of the prototype of LePlanner.

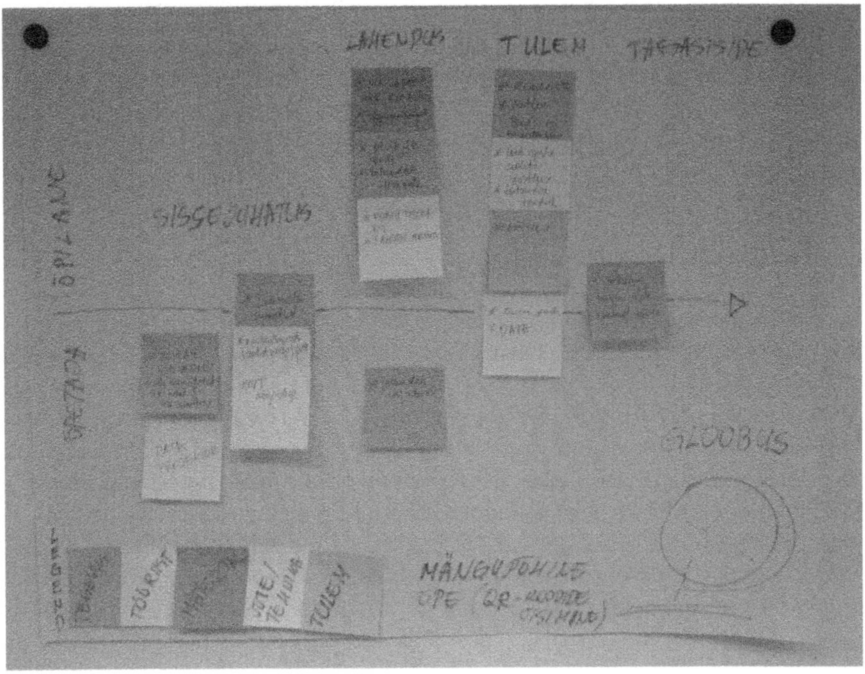

Fig. 2. Representing pedagogical scenario using stickers in the first design session.

identify their understanding of the pedagogical scenario and its related elements. During the iteration, it became evident that the pedagogical scenario is more convenient to present as a timeline. Also the scenario was divided into two views that described the activities of the students and the teacher (Fig. 2).

During the second iteration, we worked with Estonian educational technologists in order to determine their expectations of a tool for describing a pedagogical scenario. For these tasks, we asked them to describe one pedagogical scenario using one of the templates we presented. The templates were created with Google Draw and Lucidchart (Fig. 3). Each of the templates allows the teacher to represent a pedagogical scenario in a different way. The first of these was a narrative form (it contained fields for describing the topic of the lesson, goals, learning process, environment, methods, tools and assessment) that allowed the teachers to freely describe the learning activities. The second template was a block diagram (containing fields for describing the topic of the lesson and its goals, and different shapes for describing the learning activities) that allowed the teachers to build a sequence of the parts of the lesson in a free order. The last template was in the form of a timeline with different types of blocks: learning materials, software/web-tools, display/medium, technique/method. This template allowed the teacher to construct their own scenario by using the blocks and arranging them along the timeline.

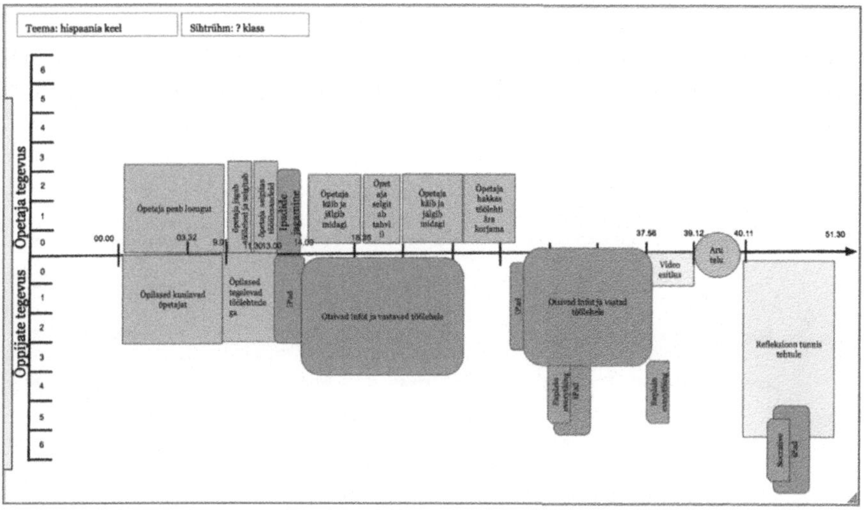

Fig. 3. Representing pedagogical scenario using Google Draw in the second design session.

These two iterations showed that, for the purpose of supporting the teachers in changing their approach and in using innovative pedagogical scenarios, there should be a fundamentally different tool for creating and sharing pedagogical scenarios. It should be a visual, clear and structured tool, that displays the actions of the teacher and the students. This tool should give the teacher a visual understanding of the innovative approach of the pedagogical scenario and the structure of each scenario should be visually different from the others.

As we mentioned above, it is important that the tool used for creating the innovative pedagogical scenario is not pedagogically neutral. Therefore, in the third iteration our goal was to develop such a tool for creating and sharing an innovative pedagogical scenario according to the new learning theories; for example, the concept of trialogical learning. The fully functional prototype of the LePlanner was tested with a group of teachers, who described and visualised their pedagogical scenarios with it. The teachers gave us qualitative feedback through a group interview and they filled in an online survey questionnaire.

The design of LePlanner includes functionalities typical of social networking platforms, which should be a good premise for spreading the knowledge within various communities of teachers. For instance, LePlanner allows any user to follow other users, while the feeds of the pedagogical scenarios published recently by inspiring colleagues are presented on the user's dashboard. It is also possible to like and comment on certain scenarios, in which case the author of the scenario received a notification. The main action of creating the pedagogical scenario is divided into parts. First, primary information such as the title, description, subjects, grade, total duration and the learning outcomes have to be provided. Next, the pedagogical scenario is divided into activities. As is shown in Fig. 4, the user can add the following information for each activity: the title and duration of the activity; whether it is a face-to-face (default) or a classroom activity; and whether the activity is done individually, in pairs, in small group or involving whole class. Each activity can be linked to previously defined learning outcomes from the national curriculum.

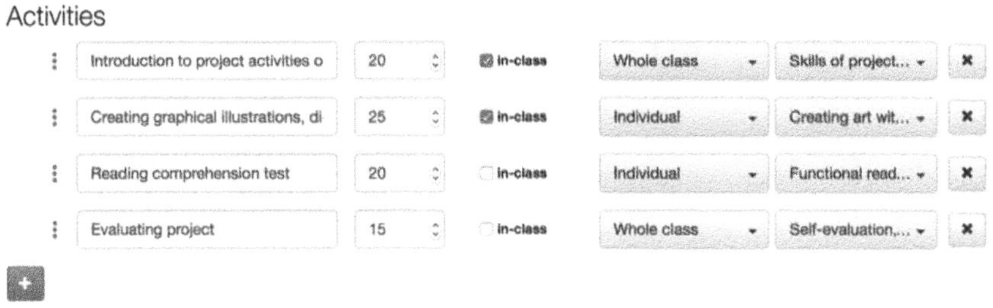

Fig. 4. Editing details view for describing scenario activities.

After the activities are added, they are visualised on the timeline which is divided horizontally into two parts: above the timeline is a space for teacher resources and below is a space for student resources. The next step is to add learning resources to the activities. For the student resources, it is possible to add the title of the resource and the URL where it can be accessed. The Level of Co-Authorship (LoCA) for the resource can be defined, which makes it visually easy to grasp whether the students are only listening or reading in the lesson, or are actively engaged in trialogical knowledge creation. The use of LoCA in visualising the pedagogical scenarios takes the students' interactions with the digital resources into consideration by dividing the interactions into seven levels [29]. The chosen level is reflected by the height of the student resource bar, with the higher level results in a higher box. Next, multiple conveyors that describe the tools or software that will mediate a given resource can be added. Display options for viewing or creating the resource can be selected, including a projector/TV, smart board, computer, tablet and smartphone. It is also possible to add other display options. Adding resources for the teachers differs only by not including the LoCA selection. Figure 5 hows activities with two added resource linked with conveyors and displays – one for the teacher and one for the student.

When the scenario is ready, it is published and visualised as timeline. As Fig. 5 shows, it is possible to see an overview of the resources for each activity with the use of conveyors and displays. The LoCA makes it possible to make conclusions about the students' interactions with the resources and how much they are involved in the activities. This is done by evaluating the height of the student resources box. If necessary, the created scenario can also be accessed in a text outline view, where the activities and resources used, with all the other data, are represented in a multilevel list.

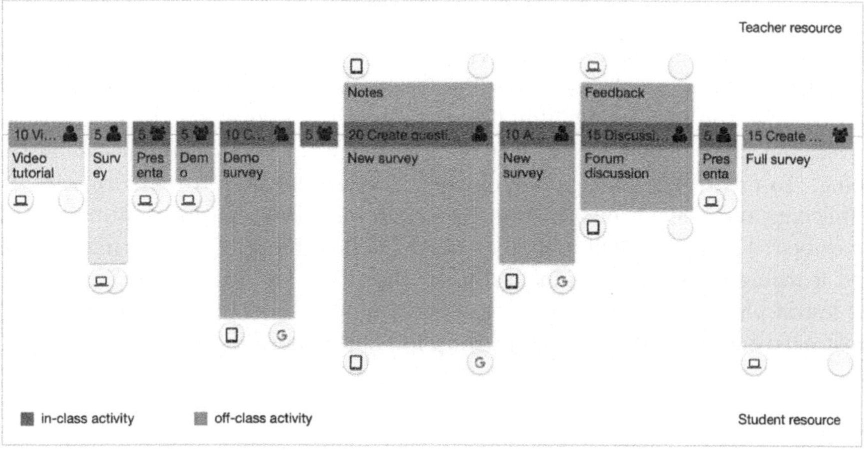

Fig. 5. Visualised Flipped Classroom scenario with related activities and resources.

LePlanner is an open source software released under an MIT licence and its source code can be found in the GitHub repository at https://github.com/romilrobtsenkov/leplanner-beta. It is currently available in the Estonian, English and Croatian languages. Additional think-aloud testing with multiple first-time users was carried out to improve the software's usability. In one phase of the evaluation, a survey was carried out among LePlanner users, who were mostly teachers and educational technologists. The goal of the survey was to get an overview of the disadvantages and opportunities of the tool. The survey was conducted with 53 users of LePlanner, from which 33 were used to measure if the teachers believe that LePlanner can help them to do their job better. Most of the respondents agreed that LePlanner has important extra benefits over traditional lesson plans ($M = 3.79$; $SD = 0.93$) and that it is useful in their everyday work

(M = 3.52; SD = 1.00). The respondents agreed less with the statements that LePlanner enables them to save time (M = 3.21; SD = 0.99) and makes it possible to plan their lessons with less effort. To summarise the results of the TAM2 for the perceived usefulness, it is possible to say that the respondents agreed to a small degree (M = 3.37; SD = 0.85) that LePlanner allows them to do their job better. The evaluations for all the statements were reliable (=0.90). The respondents considered the visualisation based on the LoCA taxonomy as a useful feature of LePlanner. The users liked the timeline visualisation, which allowed them to have a better understanding of the duration of different activities and to plan the pedagogical scenario. The users also liked the fact that pedagogical scenario is composed of two main building blocks: activities and resources. The possibility offered by LePlanner to add and visualise the applications and services used for specific resources was received well by the respondents. It was acknowledged that this approach allows pedagogical scenarios that are innovative, technology enhanced and based on a trialogical learning concept to be described. The users expressed their need to describe more complicated pedagogical scenarios, which have parallel activities for different groups. There was also a need to be able to add multiple resources to one activity and vice versa – and to link two activities with the same single resource. The respondents indicated that because of a lack of time, the teachers wouldn't start to describe pedagogical scenarios themselves, but they would be interested in seeing what other good teachers were doing. To create the best opportunities, it would be best to pair up with the publishers and make it possible for teachers to use the scenarios that are already described. The respondents mostly valued the possibility of integrating teaching and learning analytics to gain feedback, improve scenarios and get suggestions for lesson planning. In the future, teacher training students are considered to be most active and interested target group for LePlanner.

6 Discussion

We argue that a digital tool for creating and sharing innovative pedagogical scenarios should be based on the new learning theories; for example, the trialogical approach to learning, and it cannot be pedagogically neutral. The tool has to guide and support teachers in the implementation of innovative practices. It should be visual and structured, display the actions of both teachers and students, and offer a visual understanding of the innovative aspect of the pedagogical scenario. The tools based on the IMS LD focus on the opportunity for teachers to construct the sequence of a learning activity so that it provides learners with the opportunity to perform tasks. Using these kinds of tools, the teacher can still create scenarios according to the traditional approach to teaching. That is why we argue that the IMS LD specification is not suitable for the development of an authoring tool designed for creating innovative pedagogical scenarios. We believe that the standard is used only for some PhD work in applied computer science. Nevertheless, we have found many articles that praise the IMS LD and not so many that have expressed criticism. This paper introduces the framework and the online tool called LePlanner that has been designed as a result of this line of thinking. The pedagogical foundation of LePlanner is the concept of trialogical learning. According to this concept, the tool has a taxonomy based on the Levels of Co-Authorship, which support teachers in the process of planning the learning activity, whereby students become more active in relation to the learning materials. We summarised the results of the first evaluation study, in which 20 teachers were engaged in actively using the tool for a period of 4 months. As we have shown, the results of the study revealed that a more complicated task for teachers in describing a pedagogical scenario was applying a level of co-authorship. It is important to note that it is exactly this opportunity that gives a better visual overview of the level of the learner's activity. Another difficulty for teachers in describing a pedagogical scenario is a lack of time. Therefore, in designing the framework and in the development a tool for creating a pedagogical scenario it was important for us to keep this fact in mind. Using LePlanner, a teacher has the opportunity to plan the learning process with a focus on students engagement and to help develop skills such as creativity and collaboration. There is one more point that is important to pay attention to: the main task of the teachers is to create learning opportunities and conditions in which the learner is active, involved in the learning process and can develop self-regulation. At the moment, the teacher himself prescribes all the activities and tasks for the learners in LePlanner, so the students don't have enough freedom in terms of planning their own activities and performing their own tasks. But it does offer the necessary conditions for developing the student's self-regulation skills. Most likely, in order to reflect the activities of the learners in LePlanner that they design for themselves, the principles of emergent design should be used.

7 Conclusions

A multitude of authors have expressed a similar agenda for a pedagogical innovation that changes the role of the teacher, who should become a facilitator of self-directed, creative and collaborative knowledge creation by the student. Instead of transmitting information to the students and controlling their behaviour, the teacher should guide and support the learners, to engage them in deep meaningful learning. While there are some teachers who already practice such innovative pedagogies, their experience is not easily spread among the wider communities of teachers. After developing and piloting LePlanner, we believe that this tool could be used to increase and speed up the uptake of innovative practices on a wider scale. As a result of the feedback collected from the teachers who have used LePlanner, the next version of the tool will address new functionalities, such as emergent design or meta-design (a part of the pedagogical scenario that the teacher will leave for the students to design in a self-directed manner). Future research should focus on using LePlanner with students in initial teacher education. Next, we plan to enhance LePlanner to contribute to learning analytics by comparing the designed pedagogical scenarios with the actually implemented ones.

References

1. Bower, M., Craft, B., Laurillard, D., Liz, M.: Using the Learning Designer to develop a conceptual framework for linking learning design tools and systems. In: International LAMS and Learning Design Conference, pp. 61–71 (2011)
2. Caeiro, M., Anido, L., Llamas, M.: A critical analysis of IMS Learning Design. In: Wasson, B., Ludvigsen, S., Hoppe, U. (eds.) Designing for Change in Networked Learning Environments. CULS, vol. 2, pp. 363–367. Springer, Dordrecht (2003). https://doi.org/10.1007/978-94-017-0195-2_44
3. Conole, G., Fill, K.: A learning design toolkit to create pedagogically effective learning activities. J. Interact. Med. Educ. **8**, 1–16 (2005)
4. Dalziel, J.: Lessons from LAMS for IMS learning design. In: Sixth International Conference on Advanced Learning Technologies, pp. 1101–1102 (2006)
5. De-La-Fuente-Valentin, L., Leony, D., Pardo, A., Kloos, C.D.: Developing and using an IMS LD ontology to create and execute learning designs Learning Designs. In: Proceedings of the Frontiers in Education Conference, FIE (2011)
6. Emin, V., Pernin, J.-P., Aguirre, J.L.: ScenEdit: an intention-oriented authoring environnment to design learning scenarios. In: Wolpers, M., Kirschner, P.A., Scheffel, M., Lindstaedt, S., Dimitrova, V. (eds.) EC-TEL 2010. LNCS, vol. 6383, pp. 626–631. Springer, Heidelberg (2010). https://doi.org/10.1007/978-3-642-16020-2_65
7. Fullan, M., Langworthy, M.: How New Pedagogies Find Deep Learning (2014)
8. Yu, G.: An IMS learning design meta-model for learners with autism (2008)
9. Hakkarainen, K., Paavola, S.: The knowledge creation metaphor - an emergent epistemological approach to learning. Sci. Educ. **14**(6), 535–557 (2005)
10. Hakkarainen, K., Paavola, S.: From monological and dialogical to trialogical approaches to learning. A Paper at an International Workshop and Quot (2007)
11. Hernández-Leo, D., et al.: COLLAGE: a collaborative Learning Design editor based on patterns. Educ. Technol. Soc. **9**, 58–71 (2006)
12. Sørensen, B.H., Levinsen, K.T.: Digital production and students as learning designers. Des. Learn. **7**, 54–73 (2014)
13. Häkkinen, P., Mäkitalo-Siegl, K.: Educational perspectives on scripting CSCL. In: Fischer, F., Kollar, I., Mandl, H., Haake, J.M. (eds.) Scripting Computer-Supported Collaborative Learning. CULS, vol. 6, pp. 263–271. Springer, Boston (2007). https://doi.org/10.1007/978-0-387-36949-5_15
14. Jahnke, I., Mårell-Olsson, E., Norqvist, L., Olsson, A., Norberg, A.: Digital didactical designs - reimagining designs for teaching and learning. In: International Consortium for Educational Development Conference (2014)
15. Koper, R., Miao, Y.: Using the IMS LD standard to describe learning designs. In: IMS Learning Design, pp. 1–44 (2007)
16. Kozma, R.B.: Technology, Innovation, and Educational Change: A Global Perspective (2003)
17. Kurvits, M., Laanpere, M., Väljataga, T.: Analysis of tools and methods for describing and sharing reusable pedagogical scenarios. In: Li, F.W.B., Klamma, R., Laanpere, M., Zhang, J., Manjón, B.F., Lau, R.W.H. (eds.) ICWL 2015. LNCS, vol. 9412, pp. 251–257. Springer, Cham (2015). https://doi.org/10.1007/978-3-319-25515-6_24
18. Lakkala, M., Lallimo, J., Hakkarainen, K.: Teachers' pedagogical designs for technology-supported collective inquiry: a national case study. Comput. Educ. **45**(3), 337–356 (2005)

19. Mhouti, A.E., Nasseh, A., Erradi, M.: A framework to stimulate collaborative e-learning through collaborative educational games modeled using IMS-LD. Int. J. Inf. Technol. Comput. Sci. **8**, 19–27 (2016)
20. Milligan, C.D., Beauvoir, P., Sharples, P.: The reload learning design tools. J. Interact. Med. Educ. (2005)
21. Ouahabi, S., Eddaoui, A., Labriji, E.H., Benlahmar, E., El Guemmat, K.: Educational modelling in cloud computing using IMS learning design. J. Theoret. Appl. Inf. Technol. **66**, 654–660 (2014)
22. Sánchez, E., Lama, M., Amorim, R.R.: Developing and using an IMS LD ontology to create and execute learning designs. In: Learning Designs, pp. 459–464 (2006)
23. Schneider, D.K., Synteta, P., Frété, C., Girardin, F., Morand, S.: Conception and implementation of rich pedagogical scenarios through collaborative portal sites: clear focus and fuzzy edges. University of Mauritius (2003)
24. Sporer, T., Steinle, M., Metscher, J.: Evaluation of the software "e^3-Portfolio" in the context of the study program "problem-solving competencies". In: Wolpers, M., Kirschner, P.A., Scheffel, M., Lindstaedt, S., Dimitrova, V. (eds.) EC-TEL 2010. LNCS, vol. 6383, pp. 584–589. Springer, Heidelberg (2010). https://doi.org/10.1007/978-3-642-16020-2_58
25. Tattersall, C., Manderveld, J., Hummel, H., Sloep, P., Koper, R., De Vries, F.: IMS Learning Design frequently asked questions (2004)
26. The Estonian Lifelong Learning Strategy 2020. http://bit.ly/2LDuSWL. Accessed 1 July 2019
27. Venkatesh, V., Davis, F.D.: A theoretical extension of the technology acceptance model: four longitudinal field studies. Manag. Sci. **46**(2), 186–204 (2000)
28. Villasclaras-Fernández, E.D., Hernández-Gonzalo, J.A., Hernández-Leo, D., Asensio-Pérez, J.I., Dimitriadis, Y., Martínez-Monés, A.: InstanceCollage: a tool for the particularization of collaborative IMS-LD scripts. Educ. Technol. Soc. **12**, 56–70 (2009)
29. Väljataga, T., Fiedler, S.H.D., Laanpere, M.: Re-thinking digital textbooks: students as co-authors. In: Li, F.W.B., Klamma, R., Laanpere, M., Zhang, J., Manjón, B.F., Lau, R.W.H. (eds.) ICWL 2015. LNCS, vol. 9412, pp. 143–151. Springer, Cham (2015). https://doi.org/10.1007/978-3-319-25515-6_13

Automated Grading of Short Text Answers: Preliminary Results in a Course of Health Informatics

Giovanni De Gasperis[1], Stefano Menini[2], Sara Tonelli[2], and Pierpaolo Vittorini[3(✉)]

[1] DISIM, University of L'Aquila, Via Vetoio, 67100 L'Aquila, Italy
giovanni.degasperis@univaq.it
[2] FBK-DH, Via Sommarive 18, 38123 Povo, Italy
{menini,satonelli}@fbk.eu
[3] MESVA, University of L'Aquila, P.le S. Tommasi 1, 67100 L'Aquila, Italy
pierpaolo.vittorini@univaq.it

Abstract. Students learning Health Informatics in the degree course of Medicine and Surgery of the University of L'Aquila (Italy) are required – to pass the exam – to submit solutions to assignments concerning the execution and interpretation of statistical analyses. The paper presents a tool for the automated grading of such a kind of solutions, where the statistical analyses are made up R commands and outputs, and the interpretations are short text answers. The tool performs a static analysis of the R commands with the respective output, and uses Natural Language Processing techniques for the short text answers. The paper summarises the solution regarding the R commands and output, and delves into the method and the results used for the automated classification of the short text answers. In particular, we show that through FastText sentence embeddings and a tuned Support Vector Machines classifier, we obtained an accuracy of 0.89, Cohen's K = 0.76, and F1 score of 0.91 on a binary classification task (i.e. pass or fail). Other experiments including additional linguistically-motivated features, whose goal was to capture lexical differences between the students' answer and the gold standard sentence, did not yield any significant improvement. The paper ends with a discussion of the findings and the next steps to be taken in our research.

Keywords: Automated grading · Short text answers · NLP · SVM

1 Introduction

Assessment can essentially be divided into formative and summative assessment [12]. Given a course, formative assessment takes place during its execution to check on student learning progress (by the teacher or by the students themselves), while summative assessment takes place at its end to determine the learning outcomes. Within any assessment method, question types may vary from multiple-choice, open ended, or code-snippets questions.

M. A. Herzog et al. (Eds.): ICWL 2019, LNCS 11841, pp. 190–200, 2019.
https://doi.org/10.1007/978-3-030-35758-0_18

Human grading of both open ended and code-snippets questions is a tedious and error-prone task, a problem particularly pressing when such an assessment involves a large number of students. One possible solution to this problem is to automate the grading process so that it can facilitate teachers in the correction and enable students to receive immediate feedback, so as to improve their assignments before the final submission.

Many tools implementing an automated grading of open-ended and code-snippets already exist [7,25]. As for those regarding open-ended questions, the common task is to assign either a real-valued score (e.g., from 0 to 1) or to assign a label (e.g., correct or irrelevant) to a student response. As for code-snippets questions, the available systems either compile and execute the students' programs against test data (so to compare the achieved with the expected results), or statically analyse the students' source code.

Given these premises, students learning Health Informatics in the degree course of Medicine and Surgery of the University of L'Aquila (Italy) are required – to pass the final exam – to be able to execute statistical analyses in R and to explain the results in terms of clinical findings. Accordingly, in [2] the authors presented a tool for the automated grading of R code snippets (the statistical analyses) and short text answers (the clinical findings). In this paper we extend the research regarding the grading of the short text answers, that in [2] was addressed with a string similarity approach. It is clear that string similarity distances measure the lexical rather than semantic similarity [11] and therefore they can score – as different – strings conveying the

Let us consider the following dataset:

Subject	Surgery	Visibility	Days
1	A	7	7
2	A	5	7
		...	
10	B	16	12
		...	
20	C	19	4

The data regards 20 subjects (variable Subject) that underwent three different surgical operations (variable Surgery). We observe the scar visibility (variable Visibility) in terms of ranks ranging from 1 (the best) to 20 (the worst). We also measure the hospital stay (variable Days).
You are required to:

1. calculate the mean (with confidence intervals) and the standard deviation of the hospital stay;
2. calculate the absolute and relative frequencies (with confidence intervals) of the surgical operations;
3. verify if the hospital stay can be considered as extracted from a normal distribution;
4. comment on the result;
5. calculate the median, the 25th and 75th percentile of the hospital stay for the different surgical operations;
6. verify if the aspect of the scar is different within the different surgical operations;
7. comment on the result.

Submit as solution a text containing the list of R commands with the respective output, as well as your interpretation of the analyses 3 and 6.

Fig. 1. A sample exam

same concept (and viceversa). For instance, given the sentence "The difference is statistically significant", a string similarity distance would consider the sentence "The difference is not statistically significant" (that conveys the opposite concept) only 0.085 distant[1]. Consequently, in this paper we present an approach based on sentence embeddings [5] and supervised binary classification [24], which resulted in a tool with a good ability of predicting the pass/fail grading of the short text answers.

2 Application Scenario and Educational Impact

The course of Health Informatics in the degree course of Medicine and Surgery of the University of L'Aquila (Italy) is organised in two parts. The first part regards the theoretical aspects of Health Informatics, the second part focuses on how to execute statistical analyses in R and how to correctly interpret the results into the corresponding clinical findings. With specific regard on the second part of the course, students – after having followed the lessons – complete several exercises as homework and finish the part with a practical assessment. The exercises and the final exam have the same structure: they start with the definition of the dataset and list the analyses and technical/clinical interpretations that should be performed. The analyses must be performed through R commands and can be both descriptive (e.g., mean, sd), inferential (e.g., t.test, wilcox.test) and for testing normality (e.g., shapiro.test). For the interpretation of the results, students must be able to understand e.g. if the test for normality suggests that the distribution should be considered normal or not, or if a test for hypothesis is statistically significant or not. For instance, see Fig. 1 and let us take into account the sixth point of the assignment. Since the scar visibility is qualitative and the number of different surgeries is three, the student should use a Kruskal-Wallis test. Such a test is executed in R through the command:

```
kruskal.test(data = exam, Visibility ~ Surgery)
```

which would return the following output:

```
	Kruskal-Wallis rank sum test

data:  Visibility by Surgery
Kruskal-Wallis chi-squared = 9.8959, df = 2, p-value = 0.007098
```

By looking at the p-value, which is less than 0.05, the student should then conclude that the difference in Visibility is very unlikely that took place by chance, and therefore it should be caused by the different surgeries. Such a conclusion is the solution to point 7 of the assignment.

In such an educational scenario, the tool we are working on supports both formative and summative assessment as follows (see Fig. 2). As a formative assessment instrument, it is able to provide students with both a textual feedback and

[1] By using a normalised Levenshtein string similarity distance [17].

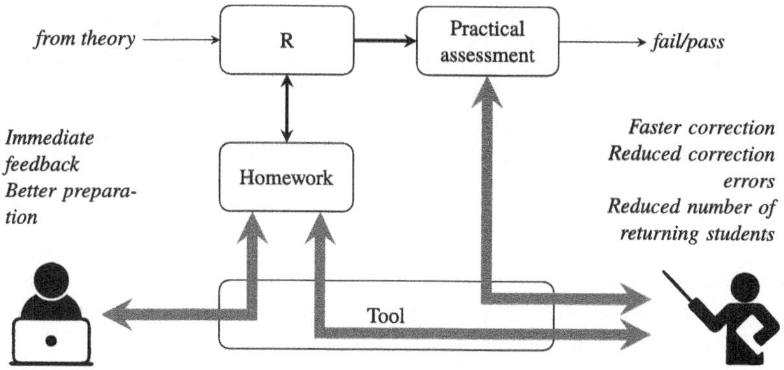

Fig. 2. Application scenario and educational impact

an estimated evaluation of the quality of the submitted solution, and enables teachers to monitor the students' progresses with the homework. As a summative assessment instrument, the tool is used by the teacher to support the manual correction activities. Accordingly, the foreseen educational benefits are manifold. For students, to support their understanding of the commands, the interpretation of the results, and – as a consequence – a desirable increase of the final learning outcomes. For professors, the tool should be able to reduce their workload, both in terms of correction times and errors, but also in a decreased number of returning students.

3 Automated Grading

3.1 Automated Grading of R Code Snippets

The specific problem of the automated grading of R code snippets is only summarised in the paper, since already presented in [2]. To grade the R code, the tool:

- compares the solution given by a student with that given by the professor (i.e., the gold standard);
- calculates the number of correct commands with correct solution, correct commands with wrong solution (e.g., because of wrong input data), missed commands;
- returns as grading the weighted sum of the numbers above.

In [2], the task of grading the comments was addressed with an oversimplified approach (i.e., string similarity). Nevertheless, the results of the comparison of the automated and the manual grading were almost acceptable:

- the intraclass correlation coefficient was measured as 0.784: such a value can be interpreted as an excellent indication of agreement between the two sets of grades [9];

- in terms of predicting the manual grading from the automated one, we obtained – with a linear regression model – an $R^2 = 0.740$: this result indicates a good linear relationship between what is measured automatically and what was assessed by the professor;
- by transforming the numerical grades into dichotomic pass/fail outcomes, the agreement measured with the Cohen's Kappa was 0.52: such a value is not very satisfactory.

The next subsection, which contains the actual novel research, shows the approach to the automated grading of the short text answers, that improves on the previous approach based on string similarity.

3.2 Automated Grading of Short Text Answers

Although several works have explored the possibility to automatically grade short text answers [7], these attempts have mainly focused on English. Furthermore, the best performing ones strongly rely on knowledge bases and syntactic analyses [20], which are hard to obtain for Italian. We therefore test for the first time the potential of sentence embeddings to capture pass or fail judgements in a supervised setting, where the only required data are *(a)* a training/test set and *(b)* pre-trained sentence embeddings [5] using fastText[2].

Dataset. The dataset available at [1] contains the list of sentences written by students, with a unique ID, its type (if either given for the hypothesis or normality test), its degree in a range from 0 to 1, and its fail/pass result, flanked with (i) the gold standard (i.e. the correct answer) and (ii) an alternative gold standard. In order to increase the number of training instances and achieve a better balance between the two classes, we also manually negated a set of correct answers and reversed the corresponding fail/pass result, therefore adding a set of (iii) negated gold standard sentences. All students' and gold standard's sentences are in Italian language. Overall, the dataset contains 1069 student/gold standard answer pairs, 663 of which are labelled as "pass" and 406 as "fail".

Method. Since we cast the task in a supervised classification framework, we first need to represent the pairs of student/gold standard sentences as features. Two different types of features are tested: *distance-based features*, which capture the similarity of the two sentences using measures based on lexical and semantic similarity, and *sentence embeddings* features, whose goal is to represent the semantics of the two sentences in a distributional space.

All sentences are first pre-processed by removing the stop-words such as articles and prepositions, and by replacing mathematical notations with their transcription in plain language (e.g. ">" with "*maggiore*" (*greater*)). We also perform part of speech tagging, lemmatisation and affix recognition using the

[2] https://fasttext.cc/ (last accessed July, 2019).

TINT NLP Suite for Italian [3]. Then, on each pair of sentences the following distance-based features are computed:

- Token overlap: a feature representing the number of overlapping tokens between the two sentences normalised by their length. This feature captures the lexical similarity between the two strings.
- Lemma overlap: a feature representing the number of overlapping lemmas between the two sentences normalised by their length. Like the previous one, this feature captures the lexical similarity between the two strings.
- Presence of negations: this feature represents whether a content word is negated in one sentence and not in the other. For each sentence, negations are recognised based on the NEG PoS tag or the affix 'a-' or 'in-' (e.g. "*indipendente*"), and then the first content word occurring after the negation is considered. We extract two features, one for each sentence, and the values are normalised by their length.

Other distance-based features are computed at sentence level, and to this purpose we employ fastText [5], an extension of word embeddings [19,21] – developed at Facebook – that is able to deal with rare words by including sub-word information, and representing sentences basically by combining vectors representing both words and sub-words. To generate these embeddings we start from the pre-computed Italian language model[3], trained on Common Crawl and Wikipedia. The latter, in particular, is suitable for our domain, since it includes also scientific content and statistics pages, therefore the language of the exam should be well represented in our model. The embeddings are created using continuous bag-of-word with position-weights, a dimension of 300, character n-grams of length 5, a window of size 5 and 10 negatives. Then, the embedding of the sentences written by the students and the gold standard ones are created by combining the word and the sub-word embeddings with the fastText library. Each sentence is therefore represented through a 300 dimensional embedding. Based on this, we extract four additional distance-based features:

- Embeddings cosine: the cosine between the two sentence embeddings is computed. The intuition behind this feature is that the embeddings of two sentences with a similar meaning would be close in a multidimensional space;
- Embeddings cosine (lemmatized): the same feature as the previous one, with the only difference that the sentences are first lemmatised before creating the embeddings;
- Word Mover's Distance (WMD): WMD is a similarity measures based on the minimum amount of distance that the embedded words of one document need to move to reach the embedded words of another document [16]. Compared with other existing similarity measures, it works well also when two sentences have a similar meaning despite having few words in common. We apply this algorithm to measure the distance between the solutions proposed by the students and the ones in the gold standard;

[3] https://fasttext.cc/docs/en/crawl-vectors.html (last accessed July, 2019).

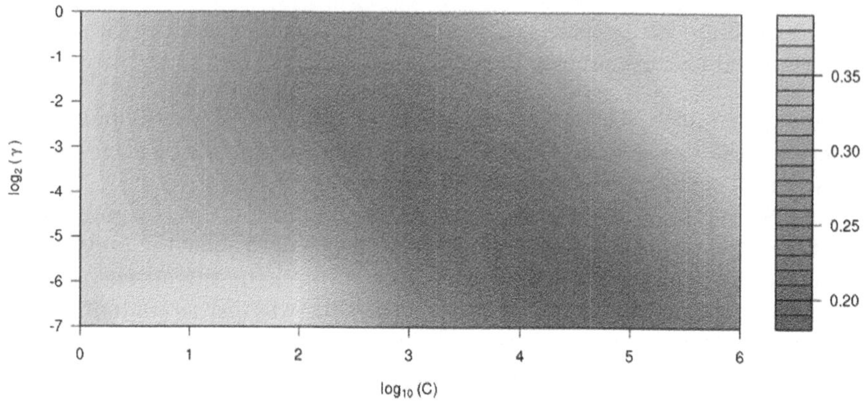

Fig. 3. Tune plot

- Word Mover's Distance (lemmatised): the same feature as the previous one, with the only difference that the sentences are first lemmatised before creating the embeddings.

The sentence embeddings used to compute the distance features are also tested as features in isolation: a 600 dimensional vector is indeed created by concatenating each sentence embeddings composing a student answer – gold standard pair. We adopt this solution inspired by recent approaches to natural language inference using the concatenation of premise and hypothesis [6,14].

As for the supervised classifier, we used Support Vector Machines (SVM) [24]. We then proceeded to find the best C and γ parameters by means of grid-search tuning [13], through a 10-fold cross-validation to prevent to overfit the model. Finally, with the parameters that returned the best performance, we finalised the classifier and calculated its accuracy, F1 score and Cohen's K. Such a process was performed using R 3.6.0 with CARET V6.0-84 and E1071 V1.7-2 packages [15,18,23].

Results. Figure 3 shows the plot summarising the tuning process. In summary, within the explored area, the best parameters were $C = 10^4$ and $\gamma = 2^{-6}$. The resulting tuned model produced the following results:

- Accuracy = 0.891 (balanced accuracy = 0.876);
- F1 score = 0.914;
- Cohen's $K = 0.764$.

With the same approach, we also tuned the classifier when fed with only the concatenated sentence embeddings as features (i.e., without distance-based features). With best parameters $C = 10^3$ and $\gamma = 2^{-3}$, the results were:

- Accuracy = 0.885 (balanced accuracy = 0.870);

- F1 score = 0.909;
- Cohen's $K = 0.752$.

The results show that the concatenated sentence embeddings yield a similar result with and without additional distance-based features.

Software Design. The classifier is under development in the UnivAQ Test Suite (UTS) [4]. The UTS system is implemented as Java web application, and has been used during the last year by more than 200 students, which took advance of the automated grading module with the string similarity approach [2].

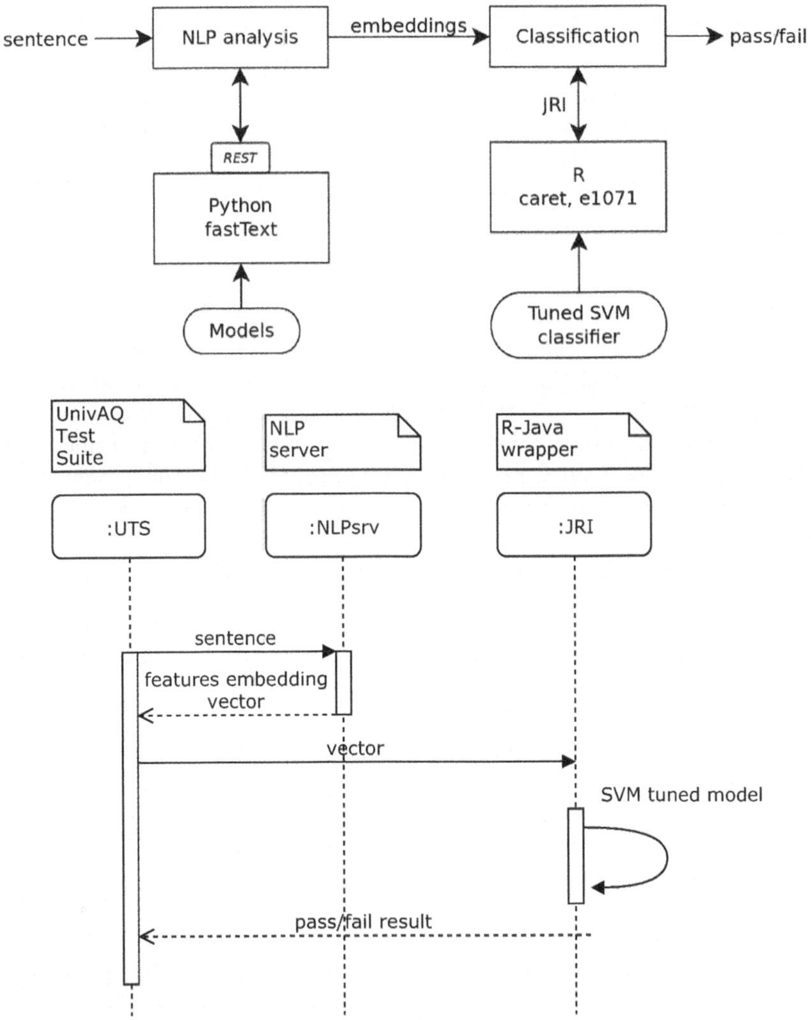

Fig. 4. Implementation of the automated grading of short text answers: on top the software design, on bottom the respective sequence diagram.

On the other hand, the automated grading module with the NLP analysis and the SVM classifier is in an alpha release. Its software design and sequence diagram are depicted in Fig. 4. The idea is straightforward. A sentence is firstly processed by an NLP module, working as explained above. The module is available as a REST service, since loading the models is a long task and – in such a way – it is performed only at service startup. The resulting embeddings are passed to the classification module, which in turn uses the Java/R Interface (JRI) [26] to actually proceed with the classification. Finally, the classification result is returned as the pass/fail grading.

4 Conclusions and Future Work

For the automated grading of solution to assignments containing R code and comments written in natural language, the paper discussed on a supervised classifier fed with embeddings and features that resulted in high accuracy, F1 score and good agreement between the reference and predicted fail/pass outcomes. The results also showed that the added value given by the features is quite limited and on the other hand requires a tuning with a larger value of C and a smaller value of γ.

The surprisingly good results may be partially due to the following reason. During the course, the professor explained to students how to understand the result of a test in terms of a process that (i) starts by finding the p-value in the R command output, (ii) then assessing whether the p-value is below or over the threshold of 0.05, (iii) if this imply that the null hypothesis has to be rejected or not, and (iv) finally give the interpretation in terms of statistical and/or clinical meaning. Also the gold standard sentences are written in terms of such a "template". Accordingly, it is reasonable to expect that also the comments given by the students will follow a similar structure, and therefore be "easy" to be classified correctly.

In terms of future work, the necessary steps are manifold:

- to measure the overall accuracy of the tool to assign the final grades (with respect to the manual grades given by the professor), i.e., how and to which extent the results reported in Subsect. 3.1 are improved;
- in terms of both formative and summative assessment:
  - from a teacher perspective, to measure whether the tool enables faster manual correction and prevents correction mistakes;
  - from a student perspective, to measure if the feedback received by the tool results in improved didactic outcomes.
- to experiment with different types of sentence embeddings, e.g., by comparing our features with ELMo-based representations [22], BERT [10] and Google Universal Sentence Encoder [8];
- given that embeddings alone proved effective in identifying pass and fail answers, it could be interesting to use them in combination with a neural network classifier. To this purpose, however, more training data should be retrieved from past years exams.

As a final consideration, we would point out that such a kind of assignment (i.e., statistical analyses in R and comments regarding the results) should not be considered as limited to the Health Informatics subject, but it can be suitable in all those disciplines in which a practical knowledge on how to perform statistical analyses is mandatory. Consequently, this research and the achieved results could be helpful also in different scientific areas belonging to the more general data science domain.

Additional Material: The initial sentence pairs, the embeddings (also lemmatized and with features), and the R script for the tuned classifier are available at URL https://vittorini.univaq.it/uts/.

References

1. Angelone, A.M., Menini, S., Tonelli, S., Vittorini, P.: Dataset: short sentences on R analyses in a health informatics subject, June 2019. https://doi.org/10.5281/ZENODO.3257363
2. Angelone, A.M., Vittorini, P.: The automated grading of R code snippets: preliminary results in a course of health informatics. In: Gennari, R., et al. (eds.) MIS4TEL 2019. AISC, vol. 1007, pp. 19–27. Springer, Cham (2020). https://doi.org/10.1007/978-3-030-23990-9_3
3. Aprosio, A.P., Moretti, G.: Tint 2.0: an all-inclusive suite for NLP in Italian. In: Proceedings of the Fifth Italian Conference on Computational Linguistics (CLiC-it 2018), Torino, Italy, 10–12 December 2018 (2018). http://ceur-ws.org/Vol-2253/paper58.pdf
4. Bernardi, A., et al.: On the design and development of an assessment system with adaptive capabilities. In: Di Mascio, T., et al. (eds.) MIS4TEL 2018. AISC, vol. 804, pp. 190–199. Springer, Cham (2019). https://doi.org/10.1007/978-3-319-98872-6_23
5. Bojanowski, P., Grave, E., Joulin, A., Mikolov, T.: Enriching word vectors with subword information. Trans. Assoc. Comput. Linguist. **5**, 135–146 (2017). https://doi.org/10.1162/tacl_a_00051, https://www.aclweb.org/anthology/Q17-1010
6. Bowman, S.R., Angeli, G., Potts, C., Manning, C.D.: A large annotated corpus for learning natural language inference. In: Proceedings of the 2015 Conference on Empirical Methods in Natural Language Processing, pp. 632–642. Association for Computational Linguistics, Lisbon, September 2015. https://doi.org/10.18653/v1/D15-1075, https://www.aclweb.org/anthology/D15-1075
7. Burrows, S., Gurevych, I., Stein, B.: The eras and trends of automatic short answer grading. Int. J. Artif. Intell. Educ. **25**(1), 60–117 (2015)
8. Cer, D., et al.: Universal sentence encoder. In: Submission to: EMNLP Demonstration, Brussels, Belgium (2018). https://arxiv.org/abs/1803.11175
9. Cicchetti, D.V.: Guidelines, criteria, and rules of thumb for evaluating normed and standardized assessment instruments in psychology. Psychol. Assess. **6**(4), 284–290 (1994)
10. Devlin, J., Chang, M.W., Lee, K., Toutanova, K.: BERT: pre-training of deep bidirectional transformers for language understanding. In: Proceedings of the 2019 Conference of the North American Chapter of the Association for Computational Linguistics: Human Language Technologies, Volume 1 (Long and Short Papers), pp. 4171–4186. Association for Computational Linguistics, Minneapolis, June 2019. https://www.aclweb.org/anthology/N19-1423

11. Gomaa, W.H., Fahmy, A.A.: A survey of text similarity approaches. Int. J. Comput. Appl. **68**(13), 13–18 (2013). https://doi.org/10.5120/11638-7118
12. Harlen, W., James, M.: Assessment and learning: differences and relationships between formative and summative assessment. Assess. Educ.: Principles Policy Pract. **4**(3), 365–379 (1997). https://doi.org/10.1080/0969594970040304
13. Hsu, C.W., Chang, C.C., Lin, C.J.: A practical guide to support vector classification. Technical report, National Taiwan University (2016)
14. Kiros, J., Chan, W.: InferLite: simple universal sentence representations from natural language inference data. In: Proceedings of the 2018 Conference on Empirical Methods in Natural Language Processing, Brussels, Belgium, 31 October–4 November 2018, pp. 4868–4874 (2018). https://aclanthology.info/papers/D18-1524/d18-1524
15. Kuhn, M.: Building predictive models in R using the caret package. J. Stat. Softw. **28**(5), 1–26 (2008). https://doi.org/10.18637/jss.v028.i05
16. Kusner, M., Sun, Y., Kolkin, N., Weinberger, K.: From word embeddings to document distances. In: International Conference on Machine Learning, pp. 957–966 (2015)
17. Levenshtein, V.I.: Binary codes capable of correcting deletions, insertions and reversals. In: Soviet Physics Doklady, vol. 10, p. 707 (1966)
18. Meyer, D., Dimitriadou, E., Hornik, K., Weingessel, A., Leisch, F.: e1071: Misc Functions of the Department of Statistics, Probability Theory Group (Formerly: E1071), TU Wien (2019). https://CRAN.R-project.org/package=e1071. Accessed July 2019
19. Mikolov, T., Chen, K., Corrado, G., Dean, J.: Efficient estimation of word representations in vector space (2013)
20. Mohler, M., Bunescu, R., Mihalcea, R.: Learning to grade short answer questions using semantic similarity measures and dependency graph alignments. In: Proceedings of the 49th Annual Meeting of the Association for Computational Linguistics: Human Language Technologies - Volume 1, HLT 2011, pp. 752–762. Association for Computational Linguistics, Stroudsburg (2011). http://dl.acm.org/citation.cfm?id=2002472.2002568
21. Pennington, J., Socher, R., Manning, C.D.: GloVe: global vectors for word representation. In: Proceedings of EMNLP (2014)
22. Peters, M.E., et al.: Deep contextualized word representations. In: Walker, M.A., Ji, H., Stent, A. (eds.) NAACL-HLT, pp. 2227–2237. Association for Computational Linguistics (2018). http://dblp.uni-trier.de/db/conf/naacl/naacl2018-1.html#PetersNIGCLZ18
23. R Core Team: R: A Language and Environment for Statistical Computing (2018). https://www.R-project.org/
24. Scholkopf, B., Smola, A.J.: Learning with Kernels: Support Vector Machines, Regularization, Optimization, and Beyond. MIT Press, Cambridge (2001)
25. Souza, D.M., Felizardo, K.R., Barbosa, E.F.: A systematic literature review of assessment tools for programming assignments. In: 2016 IEEE 29th International Conference on Software Engineering Education and Training (CSEET), pp. 147–156. IEEE, April 2016. https://doi.org/10.1109/CSEET.2016.48
26. Urbanek, S.: rJava: Low-Level R to Java Interface, R package version 0.9-11 (2019). https://CRAN.R-project.org/package=rJava. Accessed July 2019

E-learning Platforms and Tools

Audience Response Systems Reimagined

Sebastian Mader(✉) and François Bry

Institute of Informatics, Ludwig Maximilian University of Munich, Munich, Germany
sebastian.mader@ifi.lmu.de

Abstract. Audience response systems (ARS) allow lecturers to run quizzes in large classes by handing to technology the time-consuming tasks of collecting and aggregating students' answers. ARSs provide immediate feedback to lecturers and students alike. The first commercial ARSs emerged in the 1990s in form of clickers, i.e., transmitters equipped with a number of buttons, which impose restrictions on possible questions – most often, only multiple choice and numerical answers are possible.

Starting from the early 2010s, the ubiquity of smartphones, laptops, and tablet computers paved the way for web-based ARSs which, while running on technology that provides more means for input and a graphical display, still have much in common with their precursors: Even though more types of questions besides multiple choice are supported, the full capability of web-based technology is still not fully exploited. Furthermore, they also do not adapt to a student's needs and knowledge, and often restrict quizzes to two phases: Answering a question and viewing the results.

This article first examines the current state of web-based ARSs: Question types found in current ARSs are identified and their support in a variety of ARSs is examined. Afterwards, three axes on which ARSs should advance in the future are introduced: Means of input, adaption to students, and support for multiple phases. Each axis is illustrated with concrete examples of quizzes.

Keywords: Audience response systems · Adaptive learning environments · Large classes

1 Introduction

Audience response systems (ARS) allow lecturers to run quizzes even in large classes by handing the time-consuming tasks of collecting and aggregating students' answers to technology. ARSs provide immediate feedback to lecturers and students alike. The first commercial ARSs emerged in the 1990s in form of clickers [15], i.e., transmitters equipped with a number of buttons, which impose restrictions on possible questions – most often, only multiple choice and numerical answers are possible [17,25].

Starting from the early 2010s, the ubiquity of smartphones, laptops, and tablet computers paved the way for web-based ARSs which – while running on

M. A. Herzog et al. (Eds.): ICWL 2019, LNCS 11841, pp. 203–216, 2019.
https://doi.org/10.1007/978-3-030-35758-0_19

technology that provides more means for input and a graphical display – still have much in common with their precursors: While question types besides multiple choice are supported, those are still not exploiting what is possible with today's web technology [3,7]. Furthermore, they also do not adapt to a student's needs and knowledge, and often restrict quizzes to two phases: Answering a question and viewing the results.

Giving answers that go beyond selecting one or more options from a list of options requires more involvement from students and allows to move from checking students' fact knowledge to checking their application skills. Recall that it is a debated issue whether the latter is possible at all with multiple choice questions [10,28,31]. Cooper et al. found that students require different skills for selecting a correct chemical structure from a list of structures (i.e., multiple choice) and for creating a correct structure [5]. Furthermore, Jensen et al. showed that students who have been tested with higher-level thinking tasks throughout a term have significantly better examination results [18].

Large class lectures are the predominant form of teaching in higher education and the larger an audience becomes, the more heterogeneous an audience's abilities become. With multiple choice or similar questions, each student is able to submit an answer – even if it might be wrong. The more complex quizzes become, the more work and knowledge are required for submitting an answer, what could lead to low-ability students being unable to give an answer which subsequently could result in their demotivation and drop-out. Therefore, an ARS should adapt to each student, in the best case providing each student with a variation of the same task at a different level of difficulty that they are able to solve, so that the majority of students are empowered to achieve their best.

With web technology, the students' responses and a quizzes' results are available for further use, which allows quizzes that span multiple phases and reuse results or submission from previous phases: Assigning each student another student's submission for peer review or letting students vote on their peers' submissions are new forms of classroom interactions that are enabled by quizzes spanning multiple phases. There are already teaching formats that consist of multiple phases, such as peer instruction [6] that could easily be implemented with ARSs that support multiple phases.

This article first gives an overview of current ARSs in form of a structured survey and then proposes three axes on which ARSs should advance in the future: Means of input, adaption to students, and support for multiple phases.

The rest of the paper is organized as follows: Sect. 2 discusses related work. Section 3 gives an overview of the current state of ARSs by means of a structured survey. In Sect. 4 three axes on which ARS should advance in the future that leverage the technology's affordances are introduced, and Sect. 5 concludes the article and proposes avenues for future research.

2 Related Work

This article is a contribution to audience response systems and relates to feedback, scaffolding, and adaptive learning environments.

2.1 Audience Response Systems

Audience response systems allow students to give their response to questions posed by a lecturer (a *quiz*) using clicker devices. Responses are then aggregated by software and shown to the lecture hall [4]. While, initially, clickers and software that aggregates the results were task-specific technology, nowadays most ARSs are web-based and run on students' and lecturers' personal devices [15]. ARSs allow students to give their answer anonymously and unseen by their peers, which diminishes two effects that can be seen with other quizzing methods, such as hand raising: Only high-achieving students provide answers [23,24] and unsure students tend to answer like the majority [26]. Both effects skew the results, preventing an accurate assessment of the classroom's understanding by lecturers. For lecturers, ARSs take over the time-consuming task of aggregating students' responses, which allows quizzes to be run in large lecture halls [4].

Kay and LeSage [20] identified in their literature review a number of areas in which classrooms benefit from the use of hardware-based clickers, among other a positive effect on attendance, participation, and engagement of students [20]. Attendance, participation, and engagement are classified in Hunsu et al.'s [15] meta-survey among others as *non-cognitive outcomes* of using ARSs. Their meta-survey showed that the use of ARSs has a significant positive effect on non-cognitive outcomes. On the other hand, their survey showed that the use of ARSs only has a small positive effect on cognitive outcomes such as knowledge transfer, but no effect on knowledge retention [15].

2.2 Pedagogical Foundations

In this section, the concepts feedback, scaffolding, and adaptive learning environments are introduced as they constitute the pedagogical foundation for the remainder of the article.

Feedback. Hattie and Timperley [11] divide feedback into the three dimensions feed *up*, feed *back*, and feed *forward*. Feed up is giving students a clear goal that they are working towards through performing a task, feed back provides "information relative to a task or performance goal" [11, p. 89], and feed forward provides information about where to go next after having attained a goal [11].

Each of the aforementioned three dimensions can be given on the four levels *task*, *process*, *self-regulation* and *self*. Feedback on the self-level only pertains the student and not the task. On the task level, feedback is given about "how well a task is being accomplished or performed" [11, p. 91]. On the process level feedback provides information about the underlying processes, e.g., learning how to solve similar exercises. Feedback on the self-regulation level aims to teach students to self-regulate their learning, e.g., making them capable of reflecting on their own learning and assessing their own work [11].

Kulik and Kulik [21] examined in their meta-study the differences between immediate and delayed feedback in two scenarios: In *applied studies*, i.e., in real classrooms, immediate feedback has been shown to be superior to delayed feedback, whereas in *experiments*, i.e., under simulated conditions, delayed feedback has been shown to be superior to immediate feedback [21].

Scaffolding. Wood et al. [32] define scaffolding as a "process that enables a child or novice to solve a problem (...) which would be beyond his unassisted efforts" [32, p. 90] with the goal of developing "task competence (...) at a pace that would far outstrip his unassisted efforts" [32, p. 90]. While Wood et al. examine a scaffolding process tailored to children, the different phases can easily be adapted to other education scenarios. Among the elements of their scaffolding process are "reduction in degrees of freedom", "direction maintenance", and "frustration control" [32, p. 98]. Reduction in degrees of freedom simplifies the task by reducing the required actions or the number of actions required for task completion [32], which makes it similar to Grüner's idea of *didactic reduction*, which refers to removing certain aspects from a task, leaving only the most important aspects, while later on reintroducing removed aspects step by step [9]. Direction maintenance refers to keeping students on track, i.e., intervening, if solutions are heading into wrong directions. Frustration control refers to a tutor's goal to prevent or minimize the frustration of students working on a task [32].

Scaffolding can be done by adapting the task itself as well, as suggested by Merriënboer et al. [30], who mention among various manners of scaffolding a task the option of providing *worked-out examples*, i.e., model solutions or *completion tasks*, i.e., providing tasks where a number of steps are already correctly completed.

The advent of online learning environments moved scaffolding from face-to-face scenarios to scenarios where lecturers and students are connected through software, or scaffolding provided by software with no intervention from lecturers at all [1,19].

Adaptive Learning Environments. Hwang [16] defines adaptive learning systems as systems that adapt "the learning interfaces or materials based on their [the students] needs" [16, p. 1] Hwang's framework for adaptive learning systems encompasses three criteria, the ability to detect learning status, "to adapt the user interface" and to "to offer instant and adaptive support to learners" [16, p. 6]. Therefore, adaptive learning systems are related but not limited to computer-provided scaffolding, which provides a student with immediate support when the system detects that the student is off-track or requires help, e.g., by adapting the user interface. When and how to adapt to a learner is most often determined by a user model [2].

3 State of Audience Response Systems

To assess the current state of web-based ARSs, a survey was conducted that identified systems and classified them according to their supported question types.

3.1 Method

Google Search with language set to English was queried with all possible combinations of the following two keyword sets:

- {Audience Response System, Classroom Response System, Personal Response System}
- {Laptop, Smartphone, Tablet, Personal Device, Bring Your Own Device, Web based}

The first 100 search results (including ads, as those are relevant for the state of ARSs as well) were extracted for each query. Using results from Google Search instead of using results from scientific databases was done so as to represent the current state of actively used ARS. From the collected links, duplicates were removed, and the remaining links were classified as follows:

1. *self-reference*: A website of an ARS or its developer.
2. *foreign reference(s)*: A website that mentions at least one ARS or a developer of an ARS.
3. *no references*: A website that has ARSs as content, but mentions no ARS or developers.
4. *article*: A link that points to a scientific article.
5. *unrelated*: A website that is not available or its content is unrelated to ARS.

From links classified as (1), (2), or (3) systems' names were taken and added to the list of ARSs to classify. In case of developers being mentioned, the developer's website was visited and systems developed by them were added to the list. Peer reviewed articles were read and systems and developers mentioned in those were treated the same way as links.

Each ARS' website was visited and using the information available on the website the question types supported by the ARS were determined. For identifying question types, only the way students enter their answers was regarded. That lead, e.g., to quizzes where students enter terms that are subsequently organized as a word cloud being classified as *open answer*. If a system only supported hardware clickers, was no longer available, was exclusively marketed for corporate use, or the website provided not enough information on the available question types, the corresponding ARS was not further examined. Starting from a list of two question types (choice and open answer), each time at least two ARSs supported a new question type that type was added as a question type. Classification was done by a single judge who in case of uncertainty discussed with a second person until a decision was reached. The classification yielded the following twelve question types:

- *Choice*: Users select one or more answers from a list of answers.
- *Open answer*: Users enter their own answer.
- *Region*: Users select a point or a region on an image as answer.
- *Sketch*: Users sketch their answer using a drawing tool running in the browser.

- *Fill-in-the-blank*: Users fill blanks in a text, either by entering terms or selecting those from an list of options.
- *Scale*: Users select their answers in a certain range of values using a slider element.
- *Order*: Users arrange a number of items in sequence.
- *Sort*: Users select from pre-defined classes for pre-defined items.
- *Graph*: Users give their answers as a graph created by graphing software running in the browser.
- *Text highlight*: Users select part of a text as their answer.
- *Match*: Users create pairs from an even number of items.

A number of question types were unique to certain systems and will be discussed in Results as well.

3.2 Results

A total of 2.417 links were collected using the process described above yielding a list of 126 ARSs, 81 of which were completely classified.

In Fig. 1, the percentage of systems implementing a certain question type can be seen: *Choice* is implemented by the majority of systems, with only two systems implementing nothing resembling that question type. *Choice* is followed by *open answer* which is still implemented by the majority of systems. Overall, 50.62% of the systems only implement *open answer*, *choice*, or a combination of both. When looking at the question types implemented in the minority of ARSs, *order* with about 26% of systems implementing that type is the only outlier amongst questions types that are generally implemented only by few systems.

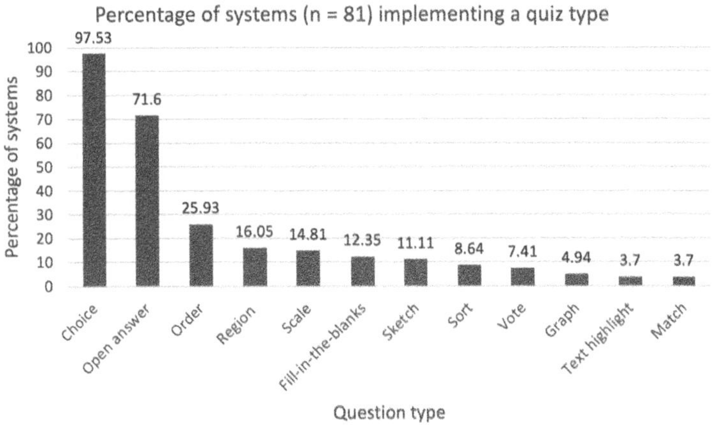

Fig. 1. Percentage of systems implementing a question type.

Figure 2 shows how many question types were implemented by the systems: The majority of systems implements two question types and among the 29 systems implementing two question types, 24 implement *choice* and *open answer*.

With a single exception, systems implementing only a single question type implement *choice*. Most systems implement no more than two question types, and only 7 systems implement six or more question types.

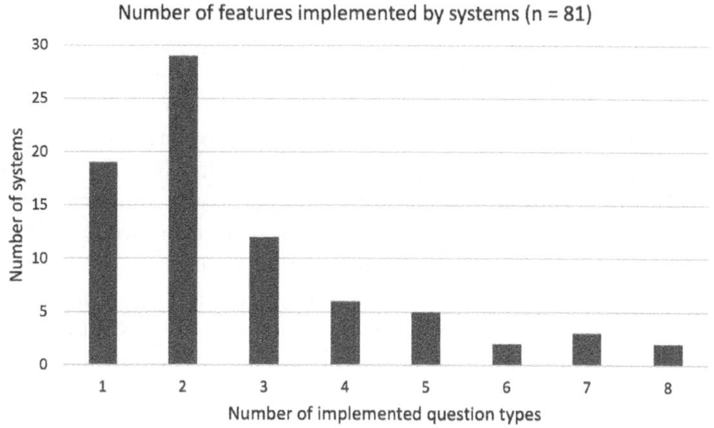

Fig. 2. Number of systems implementing a number of question types.

The following list contains question types that were unique to a single platform or question types that could not be classified using the proposed classification:

- Schön et al. [27] introduces a framework for ARSs which moves away from predefined question types and considers a question a combination of inputs and rules: Inputs from users (e.g., checking a checkbox or entering something into an input field) are automatically synchronized with all other users, and rules work with the values of those inputs, changing the quizzes' view [27]. Their model is much more flexible in regards to what is possible with current ARSs, but its inputs are still restricted to what is available in HTML: checkboxes, radio buttons, and input fields.
- Informa is a system that can be extended with additional editors for user input and offers (besides a few of the aforementioned question types) specialized editors for inputting an answer in form of flow graphs, UML diagrams, heap and stack diagrams, as well as regular expressions [12–14].
- Bryfczynski et al. [3] introduce uRespond, an ARS that supports quizzes which provide students with a specialized editor for creating chemical structures.
- A similar editor for chemical structures is provided by Top Hat, as well as two editors that allow to give answers in form of chemical and mathematical equations.
- In addition to to scale quizzes, Mentimeter offers a *2x2 Pairs* quiz where a number of items have to be placed into a coordinate system where each axis represents a dimension on which the item is to be rated.

- *Scrambled Answers* from Quizalize scrambles the letters of a word and users have to bring the letters back in the correct order.

3.3 Discussion

The fact that *choice* is implemented by the majority of systems and the fact that half of the systems implement only *choice* and *open answer* show that ARSs still have much in common in terms of possible input with their hardware precursors. While there are systems that exploit more of the possibilities offered by today's web technology, such systems are the minority. The results for the number of question types implemented by systems show a similar pattern: While there are few systems that implement three question types, only around 20% of the systems implement more than three question types.

There are limitations to this study: First, the classification of the ARSs was carried out by a single judge which could have influenced the results, and second, for identifying ARSs and question types only Google Search was used. Extending the search to scientific databases could yield concepts and question types that were not found using only Google Search.

4 Audience Response Systems Reimagined

Around half of the systems only provided support for the question types *choice* and *open answer* both of which have disadvantages:

- The ability of choice questions being able to foster higher order thinking abilities is still debated [10,28,31].
- As stated by Hauswirth and Adamoli [14], choice questions give students less room for errors and making errors is something students learn from.
- In open answer questions, students are more free to formulate their answers, but an automatic check for correctness is usually only possible for short answers – as soon as a potential answer spans a whole sentence or more, an automatic check might no longer be possible.

While many of the question types mentioned in Sect. 3 can somewhat be mapped to choice or open answer questions (e.g., enter the correct order/choose the correct order from a list of orders, ...), those mappings feel artificial, because they are the same question type in a different coat.

The easiest way to give students the means for inputting anything as their answers would be a blank canvas and a set of drawing tools as that approach is the digital approximation that is most similar to working on a sheet of paper. Yet, that approach has disadvantages: On the computational side, only a fraction of submissions and only specific types of exercises can be automatically checked for correctness, and, on the human side, not every student might be able to start solving exercises from a blank slate. Both disadvantages are not an issue in small classes, where a lecturer stands ready to help the struggling students and can correct a manageable size of submissions to assess a classes' progress. Yet, those two tasks become more difficult, the larger classes get.

To overcome those issues, the following section introduces three axes on which ARSs should advance in the future: In terms on input, through problem- or subject-specific editors, in terms of adaption to the student to empower every student to achieve their best, and through phases, making more complex classroom interactions possible.

4.1 Input

Problem- or subject-specific editors are applications that enable students to solve exercises of a specific type or of a specific subject, while supporting the students throughout the process, e.g., by feedback on their submissions' correctness or scaffolding. Using such editors as input means in an ARS allows students to work on problems that go beyond multiple choice.

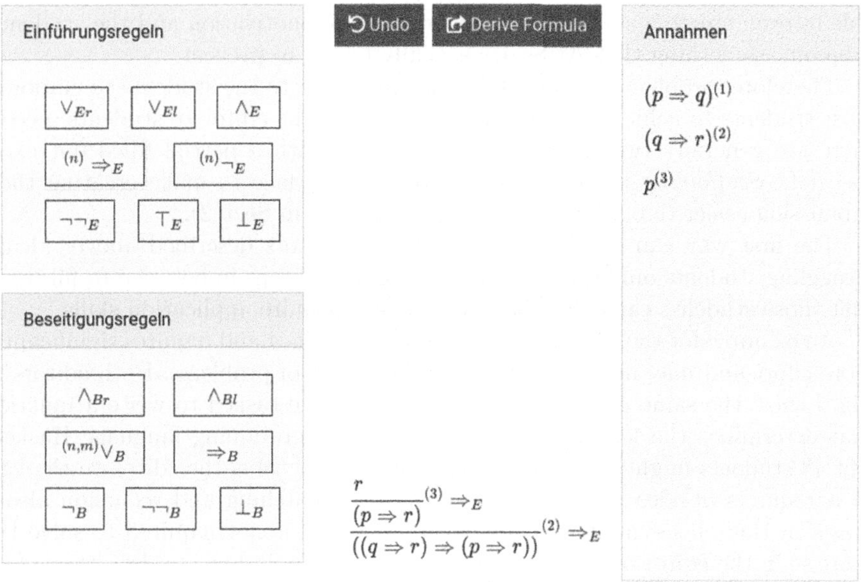

Fig. 3. An example for a problem-specific editor which allows students to create proofs using the proof technique Natural Deduction (taken from [29, p. 4]).

An example for a problem-specific editor can be seen in Fig. 3 which shows an editor for creating logical proofs using the proof technique Natural Deduction. Throughout the process of working on an exercise, students are provided with immediate feedback on a rule's applicability. Students are guided through the process of applying a rule by first having to select formula(s), a rule, and potentially assumptions, which acts as a form of scaffolding. The editor assumes responsibility of building a syntactically correct proof tree and management of assumptions, which allows students to focus on applying rules what provides them didactic reduction [29].

By now, web-based technologies can do nearly anything previously reserved to desktop applications which allows to create problem-specific editors that run in browsers. Among already existing editors are GeoGebra,[1] an editor for geometry, Top Hat's editor for mathematical formulas, various coding environments with unit tests, and editors for chemical structures, as found in uRespond [3] or Top Hat's ARS.

4.2 Adaptive Quizzes

Even if students are supported by problem-specific editors while creating their submissions to quizzes, they still might not be able to turn in a submission or even be able to make a first step as – when doing an exercise immediately after learning the associated concept – factors such as previous knowledge or short lapses in attention during the lecture come into effect much stronger. Not being able to even create a submission could result in demotivation and the student's drop out, something that ARSs are actually trying to prevent.

Therefore, problem-specific editors should adapt to the students to empower most students to achieve their best. For adapting the editor to students' needs, there are generally two ways: Provide students with a partial filled out exercise (c.f., *Scaffolding* in Sect. 2) or adapt the interface to make creating their submission easier (c.f., *Adaptive Learning Systems* in Sect. 2).

The first way can easily be done with the editors described above – leave struggling students only the last few steps or a few steps in between to fill in, so that those students can solve the quiz and still acquire application skills.

An example for the second way can be seen in Fig. 4 and requires significantly more effort and may not be applicable to all kinds of problems. Both editors in Fig. 4 show the same exercise in which students are tasked to write a function that determines the length of a list using the programming language Haskell. Not all students might be able to solve that exercise using the editor on the left, as it requires besides understanding of pattern matching and recursion also a grasp on Haskell's syntax, which is something that is not required to solve the exercise in the editor on the right side, as students only have to drag the puzzle pieces into the correct parts of the otherwise syntactically correct function.

Knowing when and how to adapt is most often done using a user model (c.f., *Adaptive Learning Systems* in Sect. 2), the discussion of which is out of the scope of this article. In case of an ARS, those models could be built from values such as the correctness of previous quizzes or time idle or without progress. It is imaginable to let users chose by themselves on which level of adaption they want to solve a certain exercise as well.

[1] https://www.geogebra.org/?lang=en.

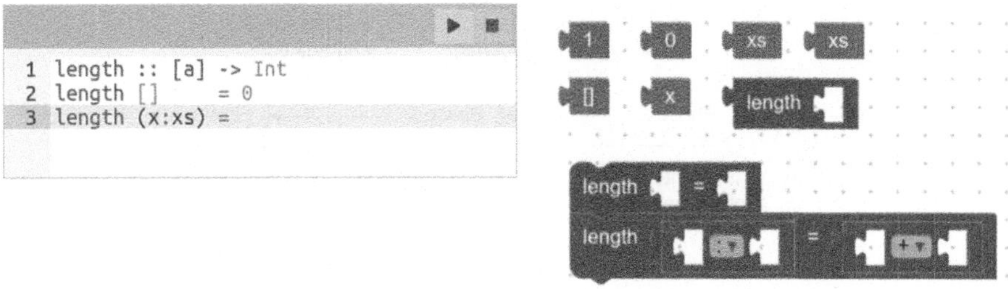

Fig. 4. The same exercise, two different students: Different representations of the same exercise can be shown to different students depending on their knowledge and skills.

4.3 Phases

In the majority of examined systems, quizzes consist of exactly two phases: A phase in which students prepare their submissions and a phase in which the results are shown. While not every quiz needs more than two phases, limiting quizzes to two phases excludes various classroom interactions.

Two features were identified during the study described in Sect. 3 that are similar to phases as envisioned in this article: There were systems where instructors prepared a number of quizzes which are posed the student in succession, each answer immediately followed by the next quiz. Schön et al. [27] propose a concept of phases in quizzes as well: In their implementation, a quiz consists of a number of smaller quizzes with a lecturer deciding when the next quiz in a series is starting. Lecturers are shown an overview of the correctness of all students' answers and can use that overview to identify struggling students or general knowledge gaps or misunderstandings of the class.

Both approaches have in common that they do not use the submissions created by the students for more than a correctness feedback. Having all the submissions available in a web-based system allows to use that data in consecutive phases, e.g., for peer review. The concept of phases introduced in this section allows phases to either be controlled by the student (see the aforementioned chain quizzes) or controlled by the lecturer (see Schön et al.'s concept), but uses submissions and results generated in previous phases for subsequent phases as well.

An example for a quiz consisting of two phases can be seen in Fig. 5: In a first phase, students prepare their submissions, each of which is assigned in a second phase to another student for peer review. A similar concept was explored by Hauswirth and Adamoli [14]: In their ARS, the peer review phase runs concurrently to the submission phase to give students who already completed a quiz something to do. Therefore, its somewhat controlled by students but not every student takes part in the peer review. The aforementioned three-phase quiz spanning a submission and a peer review phase was evaluated in a course on JavaScript programming, where students turned in larger pieces of code as their submissions which where subsequently reviewed by their peers [22].

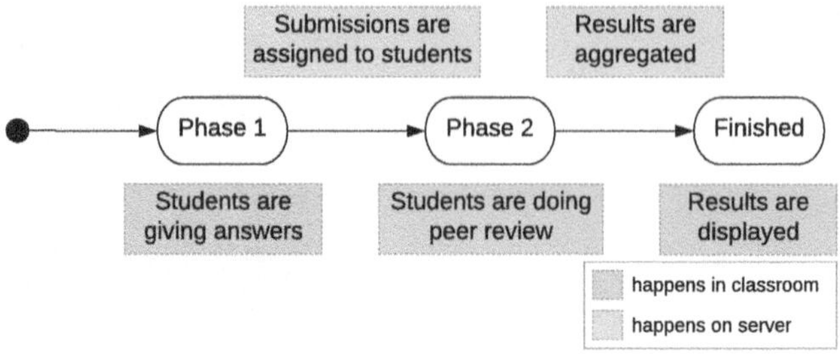

Fig. 5. An example for a quiz consisting of two phases where the submissions generated by students in the first phase are used for peer review in the second phase.

Another idea for a quiz spanning three phases was introduced by Gross in [8]: In a first phase, students turn in their submissions to a small coding task, which are up- or downvoted by their peers in a second phase. The rationale behind this quiz is to let students see and evaluate different approaches to the same problem.

An instruction format often used in conjunction with ARSs is peer instruction, a format after which students provide a first answer, which they then subsequently discuss with their peers, and finally provide a second answer [6]. Implementing peer instruction as a three-phase quiz allows to show comparisons between before-discussion and after-discussion results.

5 Conclusion and Perspectives

This article first provided a survey on the current state of ARSs which showed that, with exceptions, most ARSs are limited to few question types, even though today's web-based technology provides possibilities for creating richer interactions. This article then introduced three axes on which ARSs should advance in the future: Providing students more means for input, adapting to students' needs and knowledge, and lastly, providing quizzes that encompass multiple phases. Further research should focus on how to combine the three axes in ways that empower the majority of students to achieve their best. Most of the technology described in the article is implemented in the learning and teaching system Backstage,[2] using which many of the concepts and ideas introduced in the article currently are and will be further evaluated in the future.

Those three axes on which ARSs should advance in the future involve a significant amount of work: Creating a concept for and implementing problem- or subject-specific editors, user models, different visualizations of a same task, and multi-phase quizzes are time consuming tasks. Nonetheless, to still be able to teach appropriately in a time where ever-increasing numbers of students often leave the traditional lecture as the last resort, that work seems without any alternative.

[2] https://backstage2.pms.ifi.lmu.de:8080.

References

1. Azevedo, R., Hadwin, A.F.: Scaffolding self-regulated learning and metacognition-implications for the design of computer-based scaffolds. Instr. Sci. **33**(5), 367–379 (2005)
2. Brusilovsky, P., Millán, E.: User models for adaptive hypermedia and adaptive educational systems. In: Brusilovsky, P., Kobsa, A., Nejdl, W. (eds.) The Adaptive Web. LNCS, vol. 4321, pp. 3–53. Springer, Heidelberg (2007). https://doi.org/10.1007/978-3-540-72079-9_1
3. Bryfczynski, S.P., et al.: uRespond: iPad as interactive, personal response system. J. Chem. Educ. **91**(3), 357–363 (2014)
4. Caldwell, J.E.: Clickers in the large classroom: current research and best-practice tips. CBE-Life Sci. Educ. **6**(1), 9–20 (2007)
5. Cooper, M.M., Grove, N., Underwood, S.M., Klymkowsky, M.W.: Lost in Lewis structures: an investigation of student difficulties in developing representational competence. J. Chem. Educ. **87**(8), 869–874 (2010)
6. Crouch, C.H., Mazur, E.: Peer instruction: ten years of experience and results. Am. J. Phys. **69**(9), 970–977 (2001)
7. González-Tato, J., Llamas-Nistal, M., Caeiro-Rodríguez, M., Mikic-Fonte, F.A., et al.: Web-based audience response system using the educational platform called BeA. J. Res. Pract. Inf. Technol. **45**(3/4), 251 (2013)
8. Gross, M.: Collective peer evaluation of quiz answers in large classes through pairwise matching, Institute of Informatics, Ludwig Maximilian University of Munich. Bachelor thesis (2017)
9. Grüner, G.: Die didaktische Reduktion als Kernstück der Didaktik. Die Deutsche Schule **59**(7/8), 414–430 (1967)
10. Haladyna, T.M.: Writing Test Items to Evaluate Higher Order Thinking. ERIC, New York (1997)
11. Hattie, J., Timperley, H.: The power of feedback. Rev. Educ. Res. **77**(1), 81–112 (2007)
12. Hauswirth, M.: Informa: an extensible framework for group response systems. In: Bertino, E., Joshi, J.B.D. (eds.) CollaborateCom 2008. LNICST, vol. 10, pp. 271–286. Springer, Heidelberg (2009). https://doi.org/10.1007/978-3-642-03354-4_21
13. Hauswirth, M.: Models and clickers for teaching computer science. In: 7th Educators' Symposium@ MODELS (2011)
14. Hauswirth, M., Adamoli, A.: Teaching java programming with the informa clicker system. Sci. Comput. Program. **78**(5), 499–520 (2013)
15. Hunsu, N.J., Adesope, O., Bayly, D.J.: A meta-analysis of the effects of audience response systems (clicker-based technologies) on cognition and affect. Comput. Educ. **94**, 102–119 (2016)
16. Hwang, G.J.: Definition, framework and research issues of smart learning environment - a context-aware ubiquitous learning perspective. Smart Learn. Environ. **1**(1), 4 (2014)
17. Imazeki, J.: Bring-your-own-device: turning cell phones into forces for good. J. Econ. Educ. **45**(3), 240–250 (2014)
18. Jensen, J.L., McDaniel, M.A., Woodard, S.M., Kummer, T.A.: Teaching to the test or testing to teach: exams requiring higher order thinking skills encourage greater conceptual understanding. Educ. Psychol. Rev. **26**(2), 307–329 (2014)
19. Jumaat, N.F., Tasir, Z.: Instructional scaffolding in online learning environment: a meta-analysis. In: 2014 International Conference on Teaching and Learning in Computing and Engineering, pp. 74–77. IEEE (2014)

20. Kay, R.H., LeSage, A.: Examining the benefits and challenges of using audience response systems: a review of the literature. Comput. Educ. **53**(3), 819–827 (2009)
21. Kulik, J.A., Kulik, C.L.C.: Timing of feedback and verbal learning. Rev. Educ. Res. **58**(1), 79–97 (1988)
22. Mader, S., Bry, F.: Phased classroom instruction: a case study on teaching programming languages. In: Proceedings of the 11th International Conference on Computer Supported Education, CSEDU, vol. 1, pp. 241–251. SciTePress (2019)
23. Maheady, L., Mallette, B., Harper, G.F., Sacca, K.: Heads together: a peer-mediated option for improving the academic achievement of heterogeneous learning groups. Remedial Spec. Educ. **12**(2), 25–33 (1991)
24. Martyn, M.: Clickers in the classroom: an active learning approach. Educ. Q. **30**(2), 71 (2007)
25. McLoone, S., Brennan, C.: A smartphone-based student response system for obtaining high quality real-time feedback-evaluated in an engineering mathematics classroom: National university of ireland maynooth. Thinking Assessment in Science and Mathematics, p. 148 (2013)
26. Roselli, R.J., Brophy, S.P.: Experiences with formative assessment in engineering classrooms. J. Eng. Educ. **95**(4), 325–333 (2006)
27. Schön, D., Klinger, M., Kopf, S., Weigold, T., Effelsberg, W.: Customizable learning scenarios for students' mobile devices in large university lectures: a next generation audience response system. In: Zvacek, S., Restivo, M.T., Uhomoibhi, J., Helfert, M. (eds.) CSEDU 2015. CCIS, vol. 583, pp. 189–207. Springer, Cham (2016). https://doi.org/10.1007/978-3-319-29585-5_11
28. Stanger-Hall, K.F.: Multiple-choice exams: an obstacle for higher-level thinking in introductory science classes. CBE-Life Sci. Educ. **11**(3), 294–306 (2012)
29. Staudacher, K., Mader, S., Bry, F.: Automated scaffolding and feedback for proof construction: a case study. In: Proceedings of the 18th European Conference on e-Learning (ECEL 2019). ACPI (2019, to appear)
30. Van Merriënboer, J.J., Kirschner, P.A., Kester, L.: Taking the load off a learner's mind: instructional design for complex learning. Educ. Psychol. **38**(1), 5–13 (2003)
31. White, E.M.: Assessing higher-order thinking and communication skills in college graduates through writing. J. Gen. Educ. **42**(2), 105–122 (1993)
32. Wood, D., Bruner, J.S., Ross, G.: The role of tutoring in problem solving. J. Child Psychol. Psychiatry **17**(2), 89–100 (1976)

ULearn: Personalized Medical Learning on the Web for Patient Empowerment

Marco Alfano[1,5(✉)], Biagio Lenzitti[2], Davide Taibi[3(✉)], and Markus Helfert[4]

[1] Lero, Dublin City University, Dublin, Ireland
marco.alfano@lero.ie
[2] Dipartimento di Matematica e Informatica, Università di Palermo, Palermo, Italy
biagio.lenzitti@unipa.it
[3] Istituto per le Tecnologie Didattiche, Consiglio Nazionale delle Ricerche, Palermo, Italy
davide.taibi@itd.cnr.it
[4] Lero, Maynooth University, Maynooth, Co. Kildare, Ireland
markus.helfert@lero.ie
[5] Anghelos Centro Studi sulla Comunicazione, Palermo, Italy

Abstract. Health literacy constitutes an important step towards patient empowerment and the Web is presently the biggest repository of medical information and, thus, the biggest medical resource to be used in the learning process. However, at present, web medical information is mainly accessed through generic search engines that do not take into account the user specific needs and starting knowledge and so they are not able to support learning activities tailored to the specific user requirements. This work presents "ULearn" a meta engine that supports access, understanding and learning on the Web in the medical domain based on specific user requirements and knowledge levels towards what we call "balanced learning". Balanced learning allows users to perform learning activities based on specific user requirements (understanding, deepening, widening and exploring) towards his/her empowerment. We have designed and developed ULearn to suggest search keywords correlated to the different user requirements and we have carried out some preliminary experiments to evaluate the effectiveness of the provided information.

Keywords: Patient empowerment · Search as learning · e-health · Health literacy · Health seeking behavior

1 Introduction

"Engaging and empowering people & communities" constitutes the first of the five strategies of the "Framework on integrated people-centred health services" of the World Health Organization (WHO). It calls for a fundamental shift in the way health services are funded, managed and delivered and presents a compelling vision of a future in which all people have access to health services that are coordinated around their needs, respects their preferences, and are safe, effective, timely, affordable, and of acceptable quality [1].

M. A. Herzog et al. (Eds.): ICWL 2019, LNCS 11841, pp. 217–228, 2019.
https://doi.org/10.1007/978-3-030-35758-0_20

In this perspective, the way in which people access, understand and learn about health information plays a key role in enabling patient empowerment [2, 3].

When it comes to the access of online information, search engines are more and more used as a tool to support users in finding information in the non-homogeneous and continuously evolving World Wide Web. In particular, when users look for information on a new topic, related either to health or other subjects, generic search engines, such as Google™ or Bing™, are undoubtedly the most used tools as a starting point. However, the amount of information published on the Web has reached a huge dimension and the number of search results can be potentially enormous so leading users to spend a lot of time in searching what they are looking for, even with the risk of not finding the expected information. This is worsened by the fact that the majority of users take into account only the first results retrieved by the search engines (at most the first 20–30 results). Consequently, those results are crucial and play a key role in influencing users understanding in a specific domain, even though might not contain all the real "useful" information.

At the same time, the connection among search processes, learning and knowledge building is emphasized in several works in literature [4, 5]. This is bringing, as a natural consequence, to the development of a new research field which connects the educational sphere with information seeking. In particular, "search as learning" investigates the relationship between searching and learning where "the information seeking is conceptualized as a learning process, and learning as an outcome of the information seeking process" [6].

Generic search engines have not been designed to support learning processes, therefore it is necessary to develop more suitable tools that, on one hand offer the possibility to search for information on the whole Web, as the generic search engines do, and, on the other hand, are able to support learning activities based on effective searching processes [7, 8].

This paper, based on a previous work presented in [9], aims to evolve the idea of using a meta engine to create knowledge paths on the web. In particular, we present "ULearn", a new version of the meta engine that supports learners in achieving the objective of a "*balanced learning*" through personalized learning paths in the medical domain, based on specific user requirements. To this end, we consider four different learner categories: "basic", "deep", "wide" and "explorer", each of them with different objectives and needs. ULearn suggests words correlated to each of those learner categories thus supporting the creation of medical learning activities tailored to the real user needs.

The paper is organized as follows. Section 2 describes the basic principles upon which ULearn is based with particular respect to the "balanced learning" approach. Section 3 presents the software architecture of ULearn and Sect. 4 describes its implementation and preliminary experimental results. The final section presents some conclusions and ongoing work.

2 Balanced Learning Methodology

The research field of "search as learning", recently developed, highlights the connections between the information seeking and the learning processes [4, 5]. Users, generally, have different needs when performing a search especially for knowing and learning, and that is particularly emphasized when users want to shape their understanding on a new topic in the medical domain.

In what follows we distinguish "learning searchers" from "focused searchers": a "learning searcher" is not looking for a specific information but explores and navigates the web to increase his/her knowledge (e.g., a user who wants to learn more about *diabetes*), a "focused searcher", instead, is looking for a specific piece of information and uses a general-purpose search engine to find it (e.g., a hospital that deals with a specific disease). For what concerns the learning process for patient empowerment, the "learning searcher" is the category directly involved and it is the main target of this study.

With regards to the "learning searchers", we consider four main categories for four different learning needs. They have been identified starting from the categorizations presented in [9–11]:

- a "basic learner" who knows little about a medical topic and desires to learn the fundamental aspects of the topic, i.e., looks for medical information strictly correlated to the searched keyword(s);
- a "deep learner" who wants to learn more specific details on a medical topic he/she already knows, i.e., looks for medical information that provides the details of the searched keyword(s);
- a "wide learner" is not so interested in focusing on the details of a medical topic but rather prefers to expand his/her medical knowledge domain with topics that are partially related to the starting topic;
- an "explorer" who considers the initial keyword(s) just as a starting point and wants to expand his/her medical knowledge domain with topics that are loosely related to the initial keyword(s).

Each searcher category has different objectives influencing the learning process. However, since patient empowerment calls for autonomy from the user, it is he/she who will decide whether, when and how to cover the different learning aspects, in order to reach what we call a "balanced learning". Figure 1 presents the pyramid that leads to the "balanced learning" where the four sides of the pyramid (Fig. 1 only shows two sides of the pyramid for graphical simplicity) correspond to the four learning needs, related to basic, deepening, widening and exploring categories. Figure 1 also shows the knowledge already acquired on each specific dimension and, consequently, the learning gap to the pyramid top and, then, to the balanced learning.

Even though, a balanced learning, in terms of a learning process that evenly covers the four different categories, is desirable, it is the user who, ultimately, establishes his/her learning goals for achieving empowerment and what are the learning needs (if any) on each side of the pyramid to reach a "balanced learning". Thus, the top of the pyramid is not reached when specific knowledge levels are reached in each side of the pyramid but, rather, when the user has satisfied all his/her learning needs with the learning activities in the four categories.

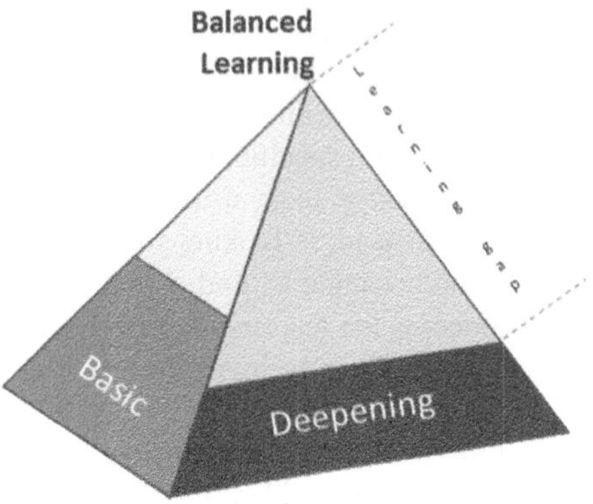

Fig. 1. Learning pyramid.

3 ULearn Meta Engine

ULearn is a meta engine that implements the "search as learning" methodology presented above. It allows a user to specify one or more keywords and provides words for each of the four categories presented above. Figure 2 shows its basic architecture.

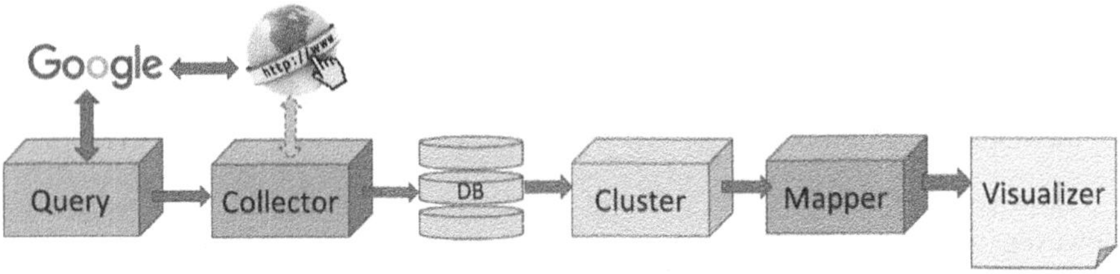

Fig. 2. ULearn architecture.

The "QUERY" module takes the keyword(s) specified by the user and the number n of documents (web pages) to be analyzed. It then uses Google™ to search the World Wide Web with this keyword(s) and takes the first n results creating a collection of n links to the related web pages.

For the found links, the "COLLECTOR" module retrieves the related web pages, cleans them (by removing tags and common words) and stores the remaining m words in the "DB" database together with the total number of pages that contain the word and the number of occurrences of a word in each web page divided by the total number of words in the page (term frequency - tf).

The "CLUSTER" module applies the K-means algorithm to a bidimensional matrix made up, for each word, by the normalized number of web pages containing the word (document frequency - df) and the normalized term frequency. The K-means algorithm creates four clusters, related to the four categories, starting from the outermost corners of the normalized matrix, i.e., C_0 (0,0), C_1 (1,0), C_2 (0,1) and C_3 (1,1).

The "MAPPER" module associates the clusters to the four learner categories, presented above, considering that each word has a specific correlation with the initial keyword(s) and will allow a specific type of navigation. Thus, the "understanding" words are likely to be conceptually close to the initial keyword(s). They will be used by a basic learner for an understanding and learning of the related knowledge domain (e.g., "insulin" and "type" for the *diabetes* keyword). The "deepening" words are terms that are likely to have a strong correlation to the initial keyword(s) (in terms of number of occurrences) but only appear in a few documents so they are likely to represent specific topics inside the semantic domain (e.g., "periodontal" and "diabetesvoice" - the latter is the online magazine of the International Diabetes Federation - for the *diabetes* keyword). The "widening" words are terms that are likely to have a loose correlation (in terms of number of occurrences) to the initial keyword(s) but appear in many documents so they are likely to represent topics at the border of the semantic domain (e.g., "obesity" and "exercise" for the *diabetes* keyword). Finally, the "exploring" words are terms that are likely to have a very loose correlation (both in terms of number of occurrences and pages) to the initial keyword(s) so they are likely to represent topics that allow the user to easily explore other semantic domains allowing him/her to increase the knowledge of those domains may be finding "something" even more interesting of the initial search thanks to a serendipitous discovery [12] (e.g., "hyperphagia" and "periodontist" for the *diabetes* keyword).

Thus, starting from the results of previous studies [9–11], we assume the following rules:

- a word that appears in many pages with many occurrences can be used for "understanding" and "basic learning";
- a word that appears in a few pages with many occurrences can be used for "deepening" the knowledge;
- a word that appears in many pages with a few occurrences can be used for "widening" the knowledge.
- a word that appears in a few pages with a few occurrences can be used for "exploring" the knowledge.

And, consequently, the following associations apply:

- the C_3 cluster is associated to the "understanding" category;
- the C_1 cluster is associated to the "deepening" category;
- the C_2 cluster is associated to the "widening" category;
- the C_0 cluster is associated to the "exploring" category.

The "VISUALIZER" module will present the user with a maximum number of m words for each category (where m has been presently set equal to five for the readability of the results but can be easily changed).

4 ULearn Implementation and Experimental Results

We have implemented the ULearn meta engine following the architecture presented in the previous section and using the PHP language and MySQL database. Figure 3 shows the input page that allows the user to specify the keyword(s) to be searched, the learning category (understanding, deepening, widening and exploring) and the number of pages to be analyzed.

We have run some experiments using six different medical keywords. Three terms are popular medical terms i.e., *Arthritis*, *Diabetes* and *Hepatitis*. The other three have been chosen among the most complex medical terms[1], i.e., *Aphthous Stomatitis*, *Bradykinesia* and *Epistaxis*.

For each term, we have used the QUERY module to take the first fifty Google results - going beyond the number of twenty-thirty results manually analysed by a user (as seen above) - and create a set of fifty links to web pages. Then, we used the COLLECTOR to retrieve the web pages, extract the words, make the computation presented in the previous section and store the results in the DB.

The next step was to run the K-means algorithm of the ANALYZER to each bidimensional matrix. Its application poses some limitations to be taken into account as described in [13]. They are the possible indeterminacy of the exact number of clusters, the potential different results in presence of outliers, the non-optimal results in presence of not well distributed data and, finally, the possible presence of empty clusters. Starting from the assumption that the aggregations sought were for the four different learning needs, the keywords of the research were excluded from the data in order to avoid outliers. Moreover, we chose, as initial centroids, the external points to ensure an initial clustering with at least one value per cluster and avoid empty clusters.

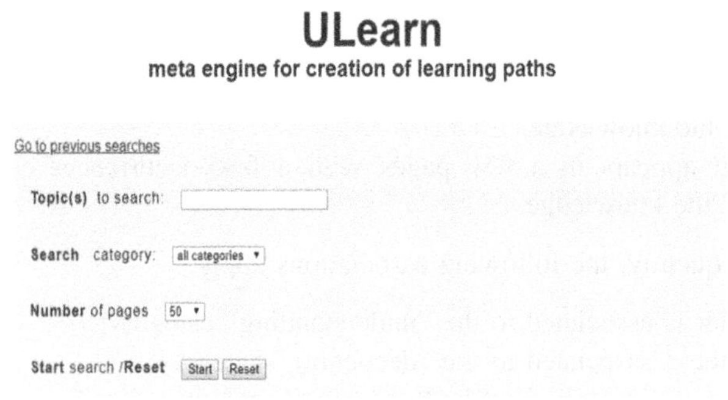

Fig. 3. ULearn input page.

Table 1 presents the results summary of the clustering algorithm for the six keywords. In particular, for each cluster it shows the X and Y coordinates of the centre and the number of word occurrences.

[1] https://www.prdaily.com/17-complicated-medical-terms-and-their-simpler-explanations/.

Table 1. Summary of results of the clustering algorithm.

Keyword	C_0	C_1	C_2	C_3
Arthritis	X = 0.042305 Y = 0.007535 No = 10803	X = 0.047727 Y = 0.444596 No = 13	X = 0.280934 Y = 0.00972 No = 593	X = 0.29404 Y = 0.012189 N0 = 344
Diabetes	X = 0.032328 Y = 0.015297 No = 13933	X = 0.025625 Y = 0.418576 No = 59	X = 0.405283 Y = 0.033976 No = 375	X = 0.786458 Y = 0.321185 No = 21
Hepatitis	X = 0.041577 Y = 0.011861 No = 11117	X = 0.031586 Y = 0.3524 No = 63	X = 0.364729 Y = 0.022705 No = 521	X = 0.725 Y = 0.145769 No = 60
Aphthous Stomatitis	X = 0.054744 Y = 0.011107 No = 8263	X = 0.029457 Y = 0.316276 No = 37	X = 0.382242 Y = 0.0127 No = 679	X = 0.674419 Y = 0.162734 No = 68
Bradykinesia	X = 0.047806 Y = 0.010522 No = 8927	X = 0.018803 Y = 0.483662 No = 10	X = 0.326734 Y = 0.011354 No = 548	X = 0.676374 Y = 0.033181 No = 60
Epistaxis	X = 0.044088 Y = 0.057612 No = 8176	X = 0.026454 Y = 0.350072 No = 461	X = 0.281967 Y = 0.047219 No = 722	X = 0.664286 Y = 0.063755 No = 92

The exam of Table 1 shows that the centres of the clusters are approximately on the same positions. The C_0 cluster presents a much higher number of words compared to C_2 (second cluster in terms of number of words) and C_1, C_3. The graphical representation of the four cluster for the *Diabetes* keyword is presented in Fig. 4. The blue dots (bottom-left) belong to C_o, the red dots (top-left) belong to C_1, the yellow dots (centre) belong to C_2 and the green dots (right) belong to C_3.

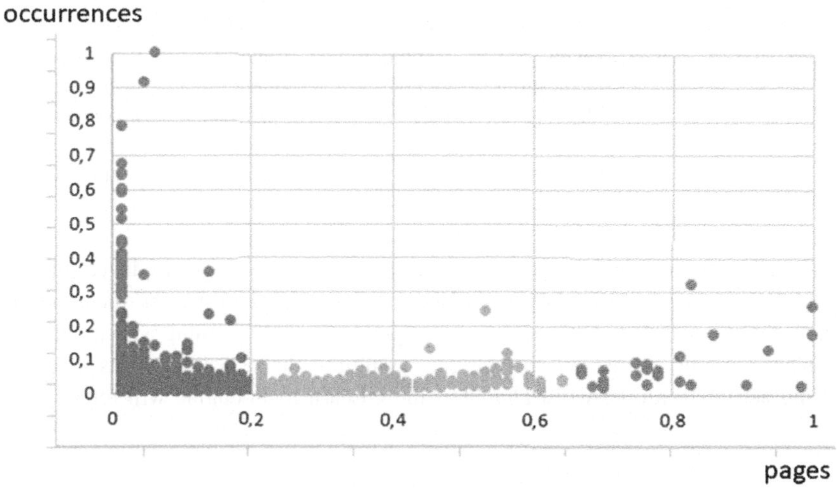

Fig. 4. The four clusters for the *Diabetes* keyword.

Considering the association between cluster and learner category presented in the previous section, Table 2 shows, for each keyword and for each category, the first five words of that category.

Table 2. ULearn results for the six medical keywords.

Keyword	Understanding	Deepening	Widening	Exploring
Arthritis	1. joint	1. lilia	1. original	1. express
	2. joints	2. proxima	2. foods	2. verywell
	3. osteoarthritis	3. ireland	3. kids	3. salute
	4. rheumatoid	4. organization	4. jia	4. assets
	5. disease	5. cleveland	5. acetaminophen	5. emmerdale
Diabetes	1. insulin	1. periodontal	1. obesity	1. hyperphagia
	2. type	2. diabetesvoice	2. exercise	2. periodontist
	3. health	3. melton	3. diabetic	3. symlinpen
	4. glucose	4. wdf	4. diet	4. flexpen
	5. disease	5. wbur	5. screening	5. summaries
Hepatitis	1. virus	1. ethanol	1. viruses	1. reg
	2. infection	2. nsw	2. hcv	2. hepatovirus
	3. viral	3. zealand	3. hav	3. nys
	4. chronic	4. parenthood	4. donor	4. fund
	5. disease	5. fibroscans	5. transplantation	5. credit
Aphthous Stomatitis	1. oral	1. wiley	1. pubmed	1. osteopathic
	2. ulcers	2. ibd	2. med	2. columns
	3. stomatitis	3. sage	3. edit	3. clinic
	4. recurrent	4. aocd	4. data	4. irbesartan
	5. ulceration	5. idcsu	5. rau	5. osmosis
Bradykinesia	1. disease	1. wiley	1. scholar	1. merriam
	2. parkinson	2. smiling	2. google	2. nursing
	3. movement	3. aps	3. training	3. appendicular
	4. patients	4. posed	4. cancer	4. xplore
	5. parkinsons	5. dictionary	5. subjects	5. univ
Epistaxis	1. health	1. institution	1. youtube	1. checker
	2. medications	2. faction	2. video	2. instagram
	3. bleeding	3. coli	3. financial	3. courses
	4. rarely	4. vulgaris	4. advice	4. committees
	5. nosebleed	5. escherichia	5. appointment	5. clogged

The ULearn meta engine supports search as learning processes by leveraging these results. Starting from an initial search keyword a learner can use the meta engine to obtain other keywords to be used in a subsequent search as learning activity according to his/her learning needs. As an example, assuming that a learner starts a search as learning activity with the word *Diabetes*, the ULearn meta-engine will return specific keywords to be used in further search activities depending on which categories (understanding, deepening, widening or exploring) the user is interested to expand for his/her empowerment. Therefore, for users who are interested in a basic understanding, ULearn suggests as related keywords: insulin, type, health, glucose, disease, that are popular terms connected to the Diabetes topic. For whom interested in widening the knowledge in the Diabetes topic ULearn will suggest to continue the online searching by using keywords such as: obesity, exercise, diabetic, diet, screening. In this perspective, the ULearn system will contribute to promote personal learning experiences based on search as learning processes (aimed at achieving learner empowerment) on the four faces of the pyramid towards the achievement of a "balanced learning".

The results presented above are quite satisfying mainly for the Understanding/Basic Learning category because they provide some basic keywords that allow a user to understand the meaning of the keyword and the related elements. The same applies to the Exploring category because the words are quite unrelated and allow an easy exploration of other subject domains. For what concerns the Deepening and Widening categories there is a mix of medical words that actually help in deepening and widening the medical knowledge domain and words that appear less correlated to the medical context.

As a further step, we have filtered the words, only taking the medical words, by means of the system presented in [2] for simplifying medical terminology and that uses the Unified Medical Language System (UMLS) metathesaurus that has been developed by the US National Library of Medicine and contains the most comprehensive collection of medical vocabulary [14]. By filtering the medical words, we noticed that "Understanding" and "Deepening" clusters got quite close as well as the "Widening" and "Exploring" clusters. This is also explained by the fact that the search now is more focused on the medical domain. As a consequence, we have grouped the four clusters to two clusters, namely the "Understanding/Deepening" cluster and the "Widening/Exploring" cluster. The first five medical words of these new clusters are reported in Table 3.

The results shown in Table 2 are used by the ULearn meta engine to support a learning process in the four categories and in other subject domains. The results shown in Table 3 allow ULearn to support a learning process in two different categories focusing more on the medical field. Although, more experiments are needed, we can preliminary assume to use the four categories for non-medical experts, who have broader needs in terms of learning, and the two categories for medical experts, who have more specific/narrow needs in terms of learning, as discussed in [3, 15]. In this case, we can assume that the balanced learning occurs when the experts mainly progress through the "deepening" and "widening" learning dimensions.

Table 3. ULearn medical results for the six medical keywords.

Keyword	Understanding/Deepening	Widening/Exploring
Arthritis	1. joint 2. disease 3. health 4. margin 5. research	1. screening 2. cells 3. national 4. kidney 5. training
Diabetes	1. type 2. health 3. disease 4. risk 5. medical	1. obesity 2. exercise 3. diabetic 4. diet 5. screening
Hepatitis	1. virus 2. disease 3. health 4. risk 5. acute	1. diseases 2. dna 3. rna 4. cells 5. infectious
Aphthous Stomatitis	1. ras 2. disease 3. mucosa 4. diseases 5. medical	1. cells 2. herpes 3. virus 4. professional 5. drug
Bradykinesia	1.disease 2.parkinson 3.medical 4.dopamine 5.health	1. cancer 2. resources 3. cells 4. data 5. gene
Epistaxis	1.health 2.support 3.medical 4.disorders 5.sinus	1. video 2. monitoring 3. community 4. oncology 5. willebrand

5 Conclusions and Future Work

This paper has presented ULearn, a new meta engine that allows a personalized medical learning process for patient empowerment based on specific user requirements. We have designed and implemented a prototype and carried out some preliminary experiments to cluster search keywords to be used for a search as learning activity.

The preliminary experimental results are satisfying but more experiments are needed to better identify the user needs and the starting knowledge level (e.g., medical expert or non-expert) so to provide the search keywords to the user and allow him/her to progress in his/her learning activity accordingly.

As a future work, we plan to use semantic analysis to overcome the limit of text elaboration (connected for instance to synonyms and acronyms) and leveraging new approaches based on interconnected knowledge graphs. Moreover, the keyword provided by ULearn can be connected to correlated web pages (or parts of them) in order to provide users not only with keywords but also with whole learning contents.

Finally, even though the k-means is one of the most popular clustering algorithms [16] used in the fields of information retrieval, computer vision and pattern recognition, other clustering techniques will be investigated to improve the results.

Acknowledgements. This work was partially supported by the European Union's Horizon 2020 research and innovation programme under the Marie Skłodowska-Curie grant agreement No 754489 and by Science Foundation Ireland grant 13/RC/2094 with a co-fund of the European Regional Development Fund through the Southern & Eastern Regional Operational Programme to Lero - the Irish Software Research Centre (www.lero.ie).

References

1. World Health Organization: Framework on integrated, people-centred health services: Report by the Secretariat. World Health Assembly, (A69/39), pp. 1–12 (2016)
2. Alfano, M., Lenzitti, B., Lo Bosco, G., Taibi, D.: Development and practical use of a medical vocabulary-thesaurus-dictionary for patient empowerment. In: Rachev, B., Smrikarov, A. (eds.) Proceedings of the ACM 19th International Conference on Computer Systems and Technologies (CompSysTech 2018), pp. 88–93. ACM, New York (2018). https://doi.org/10.1145/3274005.3274017
3. Alfano, M., Lenzitti, B., Taibi, D., Helfert, M.: Provision of tailored health information for patient empowerment: an initial study. In Proceedings of the ACM International Conference on Computer Systems and Technologies (CompSysTech 2019) (2019)
4. Eickhoff, C., Gwizdka, J., Hauff, C., et al.: Introduction to the special issue on search as learning. Inf. Retrieval J. **20**, 399–402 (2017). https://doi.org/10.1007/s10791-017-9315-9
5. Ghosh, S., Rath, M., Shah, C.: Searching as learning: exploring search behavior and learning outcomes in learning-related tasks. In: Proceedings of the 2018 Conference on Human Information Interaction & Retrieval (CHIIR 2018), pp. 22–31. ACM, New York (2018). https://doi.org/10.1145/3176349.3176386
6. Barker, J., Kupersmith, J.: Recommended search strategy: analyze your topic & search with peripheral vision (2009). http://www.lib.berkeley.edu/TeachingLib/Guides/Internet/Strategies.html
7. Taibi, D., Rogers, R., Marenzi, I., Nejdl, W., Ahmad, Q.A.I., Fulantelli, G.: Search as research practices on the web: the SaR-Web platform for cross-language engine results analysis. In: Proceedings of the 8th ACM Conference on Web Science (2016)
8. Fulantelli, G., Marenzi, I., Ahmad, Q.A.I., Taibi, D.: SaR-Web-A tool to support search as learning processes. In: SAL@ SIGIR (2016)
9. Alfano, M., Lenzitti, B.: U-search: a meta engine for creation of knowledge paths on the web. In: Proceedings of the ACM International Conference on Computer Systems and Technologies (CompSysTech 2010), pp. 442–447. ACM, New York (2010). https://doi.org/10.1145/1839379.1839457
10. Alfano, M., Lenzitti, B., Lo Bosco, G.: U-MedSearch: a meta search engine of medical content for different users and learning needs. In: Proceedings of the International Conference on e-Learning (e-Learning 2015) (2015)
11. Pang, P.C.I., Verspoor, K., Chang, S., Pearce, J.: Conceptualising health information seeking behaviours and exploratory search: result of a qualitative study. Health Technol. **5**(1), 45–55 (2015). https://doi.org/10.1007/s12553-015-0096-0

12. Campos, J., Dias de Figueiredo, A.: Searching the unsearchable: inducing serendipitous insights. In: Proceedings of the Fourth International Conference on Case-Based Reasoning, Vancouver, Canada (2001)
13. Shraddha, S., Naganna, S.: A review on K-means data clustering approach. Int. J. Inf. Comput. Technol. **4**(17), 1847–1860 (2014). ISSN 0974-2239
14. Bodenreider, O.: The unified medical language system (UMLS): integrating biomedical terminology. Nucleic Acids Res. **32**(Database issue), D267–D270 (2004). https://doi.org/10.1093/nar/gkh061
15. Alfano, M., Lenzitti, B., Taibi, D., Helfert, M.: Facilitating access to health web pages with different language complexity levels. In: Proceedings of the 5th International Conference on Information and Communication Technologies for Ageing Well and e-Health (ICT4AWE 2019), Heraklion-Crete, 2–4 May 2019, pp. 113–123 (2019)
16. Jain, A.K.: Data clustering: 50 years beyond K-means. Pattern Recognit. Lett. **31**(8), 651–666 (2010)

Visualizing Search History in Web Learning

Tetiana Tolmachova[1(✉)], Luyan Xu[2], Ivana Marenzi[1], and Ujwal Gadiraju[1]

[1] L3S Research Center, Leibniz University of Hannover, Hannover, Germany
{tolmachova,marenzi,gadiraju}@l3s.de
[2] Renmin University of China, Beijing, China
xuluyan@ruc.edu.cn

Abstract. Search history visualization provides a medium to organize and quickly re-find information in searching. Scientific studies show that a good visualization of a user search history should not only present the explicit activities represented by search queries and answers but also depict the latent information exploration process in the searcher's mind. In this paper, we propose the LogCanvasTag platform for search history visualization. In comparison to existing work, we focus more on helping searchers to re-construct the semantic relationship among their search activities. We segment a user's search history into different sessions and use a knowledge graph to represent the searching process in each of the sessions. The knowledge graph consists of all queries and important related concepts as well as their relationships and the topics extracted from the search results of each query. Especially to help searchers not get lost in complicated history graph, we provide a function wherein sub-graphs can be extracted for each topic from the session graph for deeper insights. We also provide a collaborative perspective to support a group of users in sharing search activities and experience. Our experimental results indicate that searching experience of both independent users and collaborative searching groups benefit from this search history visualization. We present novel insights into the factors of graph-based search history visualization that help in quick information re-finding.

Keywords: Search history visualization · Information re-finding · Collaborative search

1 Introduction

Searching to learn is increasingly viable as more primary materials go online. Learning searches involve multiple iterations of queries and return sets of objects that require cognitive processing and interpretation. During this process, searchers' interaction with search systems is generally recorded as search history logs. Studies found that as many of 40% of users' search queries are attempts to re-find previously encountered results [22]; a survey of experienced

M. A. Herzog et al. (Eds.): ICWL 2019, LNCS 11841, pp. 229–240, 2019.
https://doi.org/10.1007/978-3-030-35758-0_21

Web users showed that people would like to use search engines to re-find online information, but often have difficulty remembering the sequence of queries they had used when they originally discovered the content in question [1]. In this scenario, search history can be an important resource for both individuals and collaborative searching groups to preserve and recall their searching and learning process.

Search logs record explicit activities of searchers, including the submitted queries and the answers (search results) clicked. However, in reality, such explicit activities provide only partial information about an information exploration process; more intellectual activities are carried out in the searcher's mind. Studies have shown that a good visualization of a user search history should not only presents the explicit activities, represented by search queries and answers but also depict the latent relationships between them and the information exploration process in the searcher's mind [9]. Network structures (i.e. concept maps, knowledge graphs, and entity-relationship diagrams) are widely used in information visualization as a method to represent relationships between facets or concepts in a corpus [2]. Inspired by these previous work, some recent studies [8,11,24] visualize search history by applying knowledge graphs, depicting a searcher's query sequence and navigation path as well as the related concepts and their relationships extracted from the progress. However, one drawback to network structure is that when the network graph becomes huge and complicated, it is hard to get an overview of the related information graph and to navigate through the graph effectively: users are likely to get "lost" when the graph becomes complicated [10,17].

In this paper, we focus on the problem of "huge graphs" in search history visualization and present LogCanvasTag, a graph-based search history visualizing platform. Aligning with previous work [24], LogCanvasTag supports search session segmentation wherein users' search activities are segmented into sessions according to time interval; automatic search history graph construction wherein the knowledge graph is constructed based on queries and the concepts extracted from search result snippets, and quick information re-finding wherein searchers can re-find information of previous searches quickly. Especially for long search sessions and complicated session graphs that could be generated during sessions segmentation, we apply a Wikipedia-based categorization method that allows searchers to deconstruct the session graph into subgraphs of certain topics.

The visualization platform can be used in different platforms, and is currently integrated into Learnweb[1], an online environment that supports learning and sensemaking by allowing users to search and work on content retrieved from a variety of web sources.

This paper is organized as follows: in Sect. 2, we provide an overview of related literature about existing search history visualization platforms. We introduce the interface and workflow of LogCanvasTag in Sect. 3. In Sect. 4, we describe our research questions and experimental setup for platform evaluation. Results and analysis are presented in Sect. 5. We make a conclusion in Sect. 6.

[1] https://learnweb.l3s.uni-hannover.de/.

2 Related Literature

Existing works in the area of archived data visualization, information re-finding, and collaborative search are relevant to our work concerning the goals of preserving users' search data, facilitating and visualizing the history logs from different points of view.

One of the first works regarding developing an interface for collaborative learning was published in 1996 by Twidale and Nichols in their work "Interfaces to support collaboration in information retrieval" [23]. The key idea was to develop an interface, which allows to collect the user's queries and their results, and after that to visualize the search process.

A more recent solution is SearchX [18], which is based on Pineapple Search[2]. SearchX[3] is a search system, which includes a collaborative search interface. People can collaborate with each other in groups during the searching process by using different widgets, such as shared query history with the groupmates, bookmarks of useful information and sites which can be seen and used by other people in the group.

Systems such as popHistory [3] and Warcbase [12,13] save users' visit data, based on which they can extract and display the most visited websites to users. History Viewer [20] tracks processes of exploratory search and presents users with interaction data to enable them to revisit the steps that led to particular insights.

Information re-finding tools such as SearchBar [15] provide a hierarchical history of recent search topics, queries, results and users' notes to help users quickly re-find the information they have searched. The system Personal Web Library helps users to understand their Web browsing patterns, identify their topics of interest and retrieve previously visited Web pages more easily [5]. Some other tools, such as SIS (Stuff I've Seen) [6], collect users' personal data, such as email and docs, and offer a diary list to help users quickly locate past events or visited web-pages based on dates. Some recent work [4,19] has investigated how to combine context analysis and information re-finding frameworks to remind users about historical events according to users' current context.

In collaborative search systems such as Coagmento [21] and as well as Search-Together [16], visualization of search history usually involves multiple users' search logs, including their search queries, bookmarks. Interfaces of this kind display search histories separately according to data types or categories and support notepad functions which allow group members to share an experience.

By contrast to described above systems, LogCanvasTag provides a visualization of the search sessions as a knowledge graph as well as categorization of the search queries from the chosen session, that should help users easily to find and remember an information which they searched for.

---

[2] https://onlinelibrary.wiley.com/doi/full/10.1002/pra2.2016.14505301122.

[3] https://github.com/felipemoraes/searchx.

3 Our Platform

LogCanvasTag provides an interface for visualizing search history. Based on the previous LogCanvas search history interface [24], LogCanvasTag provides functions focusing on helping searchers quick refind information in long search sessions and complicated search history knowledge graphs. Figure 1 shows the overview of the interface, which includes:

(1) Search Session Quick Refinding (Fig. 1A)—session blocks can be filtered from search session list according to the queries entered in the filtering bar;
(2) Topic and Category Extraction (Fig. 1C)—queries and the related entities extracted from the search results are formed as a knowledge graph; meanwhile the most relevant categories (topics) are extracted from the search results with the help of TagTheWeb [14];
(3) Topical Concepts clustering (Fig. 1B)—topical subgraphs containing all the relevant queries and extracted entities are clustered (highlighted) according to the selected topics in 2);
(4) Search Result Acquisition (Fig. 1D)—the snippets of the top 10 search results are fetched from the archived search results.

After users carry out a search session, they can revisit the previous session using the LogCanvasTag interface. In section A they can select one search session and visualize the keywords they used to carry out the search. If the search session is very long, and the user wants to refer back to a specific keyword, s/he can type that keyword in the search field on top of section A. The system sends a request to the database and displays the filtered search results (e.g. only the search sessions including the specific query typed by the user).

When the user clicks on a search session in section A the system displays the graph of all search queries founded in the specific session in section B. On the right side of the window (Fig. 1D) a list of snippets is visualized which represents the first ten search results. The snippets give users a contextualization of the information.

If the session is very long, the graph will show a lot of nodes (search keywords) and will not be readable. In order to simplify the exploration of the graph, the user can highlight the nodes which are related to one or more categories by using a filter (Fig. 1C). To extract topics from entities we use TagTheWeb, a service developed to categorize entities or words with the use of Wikipedia categorization. We send each query from the search session as the parameter of an API endpoint of TagTheWeb, which returns the categories and probabilities that the queries belong to them. After that, we use the retrieved categories to filtering queries by categories (Fig. 1C). A user can select different categories by clicking on selection boxes close to each category in the categorization box. When they press the "Apply" button, nodes (queries), which mapped to this/these categories, are highlighted in the graph.

To get details about the search query from the visualization graph, the user clicks on the node and through the snippets viewer in section D s/he reviews

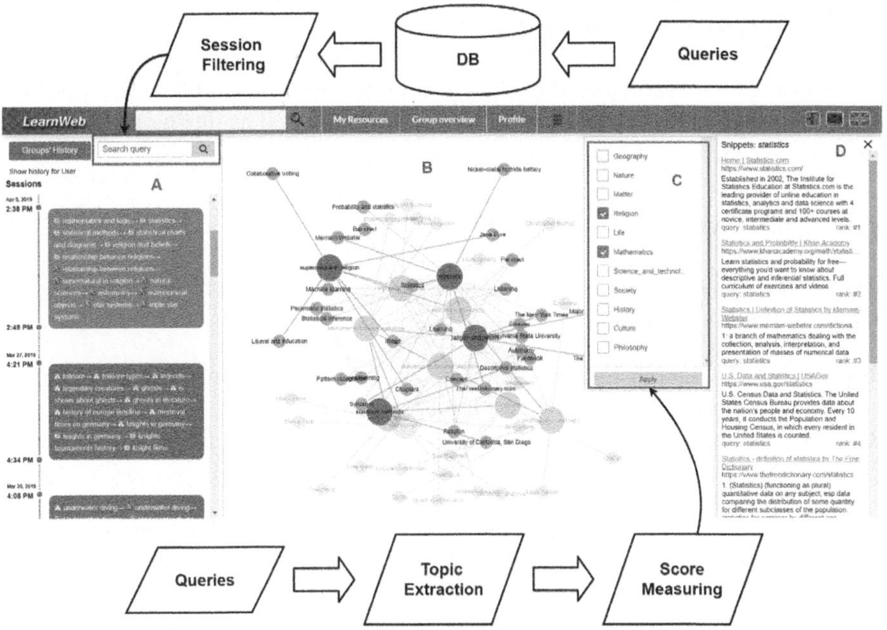

Fig. 1. LogCanvasTag interface

all filtered search result snippets that are related to the search query. To collect users' search histories, whenever a user submits a query to the platform (i.e., LearnWeb), we record the query, the search objective (text, image, video) and the search service provider (Bing, Flickr, YouTube, etc.) in the history log, and annotate them with a timestamp. These preprocessing steps are then performed offline once a certain amount of log has been accumulated - we run the edge score computation script at the end of each day.

Besides this, we added a search field in session block on top of section A, and a switcher between personal and Groups' search histories.

In general, in our dataset (Fig. 2) we have 19 top categories from Wikipedia, which are related to 659 resources. Each resource is a search query. Considering that one resource can have many categories, we found that, for example, the category "Society" consists of 652 resources. At the same time the category "Reference_works" can be found in 225 resources.

resource_id	category	precision
12,648	Science_and_technology	0.025210084033613
12,648	Society	0.10819327731092
66,168	Arts	0.025878003696858
66,168	Culture	0.13493530499076

Fig. 2. An example of the dataset

4 Experimental Design

In our work, we investigated the efficacy of LogCanvasTag and how this platform could help searchers in searching for information, as well as during the re-finding process.

4.1 Study Design

Making use of LogCanvasTag, we conducted a lab experiment investigating the following research questions:

RQ1: Does the search history visualization interface support users in remembering their search path and re-finding information?
RQ2: What impact can the new functionality have on the user learning performance?

As regards the first research question, we start from the assumption that using the Browser search history the user can easily remember what s/he searched for, but typical browser history only provide the time and the URL to the visited web page. We want to investigate whether a visual interface with link categorization can better support users remembering and re-finding information. Regarding the second question, the user, using the graph, can simplify the search for information. When the graph becomes too large though, it becomes complicated to find the required information and the learning process is affected.

To evaluate the new interface and answer the research questions, we designed a project-based study involving students from our University. The evaluation process was divided into two phases, each of them divided into two parts (pre-test and post-test), with one week break between them (Fig. 3). In order to understand how the LogCanvasTag interface can help users recover their search process, we asked students to perform a search using LogCanvasTag and, after one week, to use the interface to re-find specific information.

The first phase took place in the first week of the evaluation process and lasted 40 min. Each student received a handout with all relevant links, namely the Google Form to the pre-test, the URL to join the course in LearnWeb, a short description how to perform the search in LearnWeb and the link to the post-test. It should be noted that we set time limits for students to perform the various tasks.

In the first phase, that means during the first week of the evaluation process, we wanted to know how efficient can LearnWeb be in searching for information. The first task in this phase was a pre-test to measure the students' knowledge about a given topic. In order to motivate students to perform the task, we decided to ask 25 statements about five cities in the world (i.e. Beijing, Berlin, Brasilia, Brisbane and Cairo) which they could find interesting to learn more about, for example the statements were as "Oscar Niemeyer was best known for his design of civic buildings for Brasília" (Brasilia), "Beijing is the largest Chinese city by the urban population" (Beijing) and "The Berlin Wall fell in

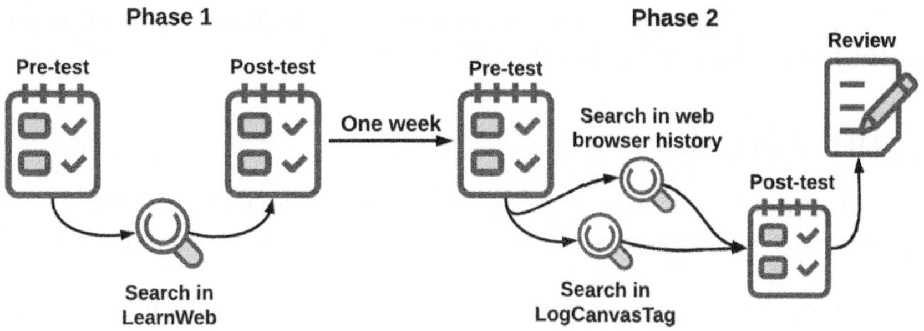

Fig. 3. Phases of the evaluation process

November 1990" (Berlin). 25 statements were divided into five sections, namely politics, art, transportation and sightseeing, religion and history. Students had to answer each statement by choosing between three options: "true", "false" or "I don't know". They had 10 min to complete the pre-test.

As a second step, students had to register to the LearnWeb platform and join a given group about a specific city. All students who joined the same LearnWeb group, could see the search history of other peers to whom the same city was assigned.

At this point, the most significant part of the task was to search for information using LearnWeb in order to proof the answers they gave to the statements in the pre-test, or to learn more and find out the correct answer. Students received a list of all statements in the printed handout in order to facilitate them during the search. The maximum duration of time, which students could spend on this part of the task was 20 min.

The last part of phase 1 was a post-test, in which students were asked to answer the same statements as in the pre-test, after the knowledge gained through the LearnWeb search.

The second phase of the evaluation process was carried out a week after. Here the first step of the evaluation was a pre-test with the same statements about the given city in order to understand how much information students remembered from the previous week. Time limits for passing the test remained the same.

After the pre-test, students were divided into two groups: the members of one group were asked to reconstruct their search history process using the Browser history, while the members of the second group could use the LogCanvasTag interface to revisit their search steps. The duration of this part of the task was ten minutes.

The last post-test was given to students to measure their knowledge at the end of the task. The ultimate goal was to compare the performance of the two groups and understand the usefulness of LogCanvasTag against the usual Browser history in reconstructing the search process and supporting students learning.

At the end of the study we collected students feedback about their experience using two different questionnaires which were assigned based on the two groups:

to give a review about LearnWeb (if students used the Browser search history), or about the LogCanvasTag interface.

4.2 Data Collection

In order to collect some experience of use of the developed search history interface and reviews of system usefulness, we decided to involve students in a lab experiment.

In the evaluation process participated 34 students, of which 22 were male and 12 female of an age between 19 and 27 years old; 22 were bachelor students, 11 master students and 1 PhD student.

Eleven students performed all the tasks, which include registration to the group regarding the given city, performing two tests (i.e. pre-test and post-test) and the given search task during the first phase, as well as two tests during the second phase with the reconstruction of the search process and a final test regarding usage LearnWeb or LogCanvasTag.

Besides the 11 users who performed all the tasks, three more users did not do one task and two users did not register to any group. In general, 23 users registered to the group of the given city, 30 users answered the pre-test questionnaire in the first phase, 21 users answered the post-test in the first phase, 20 users left answers on the pre-test in the second phase and 17 users on the last post-test.

5 Result and Analysis

5.1 Analysis of Users Data

We divided the analyses into several parts. First of all, during the various search sessions, the users performed 308 search queries using the LearnWeb platform, of which 32 about Bejing, 97 about Berlin, 120 about Brasilia, 19 about Brisbane and 40 about Cairo. Two users used the LearnWeb search also during the second evaluation phase while recovering their search from the first phase.

In general, the average time per one search session on the platform was 16 min long (M = 15.56, SD = 11.09), where for Bejing the average session was 10 min (M = 10.43, SD = 8.56), 19 min for Berlin (M = 19.25, SD = 12.79), 18 min for Brasilia (M = 18, SD = 14.27), 26 min for Brisbane (M = 26, SD = 11.31) and for 13 min for Cairo (M = 13.2, SD = 8.98). The shortest session took only one minute, while the longest one took 40 min.

For each user we can identify a specific search behaviour. While analysing the search, we found that users' queries could generally be divided into three types:

1. *Long search query* – when the user types in the search field the full statement from the given list, for example, "Egyptian Revolution against former president Hosni Mubarak was in 2010"

2. *Short search query* – when the search query consists of up to five words: "Brasilia tickets bus"
3. *Mixed* – a mixed type of search, when the user writes not only the long query but also short ones.

We established, that only two users used long search queries in the search sessions, while at the same time 12 users made short search queries and eight made a mixed variant.

5.2 Measuring Knowledge Status

The goal of this part of the analysis was to measure students' knowledge gain [7,25] by comparing the correctness of the answers per each phase and city. Based on the fact that not all users performed all the tasks, we selected only ten students, who did all of them. We removed the results from two cities (Cairo and Brisbane) because we did not have enough results to analyze the correctness of the answers. Among remaining students four were assigned to Berlin, four to Brasilia and two to Bejing.

In Table 1 we calculated the success rate by comparing the correct answers with the answers given by the users who used LearnWeb with the Browser search history in the second phase (ST in the table), and those who used LogCanvasTag (LC), with two methods: mean and standard deviation.

Table 1. The success rate of answering the questions in both phases (M, SD). M: mean of correct answers and answers by the users; SD: standard deviation; ST: standard user log system; LC: LogCanvasTag user log visualization; AVG: an average of M and SD accordingly

		Phase 1				Phase 2			
		Pre-test		Post-test		Pre-test		Post-test	
		M	SD	M	SD	M	SD	M	SD
Bejing	ST	0.52	0.51	0.44	0.5	0.52	0.51	0.44	0.5
	LC	0.48	0.51	0.68	0.48	0.84	0.37	0.88	0.33
	AVG	**0.5**	**0.51**	**0.56**	**0.49**	**0.68**	**0.44**	**0.66**	**0.415**
Berlin	ST	0.32	0.41	0.79	0.4	0.57	0.46	0.69	0.43
	LC	0.52	0.5	0.84	0.37	0.68	0.48	0.76	0.44
	AVG	**0.42**	**0.455**	**0.815**	**0.385**	**0.625**	**0.47**	**0.725**	**0.435**
Brasilia	ST	0.52	0.45	0.76	0.43	0.74	0.45	0.76	0.43
	LC	0.38	0.44	0.7	0.46	0.72	0.46	0.7	0.46
	AVG	**0.45**	**0.445**	**0.73**	**0.445**	**0.73**	**0.455**	**0.73**	**0.445**

As we can see from Table 1, the significant improvement of users answers can be found in the first phase, when before answering the post-test users used the

LearnWeb search to refind the statements; questionnaire results about Berlin and Brasilia are two times better than in the pre-test. For Bejing we don't have so good results: the average Mean from the first phase in the pre-test is 0.5 and in the post-test is only 0.56.

During the second phase, users who answered questions about Bejing using LogCanvasTag have more significant results compared to those who used the search history visualization from their browser history. Users who searched for Berlin have better results for both for ST and for LC. Despite these results, in users' answers from Brasilia questionnaire, the progress in post-test in the second phase for both ST and LC stays the same (an average of both Ms is 0.73 and of both SDs id 0.455). Such difference in the results could depend on the complexity of the questions and on the previous knowledge of each person who performed a specific search task.

6 Conclusion and Future Work

In this paper, we introduce LogCanvasTag, a graph-based search history visualization platform. Aligning with our previous work, LogCanvasTag provides graph-based search history visualization helping users re-construct the semantic relationship among their search activities. LogCanvasTag clusters a user's search history into different sessions according to the time interval. A knowledge graph is composed of the queries and the most important concepts or entities discovered by each search query, as well as their relationships. To help searchers not to get lost in a long search history session graph, we provide a search history filtering method to help searchers filter sessions containing certain queries from a long search history. To help searchers to realize the semantic relationships in complicated session graphs, we cluster queries and related entities in the graph as sub-graphs according to their extracted topics. We conducted a lab experiment to evaluate the new visual interface. Results show that the LogCanvasTag search history visualization could help searchers quickly re-find search results and efficiently increase their knowledge gain.

For the current study, we conducted a lab experiment with limited number of students, which means the results can not be fully representative for all the use-cases of LogCanvasTag. In the future, we will carry out a crowdsourcing experiment online exploring the usage of LogCanvasTag from different perspectives based on the current results and analysis.

References

1. Aula, A., Jhaveri, N., Käki, M.: Information search and re-access strategies of experienced web users. In: Proceedings of the 14th International Conference on World Wide Web, pp. 583–592. ACM (2005)
2. Cañas, A.J., et al.: A summary of literature pertaining to the use of concept mapping techniques and technologies for education and performance support. Report to the Chief of Naval Education and Training (2003)

3. Carrasco, M., Koh, E., Malik, S.: popHistory: animated visualization of personal web browsing history. In: Proceedings of the 2017 CHI Conference Extended Abstracts on Human Factors in Computing Systems, pp. 2429–2436. ACM (2017)
4. Deng, T., Zhao, L., Feng, L., Xue, W.: Information re-finding by context: a brain memory inspired approach. In: Proceedings of the 20th ACM International Conference on Information and Knowledge Management, pp. 1553–1558. ACM (2011)
5. Du, W., Qian, Z.C., Parsons, P., Chen, Y.V.: Personal web library: organizing and visualizing web browsing history. Int. J. Web Inf. Syst. **14**(2), 212–232 (2018)
6. Dumais, S., Cutrell, E., Cadiz, J.J., Jancke, G., Sarin, R., Robbins, D.C.: Stuff i've seen: a system for personal information retrieval and re-use. ACM SIGIR Forum **49**(2), 28–35 (2016)
7. Gadiraju, U., Yu, R., Dietze, S., Holtz, P.: Analyzing knowledge gain of users in informational search sessions on the web. In: Proceedings of the 2018 Conference on Human Information Interaction & Retrieval, pp. 2–11. ACM (2018)
8. Guo, H., Gomez, S.R., Ziemkiewicz, C., Laidlaw, D.H.: A case study using visualization interaction logs and insight metrics to understand how analysts arrive at insights. IEEE Trans. Vis. Comput. Graph. **22**(1), 51–60 (2015)
9. Hearst, M.: Search User Interfaces. Cambridge University Press, Cambridge (2009)
10. Komlodi, A., Marchionini, G., Soergel, D.: Search history support for finding and using information: User interface design recommendations from a user study. Inf. Process. Manag. **43**(1), 10–29 (2007)
11. Lee, J., Jeon, J., Lee, C., Lee, J., Cho, J., Lee, K.: A study on efficient log visualization using D3 component against apt: how to visualize security logs efficiently? In: 2016 International Conference on Platform Technology and Service (PlatCon), pp. 1–6. IEEE (2016)
12. Lin, J.: Scaling down distributed infrastructure on wimpy machines for personal web archiving. In: Proceedings of the 24th International Conference on World Wide Web, pp. 1351–1355. ACM (2015)
13. Lin, J., Gholami, M., Rao, J.: Infrastructure for supporting exploration and discovery in web archives. In: Proceedings of the 23rd International Conference on World Wide Web, pp. 851–856. ACM (2014)
14. Medeiros, J.F., Pereira Nunes, B., Siqueira, S.W.M., Portes Paes Leme, L.A.: TagTheWeb: using Wikipedia categories to automatically categorize resources on the web. In: Gangemi, A., et al. (eds.) ESWC 2018. LNCS, vol. 11155, pp. 153–157. Springer, Cham (2018). https://doi.org/10.1007/978-3-319-98192-5_29
15. Morris, D., Ringel Morris, M., Venolia, G.: SearchBar: a search-centric web history for task resumption and information re-finding. In: Proceedings of the SIGCHI Conference on Human Factors in Computing Systems, pp. 1207–1216. ACM (2008)
16. Morris, M.R., Horvitz, E.: SearchTogether: an interface for collaborative web search. In: Proceedings of the 20th Annual ACM Symposium on User Interface Software and Technology, pp. 3–12. ACM (2007)
17. Olston, C., Chi, E.H.: ScentTrails: integrating browsing and searching on the web. ACM Trans. Comput.-Hum. Interact. (TOCHI) **10**(3), 177–197 (2003)
18. Putra, S.R., Moraes, F., Hauff, C.: SearchX: empowering collaborative search research. In: SIGIR 2018, pp. 1265–1268 (2018)
19. Sappelli, M., Verberne, S., Kraaij, W.: Evaluation of context-aware recommendation systems for information re-finding. J. Assoc. Inf. Sci. Technol. **68**(4), 895–910 (2017)

20. Segura, V.C.V.B., Barbosa, S.D.J.: History viewer: displaying user interaction history in visual analytics applications. In: Kurosu, M. (ed.) HCI 2016. LNCS, vol. 9733, pp. 223–233. Springer, Cham (2016). https://doi.org/10.1007/978-3-319-39513-5_21
21. Shah, C., González-Ibáñez, R.: Exploring information seeking processes in collaborative search tasks. Proc. Am. Soc. Inf. Sci. Technol. **47**(1), 1–7 (2010)
22. Teevan, J., Adar, E., Jones, R., Potts, M.A.: Information re-retrieval: repeat queries in Yahoo's logs. In: Proceedings of the 30th Annual International ACM SIGIR Conference on Research and Development in Information Retrieval, pp. 151–158. ACM (2007)
23. Twidale, M., Nichols, D.: Interfaces to support collaboration in information retrieval. Inf. Retr. Hum. Comput. Interact. 25–28 (1996)
24. Xu, L., Fernando, Z.T., Zhou, X., Nejdl, W.: LogCanvas: visualizing search history using knowledge graphs. In: The 41st International ACM SIGIR Conference on Research & Development in Information Retrieval, pp. 1289–1292. ACM (2018)
25. Yu, R., Gadiraju, U., Holtz, P., Rokicki, M., Kemkes, P., Dietze, S.: Predicting user knowledge gain in informational search sessions. In: The 41st International ACM SIGIR Conference on Research & Development in Information Retrieval, pp. 75–84. ACM (2018)

Promoting Inclusion Using OER in Vocational Education and Training Programs

Silvia Baldiris[1,2], Laura Mancera[2(✉)], Levintón Licona[1], Cecilia Avila[3], Jorge Bacca[3], Yurgos Politis[4], Lizbeth Goodman[4], and Jutta Treviranus[5]

[1] Fundación Universitaria Tecnológico Comfenalco, Sede a Barrio España Cr 44 D N° 30A – 91, Cartagena, Colombia
sbaldiris@tecnologicocomfenalco.edu.co
[2] Universidad Internacional de la Rioja, Rectorado – Avda. de la Paz, 137, Logroño, Spain
{silvia.baldiris, laura.mancera}@unir.net
[3] Facultad de Matemáticas e Ingenierías, Fundación Universitaria Konrad Lorenz, Cra. 9 Bis # 62-43, Bogotá, Colombia
{cecilia.avilag, jorge.bacca}@konradlorenz.edu.co
[4] University College Dublin, Dublin, Belfield, Ireland
{gos.politis, lizbeth.goodman}@ucd.ie
[5] Inclusive Design Research Centre, OCAD University, Toronto, Canada
jtreviranus@ocadu.c

Abstract. Open Educational Resources (OER) have been declared by UNESCO as a promising tool to address inclusion in educational settings. However, recent studies support the need to pay more attention to the accessibility and inclusion capacity of OER. In this context, this paper provide evidence about the benefits of adopting Universal Design for Learning and the Web Content Accessibility Guidelines to support the OER creation considering the variability of students in Vocational Education and Training (VET) programs. For doing so, it was created some OER using CO-CREARIA model and it was validated on VET setting in Colombia. Results evidence that the OER created support the achievement of high level of motivation and academic performance.

Keywords: Inclusion · Co-creation · Accessibility · Open Educational Resource · Universal Design for Learning

1 Introduction

VET programs are considered a great instrument to achieve social inclusion because they provide people with specific conceptual and practical knowledge that facilitate employment. In this sense, since 1987 UNESCO promotes international congresses that aim to make these programs more attractive and pertinent for young people, including those with diverse educational needs. Within this general aim, the Shanghai Consensus [1] recommended: To promote a better understanding of the contribution of VET programs to the achievement of sustainable development; To define strategies for cooperation among countries in order to promote VET for all; and to favor access,

M. A. Herzog et al. (Eds.): ICWL 2019, LNCS 11841, pp. 241–249, 2019.
https://doi.org/10.1007/978-3-030-35758-0_22

inclusion, and equity in educational environments for sustainable development and a culture of peace.

In this context, this study aims to contribute to UNESCO's call for more inclusive VET programs [2], by providing a validation of CO-CREARIA, a model to build inclusive and accessible OER. As an important part of the model the Universal Design for Learning (UDL) framework and the Web Content Accessibility Guidelines (WCAG) are adopted.

The UDL framework is considered based on the successfully results at different levels of education to attend students' variability [3–5]. Capp [3] conducted a meta-analysis on the effectiveness of the UDL and found that "UDL is an effective teaching methodology for improving learning" (p. 1). The target groups in the meta-analysis were kindergarten children, students from primary and secondary education (with or without disabilities) and pre-service or In-service teachers. Al-Azawei, Serenelli, and Lundqvist [5] analysed the content of 12 papers and concluded "UDL is an efficient approach for designing flexible learning environments and accessible content" (p. 1). The samples identified in the studies were K − 12 students, university students, and teacher candidates. Rao, Ok, and Bryant conducted a literature review from which they concluded there is a lack of research about UDL effectiveness in VET programs settings [4].

The present study extends previous research on the field of UDL application to support the attention to students' variability in VET settings. Thus, the main contribution of this paper is to give insights about the benefits of using OER that adopts UDL for improving the learning experience of all students. In this way, the study also contributes to enrich the research on OER adoption for inclusion as was promoted by the UNESCO & Government of Slovenia [6].

The manuscript is organized as follows. In the Sect. 2 the creation of the OER using CO-CREARIA is presented. The third section describes the evaluation carried out in a vocational educational program in Colombia. The fourth section presents the results and discusses the meaning of such results. Finally, the fifth section outlines the conclusions and future work.

2 OER Implementation Using CO-CREARIA

CO-CREARIA is a collaborative creation model of OER that promotes the active participation of teachers and other actors involved in the teaching-learning process – including students – in identifying and addressing the educational learning needs and preferences that must to be met through the co-created resources. The model adopts openness as a value and an opportunity to promote educational inclusion. Technology is used as a tool in a way that helps the educational process and aids all students in achieving their educational goals. The model and its phases are clearly detailed in [7]. Next paragraphs explain the process follow to create the OER "Implementing a Network Structure" using CO-CREARIA.

During the Analysis phase the instructors characterized the OER, identified the competences to develop during the course and done a whole profile of the course under the base of UDL (neuronal networks analysis).

This being so, for "Implementing a Network Structure" OER the instructor defined four learning units. Unit 1 introduces an overall description of the learning goals, expected results, skills, and activities and their corresponding evaluation. And the other three learning units were created in order to support students' acquisition of specific competences associated to the course: (1) Numerical systems, (2) Network models, and (3) Optical media communication. On the other hand, with respect to the course profile, the instructor managed to build the profile shown in Table 1.

Table 1. Profile of the course.

Recognition networks resume		
Strengths	Weaknesses	Preferences
Experts in oral presentations Good vocabulary	Blindness, Low vision, Dyslexia, Difficulties to recognize words Reading and comprehension difficulties, Hypermetropia, Low audition	Preference for drawing Work with graphics
Strategic network resume		
Experts in computer-based graphic design Experts in handmade graphics Experts in building things (build, assembly, repair, design) Experts in analysing and solving problems	Fine mobility problems Some students do not like oral presentations. Problems in self-regulated learning Problems to sustain attention over time	Preference for music and composition Preference for autonomous tasks Preferences for activities where they can build things Preference for collaborative work
Affective network resume		
Good collaboration Enjoy learning Looking for deep learning experiences Looking for interesting challenges Leaders Good attitude to help others Confidence	Team work difficulties Low motivation to face learning problems, Frustration	Preference for music and composition Preference for artistic activities

Once the competences and course profile were defined, the instructor designed the course teaching. In this case, each learning unit consisted of learning content and activities that include teamwork, independent work, the use of ICT tools, and co-evaluation with the purpose of stimulating the collaborative learning. Moreover, at the end of each unit, the instructor proposed that students carry out interactive activities made with Hotpotatoes or Educaplay (externals authoring tools to Atutor) to reinforce the acquired knowledge and engage students.

During the Design phase, teachers together with UDL experts identified possible barriers that OER could present to the students and barriers of the traditional process carried out by the instructor in the past. These barriers must be addressed in order to promote a better learning process to all students. Subsequently, the teacher defined strategies to overcome those barriers; in this case it was considered alternatives to visual forms in presenting the content to students. It also provided different types of support, including translation of text to speech systems, speech and text recognition on the screen, and the use of tools to expand images for the students with visual impairment. For doing so, the teacher described each resource that was planned to be used in the OER development, considering the needs and preferences of each student. In the description of the materials, the teacher described the accessibility considerations that need to be addressed in each resource. Table 2 shows an example of a video resource description.

Table 2. Video resource description

Information	Description
Digital Resource Title	Video of Numbering Systems and Conversions
Type of material	Video
Description	Present a brief explanation of the characteristics of different numbering systems and talks about the process of converting from one system to another
Justification	This is a multimedia resource. Audio can be very useful for visually impaired people and video supports people with attention deficit disorder
Description of accessibility elements to consider:	Video must have subtitle and transcripts

The Development phase was carried out considering accessibility guidelines correspond with the basic of WCAG 2.0. The instructor, helped by the developer, considered the accessibility criteria in the development of the OER (Text alternatives for non-text content, appropriate headings structures, links descriptions, definition of abbreviations and acronyms, well-structured tables).

The teacher and two experts in web accessibility carried out the Evaluation phase considering two dimensions: Quality and Accessibility. The results of the evaluation are shown in Table 3.

The narrative presented evidence that the instructor carried out all the phases defined in the CO-CREARIA model, which allowed the instructor to develop an accessible and inclusive OER by considering the diverse needs of his student.

Table 3. Accessibility Evaluation results.

HTML element	Evaluation result	Teacher's solution
Headings	Correct order but there are some empty headings	There were empty headings because of blank spaces with heading format. Those empty headings were removed
Images	Long descriptions were missing in some images with complex contents	A file with the long description of each image was created in the ATutor platform. Then, the link to the long description was added to each image
Tables	All tables have a caption, summary, and the corresponding table headings	Solution wasn't needed
Links	All links have a descriptive title but some of them are broken links	Broken links were verified and fixed, and the link to the Word "Binario" was deleted because it was not necessary
Definitions lists	The OER has no definitions lists	As there are not definitions lists, solution is not needed
Videos	All videos have subtitles and are described in context	As all videos are accessible, solution is not needed
Abbreviations and Acronyms	Some acronyms such as "TCP" and "IP" are not defined	The meaning of each undefined acronym was added in its title field

3 Evaluation

The Evaluation was oriented towards obtaining insights about the benefits of using OER created following CO-CREARIA model, in VET settings, for both students and instructors. In this regards, a complete evaluation was carried out in the context of a VET program offered by the National Training Service (SENA) [8] in Colombia. The evaluation scenario was the course called Implementing a Network Structure offered by the SENA. This course is part of a Technical Educational Program called Network Installation. The main desired competence to promote in the students in this course is to "implement the structure of the network according to a pre-established design based on international technical standards". An OER was developed by the teacher in charge of the course with the support of experts in the field of diversity (pedagogues, psychologists, etc.) and experts in web content accessibility. Subsequently, students from the course used the developed OER as a pedagogical tool during their learning process. This course was selected due to the diversity of students registered in it, and because of the teacher's desire to offer his students a truly inclusive learning experience.

Method. The research design was split in two steps as follows:

(1) A descriptive experimental Pre-test and Post-test design", that corresponded to a Pre-test and Post-test design. In the Pre-test, students were presented with a 20-item questionnaire about the course content to be answered in 20 min. Moreover, the Pre-test results were used in order to define the participants' level of

competence for the course. Post-test involved a similar 20 items questionnaire after the completion of the course. To measure the performance of the students in of both pre-test and post-test a 1–100 scale was used.

(2) Analysis of students' motivation". At the end, students were presented with the Instructional Materials Motivation Survey (IMMS) (Cronbach = 0,96) [9]. This was done in order to evaluate the motivation of the students using the created OER over four dimensions: Attention, Relevance, Confidence and Satisfaction. The instrument uses a 5-point Likert scale over a set of 36 questions. The questionnaire was completed in 40 min.

Participants. The evaluation was conducted with 16 students who were formally registered in the Implementing a Network Structure Course at SENA. Demographic results show that 56,25% (N = 9) of the sample were male participants, whereas 43,75% (N = 7) were female participants. This distribution can be considered as an adequate gender balance in our sample because in the particular case of Colombia, men tend to prefer technical careers, whereas women prefer humanistic careers.

4 Results

This section presents the results of the evaluation described previosly. The first stage "Students' performance" describes the results obtained with respect to students' performance using the OER. The second stage "Students' motivation" shows the results regarding students' motivation.

4.1 Students' Performance

Table 4 presents quantitative data analysis results of the Pre-test and Post-test scores obtained by the students in the "Implementing a Network Structure" course. Note that the maximum value of each test is 100.

Table 4. Statistical data of the Pre-test and Post-test for Students registered in the course.

Students	PreTest	PostTest	Gain
Mean Scores	27.06	76	49
Standard Deviation	6.50	13.05	16.51

A paired-sample t-test was conducted to analyse the gains between the Pre-test and Post-test scores. A significant increase ($M = 49$, $SD = 16.51$) in the Post-test scores was found: $t(15) = 11.85$; $p < .001$; two tailed. Cohen's d effect size was found to be large ($d = 3$). All students demonstrated a considerable amount of growth between Pre-test and Post-test with respect to the competence associated to the OER. This could indicate the added value of the created OER to support the acquisition of the required competences.

Students' Motivation. As mentioned before, the ARCS model was used to measure student's motivation. Table 5 summarizes the results for each dimension of motivation.

Table 5. Global scores for each dimension of motivation.

Dimension	Mean score	Standard deviations (SD)
Attention	4.3	0.6
Relevance	3.9	0.6
Confidence	3.8	0.7
Satisfaction	4.3	0.9

It can be concluded that the results are promising because they indicate that working with the OER has a positive impact on students for all motivation dimensions. Attention and Satisfaction dimensions rated better than Relevance and Confidence. The Attention dimension (M = 4.3, SD = 0.6) is about engaging the learners and capturing their interest. As pointed out by [9] an important pre-requisite of a learning process is that student's attention must be engaged. In this regard, the results show that the created OER seems to capture student's attention by triggering their curiosity and creating opportunities to sustain it.

The Satisfaction dimension (M = 4.3, SD = 0.9) is about reinforcing accomplishments and is the result of feelings of mastery and having successfully completed a task. The results in this dimension indicate that the OER has created an environment that sustains intrinsic satisfaction including activities with an optimal level of challenge for all students and activities perceived to be worthwhile. Moreover, the structure and clarity of the OER is positively related to students' satisfaction [10].

Regarding the Relevance dimension (M = 3.90, SD = 0.6), the results are also promising. The Relevance dimension is about meeting personal needs and goals and discovering the meaningfulness of the learning activity. This means that students need to identify the importance of studying the content, and how it meets their personal interests. The results in the dimension of Motivation show that perceiving the content as being right for them, is one of the factors that influence students' motivation [11]. According to Keller [9] there are three tactics for supporting relevance. The first tactic is goal orientation, which is about addressing the learning needs in terms of goals. This was addressed by clearly defining the desired competences to be achieved by the students in the OER.

Finally, the Confidence dimension is about helping students feel that they can succeed and control their success. Moreover, providing the possibility of succeeding in challenging tasks is important to foster motivation. Confidence is directly related to the perceptions of control and according to [18], the perceptions of autonomy are influenced by the design of the learning activities and some factors in the learning context. The strategies for building confidence are: creating a positive expectation for success, creating success opportunities, and creating personal control. By analysing the results of the Confidence dimension, it can be concluded than the OER promoted autonomy in students, giving a feeling of control, as they were able to decide how and when they want to learn using the OER.

5 Conclusions and Future Work

This paper gives insights about the benefits of using OER that adopts UDL and WCAG for improving the learning experience of all students and contributes to the research on OER adoption for inclusion purposes. In addition, the paper introduces CO-CREARIA as a model for the creation of OER, as well as its validation process in VET settings.

Results show that by analysing students' needs and preferences, the instructor is able to create a better curriculum by deciding what strategies could benefit each student. The analysis of learning strategies according to UDL principles allowed teachers to identify potential barriers at different stages of the learning process. Teachers found different solutions that address those barriers with respect to the methods, materials, and teaching strategies used as part of the created OER.

The results of the evaluation of accessibility and quality show that the creation of the OER considered most accessibility and quality guidelines, which proved to be very important to improve the OER.

Performance results show that the consideration of students' needs and preferences in the learning experience design influenced the students' performance in a significant way. Because motivation is highly related to learning, the importance of motivational aspects in OER is high and it may help boost learning. In terms of students' motivation, the results show high levels of motivation in four dimensions: Attention, Relevance, Confidence, and Satisfaction. Attention and Satisfaction rated higher than Relevance and Confidence. The variety of learning activities included in the OER helped to capture students' attention, which is also in-line with the recommendations of the UDL in terms of providing multiple means of representation, multiple means of action and expression and multiple means of engagement.

References

1. UNESCO: Consenso de Shanghái. Shanghái, República Popular de China (2012)
2. UNESCO: 2012 Paris OER declaration. In: World Open Educational Resources (OER) Congress, France (2012)
3. Capp, M.J.: The effectiveness of universal design for learning: a meta-analysis of literature between 2013 and 2016. Int. J. Inclusive Educ. **21**(8), 791–807 (2017)
4. Rao, K., Ok, M.W., Bryant, B.R.: A review of research on universal design educational models. Remedial Spec. Educ. **35**(3), 153–166 (2014)
5. Al-Azawei, A., Serenelli, F., Lundqvist, K.: Universal design for learning (UDL): a content analysis of peer reviewed journals from 2012 to 2015. J. Sch. Teach. Learn. **16**(3), 39 (2016)
6. UNESCO & Government of Slovenia: Ljubljana OER Action Plan 2017. In: Second World OER Congress, Slovenia (2017)
7. Baldiris, S., Mancera, L., Saldarriaga, G.L.V., Treviranus, J.: Co-evaluation, to scaffold the creation of open educational resources. In: Xie, H., Popescu, E., Hancke, G., Fernández Manjón, B. (eds.) ICWL 2017. LNCS, vol. 10473, pp. 168–176. Springer, Cham (2017). https://doi.org/10.1007/978-3-319-66733-1_18
8. Servicio Nacional de Aprendizaje – SENA. www.sena.edu.co. Accessed 27 June 2016

9. Keller, J.M.: Motivational Design for Learning and Performance. Springer, New York (2010)
10. Kim, K.-J., Frick, T.W.: Changes in student motivation during online learning. J. Educ. Comput. Res. **44**(1), 1–23 (2011)
11. Hartnett, M.: Facilitating motivation through support for autonomy. In: Annual conference of the Australian Society for Computers in Tertiary Education - ASCILITE 2012, Wellington, New Zealand (2012)

SALMON: Sharing, Annotating and Linking Learning Materials Online

Farbod Aprin(✉), Sven Manske, and H. Ulrich Hoppe

COLLIDE Research Group, University of Duisburg-Essen,
Lotharstr. 63, 47045 Duisburg, Germany
farbod.aprin@stud.uni-due.de,
{manske,hoppe}@collide.info

Abstract. In consideration of the growing availability of mobile devices for students, web-based and shared annotations of learning materials are becoming more popular. Annotating learning material is a method to promote engagement, understanding, and independence for all learners in a shared environment. Open educational resources have the potential to add valuable information and close the gap between learning materials by automatically linking them. However, current popular web-based text annotation tools for learners, such as Hypothesis and Diigo, do not support learners in discovering new learning resources based on the context, metadata and the content of the annotated resource. In this article, we present SALMON, a collaborative web-based annotation system, which dynamically links and recommends learning resources based on annotations, content and metadata. It facilitates methods of semantic analysis in order to automatically extract relevant content from lecture materials in the form of PDF web documents. SALMON categorizes documents automatically in a way that finding similar resources becomes faster for the learners and they can discover communities for interesting topics.

Keywords: Open educational resources · CSCL · Recommender system · Annotation · PDF annotator · Semantic analysis · Web-annotation · Education · OER · TEL

1 Introduction

The digital annotation of learning materials is a common activity in the process of self-regulated learning and has a long tradition in the field of technology-enhanced education. Collaborative annotation systems like *Hypothesis* allow learners to share their annotations and create annotations of web resources together. Such annotations can encompass explanations on text, excerpts, or individual highlights. Incorporating digital technologies can be beneficial when it comes to the (automatic) enrichment of such annotations. Open Educational Resources (OER) have the potential to add valuable information and to connect learning materials by automatically linking them. With an increased level of digital technology in education, quick access to information and learning resources has become more relevant. To access a large number of digital texts, the learners need robust information systems and search engines to find appropriate

M. A. Herzog et al. (Eds.): ICWL 2019, LNCS 11841, pp. 250–257, 2019.
https://doi.org/10.1007/978-3-030-35758-0_23

resources. Today the collection of OER found on YouTube, Vimeo or wikis has become an inevitable part of information seeking procedure for learners to enrich their knowledge in a specific area. Without the need to search actively for related OERs, recommendations based on an automatic tagging of the respective learning materials might be supportive in this context.

The Semantic Web (SW) can be considered in designing learning tools. SW is an extension of the current interactive web, which means: "Information is given well-defined meaning, better enabling computers and people to work in cooperation" [1]. Web 3.0 technologies will assist online learning instructors in the areas of course development, learner support, assessment, and record keeping [2]. The outcome of such a shared environment could be distributing knowledge among learners with different expertise level. The critical aspects behind achieving the SW vision are enabling metadata and the mapping of it onto learning resources.

In this article, SALMON has been presented, a collaborative web application to share, annotate and automatically link learning materials with each other and with external OERs. Tags, metadata and annotations are extracted automatically from learning materials. Links between resources are based on semantic similarity of the aspects of the materials. This linking is facilitated to recommend OERs to learners in order to expand their collections of learning materials.

2 Related Work

2.1 Generating Metadata in Collaboration Learning Systems

The information extraction process is observed as the method of identifying essential parts of the learning document and content of the annotation [3]. Knowledge about documents has traditionally been accomplished through the use of metadata that can involve the world around the document like a cloud. A learning object is an entity such as digital or non-digital object that may be used for learning, education or training [4]. Metadata is used to describe the learning object and make it possible to select and integrate relevant learning experiences from a collection of learning objectives. This will provide reusable learning objects permitting in the lessons to be generated and customised for specific groups [5]. Learning Object Metadata (LOM) is a standard to integrate educational metadata into learning objects. Such metadata makes learning objects shareable and accessible through indexing and a description of the specific context it occurs. Cardinaels, Michael, and Duval presented a method to automatically extract metadata and transform it into LOM [6, 7]. The automatically generated metadata can be approved by filtering and observation to retrieve more relevant learning objects. Open-Calais and CiceroLite are two tools that enable API to generate semantic tags from the extracted text. This metadata can be utilised for enriching the LOM [16].

Collaborative tagging is the process wherein learners work on the shared resource and assign keywords to it. If it were possible to generate tags to aid learners also enable them to have feedback on the shared tags, then we would have a common understanding of target learning material. The integration of collaborative e-learning systems and SW, which includes application and platform for social and collaborative exchange is increasing the quality of learning experience [8].

2.2 Learning Resource Recommendation

Open educational resources can be seen as an educational paradigm based on a simple but powerful idea that the knowledge of the world is a public good. OER provides a great possibility for learners to share, use, and reuse knowledge [9]. Integration of this idea to the daily learning procedure would add valuable free accessible information for learners to enhance their knowledge. A recommender system in a learning context is an information system examining what a learner is doing and tries to support actions [10]. Popular search engines are currently quite powerful regarding retrieval OER, but they still return the huge instructional list of information; in that, they can be easier by embedding recommender systems in the learning application.

Based on Almudena Ruiz-Iniesta research, integration of OER resources into educational tool helps students find resources faster. It also helps to retrieve the resources that matched with their interest and knowledge. According to evaluations, users are interested in using tools with OER repositories in different domains and mostly had positive feedback. Besides, the supplementary qualitative analysis evaluation showed promising improvements in learning performance and a considerable decrease in dropout rates of the students using OER in learning environment [11].

2.3 Related Collaborative Annotation Tools

A digital annotation learning tool provides an explanation, comment or feedback that is added to a text or diagram on the learning material. The semantic web envisions that technologies can make it possible to generate a kind of "intelligent" documents that were imagined almost twenty-five years ago [12]. There are specific tools that can generate semantic digital annotation automatically or manually to assist users.

One user-friendly interface tool is Mangrove system from the University of Washington that supports automated tagging of HTML documents. The first requirement is the facility of authoring. MANGROVE presents a graphical webpage annotation tool allowing users to immediately and accumulatively annotate the HTML content [13].

Hypothesis[1] is a web-based annotation tool where the users annotate a web resource (as URL) collaboratively in a textual representation [14]. It provides a second layer on the web to enable teachers and students to highlight and annotate on web-based links. Diigoo[2] is a web-based annotation tool that lets students bookmark and tag web pages. It would also be able to highlight a part of a webpage like *Hypothesis*, and for more emphasis attaching the sticky notes to the text is considered.

The Open Annotation and Tagging System (OATS) is a multi-purpose annotation tool that can be integrated into any e-learning system. It will allow the students to tag and annotate HTML based on learning materials. Also, annotation in OATS consists of notes and tag categories on a highlighted section in a selected learning material [15]. Contrary to other systems, OATS provided retrieval functionalities. The user can search for pages, notes and tags among the index of the whole OATS system.

[1] Hypothesis website, hypothesis project (2013), https://web.hypothes.is/, retrieved:2019-6-25.

[2] Diigo Blog, https://blog.diigo.com/2014/09/03/annotating-PDF-docs-with-diigo-a-tutorial/.

All the mentioned tools focus on collaboration on the textual annotation tool. They are not integrating OER by recommendation. Besides, they are unable to provide an implementation for automatic metadata extraction and tagging.

3 SALMON Approach

The SALMON web application offers a collaborative textual annotation environment, which makes use of semantic methods for linking and recommending and learning open educational resources. In SALMON, collaboration is through the artefact. Learners can work together in a group around the learning material, for example, PDF slides of a lecture at university. The PDF format can be seen as the de facto standard for delivering digital lecture materials. Thus, the web-based environment consists of a PDF document viewer in the annotation component. On this material, learners perform different activities in a collaborative space, supports them in creating mutual knowledge. Such activities encompass tagging, immediate feedback on automatically generated semantic tags, highlighting and notes on the text in public or anonymous mode. The initial document of the learning material used that serves as a seed for the recommendation and discovery of new resources is called Pdf-core in this work. Besides, the learners can browse different topics of interest, vote on the recommended OER links to provide relevant feedback and watch multimedia formats in annotation environments. The application generates metadata based on the semantic tags extracted from the content and the from the interaction data obtained from the learners. Consequently, it categorises learning material into different topics by calculating the cosine similarity between semantic metadata.

3.1 Scenario in SALMON

As a scenario, a student called Sara participating in application desires to annotate collaboratively with other students in the learning document environment online. The teacher added the document link with virtual reality topic to the application. After registration via email, Sara and others can access the Pdf-core environment by scanning a QR-code or by entering directly via URL. They can highlight text or capture screenshot of the document and annotate it. Sara can post under her username or as anonymous. This note will be shown in the sidebar. Adding the new Pdf-core is possible, but the content of the new material must be unique; otherwise, Sara will get a warning that the target resource is added before. Furthermore, the application automatically redirects her to the existing collaboration Pdf-core environment. Once she adds new unique Pdf-core, the system searches in local Pdf-core collections to find a match according to similarity function and assigns the new link to an associated collection. If it does not match with any current stored collection, then the system will generate a new collection with the title of the highest rank tag. Recommending relevant OER and Pdf-cores from other remote or local collections in SALMON could assist Sara and her friends to find their answers more quickly and enable them to find other communities for other related Pdf-cores in the same collection. Sara can pin a visual card to save it in her own private collection. These personalisation features prevent repeating the information-seeking procedure. The annotation will be stored and usable for the next semester students (Figs. 1 and 2).

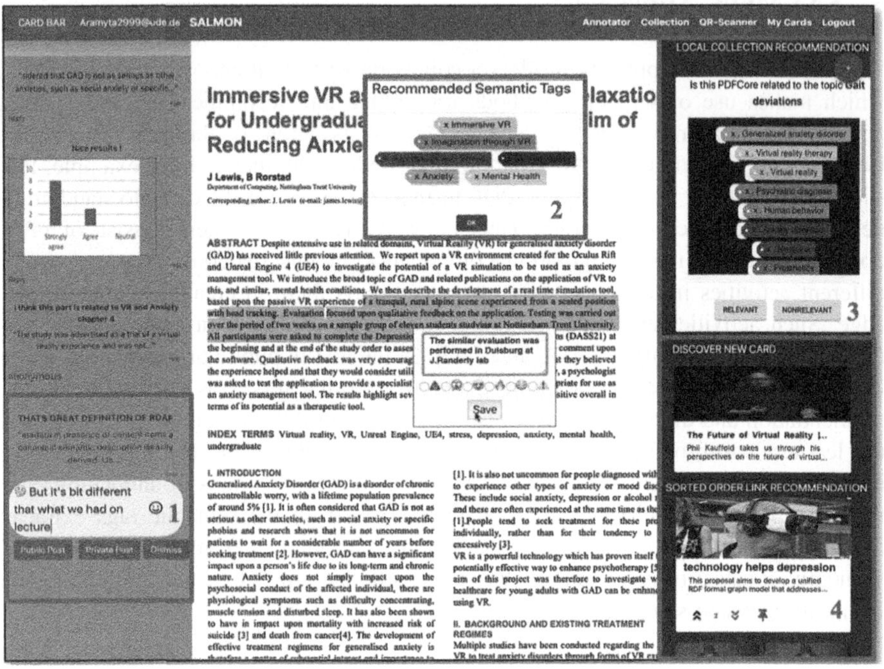

Fig. 1. Annotating PDFs: learners can add a new PDF file and annotate it. **1.** Comment part: learners can ask questions or reply to it. **2.** Automatically generated tags based on the se-mantic text analysis, learners can add or remove tags. **3.** Recommended similar collection in SALMON **4.** Recommended Open Educational Resources.

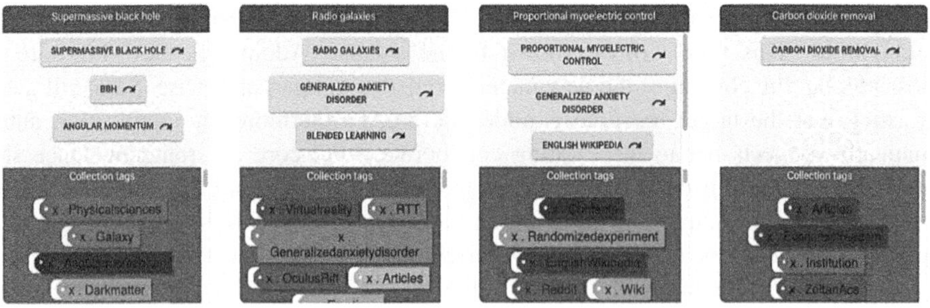

Fig. 2. A collection is a set of similar Pdf-cores (cosine similarity) and contains the union of their tags. Users can find a specific collection by querying the system and navigating through topics.

3.2 SALMON Life Cycle

SALMON is designed to act dynamically by modifying the metadata when the data is changed by each API service provider or by user interaction. The application receives the input data from learning material content, user activities, and feedback in different nonlinear steps. Afterwards, it filters and stores input data as metadata for the added Pdf-core. This data is needed for generating procedure of semantic tags. With the usage of extracted data, the system utilises external knowledge extraction services engines via the application user interface (API). We used Open-Calais[3] to generate semantic tags from extracted filtered text and then added that to enrich metadata [16]. These keywords are exploited to index the OERs in the domain ontology of Pdf-cores and are exploited for retrieval and classification purposes.

SALMON also obtains metadata from a particular part of the Pdf-core content and the keywords that have been set previously to the PDF file by the author. This metadata can be enriched through lifecycle. The current version of SALMON determines similarity by utilising the *DKPro* Similarity package for estimating the similarity between two sets of metadata text [17]. "The Semantic Web offers learners the possibility of having a wealth of related content delivered to their desktop without explicitly identifying or requesting it" [18].

Morris indicates that semantic web-based learning software system agents can provide instructors new information relevant to expertise area and professional interests [2]. A Semantic search will return multimedia rather than just a list of URLs. A smart agent can return relevant blogs and multimedia about the topic to the user [19].

Brindley stated, "Quality learning environments include opportunities for students to engage in interactive and collaborative activities with their peers" [20]. As illustrated, visual cards can be rated by the learners and pined; pined cards will be kept in layout and stored in learner personal collection. Semantic web technologies are used to provide contextualised feedback to instructors about learner personalisation [15].

4 SALMON Architecture

SALMON architecture follows the variant of the service-oriented architecture (SOA). It introduces a modular architecture that has the benefit of decomposing application into different smaller services besides improving modularity. These microservices (MS) are compiling and running independently with various application servers. "In short, the MS architectural style is an approach to developing a single application as a suite of small services, often an HTTP resource API[4]." One benefit of utilising microservice architectures is that if one of the services is disrupted even for a short period, other services will continue their functioning independently.

Each microservice can be tested and run independently. SALMON has three main modules that include two services: SALMON-API microservice (MS), SALMON

[3] Semantic knowledge extractor, Thomson Reuters (2018), http://www.opencalais.com/opencalais-api/, retrieved:2019-6-25.

[4] Microservice architecture, Martin Fowler (2012), https://martinfowler.com/, retrieved: 2019-6-25.

backend MS and SALMON frontend module (Fig. 3). The user interacts with a ReactJs application and can add new data or modify the system status via environment interface. For instance, as the user adds new material and desire to annotate it, the state in the SALMON-Front will be changed. Besides, SALMON-Front talks to SALMON-Backend MS via REST-API to post the PDF link to the Backend MS[5].

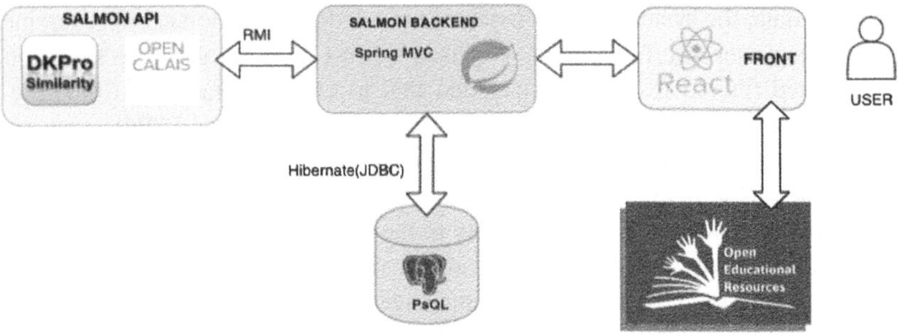

Fig. 3. SALMON architecture consists of three main modules: SALMON API microservices, SALMON backend microservices and SALMON frontend module.

5 Discussion and Conclusion

In this work, we have presented SALMON, a collaborative web-based text annotation tool with recommender systems. The system extracts the metadata for added learning material, which can add the valuable potential for integrating the OER and similar local resources, as a recommendation for learners.

In the SALMON environment, we have considered the nonlinear procedure to enrich the learning material metadata which can be updated, according to learner interaction and feedback and updating resources. This feature can increase the level of relevancy in the recommended resources for the learners. To find similarity for the local document recourses, cosine-similarity which is a useful method, was used to approximate the similarity between metadata for materials. By finding the similarity of metadata, we demonstrate categorizing learning materials into different associated collections. This feature will facilitate the procedure of discovering similar documents for learners. Also, classification helps to find other peers in the interested topic easier.

For future work, the application will be evaluated empirically in the context of a university course. In order to support internationalisation and multiple languages, future versions of SALMON will be connected to different text analysers like FRED[6] to increase the preciseness of the extracted keyword and for using it for extracting more different languages, e.g., Russian and German. We will update the interaction features like an instant recommendation for highlighted text in the annotation tool.

[5] SALMON GitHub repository, 02-06-2019, https://github.com/SALMON2PROJECT.

[6] Keyword extraction Framework, Machine Reading for the Semantic Web, STlab 2015 http://wit.istc.cnr.it/stlab-tools/fred/.

References

1. Berners-lee, T., Hendler, J., Lassila, O.: The Semantic web a new form of web content that is meaningful to computers will unleash a revolution of new possibilities (2001)
2. Morris, R.D.: Web 3.0: implications for online learning. TechTrends **55**, 42–46 (2011). https://doi.org/10.1007/s11528-011-0469-9
3. Bittencourt, I.I.M., Costa, E., Isotani, S., Mizoguchi, R.: Towards a reference model to semantic web-based educational systems (2008)
4. Barker, P., Campbell, L.M.: Metadata for learning materials: an ovierview. Technol. Instr. Cogn. Learn. **7**, 225–243 (2010)
5. Baker, T.: Library Hi Tech Libraries, languages of description, and linked data: a Dublin Core perspective Article information. https://doi.org/10.1108/07378831211213256
6. Barker, P.: What is IEEE learning object metadata/IMS learning resource metadata? Cetis Stand. Briefings Ser. **1**, 4 (2005)
7. Learning Technology Standards Committee, IEEE Computer Society: IEEE Standard for Learning Technology — Extensible Markup Language (XML) Schema Definition. Institute of Electrical and Electronics Engineers (2005)
8. Torniai, C., Jovanović, J., Gašević, D., Bateman, S., Hatala, M.: E-learning meets the Social Semantic Web. In: Proceedings of 8th IEEE International Conference on Advanced Learning Technologies, ICALT 2008, pp. 389–393 (2008). https://doi.org/10.1109/ICALT.2008.20
9. Deimann, M., Bastiaens, T.: Special session OER: integrating OER and instructional design – towards a more holistic view keywords: open educational resources, instructional design abstract: 1 introduction 2 the claim of open educational resources (OER). Learning **1**, 1–10 (2007)
10. Schafer, J.B.: The application of data-mining to recommender systems. In: Encyclopedia of Data Warehousing and Mining, Second Edition, pp. 45–50 (2011). https://doi.org/10.4018/978-1-60566-010-3.ch008
11. Ruiz-Iniesta, A., Jiménez-Díaz, G., Gomez-Albarran, M.: A semantically enriched context-aware OER recommendation strategy and its application to a computer science OER repository. IEEE Trans. Educ. **57**, 255–260 (2014)
12. Delphi Group: The document process (1994). https://bit.ly/2MgNJYK
13. McDowell, L., et al.: Mangrove: enticing ordinary people onto the semantic web via instant gratification, pp. 754–770 (2010). https://doi.org/10.1007/978-3-540-39718-2_48
14. Te Whaley, D.: Annotation is now a web standard. hypothesis Blog (2017). https://web.hypothes.is/blog/annotation-is-now-a-web-standard/. Accessed 12 June 2017
15. Brooks, C., Bateman, S., Greer, J., Mccalla, G.: Lessons Learned Using Social and Semantic Web Technologies for E-Learning (2009). https://doi.org/10.3233/978-1-60750-062-9-260
16. Gangemi, A.: A comparison of knowledge extraction tools for the semantic web. In: Cimiano, P., Corcho, O., Presutti, V., Hollink, L., Rudolph, S. (eds.) ESWC 2013. LNCS, vol. 7882, pp. 351–366. Springer, Heidelberg (2013). https://doi.org/10.1007/978-3-642-38288-8_24
17. Bär, D., Zesch, T., Gurevych, I.: DKPro Similarity: An Open Source Framework for Text Similarity. (2013). www.aclweb.org/anthology/P13-4021
18. Daly, C.: The semantic web and e-Learning. eLearn. (2009). https://doi.org/10.1145/1595384.1555528
19. Ohler, J.: The semantic web in education: what happens when the read-write web gets smart enough to help us organize and evaluate the information it provides?, pp. 7–9 (2008)
20. Brindley, J., Blaschke, L.M., Walti, C.: Creating effective collaborative learning groups in an online environment. Int. Rev. Res. Open Distrib. Learn. **10**, 1–18 (2016). https://doi.org/10.19173/irrodl.v10i3.675

WEBLORS – A Personalized Web-Based Recommender System

Mohammad Belghis-Zadeh[1(✉)], Hazra Imran[2], Maiga Chang[1], and Sabine Graf[1]

[1] Athabasca University, Edmonton, AB, Canada
mobelghis@yahoo.ca, {maigac, sabineg}@athabascau.ca
[2] University of British Columbia, Vancouver, BC, Canada
hazra@cs.ubc.ca

Abstract. Nowadays, personalization and adaptivity becomes more and more important in most systems. When it comes to education and learning, personalization can provide learners with better learning experiences by considering their needs and characteristics when presenting them with learning materials within courses in learning management systems. One way to provide students with more personal learning materials is to deliver personalized content from the web. However, due to information overload, finding relevant and personalized materials from the web remains a challenging task. This paper presents an adaptive recommender system called WEBLORS that aims at helping learners to overcome the information overload by providing them with additional personalized learning materials from the web to increase their learning and performance. This paper also presents the evaluation of WEBLORS based on its recommender system acceptance using data from 36 participants. The evaluation showed that overall, participants had a positive experience interacting with WEBLORS. They trusted the recommendations and found them helpful to improve learning and performance, and they agreed that they would like to use the system again.

Keywords: Recommender systems · Web mining · Personalization

1 Introduction

Although different students have different needs, learning management systems (LMSs) usually have fixed content that is presented to all students in the same way [1]. However, these systems can be enriched with personalization through recommender systems (RS). To date, many RSs are limited to recommend the available learning objects (LOs) that either have been created in the course, which greatly limits the variety of the recommendable objects, or have been collected in LO repositories (LOR) [2]. Using LORs provides RSs with access to a larger pool of LOs, however, the quality of recommendations is highly impacted by the quality of the metadata that was provided by users who created the objects [3]. Moreover, the available pool of LOs in a LOR could still be limited based on topics and types of LOs. However, there are more LOs and learning materials openly and freely available on the web that can be targeted

M. A. Herzog et al. (Eds.): ICWL 2019, LNCS 11841, pp. 258–266, 2019.
https://doi.org/10.1007/978-3-030-35758-0_24

by RSs [4]. However, due to the vast number of these objects on the web, different techniques need to be utilized to overcome the information overload and find relevant and personalized learning materials that fit students' needs [5].

In this paper, we introduce WEBLORS, a recommender system that aims at helping students by considering their individual needs and the ratings given by other learners to present the learner with additional learning materials from the web that are relevant to the learner and the topic he/she is currently learning. This paper also presents the evaluation of WEBLORS based on its recommender system acceptance.

The remainder of this paper is structured as follows: Sect. 2 presents related work. Section 3 discusses WEBLORS' architecture and approach. Section 4 explains the evaluation methodology and the results of the WEBLORS' evaluation and, Sect. 5 concludes the paper.

2 Related Work

The idea of RSs in the learning domain has been around for decades and different recommendable objects such as courses, learning materials and academic papers have been targeted [6]. However, most literature in this area has been about LO recommendations, and one of the new research trends for LO recommendations is to broaden the search and recommend LOs from web-based LORs, social networks or even from the web. There are different ways how RSs decide which LOs to recommend. Many RSs recommend learning content based on users' past activities [7, 8]. For example, Dahdouh and colleagues proposed a recommender system that generates recommendations by considering learners' historical data as a factor and finds similarities between learners past activities collected from system logs [7]. Another example is the system built by Bourkoukou and colleagues that generates recommendations for learners based on the user's historical data collected from server logs and other attributes of learners [8]. Some other systems generate recommendations based on the keywords that are passed by the users [9–11]. For example, the RS built by Zapata and colleagues considers the keywords that are specified by a user and finds relevant LOs from a LOR called AGORA [9]. Similarly, Atkinson and colleagues proposed a system that accepts the queries as input from users and uses focused crawling and metadata extraction to find relevant web resources [10]. Rahman and colleagues also proposed a group-based recommender system that accepts users' queries, considers users' profiles, and uses Google search engine to recommend learning materials to learners based on their profiles [11]. After reviewing the existing literature, we identified some gaps for RSs in education that we addressed in our system. First, WEBLORS recommends LOs from the web and therefore, aims at advancing our knowledge in this new trending area. Second, many RSs consider past activities of learners as a major factor when generating recommendations. Therefore, cold start is a problem in these systems. To address this issue, WEBLORS does not rely on users' past activities and instead uses learners' learning styles, the opinions of other learners (if available) and the topic that is being studied. Third, many RSs with a broad search space often work similar to search engines and heavily rely on the search criteria that are passed by the users.

In WEBLORS, this issue is avoided by creating keywords automatically through extracting them from the content that a learner is learning.

3 Architecture of WEBLORS

WEBLORS consists of two main parts that are shown in Figs. 1 and 2 and are further described in the next two subsections.

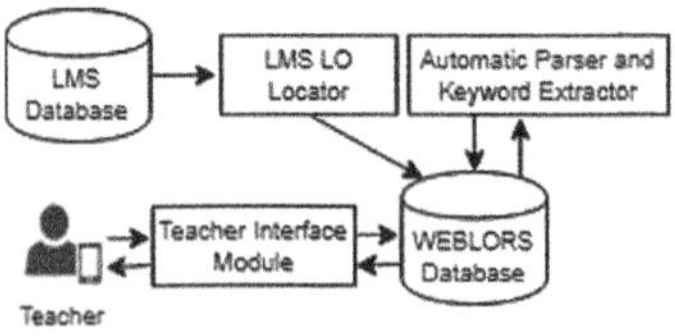

Fig. 1. Architecture of CLOA

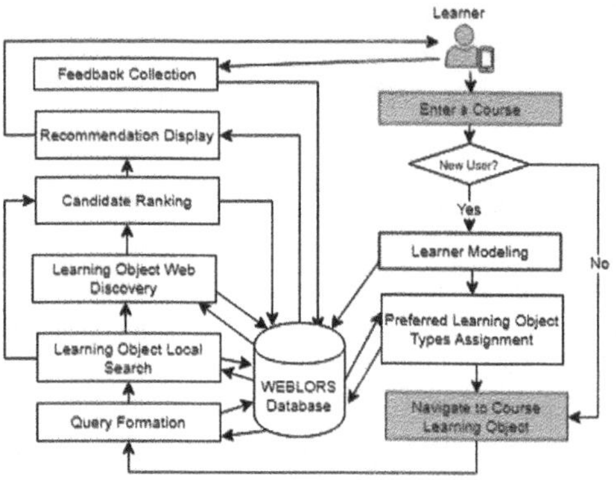

Fig. 2. Architecture of ALORS

3.1 Course LOs Analyzer (CLOA)

As shown in Fig. 1, CLOA contains a set of modules and components. The aim of the **LMS LO Locator** module is to locate all LOs within the LMS and extract their content. As part of the installation process of WEBLORS, this module searches through each course and LO in the LMS database and stores its content and the searchable criteria into the WEBLORS database (DB). Also, when a new LO is added to the LMS by a teacher, this module stores the content and the searchable criteria of the newly added LO into the DB. The aim of the **Automatic Parser and Keyword Extractor** module is to parse the content of each LO, extract a set of candidate keywords and store the keywords into the DB. This module uses the RAKE algorithm [12] to discover the keywords and key phrases that best fit the LO. The aim of the **Teacher Interface** module is to display each LO and its extracted keywords to the instructor where he/she can confirm the accuracy, relevance and the importance of the keywords or overwrite them with a set of new keywords if required.

3.2 Adaptive LO Discovery and Recommender System (ALORS)

As shown in Fig. 2, ALORS contains several modules and activities. The aim of the **Learner Modeling Module** is to capture learners' learning styles (LSs) based on Felder-Silverman Learning Style Model [13], a widely known and commonly used LS model. Based on this model, learners are classified in four dimensions: (1) active/reflective (Act/Ref), (2) sensing/intuitive (Sen/Int), (3) visual/verbal (Vis/Ver) and (4) sequential/global (Seq/Glo). This module uses a questionnaire called Index of Learning Styles (ILS) [14] that contains 44 questions. ILS was developed by Felder and Soloman and was found to be valid, reliable and suitable for identifying LSs [15]. ILS is presented to each user when he/she enters his/her first course for the first time and based on the provided answers, his/her LSs are calculated as four numeric values (each for one LS dimension). This module then builds a profile *(sp)* for each student *(s)* which is represented as a vector of 8 elements and is formed as *sp(s)* = (Act, Ref, Sen, Int, Vis, Ver, Seq, Glo). In *sp*, each LS dimension is represented with 2 elements where each element has a value between 0 and 2, representing the strength of the LS preference.

The aim of the **Preferred Learning Object Types Assignment** is to identify a set of preferred LO types (PLOTs) and their associated keywords for each learner based on their LSs. This module uses a mapping table (Table 1) that has been created based on the mapping proposed by El-Bishouty and colleagues [16] and has been extended with the LO type of videos that according to Felder and Silverman is suitable for visual and verbal learners [13]. In this module, each LO type (*lot*) is represented by a LO type profile (*lp*) which is a vector with the same 8 elements as the *sp*. Each element of *lp* is either 0 or 1 and is assigned per Table 1, indicating whether (1) or not (0) the LO is beneficial for that LS.

Table 1. Mapping table (based on [16])

LO type	LO type keyword	Act	Ref	Sen	Int	Vis	Ver	Seq	Glo
Exercises	exercise 1	1	0	1	0	0	0	0	0
Examples	example 1	0	1	1	0	0	0	0	1
Real Life Application	real world application	0	0	1	0	0	0	0	1
Video	video	0	0	0	0	1	1	0	0
Self-Assessment Test	questions and answers	1	0	1	0	0	0	0	0
Additional Reading Material	pdf	0	1	0	1	0	1	1	0

Next, this module calculates a numeric value for each LO type that is called **Relevance** value (Rel(*s*,*lot*)) which is the scalar product of *sp(s)* and *lp(lot)*, and is used to determine the most preferred LO types for a given student with a certain LS. All LO types that have a positive Rel(*s*,*lot*) form the student's preferred LO types (PLOT).

The aim of the **Query Formation Module (QFM)** is to take the previously extracted keywords from the LO that the student is currently visiting and the LO type keywords associated with each PLOT of the student (per Table 1) as input and form one query per PLOT. WEBLORS considers three different categories of LOs when generating recommendations: (1) course LOs, (2) local LOs and (3) web LOs. Course LOs are objects that are created by the teacher and are part of the course. Local LOs are the objects that have been previously discovered from the web, recommended to learners and stored in the DB. Web LOs are the objects that are discovered from the web for the first time.

The aim of **Learning Object Local Search Module (LOLSM)** is to select a set of local LOs for each query that has been formed by the QFM and mark them as candidate local LOs and pass them to the Candidate Ranking module for further processing. Local LOs are considered to be a candidate local LO if they are of a LO type that the given query has been created for and satisfy one of the following conditions: (1) local LOs that have been previously rated (with values between 1 and 5) by five or more users and the weighted average rating for them (WAvg(*lo*)) is greater than or equals to 3.5 out of 5 (i.e., $\geq 70\%$ of agreement) or (2) all local LOs that have been rated less than five times (to give enough chance to new local LOs to be recommended and rated by users).

The **Learning Object Web Discovery Module (LOWDM)** aims at using the Google API to execute the queries that are created by the QFM on the web and finding the candidate web LOs. To ensure that only educational materials are being targeted, a new Google Custom Search Engine (CSE) was created and configured to only target learning resources, scholarly articles and educational materials on the web. Also, to narrow down the search and control the number of results that are returned from the web, this module appends the index of the first result that should be returned (*start*) and the number of results that should be retrieved (*num*) to each query before running them. Both *num* and *start* parameters can be configured. The *num* parameter is set to 5 by default to enforce the query to return only 5 results at a time. In order to find at least one web LO that has not been recommended before, the *start* parameter is used in a way that if all 5 LOs that are returned by the query exist in the DB, then the system increases the *start* parameter by 5, reruns the query and returns the next 5 results until at least one new LO is found in those 5 results. At this point, the 5 results are checked and those that have not been previously recommended to any user (1 to 5 web LOs) are considered as candidate web LOs and are passed to the Candidate Ranking module. This process is repeated for each query so that there are 1–5 web LOs passed to the Candidate Ranking module for each query.

The aim of the **Candidate Ranking Module** is to accept the candidate local and web LOs from the LOLSM and LOWDM as input and decide which of them should be recommended to the learner. To generate the list of recommendations for a given student (*s*), this module calculates an **Importance** value (Imp*(lo)*) as the scalar product of the relevance value (Rel*(s,lot)*) and the weighted average rating for each candidate

LO (WAvg(*lo*)). A default value of 2.5 (average rating) is used as WAvg(*lo*) for web LOs and the local LOs with less than five ratings. Next, all candidate LOs are ranked in ascending order in a way that the candidate LO with the lowest Imp(*lo*) gets the rank of 1. Subsequently, the Fitness Proportionate Selection algorithm (FPS) [17] is used to select the recommendable objects in a way that the LOs with a higher Importance value have higher chance to be selected, but LOs with lower Importance value still have a small chance to be recommended. In order to select N candidate LOs where N is the number of LOs that should be recommended to the student, FPS is applied $N - 1$ times. Next, the list of already selected LOs is checked. If at least one LO from the web is already selected, FPS is applied one more time. Otherwise the web LO with the highest Importance value is selected as the Nth LO.

The aim of the **Recommendation Display Module** is to accept the recommendation list from the Candidate Ranking module and display them to the learner. Also, a five-star rating system is presented for each recommended LO where the learner can rate the quality of the recommendation. The aim of the **Feedback Collection Module** is to collect the ratings that were provided by the users and store them in the DB.

4 Evaluation

In this section, the methodology used to evaluate the users' acceptance of the system is introduced. The research design, participants selection, and the results are explained in the next three subsections.

4.1 Research Design

For this evaluation, WEBLORS was integrated into an instance of Moodle [18] and a sample course on the topic of Data Presentation in Computers was created that contained 5 LOs. Also, a four-step process was designed and published on the evaluation website where participants were asked to complete the following tasks: (1) watch a video that contains a demo of the system, (2) complete a pre-test that contains 9 questions about the course topic and one trick question, (3) login to the course, fill out the ILS, read and learn each of the LOs, and read, learn and rate the generated recommendations (5 recommendations are generated for each LO), (4) complete a post-test, which consisted of the same questions as the pre-test and can demonstrate a students' knowledge increase, (5) complete a feedback questionnaire that contains one trick question and 6 multiple-choice questions (created based on [19] and [20]) where users could rate their experience on a scale of 1 (strong disagreement) to 5 (strong agreement). Questions 1 to 6 are listed in Table 2.

4.2 Participants Selection

For this evaluation, a new task was created on Amazon Mechanical Turk and 95 users accepted the task. To ensure that only valid data is included in the analysis, the following acceptance criteria were defined. Users should have completed all steps of the evaluation, answered all trick questions correctly, read at least 3 out of 5 LOs in the course, read and rated more than one third of the generated recommendations (9 or more out of 25), and spent at least 35 min on the sample course. Based on our assessment, at minimum, 35 min are required to complete the ILS, read at least 3 out of 5 LOs and 9 out of 25 recommendations and complete the post test. Although extracted times spent gathered from data logs might not be the exact time that users spent on the resources, it still provides valuable insights into the reliability of the collected data. After validating the collected data, responses from 36 participants (out of 95) met the acceptance criteria, and the rest were excluded from the evaluation.

4.3 Results

In order to analyze the data, the answers given to the 6 multiple-choice questions (Q1–Q6) by the 36 accepted participants were aggregated. Each question has five possible answers that are shown in Table 2 with respective scores provided in brackets. In addition, the weighted average score was calculated for each question. Based on the

Table 2. Results of quantitative analysis

Question	Total	Strongly agree (5)	Agree (4)	Neither agree nor disagree (3)	Disagree (2)	Strongly disagree (1)	Weighted average score
Q1 - I would like to use WEBLORS frequently	36	16	16	1	2	1	4.22
Q2 - I would like to see such recommendations in other courses as well	36	16	16	3	1	0	4.31
Q3 - I trusted the recommendations provided by WEBLORS	36	21	13	1	1	0	4.50
Q4 - I think recommendations provided by WEBLORS will be helpful in increasing students' performance	36	20	15	1	0	0	4.53
Q5 - I think WEBLORS will put extra work on students for providing ratings	36	4	2	4	6	20	2.00
Q6 - I think recommendations provided by WEBLORS will be helpful in increasing students' learning	36	17	17	1	1	0	4.39

results shown in Table 2, very high average scores have been given to Q1, Q2, Q3, Q4 and Q6 indicating that overall users agreed with the statements in these questions. These scores show that most users trusted the recommendations, found the system very useful, and believed that this system can increase learners' performance and help them in their learning process. In addition, users stated that they like to use WEBLORS frequently and have such system available to them while studying other courses. Q5 was a negative question and the low score that was given to this question shows that on average users disagreed with the statement in this question and believed that WEBLORS does not put much extra work on users to provide ratings.

5 Conclusion

The focus of this paper is on explaining the architecture of WEBLORS as well as the evaluation of the system in terms of recommender system acceptance. WEBLORS is a RS that considers the topic that the learner is learning as well as the ratings of LOs given by other learners and provides the learner with relevant learning materials from the web that are beneficial for him/her based on his/her LSs. Recommended materials are selected from a set of relevant LOs that are either discovered from the web for the first time or have been previously recommended to other learners and were given high ratings (or have been rated by less than 5 users), with the condition that at least one new LO from the web is recommended every time that WEBLORS generates recommendations. The results of the evaluation show that the 36 users provided promising feedback with respect to recommender system acceptance. Based on the result, users like to use WEBLORS frequently and are interested to have such system available to them in other courses as well. Also, users trusted the generated recommendations and believed that the provided recommendations can help students in their learning process and will have a positive impact on students' performance. Also, the results show that most users believe that asking users to rate the recommendations does not add lots of overhead and does not put much extra work on students. To conclude, the results show that WEBLORS fills a gap in LMSs by recommending extra personalized learning materials from the web and helping with information overload by only recommending LOs relevant to the topic that is being studied and which fits students' LSs. Future work will deal with evaluating the system further based on other aspects such as ease of use, user friendliness, knowledge increase of users after using WEBLORS, and others. In addition, future work will deal with the broad use of the system in different courses.

Acknowledgment. The authors acknowledge the support of Athabasca University, Alberta Innovates – Technology Futures (AITF), Ministry of Advanced Education of Canada, the National Science and Engineering Research Council of Canada (NSERC) [funding reference number: 402053-2012-RGPIN], and Mitacs.

References

1. Imran, H., Belghis-Zadeh, M., Chang, T.-W., Kinshuk, Graf, S.: PLORS: a personalized learning object recommender system. Vietnam J. Comput. Sci. **3**(1), 3–13 (2016)
2. Dwivedi, P., Bharadwaj, K.: e-Learning recommender system for a group of learners based on the unified learner profile approach. Expert Syst. **32**(2), 264–276 (2015)
3. Sabourin, J., Kosturko, L., McQuiggan, S.: Where to next? A comparison of recommendation strategies for navigating a learning object repository. In: Ricci, F., Bontcheva, K., Conlan, O., Lawless, S. (eds.) UMAP 2015. LNCS, vol. 9146, pp. 208–215. Springer, Cham (2015). https://doi.org/10.1007/978-3-319-20267-9_17
4. Al Abri, M., Dabbagh, N.: Open educational resources: a literature review. J. Mason Grad. Res. **6**(1), 83–104 (2018)
5. Akhtarzada, A., Calude, C.S., Hosking, J.: A multi-criteria metric algorithm for recommender systems. Fundamenta Informaticae **110**, 1–11 (2011)
6. Manouselis, N.: Recommender Systems for Learning. Springer, New York (2013)
7. Dahdouh, K., Oughdir, L., Dakkak, A., Ibriz, A.: Building an e-learning recommender system using association rules techniques and R environment. Int. J. Inf. Sci. Technol. **3**(2), 11–18 (2019)
8. Bourkoukou, O., Bachari, E.E.: Toward a hybrid recommender system for e-learning personnalization based on data mining techniques. Int. J. Inform. Vis. **2**(4), 271–278 (2018)
9. Zapata, A., Menéndez, V.H., Prieto, M.E., Romero, C.: A framework for recommendation in learning object repositories: an example of application in civil engineering. Adv. Eng. Softw. **56**, 1–14 (2013)
10. Atkinson, J., Gonzalez, A., Munoz, M., Astudillo, H.: Web metadata extraction and semantic indexing for learning objects extraction. Appl. Intell. **41**(2), 649–664 (2014)
11. Rahman, M.M., Abdullah, N.A.: A personalized group-based recommendation approach for web search in e-learning. IEEE Access **6**, 34166–34178 (2018)
12. Rose, S., Engel, D., Cramer, N., Cowley, W.: Automatic keyword extraction from individual documents. In: Text Mining, pp. 1–20. Wiley (2010)
13. Felder, R., Silverman, L.: Learning and teaching styles in engineering education. Eng. Educ. **78**(7), 674–681 (1988)
14. Felder, R.M., Soloman, B.A.: Index of learning style questionnaire. https://www.webtools.ncsu.edu/learningstyles/. Accessed 20 July 2019
15. Felder, R., Spurlin, J.: Applications, reliability and validity of the index of learning styles. Int. J. Eng. Educ. **21**, 103–112 (2005)
16. El-Bishouty, M.M., Saito, K., Chang, T.W., Kinshuk, Graf, S.: An interactive course analyzer for improving learning styles support level. In: Holzinger, A., Pasi, G. (eds.) HCI-KDD 2013. LNCS, vol. 7947, pp. 136–147. Springer, Cham (2013). https://doi.org/10.1007/978-3-642-39146-0_13
17. Bäck, T.: Evolutionary Algorithms in Theory and Practice: Evolution Strategies, Evolutionary Programming, Genetic Algorithms. Oxford University Press, New York (1996)
18. Dougiamas, M.: Moodle. http://moodle.org/. Accessed 20 July 2019
19. Brooke, J.: SUS: a quick and dirty usability scale. In: Jordan, P.W., et al. (eds.) Usability Evaluation in Industry, pp. 189–194. Taylor and Francis, London (1996)
20. Lewis, J.R., Sauro, J.: The factor structure of the system usability scale. In: Kurosu, M. (ed.) HCD 2009. LNCS, vol. 5619, pp. 94–103. Springer, Heidelberg (2009). https://doi.org/10.1007/978-3-642-02806-9_12

Automatic Topic Labeling for Facilitating Interpretability of Online Learning Materials

Jun Wang(✉) and Kanji Uchino

Fujitsu Laboratories of America, Sunnyvale, CA 94085, USA
{jun.wang,kanji}@us.fujitsu.com

Abstract. To reduce the cognitive overhead of understanding and organizing online learning materials using topic models, especially for new learners not familiar with related domains, this paper proposes an efficient and effective approach for generating high-quality labels as better interpretation of topics discovered and typically visualized as a list of top terms. Compared with previous methods dependent on complicated post-processing processes or external resources, our phrase-based topic inference method can generate and narrow down label candidates more naturally and efficiently. The proposed approach is demonstrated and examined with real data in our corporate learning platform.

Keywords: Topic model · Interpretability · Automatic topic labeling

1 Introduction

The Web can be described as an ocean of information and knowledge usable for learning. However, online learning materials are usually scattered around the Web, and not well described and structured so causing problems in their use, search, organization and management [9]. Topic models are a useful tool for understanding large document collections, which can be used to discover the hidden themes that pervade the collection and annotate the documents according to those themes, and further organize, summarize, and search learning materials. It is of interest to visualize these topics in order to facilitate human interpretation and exploration of the large amounts of unorganized documents, and a list of most probable terms is the de facto representation of individual topics as shown in Table 1. Most existing topic models are represented with unigrams as shown in the first column of Table 1, which often provide ambiguous representation of the topic and poor interpretability for new learners. Human interpretation often relies on inherent grouping of words into phrases, and augmenting unigrams with a list of probable phrases offers a more intuitively interpretable topic description as shown in the second column of Table 1. Several phrase-based topic models [3,9] have been proposed to discover topical phrases and address the prevalent deficiency in visualizing topics using unigrams. However, the cognitive overhead

M. A. Herzog et al. (Eds.): ICWL 2019, LNCS 11841, pp. 267–273, 2019.
https://doi.org/10.1007/978-3-030-35758-0_25

in interpreting a topic presented as a list of phrases can still be very high if learners are not familiar with the related domains, and has lead to interest in the task of automatically generating appropriate and meaningful phrases as topic labels which can explicitly and clearly identify the topic themes [1,4,5]. For example, if we can generate the label **natural language processing** for the topic in Table 1, and it would be easy to answer fundamental questions from learners such as "What is the topic about?" [5]. All existing automatic topic labeling methods [1,4,5] are using unigram-based topic inference under the 'bag-of-words' assumption. Phrases are decomposed into unigrams and a phrase's meaning may be lost, and that causes difficulty in finding appropriate phrases as candidate labels efficiently. These methods have to use additional complicated post-processing processes or external resources as shown in Sect. 2.

Table 1. Real example of the topic on **natural language processing** discovered and visualized by the unigram-based topic model and the phrase-based topic model, respectively.

Unigram-based	Phrase-based
Model	Word embeddings
Language	Natural language
Word	Language model
Text	Question answering
Task	Machine translation
Question	Sentiment analysis
Sentence	Neural machine translation
Translation	Natural language processing
Neural	Text classification
Natural	Word representation

This paper proposes an efficient and effective approach for generating high-quality labels as better interpretation of topics discovered and typically visualized as a list of top terms. Our phrase-based topic inference method can generate and narrow down label candidates more naturally and efficiently. The proposed approach is demonstrated and examined with real data in our corporate learning platform.

2 Related Work

Mei et al. [5] introduced the method based on first extracting bigram collocations from the topic-modelled document collection using a lexical association measure, and then ranking them based on KL divergence with each topic. The quality of phrase label candidates produced by [5] often are not stable, and in order to address the problem, Lau et al. [4] proposed using Wikipedia to automatically label topics. First, they map the topic to a set of concepts by querying Wikipedia using the top topic terms, and the top document titles from search results are pooled to generate the label candidates, and label candidates are then ranked using a number of lexical association features. Bhatia et al. [1] also proposed a method using Wikipedia document titles as label candidates, which selects the most relevant labels based on measuring distance between top topic terms and Wikipedia document titles in terms of their corresponding neural embeddings pre-computed using word2vec and doc2vec. Because their label candidates are from Wikipedia document titles, [1,4] may not be applied to vertical domains not well covered by Wikipedia. In addition, [4] is dependent on external search APIs which also limits the general-purpose utility, and in [1] the scalability may become an issue due to measuring similarity between topic terms and almost all Wikipedia document titles.

3 Topic Labeling with Phrase-Based Topic Inference

As discussed in the previous section, separation of the phrase mining and topic inference processes in the existing unigram-based methods [1,4,5] often produces low-quality phrase candidates or suffers from poor scalability. The better method is first mining phrases and segmenting each document into single and multiword phrases, and then organically integrates phrase constraints into topic inference [3,9]. Our method for topic labelling is briefly illustrated as follows.

3.1 Phrase Mining

Phrase mining is a text mining technique that discovers semantically meaningful phrases from massive text. Recent data-driven approaches opt instead to make use of frequency statistics in the corpus to address both candidate generation and quality estimation [7,9]. They do not rely on complex linguistic feature generation, domain-specific rules or extensive labeling efforts. Instead, they rely on large corpora containing hundreds of thousands of documents to help deliver superior performance several indicators, including frequency, mutual information, branching entropy and comparison to super/sub-sequences, were proposed to extract n-grams that reliably indicate frequent, concise concepts [7,9].

3.2 Phrase-Based Topic Inference

After inducing a partition on each document, we perform phrase-based topic inference [3] to associate the same topic to each word in a phrase and thus naturally to the phrase as a whole. The inference process almost same as LDA but with constraints on topics of phrases, and can be smoothly updated from unigram-based topic inference of LDA with similar complexity. In addition, the discovered topics can also be further refined in interactive processes based on user feedbacks [10].

3.3 Topic Label Generation

Presumably, a good label should be understandable to human, could capture the meaning of the topic, and distinguish a topic from other topics [5]. As shown in Table 1, the phrase-based topic models generate topics represented with more meaningful and interpretable topical phrases for human instead of ambiguous unigrams, which themselves offer natural candidates of topic labels without complex and costly post-processing in [1,4,5]. For ranking and selecting topic labels, the two methods in [1,5] are easily extended to support phrases in addition to unigrams as shown in Sect. 4.

4 Experiments

The above topic labeling method with phrase-based topic inference was deployed as a part of our corporate learning platform for data scientist training programs, in which a database contains 39191 recent machine learning related papers. The titles and abstracts of all papers were segmented into a collections of meaningful phrases using the tool based on generalized suffix tree (GST) [9], and 20 topics were extracted using our phrase-based topic models. The top-20 phrases from each topic as label candidates are ranked using neural embedding distance [1] and KL divergence [5], respectively. The ranking method based on neural embedding distance supports both supervised and unsupervised modes, and the pre-trained parameters in [1] were used. The existing unigram-based methods[1] in [1,5] with 20 topics were also applied to the same corpus and compared with our method by evaluations of three machine learning experts as shown in Table 2.

Table 2. The numbers of topics with appropriate labels well covering their themes in top-1 and top-3 ranking results by phrase-based and unigram-based methods, respectively.

Method	Neural embeddings				KL divergence	
	Supervised		Unsupervised			
	Top-1	Top-3	Top-1	Top-3	Top-1	Top-3
Phrase	8	11	6	12	2	5
Unigram	5	9	1	7	0	0

The results in Table 2 show that our phrase-based method is significantly better than the existing unigram-based methods. For the unigram-based methods, the supervised mode is much better than the unsupervised mode, but for our phrase-based method, the supervised mode is only slightly better than the unsupervised mode. It shows that the meaningful and interpretable phrases

[1] One of search APIs used by [4] is not available any more, so it is skipped in the experiments.

themselves encoded with semantic information can partially offset the missing supervision. The ranking method based on neural embedding distance is generally better than the method using KL divergence, and especially, the unigram-based method with KL divergence ranking is very unstable and cannot find appropriate labels for all 20 topics. The neural embeddings are very useful representation for topic labeling, and currently we only use a naive way to average

Table 3. Real examples of topic label candidates generated by [1] using supervised ranking based on neural embedding.

Topic Label assigned by experts: **reinforcement learning**
Top-20 topical terms (unigrams)
learning, reinforcement, policy, control, decision, agents, agent, state, approach, learn, game, robot, planning, problem, value, reward, actions, optimal, policies, algorithm
Top-3 label candidates
policy, problem solving, optimization problem

Table 4. Topic labels generated by our phrase-based method using supervised ranking based on neural embedding.

Topic Label assigned by experts: **visual recognition**
Top-20 topical terms (phrases)
object detection, face recognition, object recognition, semantic segmentation, action recognition, face images, pose estimation, image classification, image captioning, video frames, image and video, visual features, face detection, facial expression, video sequences feature extraction, saliency map, PASCAL VOC, visual recognition, object categories
Top-3 label candidates
action recognition, object recognition, face recognition

Topic Label assigned by experts: **N/A**
Top-20 topical terms (phrases)
time series, anomaly detection, community detection, outlier detection, gene expression, human brain, time series data, breast cancer, spiking neurons, pattern mining, concept drift, Alzheimers disease, brain activity, multivariate time series, EEG signals, synaptic weights, biologically plausible, fMRI data, detect anomalies, firing rates
Top-3 label candidates
outlier detection, community detection, detect anomalies

the embeddings of all words contained for the corresponding phrase embedding, so there is a lot of space to improve with the latest progress on neural embedding of phrases and sentences [2,6].

As shown in Table 3, the unigram-based methods of [1] often generate topic labels which are susceptible to deviate from the topic themes. The topic labels are prone to be too general for appropriately describing topic themes due to limitation of Wikipedia document titles, and not informative for human interpretation. For the two topics in Table 4, although our phrase-based method sometimes do not generate topic labels fully covering topic themes, but still presents important aspects which are informative for human interpretability. Actually, even a human is hard to interpret and assign a succinct and meaningful label with one single phrase for the second topic in Table 4.

5 Conclusion and Future Work

This paper presents an efficient approach to generate high-quality topic labels using phrase-based topic models in order to reduce the cognitive overhead understanding and organizing online learning materials using topic models, and the experimental results also showed the effectiveness of the proposed method. In the future, the phrase neural embeddings can be refined and updated with the latest pre-trained contextualized representations such as ELMO or BERT [2,6], which capture semantics of phrases and topics more accurately and are highly likely to improve topic labeling. Recently, Vilnis et al. [8] advocated moving beyond vector point representations to continuous densities in latent space such as Gaussian embeddings, and found its ability to learn unsupervised entailment between concepts of corresponding phrases, which may also offer informative cues for better topic labeling with a succinct phrase.

References

1. Bhatia, S., Lau, J.H., Baldwin, T.: Automatic labelling of topics with neural embeddings. In: Proceedings of COLING 2016, The 26th International Conference on Computational Linguistics: Technical Papers, pp. 953–963. The COLING 2016 Organizing Committee (2016). http://aclweb.org/anthology/C16-1091
2. Devlin, J., Chang, M., Lee, K., Toutanova, K.: BERT: pre-training of deep bidirectional transformers for language understanding. CoRR abs/1810.04805 (2018)
3. El-Kishky, A., Song, Y., Wang, C., Voss, C.R., Han, J.: Scalable topical phrase mining from text corpora. Proc. VLDB Endow. **8**(3), 305–316 (2014)
4. Lau, J.H., Grieser, K., Newman, D., Baldwin, T.: Automatic labelling of topic models. In: Proceedings of the 49th Annual Meeting of the Association for Computational Linguistics: Human Language Technologies, HLT 2011, vol. 1, pp. 1536–1545. Association for Computational Linguistics, Stroudsburg, PA, USA (2011)
5. Mei, Q., Shen, X., Zhai, C.: Automatic labeling of multinomial topic models. In: Proceedings of the 13th ACM SIGKDD International Conference on Knowledge Discovery and Data Mining, KDD 2007, pp. 490–499. ACM, New York (2007). https://doi.org/10.1145/1281192.1281246

6. Peters, M., et al.: Deep contextualized word representations. In: Proceedings of the 2018 Conference of the North American Chapter of the Association for Computational Linguistics: Human Language Technologies, Volume 1 (Long Papers), pp. 2227–2237. Association for Computational Linguistics (2018). https://doi.org/10.18653/v1/N18-1202. http://aclweb.org/anthology/N18-1202
7. Shang, J., Liu, J., Jiang, M., Ren, X., Voss, C.R., Han, J.: Automated phrase mining from massive text corpora. IEEE Trans. Knowl. Data Eng. **30**(10), 1825–1837 (2018)
8. Vilnis, L., McCallum, A.: Word representations via Gaussian embedding. ICLR abs/1412.6623 (2015)
9. Wang, J., Xiang, J., Uchino, K.: Topic-specific recommendation for open education resources. In: Li, F.W.B., Klamma, R., Laanpere, M., Zhang, J., Manjón, B.F., Lau, R.W.H. (eds.) ICWL 2015. LNCS, vol. 9412, pp. 71–81. Springer, Cham (2015). https://doi.org/10.1007/978-3-319-25515-6_7
10. Wang, J., Zhao, C., Uchino, K., Xiang, J.: Interactive topic model with enhanced interpretability. In: Proceedings of the 2nd Workshop on Explainable Smart Systems, EXSS 2019 (2019)

Forward-Looking Activities Supporting Technological Planning of AI-Based Learning Platforms

Andrzej M. J. Skulimowski[1,2(✉)]

[1] AGH University of Science and Technology, al. Mickiewicza 30, 30-059 Kraków, Poland
ams@agh.edu.pl
[2] International Centre for Decision Sciences and Forecasting, Progress and Business Foundation, ul. Lea 12B, 30-048 Kraków, Poland

Abstract. AI-based learning platforms (AILPs) are becoming an increasingly important component of knowledge-based societies. AILP development and exploitation is deeply rooted in the PEST environment and requires a thorough strategic plan of the social, and research impacts over a mid to long-term perspective. This paper presents the learning technology-profiled part of the strategic impact planning for an innovative intelligent learning platform and knowledge repository, referred to as 'the Platform', developed within a Horizon 2020 project. It also discusses selected results of the recent Delphi survey on the learning platform's future and the methodological background of the strategy building process for an AILP. This four-round/real-time forward-looking activity combined policy and decision Delphi focused on the identification of factors influencing the future performance and educational impact of the Platform. The strategy building involved two stages. Stage 1 was devoted to establishing the boundary conditions for the Platform's activity and user community building, while Stage 2 delivered the final action plan aimed at ensuring the Platform's digital sustainability, financial viability, and social acceptance. Plausible exploitation scenarios were complemented by an impact model established with anticipatory networks. All this information was used in the final collaborative roadmapping, which situated the Platform exploitation in the real-life context.

Keywords: Learning platforms · Artificial Intelligence · Delphi survey · Technological forecasting · Strategic planning · Intelligent knowledge repositories

1 Introduction

The rapidly growing relevance of AI-based digital learning platforms (AILPs) for the development of knowledge societies and Industry 4.0 is a challenge in defining new educational, research, social, and economic policy goals from regional to European levels. AI-based digital ecosystems comprising learning communities around platforms and social media, the high-tech sector providing software and services, the related research and its governance, are crucial in ensuring a positive impact and wide acceptance of learning-related AI strategies. It is also important to select priorities for

M. A. Herzog et al. (Eds.): ICWL 2019, LNCS 11841, pp. 274–284, 2019.
https://doi.org/10.1007/978-3-030-35758-0_26

EU-financed educational projects in Horizon Europe and in other forthcoming research programmes. When supported by public funds, AILP development is deeply rooted in the PEST (Political, Economic, Social and Technological) environment, and it requires a thorough strategic plan of the social and economic impacts over a mid- to long-term perspective. Strategic planning should be aligned with technological progress, specifically in the emerging areas of Artificial Intelligence, Big Data, and Global Expert Systems [10], with an emphasis put on recommendation and decision support [12].

Despite the relevance of AILPs, very few publicly accessible AILP strategies or descriptions of strategic technological planning approaches exist. Those available refer mostly to e-learning course repositories [2, 5, 6]. When defining the policy framework for an AI-based knowledge repository developed within a Horizon 2020 EU research project [www.moving-project.eu], the above situation created a need to develop methodological foundations for AILP-oriented strategic planning in the context of future learning technology needs. An outline of this methodology is presented in the next section. Section 3 presents a novel expert knowledge elicitation and processing tool that utilizes innovative 'extrapolation Delphi' surveys [www.forgnosis.eu] to construct an AILP technological strategy and estimate its social and economic impact. In Sect. 4, we present an application of this tool to define the social, economic, market, and business-oriented research environments of learning platforms. These were applied in the technological roadmapping of the generic learning platform that stores online courses, manuals and scholarly papers, video files, economic and other information useful for learners. We will refer to this AILP as the Platform. Its operation is supported by a number of AI-based tools, from content-based automatic video annotation and retrieval, to intelligent educational recommenders and creativity stimulation tools [12]. Its primary application is to support learning and provide open guided knowledge to public administrators, students and young researchers [13].

In this presentation of the AILP strategy building process and its educational implications, we will focus on the methodology of generating future visions of the Platform, functioning with a flexible Delphi survey support system based on a novel forward extrapolation methodology. The survey offers a variety of question and/or statement types, sophisticated statistical analysis and other methods to handle uncertainties, as well as a user-friendly interface. It can be run in various modes that suit the survey goals and gather expert knowledge in multiple rounds, as a real-time Delphi or as a hybrid of both. The cloud-based Delphi application was offered to the project team in SaaS mode [11]. It can also be used as a basis for designing further customised expert information retrieval and fusion exercises for a broad spectrum of learning and research needs, as well as it can serve as an AI-based learning tool itself.

2 Methodological Approaches to AILP Impact Assessment

Impact modelling and strategy building for the Platform was designed as a generic process to serve a large class of AILPs. It was split into the following two stages:

a. Establishing the boundary conditions for AILP activity, exploitation and learning community building (Stage 1).

b. Delivering the final exploitation strategy aimed at ensuring digital sustainability, financial viability and social acceptance, taking into account plausible scenarios of the PEST environment resulting from an expert Delphi survey (Stage 2).

Forecasts were obtained from experts at both stages as outcomes of the Delphi survey and used to build an anticipatory network (AN) impact model cf. e.g. [9, 14]. The AN-based methodology has already proved useful in multicriteria strategic planning [14]. The ANs provide constructive algorithms for computing nondominated strategic plans that comply with a given anticipatory preference structure. The preferences of stakeholders, policy makers and other decision makers (i.e. those responsible for shaping the Platform's future and beneficiaries) can be taken into account. We will provide indications on how to apply anticipatory decision-making principles in constructing and filtering scenarios corresponding to rational and sustainable future AILP visions. AN-based assessment processes allow the analyst to select a subset of normative scenarios corresponding to the most preferred states of the future and subsequently run an AN-based backcasting [14]. By definition, the best normative scenario describes the most desired future elicited from AILP stakeholders, starting from the current best-compromise decision of the AILP management team and passing through the intermediate states that correspond to the interim goals of the AILP development project. The strategic goals were derived from:

- Expert information concerning future trends in education technology.
- A study of the PEST environment followed by a SWOTC (Strength, Weaknesses, Opportunities, Threats, and Challenges) analysis.
- An AN-based impact model within an analytic strategic planning process that follows a technological roadmapping scheme.

This analytical and collaborative process ensures the selection of the best-compromise decision sequence, or another scenario that comes close, in the sense of reaching the best expected values of the prescribed Platform performance criteria, under different forecasts of external circumstances. Specifically, given the forecasts or scenarios, the strategic planning algorithm computes decisions that correspond to the optimal social and economic impacts of the Platform operation. This is the core procedure of the backward planning process. As the Platform's external circumstances are policy- and technology-dependent, the above procedure allows us to determine the conditions that can make the above optimum provisions and favourite circumstances real. Assuming that AILP usage principles by an average individual user do not differ considerably worldwide, we can derive general indications on the functioning of intelligent digital repositories, learning, and other knowledge platforms.

2.1 A Delphi Support System to Elicit Forward-Oriented Expert Knowledge

Future visions of the Platform's function, its PEST environment and learning technology progress are fundamental to the strategy building process. These have been obtained from experts with a flexible Delphi survey support system (DeSS, [11]). Unknown future parameters to be inserted into the social and economic impact models resulted from a novel forward extrapolation approach used in the survey, which can be summarised as follows.

First, experts provide quantitative estimations of the relevant variables for a few predefined forecasting horizons. These estimations, together with a current state assessment, are then used to fit a regression curve that can yield significant extrapolations even beyond the farthest predefined forecasting horizon. The survey offers a variety of question and/or statement types, sophisticated statistical analysis and other uncertainty handling methods, as well as a user-friendly interface. It can be run in policy or in decision Delphi modes [11, 13] as well as gather expert knowledge over multiple rounds, as a real-time Delphi, or as a hybrid of both. The survey software used (Forgnosis^{TM}, cf. [11] for details) provides a number of features. Among other things, it can detect duplicate replies, correlated replies, as well as verify the content of each individual reply (e.g. detect random entries, check the justification consistency).

The objective nature of the information obtained from experts is ensured by the manner in which the survey is organised [4]. A preceding "Round 0" is established to allow the Platform stakeholders to determine the scope of the survey. The first stage is aimed at reaching an internal consensus among the decision makers and experts, while the main goal of the second stage is to expand the future vision and seek new opportunities and challenges, cf. [11, 15]. Both stages consist of two rounds. Rounds 1 and 2 were performed in multi-round mode [11] while Rounds 3 and 4 were organised as a real-time Delphi [3] – an adaptive advisory activity. Participation in the survey was open to the Platform owners and developers staff as well as external experts who were not directly involved in the project's execution, such as higher university management staff, members of the scientific and supervisory councils, etc.

The results of the survey are intended to evaluate the internal conditions and external circumstances under which the Platform will be exploited. This information is necessary to build its sustainability strategy. Thus, the survey touched upon development trends of AI technologies enabling the future evolution of the Platform. These included autonomic web search technologies, Internet evolution prospects, creativity support systems, data mining techniques, content-based information retrieval, and multimedia searches. Furthermore, when responding to the survey, experts provided relevant information on the anticipated economic, social, and political environments, Platform's learning services and functionalities that may be offered in the future, and feasibility of strategic goals and future business models of the Platform.

The first stage of the survey was aimed at eliciting project staff opinion on the exploitation of the Platform during the project's durability period (2019-2024) and beyond (until 2030). This stage corresponded to the 'decision Delphi' [13] type of exercise, popular in corporate foresight activities. Its characteristic feature involves decision makers that may have some influence on the future visions provided in the survey. According to the 'decision Delphi' principles, Rounds 1 and 2 were focused on internal consensus building regarding all aspects of the Platform's sustainability, in particular digital sustainability, cf. [1]. Participation in this stage of the survey allowed the project staff to better understand diverse aspects of the Platform's technological viability and the relation to its future development.

The second stage consisted of Rounds 3 and 4. They included questions that did not yield consensus during the first stage of the survey and focused on research and macroeconomic aspects of AILP development. Besides reaching a consensus on general issues, the aim of Stage 2 was also to detect any change in the internal or external circumstances that might affect the Platform's development and performance.

The cloud-based Delphi application (DeSS) was used in Software-as–a-Service (SaaS) mode, with some Platform-as–a-Service (PaaS) features. This application turns out suitable to design further customised expert information retrieval and fusion exercises for various educational and research needs. The survey has been available at the dedicated web page www.moving-survey.ipbf.eu where experts can register to participate in the ongoing activities. More details on the underlying Delphi methodology are provided in [11].

2.2 Expert Information Elicited and Analysis of Survey Results

The Delphi survey variant with confidence management was selected as best suited for this type of survey, where the participants were experts in specialised fields [10] such as learning technology, pedagogy, or sociology. According to its principles, the survey questions are presented to all participants but not all of them had to reply all questions. Experience resulting from earlier surveys within thematic areas related to e-learning and learning support systems has been taken into account (cf. [5, 7, 8]).

The replies obtained from different respondents to the same question have been fused together using weighted averaging approaches and triangular fuzzy values to account for confidence coefficients. An initial value for "degree of confidence" (usually based on a 5-value Likert scale) could be self-assessed by the respondents for each question or group of questions. This made it possible to consider opinions of those respondents who are not experts in the specific field covered by the survey but are nonetheless capable of contributing valuable ideas, yet with a lower weight. Uncertainty handling with random-fuzzy distributions turned out to be a suitable technique for this kind of data. The fuzzy factors described the uncertainty related to diversified competences, while the stochastic properties of the reply dataset were used to fuse individual replies. The overall methodology is explained in detail in a context-based online help manual available to users after logging into the survey system.

3 Analysis of Survey Results and Intra-round Convergence

A DeSS questionnaire with three subordinated questions concerning the relevance of future risk factors that may affect the Platform demonstrates the survey in action (cf. www.moving-platform.ipbf.eu: Subsect. 3, question 6). An analysis of the replies shown in Fig. 1 (next page) looks at the relevance of the six risk factors related to the implementation and operation of learning platforms (listed in the Fig. 1 legend). The risk factors with the highest potential impact on the Platform were pre-selected during the Delphi "Round-0" from about 20 candidate factors. The impact assessments (horizontal axis) are confronted with the uncertainty (vertical axis) of respondents assessing them. The latter is the standard deviation of replies. Both factors are expressed in 5-point Likert scale points, where the numerical values 1 to 5 correspond to naturally ordered scale values: "*irrelevant*" (1), "*low-relevance*" (2), to "*very relevant*" (5). One can observe that data protection and data privacy have been identified as the most relevant risk factors, with slightly decreasing relevance until 2030. The uncertainty related to risk factor assessment increases with time for the three factors (a), (b) and (e), which may be explained as a natural consequence of confidence intervals growing with more distant forecasting horizons. However, an uncertainty increase accompanied by the growing relevance of the remaining risk factors (c), (d), and (f) indicates a growing consensus regarding the expected threat growth. These results have been applied in the risk analysis component of the Platform's sustainability strategy.

A similar analysis of Delphi results was performed for the group relevance assessment of learning technologies, such as user creativity measurement and stimulation tools, augmented and virtual reality, or serious educational games.

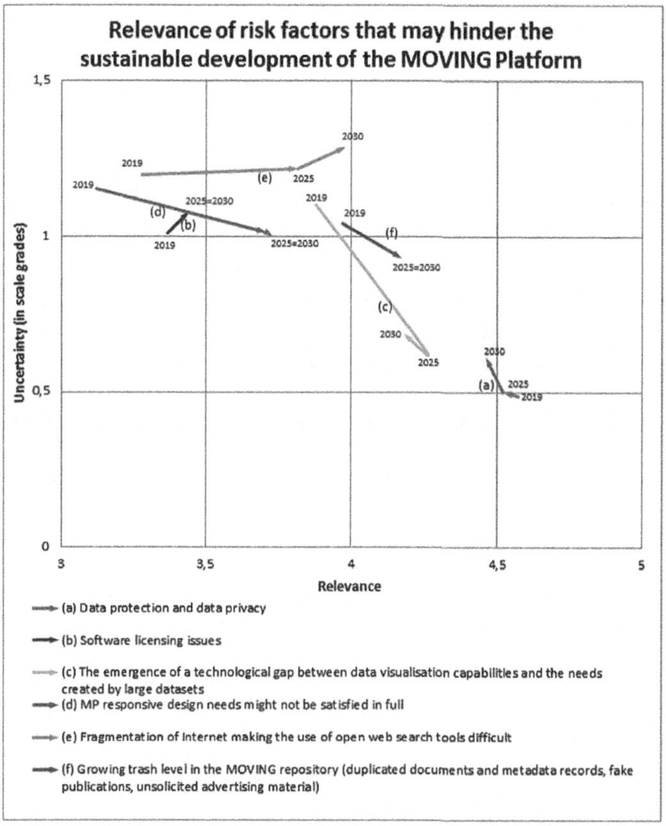

Fig. 1. Relevance/uncertainty analysis of risk until 2030. Values on both axes are expressed in 5-value Likert scale points factors with the highest potential impact on the Platform. The arrow directions coincide with time flow, ending at the state expected

Presented below is another sample set of results for the following Delphi question:

Subsection 1. Question 6. "*Integration of knowledge on the Internet with the Platform will allow for a new quality of replies to queries, which is unavailable with contemporary analysis methods. Please specify in % the share of problems which may get more relevant responses with the autonomous Platform services, compared to the queries replied by human experts*"

Table 1 contains a sample set of statistical characteristics of replies and a basic analysis. Unless indicated otherwise, table entries are given in percent or in percent points. It also provides the values of classical consensus measures y_i, $i = 1, 2, 3$, for question 1.6, where y_1 is the standard deviation σ, y_2 – the sum of standard semi-deviations, $y_2 = \sigma\_ + \sigma_+$, and y_3 *is* the *interquartile range* (IQR), by definition IQR: = 3rd quartile – 1st quartile. The above measures have been used to measure consensus achievement for all questions. The convergence between rounds has been measured as

$$\xi(y) = (1 - y(\text{round2})/y(\text{round1})) * 100\%, \text{ where } y = y_1 \text{ or } y = y_2 \text{ or } y = y_3 \quad (1)$$

or as the Kullback-Leibler divergence of the empirical reply distributions in the subsequent (n-th and (n + 1)st) rounds.

Table 1. Statistical analysis of replies to Question 1.6 of the Delphi survey (www.moving-survey.ipbf.eu); statistical characteristics calculated with respondents' competence coefficients

Share of queries which may get more relevant responses with the autonomous AILP services								
Forecast horizons	2019		2020		2025		2030	
	Round 1	Round 2	Round 1	Round 2	Round 1	Round 2	Round 1	Round 2
Average ($\bar{x}$)	50,74%	46,34%	52,60%	48,05%	57,03%	53,54%	62,08%	56,87%
No. of replies	17	15	17	15	17	15	17	15
Standard deviation (σ)	30,22	24,52	31,05	24,66	29,22	23,11	28,04	22,95
Std. semidev. left ($\sigma\_$)	19,09	14,2	19,92	15,12	19,12	15,22	19,68	16,31
Std. semidev. right (σ_+)	23,42	19,99	23,81	19,49	22,09	17,39	19,98	16,15
1. quartile ($q1$)	23,09%	30%	23,09%	30%	35,28%	39,98%	41,21%	50%
Median (2. quartile, $q2$)	38,57%	40%	39%	43,58%	45%	50%	57,50%	51,65%
3. quartile ($q3$)	65,43%	50%	75,43%	50,83%	84,07%	55,83%	89,50%	61,83%
IQR: = $q3 - q1$	42,34	20	52,34	20,83	48,79	15,85	48,29	11,83
No. of clusters of replies	2	1	2	1	2	1	1	1
Consensus reached	No	Yes	No	Yes	No	Yes	No	Yes
No. of outliers removed	2	0	2	0	2	0	2	0
Convergence between rounds $\xi(y)$: = $(1 - y(round2)/y(round1)) * 100\%$, $y = y_1$ *or* $y = y_2$ *or* $y = y_3$								
$\xi(y_1)$, where y_1: = σ	18,86%		20,58%		20,91%		18,15%	
$\xi(y_2)$, where y_2: = $\sigma\_ + \sigma_+$	19,57%		20,86%		20,87%		18,15%	
$\xi(y_3)$, where y_3: = IQR	52,76%		60,20%		67,51%		75,50%	

The quartiles provided in Table 1 are complemented by the quintiles shown in Fig. 2 (right). The left part of Fig. 2 shows the histograms of replies to question 1.6 for the forecasting horizons 2020, 2025, and 2030, showing the number of clusters of replies.

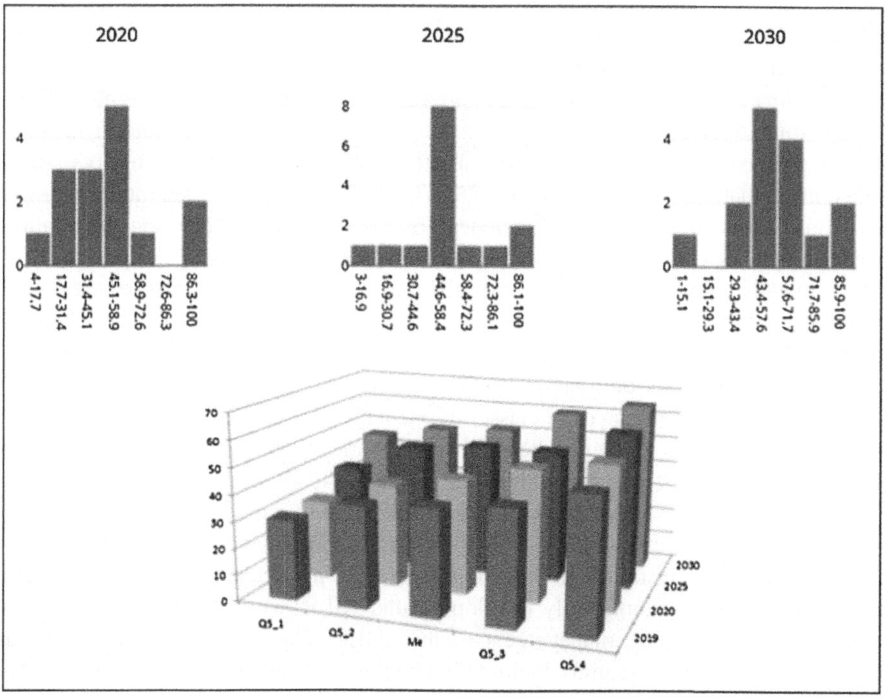

Fig. 2. Histograms (upper diagram) and the quintiles with the median (lower diagram) of replies to Question 1.6

The emergence of statistically significant clusters indicates a lack of consensus but provides indications concerning the potential existence of several exploratory scenarios of the investigated factor or variable [15]. It is worth noting that in the above question, there was only one significant cluster of replies and a consensus was reached in round 2 for all forecasting horizons. It should be noted that a consensus, in terms of IQR/2 < 20%, was reached for 48 out of 96 questions in Round 2 for the main forecasting horizon of 2025, selected as the end of the minimum durability period of the Platform. The number of questions with consensus decreased to 41 out of 96 for the year 2030. However, all but one of the Delphi statements for 2025 exhibited a convergence between subsequent Rounds 1 and 2 with respect to all the indicators (1) with $y = y_i$, $i = 1, 2, 3$, and the Kullback-Leibler divergence used as convergence measures.

4 The Strategy Building for an AILP

The information received from survey respondents was fused and analysed. The outcomes of the survey together with bibliometric, patentometric and demographics data were then used as the input needed to build an anticipatory network (AN) that models all relevant future impacts relative to the AILP analysed. The network includes all relations between actors, factors, trends, and plausible random future events. ANs are a relatively new tool in decision theory, rooted in anticipatory system theory [14]. This theory formalises and fuses multi-stage multicriteria forward planning, and multicriteria backcasting. ANs generalise earlier anticipatory models of decision impact in multicriteria problem solving and constitute an alternative decision model to utility or value function estimations and to diverse heuristics [14]. An AN is a directed multigraph with no loops, nodes modelling the decision problems, and edges modelling the relations between them. Every AN must have at least one starting node (with no predecessors) which models a present-time multicriteria strategic decision problem. The other nodes model decisions made for future multicriteria problems that will be solved by the same or other decision makers. The edges of the first kind model the causal dependence of decision problems on solutions to previous problems. There may be several causal relations and corresponding edge classes in one network. Subsequent decisions that are made along a chain of causal dependences in an anticipatory network model the consequences of decisions made at earlier nodes in the chain.

The decision is made after a constructive analysis of causal relations that link the outcomes of the current problem with their future consequences [14]. In case of the learning platform, the starting problem corresponds to the decisions of the coordinating bodies of the consortium jointly developing this AILP, while the 'next generations' correspond to the future management of this AILP. The other decision makers are responsible for user community building, technology acquisition, or development. The overall strategic technological planning process comprised of the following:

- A forward-looking activity aimed at identifying the internal and environmental factors influencing the future performance and impact of the Platform. The activity combines a four-round/real-time novel policy and decision Delphi survey with an AN impact model established with the parameters delivered as survey outcomes.
- A dynamic (2-stage, real-time) SWOTC (SWOT with Challenges) exercise, which provides additional inputs to the Risk Matrix analysis and the final roadmapping.
- Technological and anticipatory planning that delivers the final strategy with three exploitation scenarios resulting from the Delphi survey and an AN-based action plan ensuring AILP digital sustainability, economic viability and social acceptance.
- Roadmapping-based technological planning of the learning platform operation.
- Social impact analysis with ANs, cellular automata, and Bayesian network models.

A scheme of the overall generic strategy building process, which was applied for the Platform as a representative case of AILP, is presented in Fig. 3, cf. also [13].

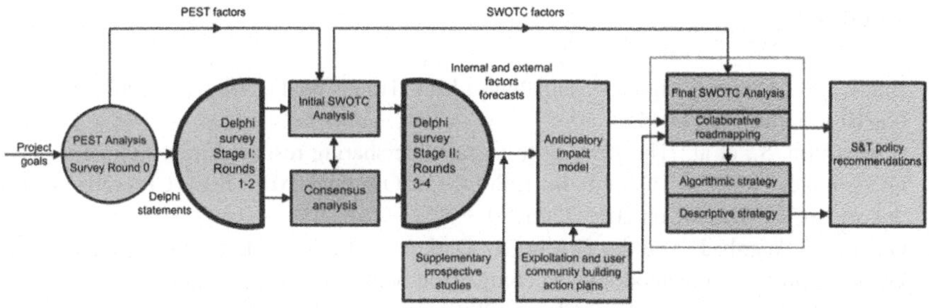

Fig. 3. A technological planning scheme for a generic AI-based digital learning platform

5 Conclusions

As a general conclusion, it should be noted that the expert knowledge acquisition and strategic decision making methods presented in this paper define a complete computing background for technological planning of an AI-based learning platform. It consists of an online Delphi survey support system (DeSS), an AN building tool, and generic roadmapping support system that form together a strategic Decision Support System (DSS) allowing an analyst to gather and efficiently deploy technological foresight results. Nevertheless, the above-presented DeSS can also be used as a stand-alone DSS. When used jointly with analytic impact modelling tools, future circumstances can be analysed quantitatively and algorithmic action plans can be defined for complex AI-based learning management systems such as AILPs. Thanks to a growing number of publicly available foresight results and an accessibility of open source web information repositories, the hitherto barely affordable strategy building processes can be performed satisfactorily as a combination of an online Delphi survey, other collaborative activities such as SWOTC, roadmapping, and interactive multicriteria decision making with anticipatory preference information and trade-offs between criteria.

The novel forward extrapolation methodology used in the above-presented DeSS offers a variety of question and/or statement types, a sophisticated statistical analysis and other uncertainty handling methods as well as a user-friendly interface. It can be run in policy as well as decision Delphi modes, gather and fuse expert knowledge in multiple rounds, as a real-time Delphi, or as a hybrid of both. The final results of outcomes was presented to the decision makers as technology or functionality rankings.

We have shown in previous sections that the overall approach proved useful in building a multiple-context learning platform strategy, exemplifying a larger class of similar applications. The Delphi survey assured a persistent deployment of contributions from experts knowledgeable in the field of technologies and AILP markets.

Finally, let us note that the models and applications presented in this paper can benefit from a synergy with other foresight and forecasting methods and IT tools such as foresight and roadmapping support systems.

Acknowledgment. The author is grateful for the support of the Horizon 2020 research project MOVING financed by the EC, contract No. 693092.

References

1. Bradley, K.: Defining digital sustainability. Libr. Trends **56**(1), 148–163 (2007). https://doi.org/10.1353/lib.2007.0044
2. Chunwijitra, S., et al.: The strategy to sustainable sharing resources repository for massive open online courses in Thailand. In: 12th ECTI-CON, June 2015. IEEE CPS (2015). https://doi.org/10.1109/ECTICon.2015.7206980
3. Gnatzy, T., Warth, J., von der Gracht, H., Darkow, I.-L.: Validating an innovative real-time Delphi approach - a methodological comparison between real-time and conventional Delphi studies. Technol. Forecast Soc. Change **78**(9), 1681–1694 (2011). https://doi.org/10.1016/j.techfore.2011.04.006
4. Hasson, F., Keeney, S.: Enhancing rigour in the Delphi technique research. Technol. Forecast Soc. Change **78**(9), 1695–1704 (2011). https://doi.org/10.1016/j.techfore.2011.04.005
5. Lopez-Catalan, B., Bañuls, V.A.: A Delphi-based approach for detecting key e-learning trends in postgraduate education: the Spanish case. Educ.+Train. **59**(6), 590–604 (2017). https://doi.org/10.1108/ET-12-2016-0186
6. Maldonado Mahauad, J.J., Carvallo, J.P., Zambrano, J.S.: Educational repositories. Study of the current situation and strategies to improve their effective use at Ecuadorian Universities. IEEE Rev. Iberoamericana de Tecnologias del Aprendizaje **11**(2), 79–86 (2016). https://doi.org/10.1109/RITA.2016.2554001
7. Meletiou-Mavrotheris, M., Koutsopoulos, K.C.: Projecting the future of cloud computing in education: a foresight study using the Delphi method. In: Koutsopoulos, K.C., Doukas, K., Kotsanis, Y. (eds.) Handbook of Research on Educational Design and Cloud Computing in Modern Classroom Settings, Chap. 12, pp. 262–290. IGI Global, Hershey (2018). https://doi.org/10.4018/978-1-5225-3053-4.ch012
8. Nworie, J.: Using the Delphi technique in educational technology research. TechTrends **55**(5), 24–30 (2011). https://doi.org/10.1007/s11528-011-0524-6
9. Ramos, J.M.: Forging the Synergy between Anticipation and Innovation: The Futures Action Model. J. Futur. Stud. **18**(1), 85–106 (2013)
10. Skulimowski, A.M.J.: Universal intelligence, creativity, and trust in emerging global expert systems. In: Rutkowski, L., et al. (eds.), Proceedings of the 12th International Conference on Artificial Intelligence and Soft Computing, Zakopane, 2013, Part II. Lecture Notes in Artificial Intelligence, vol. 7895, pp. 582–592. Springer, Heidelberg (2013). https://doi.org/10.1007/978-3-642-38610-7_53
11. Skulimowski, A.M.J.: Expert Delphi survey as a cloud-based decision support service. In: IEEE 10th SOCA 2017, 22–25 November 2017, Kanazawa, Japan, pp. 190–197. IEEE (2017). https://doi.org/10.1109/SOCA.2017.33
12. Skulimowski, A.M.J.: Cognitive content recommendation in digital knowledge repositories – a survey of recent trends. In: Rutkowski, L., Korytkowski, M., Scherer, R., Tadeusiewicz, R., Zadeh, L.A., Zurada, J.M. (eds.) ICAISC 2017. LNCS (LNAI), vol. 10246, pp. 574–588. Springer, Cham (2017). https://doi.org/10.1007/978-3-319-59060-8_52
13. Skulimowski, A.M.J.: Strategy building for a knowledge repository with a novel expert information fusion tool. In: 6th International Conference on Future-Oriented Technology Analysis (FTA): Future in the Making, 4–5 June 2018, Brussels, pp. 1–15 (2018)
14. Skulimowski, A.M.J.: Anticipatory networks. In: Poli, R. (ed.) Handbook of Anticipation, pp. 995–1030. Springer, Cham (2019). https://doi.org/10.1007/978-3-319-91554-8_22
15. Tapio, P.: Disaggregative policy Delphi: using cluster analysis as a tool for systematic scenario formation. Technol. Forecast Soc. Change **70**(1), 83–101 (2003). https://doi.org/10.1016/S0040-1625(01)00177-9

Mobile Learning

Analyzing Integrated Learning Scenarios for Outdoor Settings

Terje Väljataga(✉) and Kadri Mettis

Tallinn University, Narva Road 25, 10120 Tallinn, Estonia
{terjev,kadri.mettis}@tlu.ee

Abstract. Research suggests that an interdisciplinary approach, where students can gather and evaluate evidence, and make sense of information they receive, can enhance students' learning and better model various processes and phenomena in the real world [1]. However, it might create challenges for teachers to design integrated learning scenarios in authentic outdoor settings. The general aim of the paper is to analyze the content of integrated learning scenarios supported with technologies (mobile devices, online applications, sensors and educational robotics) in outdoor settings created by teachers from 6 K-12 schools to understand the characteristics of outdoor learning scenarios, the type of knowledge and level of contextualization these scenarios anticipate. The content analysis of the integrated learning scenarios demonstrates that the teachers tend to design learning scenarios, which hardly embrace learning contexts and enable to support higher order knowledge building types.

Keywords: Outdoor learning · Subject integration · Knowledge types · Mobile learning · Contextualization

1 Introduction

Different state level educational strategies emphasize a student-centered approach in authentic real life settings, which are supported by a set of digital technology to enrich learning processes and make learning and teaching more engaging and efficient. Taking some of the learning activities outside the classrooms into authentic settings has a great potential to connect knowledge building to the real world. This means providing students with learning experiences where they can solve complex natural problems, which require implementing knowledge and skills from different subjects. However, planning, designing and implementing learning activities outside the familiar classroom environment might be a challenging task for teachers, in particular, to design learning scenarios in which integrated knowledge building [2] happens through exploration and inquiry facilitated by mobile technologies. The study presented in this paper takes a closer look at the content of learning scenarios teachers have designed from the following perspectives: (1) What are the characteristics of outdoor integrated learning scenarios? (2) To what extent and what kind of knowledge components and context types do learning scenarios anticipate?

M. A. Herzog et al. (Eds.): ICWL 2019, LNCS 11841, pp. 287–294, 2019.
https://doi.org/10.1007/978-3-030-35758-0_27

2 Mobile and Contextualized Outdoor Learning

Mobile technologies such as smart phones, web-based applications, sensors, etc. support problem-solving and inquiry learning, inviting learners to be engaged in reflective, explorative and scientific thinking, which makes learning highly motivating [3–7]. Mobile technology can extend, enhance, enrich, challenge and disrupt existing ideas and assumptions about learning [8]. In this paper we define mobile learning as "the process of coming to know and being able to operate successfully in, and across, new and ever changing contexts and learning spaces" ([9] p. 66). A numerous physical and virtual spaces can be turned into interesting and motivational learning settings creating specific authentic contexts for learning. These contexts produce or enforce a more fluid, fragmented and transient movement between multiple spaces [8] with the support of a set of various personal and institutional mobile technologies. Operating between multiple contexts brings along one of the biggest challenges for students. They are supposed to make abstractions from their learning experience so that knowledge gained in one specific context can be successfully applied across many contexts. Sharples [10] defines three types of contextualized learning: *learning in context* means that the learner is aware of being situated within an environment that is fashioned to enable learning; *learning through context* means that the learner experiences context as a means to satisfy learning goals by deliberately or implicitly creating and augmenting interactions with people, environments and materials; *learning about context* means the natural surroundings become the object of learning [10]. Designing learning experiences for outside the classroom settings, the learning activity itself should be situational and connected to the context it takes place. According to [11] and [12] knowledge of context is the most critical feature of problem solving. The central research challenge is to reconcile these three perspectives of contextualized learning and understand the interplay between them [10].

3 Knowledge Building Components

Researchers have developed several frameworks for classifying knowledge types, such as individual/group/public, internalized/externalized, accessible/not accessible, according to modalities, etc. Burgin [13] outlines operational levels of knowledge, which are sequenced from the lowest to highest: (1) Knowledge as an ability to perceive the object; (2) Knowledge as an ability to do something with the object (3) Knowledge as an ability to use the object for some purpose. A rather typical distinction has been made between "know-that" as descriptive/declarative knowledge (explicit fundamental form of knowledge, such as facts) and "know-how" as operational/procedural knowledge (knowledge that is manifested in the use of a skill) [14]. According to Ryle [13] it is possible to have lots of knowledge-that without possessing any knowledge-how [13]. Shavelson, Ruiz-Primo and Wiley [15] have emphasized a conceptual framework for characterizing science goals and student achievement according to the level of knowledge sophistication:

- Declarative knowledge (knowing that/what/about) refers to domain-specific content, such as factual information, definitions and descriptions.
- Procedural knowledge (knowing how) refers to information that is needed to accomplish a particular task or the ability to solve a problem. This knowledge type encompasses a group of specific strategies and skills, involves understanding concepts, and applying rules and sequences that govern relationships.
- Schematic or axiomatic knowledge (knowing why) refers to explanatory knowledge enabling students to move a step beyond know-how and create opportunities to deal with unknown interactions and unseen situations applying principles, schemes, rules, etc. [13].
- Strategic or conditional knowledge (knowing when) refers to knowledge, when and where to apply and not to apply a skill, strategy, and procedure.

The aforementioned problem-oriented knowledge classification [15] has been taken as a basis for analyzing learning scenarios, which have been designed by the teachers for outdoor learning experiences.

4 Research Context

Six schools have been invited to participate in a project "Integrated mobile outdoor learning in K-12 education", which focuses on designing and testing integrated, technology supported outdoor learning scenarios. This four year project aims to co-develop with teachers 72 integrated mobile outdoor learning scenarios, which are supported by a set of mobile technological solutions: personal/institutional smart phones, a web- and location-based application Avastusrada (avastusrada.ee), Vernier sensors for measuring different environmental conditions in a chosen location point, EV3 robot's brain for reading the measures from the sensors and additional physical objects for supporting measurements in outdoor settings. According to the project focus, the scenarios should encompass applied dimension of learning and require students to combine accumulated subject specific knowledge and skills to scientifically and creatively tackle authentic real-world phenomena and problems.

Avastusrada - Avastusrada is a web-based tool for creating and playing location-based learning tracks outside the classrooms. Using Avastusrada requires a smart-phone or a tablet, which has an Internet connection (WiFi, 3G or 4G) that allows making use of GPS location services. Teachers can create questions related to chosen locations and incorporate them into meaningful holistic tracks. Questions can be textual, include photos, videos, audio or animations for additional information. The Avastusrada application offers a list of templates for creating different types of questions: multiple choice answers, free form answers, one correct answer, providing info and photos. For each location point of the track different types of tasks could be created allowing players for instance to explore the surrounding, answer the questions or carry out some measuring in the surrounding and submit the value. The location points with questions and tasks get activated when students reach the particular location (see Fig. 1) and will be turned to green as soon as the answer to the question or the task has been submitted.

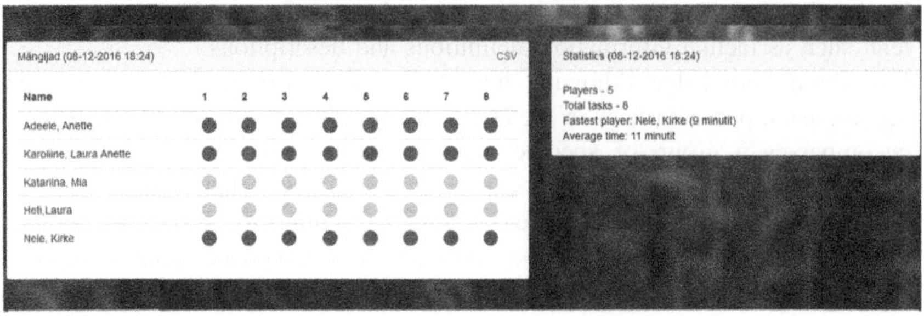

Fig. 1. A screenshot of Avastusrada.

Depending on how the track has been designed, the students can visit location points randomly or in a predefined order.

Vernier Sensors and EV3 Brain - Vernier sensors are designed specifically for active, hands-on experiments allowing carrying out various measurements in outdoor settings. Due to some economical reasons of our project, the sensors are used in combination with an EV3 robot's brain to read measured data. The data can be inserted manually by students to Avastusrada application as an answer to a question in the particular location point.

5 Methodology

The research presented in this paper aims to take a closer look at the scenarios the teachers have designed for K-12 school students. As the project is still running, 25 scenarios have been designed and tested with the students and have been included into the analysis. The content analysis focused on the following aspects: subject-integration, used question types predefined by Avastusrada, anticipated knowledge components and contextualization in these scenarios. The aim was to understand teachers' capabilities to create interdisciplinary learning scenarios for outdoor settings supported by a set of mobile applications. Regarding the interdisciplinary aspect, the subjects were divided into 4 categories. Physics, Chemistry, Biology, Geography and Science formed a group Science. Estonian and Literature, English and Russian formed a group Languages, Mathematics and Informatics were grouped as Mathematics and other subjects e.g. Physical Education, Art, Music, Traffic and Sustainability were grouped together under a category Other Subjects. For extracting potential knowledge components from these scenarios, the previously described conceptual framework by [15] was applied as a prescriptive model. The scenarios were also assessed in terms of context types according Sharples [10]. Two researchers independently analyzed the scenarios according to the aforementioned frameworks and occurred differences were discussed and agreed.

6 Results and Discussion

6.1 General Data and Subjects Integration in Learning Scenarios

Teachers from six schools have created 25 integrated outdoor learning scenarios that incorporate mobile tools. The scenarios were designed for different age levels from 1st to 9th grade. For the first school level (grades 1–3) 1 track, for second level (4–) 12 tracks, for third level (7–9) 9 tracks and for second to third level (4–9) 3 tracks were created. All the analyzed scenarios were meant for use during the class lesson and were designed as a pair or group work. The longest track was 11 km and the shortest 200 meters long. The scenario with most location points had 16 and shortest 2 different location points. In every location point it was possible to add several questions. Minimum number of questions in one scenario was 6 and maximum was 86. Total 465 questions were created.

The number of integrated subjects varied between 2–7 subjects. First school level track integrated 3 subjects: Estonian, Science and Art. The second level tracks integrated subjects in various combinations, for instance such as Science, Estonian, Physical Education, Russian. In the third level the subjects were combined, for instance, as follows: English, Russian, Estonian, Human Studies, Mathematics, Physics, Physical Education. 5–7 subjects were integrated for the second to third level scenarios, for example Physical Education, Mathematics, Science, Human Studies. Based on the collected data the teachers have designed learning scenarios with different subjects, but Math, Science and Estonian language seem to be the most popular combination. However, our initial content analysis doesn't reveal yet the meaningfulness and coherence of the subjects' integration.

6.2 Question Types in Learning Scenarios

While creating a track in Avastusrada it is possible to choose a question type (see Sect. 4). 59% of the questions were a free form answer type (see Table 1), which gives teachers a lot of freedom to develop the questions and tasks, and is the easiest type for the teachers to create.

Table 1. Question type distribution in the learning scenarios.

Total	One correct answer	Multiple correct answers	Free form answer	Photo	Info	Not marked
465	90 (20%)	39 (8%)	274 (59%)	35 (7,6%)	25 (5%)	2 (0,4%)

Out of 465 questions 64% belonged to the group Science. Within that group there was more diversity in terms of question types: free form 58%, one correct answer 19%, multiple correct answers 11%, 6% of the questions were info and 4% were photo tasks. In the group of Languages 60 questions were found, which were more homogeneous: free form answer 62%, one correct answer 33%. The group Mathematics consisted of 80% of free form answers, one correct answer 18%. The group Other Subjects contained subjects that were different from each other by their nature and that is reflected also in the used question types: photo task 46%, free form answer 43%, one correct answer and multiple correct answers were used equally in 5% of the cases. 19 questions were not related to any subjects. It seems that with other subjects than Science, the teachers have rather similar type of questions in mind. Is it because the teachers' perceived affordances of the application are limited, they lack know how or the reason is somewhere else, needs further investigation.

6.3 Knowledge Types in Learning Scenarios by Subject Groups

All the questions in the learning scenarios were categorized based on the knowledge components framework. 45% of the questions address procedural knowledge on how to use previously existing knowledge (see Table 2). 43% of the questions were about using declarative knowledge, mostly tasks about defining, describing or finding information. The questions about knowing when to use principles, existing facts or strategies related to the topic were not found. Only 10% of the questions were explanatory type that would relate the procedural knowledge to unseen relations and principles to use in other situations. As the number of questions that addresses procedural knowledge makes up almost half of the questions, then it seems that a lot of practical tasks are left without further analysis, which won't help to make relations or understanding overall principles, strategies that students could relate to in new situations.

Table 2. Distribution of knowledge types in the learning scenarios.

Total	Knowing what	Knowing how	Knowing when	Knowing why	Several types	Not marked
465	203	211	0	47	4	1

Table 3 shows that for the Science group mainly declarative and procedural knowledge types were represented. This group emphasized most the axiomatic knowledge. In overall it can be seen that the knowledge types vary in the subject groups. While declarative type is more presented in Language groups, then the procedural knowledge type in all the subject groups, however, proportionally more in Mathematics and in the Other Subjects group. This finding is in line with Crompton *et al.* [16] study where in mathematics procedural tasks were found to be the most common. The axiomatic type was mostly represented in Science group; nevertheless the number of that knowledge type is small compared to the other types.

Table 3. Distribution of knowledge types by subject groups.

	Total	Knowing what	Knowing how	Knowing why	Several types
Sciences	298	128	122	44	4
Languages	60	45	13	2	0
Mathematics	51	5	45	1	0
Other subjects	37	12	24	1	0

6.4 Contextualization of Questions in Learning Scenarios

As mentioned before, learning outside the classroom happens in different contexts enabling to design learning activities related to the chosen location point emphasizing the authenticity of learning. The data demonstrates 211 questions can be categorized as learning *in context*, which means that the students have to be in a certain location for answering the question, however, they don't need to interact with anything nor anyone in that location for solving the task. 186 questions were connected to the selected location point, where the context was perceived as a means to satisfy performing the learning task. 68 questions required interaction with the surrounding, people or materials in that location and only 15% questions were about the location point as a study object. These results are somewhat surprising. In more than half of the cases the potential of using the location for knowledge building is not used. The number of *in context* questions, which require no interaction with the location is rather big in all scenarios. As this tool gives an opportunity to move between different locations and to actually connect learning to the actual context, it can be seen that in some reasons this possibility is not used in its full potential. This raises the question of how meaningful are these learning scenarios if the context itself is not made use of and why the teachers haven't perceived the affordances of the chosen location points.

7 Conclusions

Our analysis of the existing learning scenarios has shown that designing integrated learning scenarios is a challenging endeavor for the teachers. Despite of the possibilities to use different mobile applications from smart phones to Vernier sensors, etc. the teachers lack ideas of how to develop learning scenarios, which encompass tasks that require students to implement different modalities and types of knowledge. Even though in Science subjects the questions were more diverse than in Mathematics and Languages regarding knowledge type, nevertheless, all scenarios lacked questions that would support making use of axiomatic and conditional knowledge. The scenarios follow a typical classroom structure and the affordances of mobile technology for learning in authentic settings is not perceived and used. On the other hand, the question types in the Avastusrada application might restrict teachers' creativity to design contextualized (learning about context) questions, which presume the students to apply higher knowledge types (knowing how, when and why). The reasons behind the teachers' choices need further investigation.

It is obvious that taking learning outside the classroom constraints, many new affordances and restrictions emerge. Studying an authentic phenomenon presumes involving the formulation of a question that can be answered through investigation, measurements, explorations and testing. Thinking through these questions and taking into account a variety of knowledge types students can apply, the teachers could design a more comprehensive, meaningful and rich learning scenarios for the students in which the students can create meaning within and from their surrounding. The outdoor integrated learning scenarios should shift the focus from the classroom to real environments where students use disciplinary core ideas, crosscutting concepts with scientific practices to explore, examine, and explain how and why phenomena occur and to design solutions to problems [17]. The teachers need support here in terms of meaningful subject integration and know-how of how to make use of real world contexts. Furthermore, further research is needed to understand what the constraining factors for the teachers are while designing meaningful and contextualized learning scenarios.

Acknowledgement. This project is partially funded by the European Union's Horizon 2020 Research and Innovationn Programme, grant agreement No. 669074.

References

1. Volmert, A., Baran, M., Kendall-Taylor, N., O'Neil, M.: "You have to have the basics down really well": mapping the gaps between expert and public understanding of STEM learning. FrameWorks Institute, Washington, DC (2013). http://www.frameworksinstitute.org/assets/files/PDF_STEM/STEMMTG10-1813_proofedandformatted.pdf
2. Scardamalia, M., Bereiter, C.: Knowledge building: theory, pedagogy, and technology. In: Sawyer, K. (ed.) Cambridge Handbook of the Learning Sciences, pp. 97–118. Cambridge University Press, New York (2006)
3. Hsu, Y.C., Ching, Y.H.: Mobile computer-supported collaborative learning: a review of experimental research. Br. J. Edu. Technol. **44**(5), E111–E114 (2013)
4. Hwang, G.J., Wu, P.H.: Applications, impacts and trends of mobile technology-enhanced learning: a review of 2008–2012 publications in selected SSCI journals. Int. J. Mob. Learn. Organ. **8**(2), 83–95 (2014)
5. Zacharia, Z.C., Lazaridou, C., Avraamidou, L.: The use of mobile devices as means of data collection in supporting elementary school students' conceptual understanding about plants. Int. J. Sci. Educ. **38**(4), 596–620 (2016)
6. Sung, Y.-T., Chang, K.-E., Liu, T.-C.: The effects of integrating mobile devices with teaching and learning on students' learning performance: a metaanalysis and research synthesis. Comput. Educ. **94**, 252–275 (2016)
7. Nikou, S.A., Economides, A.A.: Mobile-based assessment: investigating the factors that influence behavioral intention to use. Comput. Educ. **109**, 56–73 (2017)
8. Traxler, J., Kukulska-Hulme, A.: Contextual Challenges for the Next Generation. Routledge, New York (2016)
9. Pachler, N., Bachmair, B., Cook, J., Kress, G.: Mobile Learning. Springer, New York (2010). https://doi.org/10.1007/978-1-4419-0585-7
10. Sharples, M.: Big Issues in Mobile Learning. LSRI. University of Nottingham (2007)
11. Beyer, B.: Improving thinking skills-practical approaches. Phi Delta Kappan **65**, 556–560 (1984)
12. DeBono, E.: The direct teaching of thinking as a skill. Phi Delta Kappan **64**, 703–708 (1983)
13. Burgin, M.: Theory of Knowledge: Structures and Processes. World Scientific (2016)
14. Fantl, J.: Knowing-how and knowing-that. Philos. Compass **3**(3), 451–470 (2008)
15. Shavelson, R.J., Ruiz-Primo, M.A., Wiley, E.W.: Windows into the mind. High. Educ. **49**, 413–430 (2005)
16. Crompton, H., Burke, D., Lin, Y.-C.: Mobile learning and student cognition: a systematic review of PK-12 research using Bloom's Taxonomy. Br. J. Educ. Technol. (2018). https://doi.org/10.1111/bjet.12674
17. Krajcik, J., Delen, I.: Engaging learners in STEM education. Eesti Haridusteaduste Ajakiri **5**(1), 35–58 (2017). https://doi.org/10.12697/eha.2017.5.1.02b

Possibilities of Blended Learning to Develop Orientation and Navigation Skills of Tourism Management Students

Pavlina Chaloupska, Dagmar Hrusova(✉), and David Chaloupsky

Faculty of Informatics and Management, University of Hradec Kralove, Rokitanskeho 62, Hradec Kralove, Czech Republic
{pavlina.chaloupska,dagmar.hrusova, david.chaloupsky}@uhk.cz

Abstract. The main aim of the research was to designate and describe phases of orientation learning process in a designed theoretical model, which would integrate blended learning in the studies of tourism management. Blended learning works with advanced technologies such as smart phones, applications, smart watches, or GPS devices. On the other hand, traditional approach is based on use of paper map and compass in the terrain practice. A study (n = 55) was carried out to evaluate the level of students' spatial orientation skills, their self-estimation and to find out their experience with maps and modern IT devices in orientation and navigation. The results of the study were used to support the actual need for a blended learning model.

Keywords: Spatial orientation abilities · Navigation · Phases of orientation learning · GPS device · Tourist guide

1 Introduction

Work of a tourist guide cannot be done without specific skills. Guides should be able to navigate in an unknown terrain. Tourism management students at the University of Hradec Kralove in the Czech Republic practise these skills within the tourist guides methodology. New technologies, such as e-learning or mobile applications, have been included in the classes recently, to enhance the learning process efficiency. The blended learning concept has been implemented in tourism management study, with focus on foreign language courses. E-learning in teaching languages at the Faculty of Informatics and Management has been an important research topic [1].

Blended learning has brought many positive effects into traditional learning process. A shift to virtual environment has given the teachers the opportunity to supply students with relatively unlimited amount of study materials and better grasp the content. The teachers try to increase the learning process efficiency via virtual platforms [2]. The development of information technologies has brought a new hope for education revolution and blended learning aims at the relatively best pedagogical structure to satisfy the external needs and promote optimal learning outcomes [3].

M. A. Herzog et al. (Eds.): ICWL 2019, LNCS 11841, pp. 295–302, 2019.
https://doi.org/10.1007/978-3-030-35758-0_28

2 Theoretical Framework

2.1 Spatial Orientation Abilities and Skills

Spatial orientation is mostly defined as an ability to locate oneself in one's environment with reference to time, place and people. It depends on many endogenous and extraneous factors [4–6]. High level of spatial orientation abilities relates to effective perception, integration, and interpretation of visual, vestibular, and proprioceptive sensory information [7]. Spatial thinking includes three components: concepts of space (e.g. distance between objects, distribution and exact location of objects), tools of representation (e.g. maps, graphs, GIS), and processes of reasoning [8]. Kimura [9] described the following spatial orientation factors: spatial orientation, spatial memory, pursuit, spatial vision, simplification, and spatial perception.

One of the most frequently encountered examples of spatial behaviour is planning a route and moving through space to a destination/target point. This behaviour, known as navigation may seem to be a difficult and effortful task for some people [6]. In successful navigation or wayfinding, people first need to orientate themselves in space, namely to know where they are (location) and to which direction and cardinal point they are facing or heading. Then they need to plan a route having understood where a target point is located. Finally, they make the planned route to the given point [6]. Map interpretation is a complex, multi-stepped cognitive process [10].

This paper focuses on spatial orientation skills and abilities of tourism management students. There is not much evidence in cognitive science to have studied geoscience-relevant spatial orientation skills in students. Ormand et al. [11] evaluated students' spatial orientation skills in geoscience courses and studied the input level of spatial orientation of undergraduate students in classes and the effect of instruction on acquiring spatial skills. An individual may be excellent in some spatial thinking skills while struggling with others. To increase the efficiency, the teaching process can be divided in two parts. Teaching "about maps" means providing students with the skills necessary to read, interpret, and produce maps. While teaching "with maps" means using maps to help students to acquire key social studies concepts and relations. A key point is that spatial thinking improves with practice [11, 12].

Spatial orientation abilities play an important role in all human activities. A current theory considers the differences in men's and women's spatial cognition [13]. Gender differences are assumed to exist in spatial cognition. Sub-processes like mental rotation and spatial perception are assumed to be better in men, while memorization of object locations are assumed to be better in women [14–16]. Gender differences in everyday spatial orientation skills can depend on the given situation [5]. However, concerning younger children, at the age of four and five, significant differences between boys and girls were not verified [4].

2.2 ICT and Navigation

Spatial orientation is important when determining a target location. One needs to be able to switch between three-dimensional (3D) and two-dimensional (2D) perspective [17]. Map is an important interface technology. It can help users to get an overview of the area [18]. The development of modern technologies such as mobile phones, tablets or augmented reality have provided a new way of interpretation and interaction.

The effectiveness of Global Positioning System (GPS) navigation and map-based direct experience navigation was studied [6]. The research [6] showed that GPS users travelled longer distances and made more stops during their walk, compared to map users. Further, GPS users were slower, made bigger direction errors, had poorer topological accuracy, and rated wayfinding tasks as more difficult. Augmented reality in 3D applications give opportunity to design and implement strategies for the development of spatial orientation skills. Huang et al. [19] studied how GPS pedestrian navigation systems could help to reduce cognitive load during wayfinding. Results showed that, among different navigation prototypes (map-based, augmented reality-based, and voice-based), the map-based prototype led to higher accuracy in both the sense of direction and the sense of distance. The current research suggests that students' smart phones can be easily blended into university education to facilitate teaching and learning process [20]. Smart phones available in the hands of students represent an easy way for the teacher to implement new technologies into the lessons [21].

3 Methodology and Goal

The research study approaches the problem of learning orientation. The main aim of the research was to designate and describe phases of orientation learning process in a designed theoretical model, which would integrate blended learning in the studies of tourism management. The model follows on both from the relevant theories, but namely from the long-time experience of one of the authors (Pavlina Chaloupska) of this research paper in the field of orienteering. She has been engaged in the sports training process of the young orienteers, including the Czech Junior National Team members.

The usability and applicability of the designed blended learning model of orientation and navigation will be verified following the application of the designed model in the learning process in practice. The model will be applied in the lessons of the methods of tourist guiding, which are part of the study curriculum of the three year bachelor study, from the beginning of the academic year 2019–2020. The subsequent validation is to be carried on, in a continuous assessment, until the future participants pass their state final exams and gain a licence of a tourist guide.

The paper focuses on the students of a three-year bachelor tourism management study at the Faculty of Informatics and Management, University of Hradec Kralove in the Czech Republic. A study (n = 55) was carried out to evaluate the level of the selected orientation and navigation abilities and skills of the first year tourism management students at the beginning of their studies in the academic year of 2018–2019. The study was aimed to get a pre-modelling input information to support the actual need for a blended learning model. It concerned the students' spatial orientation skills, the self-estimation of their general orientation ability and their experience with maps and modern IT devices in orientation and navigation. The research sample comprised all the available first year students who were accepted to the tourism management study at the University of Hradec Kralove in the mentioned year. The different number of women (n = 39) and men (n = 16) reflected the fact, that there were more women-applicants to pass the 2018 entrance exams successfully. Spatial orientation was tested by the Perspective Taking Spatial Orientation Test (PTSOT), developed by Hegarty and Waller [22]. The test evaluates one's ability to imagine different perspectives and orientations in space. The test can measure the perspective involving a rotation of over 90°.

3.1 Results of the Pre-modelling Survey

A partial aim was to carry out a pre-modelling survey in the first year tourism management students (n = 55) to collect relevant data to support the actual need to make orientation learning process within tourism management studies more efficient and attractive and to keep up to the latest technologies. The research sample comprised 55 first year students of Tourism management, all the available students at the beginning of the academic year 2018–2019. Concerning the self-estimation of general orientation ability the students' average rating in marks on a four-degree scale was 2.4 (mark "1" being the best rating, mark "4" the worst, similarly to school marks). In terms of gender differences, women had lower self-estimation compared to men, the average rating counted for men was 2 and for women 2.6. The Perspective Taking Spatial Orientation Test scores showed an average mark of 2 (1.8 for men and 2.1 for women). The question of using paper maps has shown that only 38% of students have used them in their life. This was surprising, because the basics of orientation should be included the elementary school curriculum. On the other hand, 85% of the students had some experience using modern navigation technologies. The most used navigation applications were: Here, Google maps, Pedometer, Runtastic, Apple maps, Equilab, Endomondo, Waze, Samsung health. Regarding the user functions of map applications and portals, they were given by the respondents as follows: finding a place on a map, finding a route on the map, finding a particular service, checking traffic density, and sharing information. 49% of the students had experience with at least 3 of the listed functions. The most often used function was finding a place on a map (94%).

3.2 A Model of Orientation and Navigation Learning

Based on the results of the pre-modelling study, the study environment of the University of Hradec Kralove and the requirements for the acquired skills of tourism management graduates, the following methodological model was developed for tourist guides orientation and navigation learning. Orientation and navigation lessons are proceeded in two levels. The basics are explained and trained with the use of traditional navigation aids such as a paper map and compass. At the same time, students learn to use modern navigation devices, map or navigation apps and GPS. E-learning environment is used by the teachers for individual practical assignments and the students' evaluation.

Traditional Learning in Orientation and Navigation

A special paper map for orienteering is used to teach students the orientation basics around the university campus for their better insight and understanding the technique of working with a map. The orienteering map has its own specifics, it is in the scale of 1:7500 and reality is displayed in a very detailed 2D perspective. At this stage of the learning process it is important for the students to acquire the basic spatial orientation skills both with the use of a compass and without it. The first step is to orientate the map to the north and to understand the basic landmarks. The second step is to determine the right direction and the third to understand and determine the distance correctly. Students are able to handle simple paper map-based orientation in the city, by means of simple activities in practice.

Blended Learning in Orientation and Navigation

Mobile applications are included in all the phases of the designed model of orientation and navigation learning process. The phases of orientation and navigation learning are systemized and shown in the Fig. 1 below.

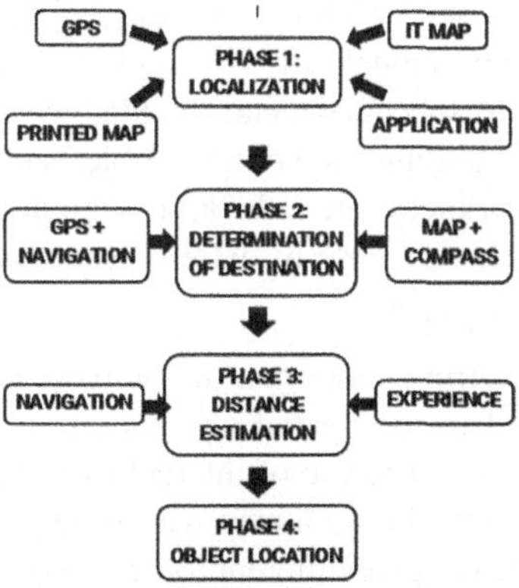

Fig. 1. Phases of orientation and navigation learning process (source: authors)

The first phase of the model of orientation and navigation learning is described as LOCALIZATION. It is possible to use a compass application that replaces the use of a classical orienteering compass. What is considered to be a most important thing is the inclusion of map applications with a GPS support. Currently the most complex and best developed portal in the Czech Republic is Mapy.cz. It is used worldwide. This is a Czech internet and mobile application developed by Seznam.cz. The base source for maps of Europe are Open Street maps. Offline maps with a GPS support are used to practice navigation in the terrain. Despite the fact that mobile technologies are very smart today, the most essential skill for students is to be able to transfer the information from mobile technologies into reality and to assign the virtual points to the real points in the terrain, by means of spatial orientation and imagination. At this stage the feature of Mapy.cz called "Panorama" can be used. The feature proceeds 3D visualization of the position in the map to support the spatial orientation.

The second phase of the model of orientation and navigation learning is called DETERMINATION OF DESTINATION. It concerns navigation from a point A to a point B, which can be done via a navigation application. It works reliably in the city and can be a useful help when driving a car. However, its terrain usability has certain limits (such as battery life or difficulties in extreme weather conditions). Tourist guides need to develop an ability to validate all the information from a critical perspective and not to rely on the technical device as the one and only source. In terms of reliability it is essential to be able to determine direction by means of a paper map and compass. In learning navigation, students should also be introduced other technologies: GPS device and GPS smart watch. These devices offer additional navigation features compared to mobile apps, such as the possibility to upload a track in the format of .gpx, possibility to return along the used track, and significantly longer battery life.

The third phase of the model of orientation and navigation learning concerns DISTANCE ESTIMATION. Students should acquire the skill to estimate the distance to the target point as exactly as possible. Navigation apps are recommended as a helpful tool to develop this skill. It helps the user to get experience in practice. A key competence of a tourist guide is to be able to compare and evaluate different route variants to the target point and to be able to choose the most optimal route.

The last phase of the model of orientation and navigation learning is OBJECT LOCATION and its success depends on the type of the object. A tourist guide must be able to locate both buildings and outdoor objects even in harsh conditions (bad weather conditions, fog, darkness, etc.). In tourist guiding the navigational devices professionalize the process and in case of extreme situations can help to save lives.

Preparation of a Tourist Guide

A phase of preparation for a trip is important in the work of a tourist guide. It requires an ability to read maps and to use spatial orientation and imagination effectively in visualizing images in 2D maps. The use of internet map data base sources has its own specifics. Students first learn to choose a map with proper map layers, relevant to their trip planning. Then they learn to plan different routes according to specific assignments, to create a chronological plan of an event, to search for sites of interest in a given destination, and to implement them in the route plan. At this level, e-learning environment is recommended to be used. It enables the students to work independently, with use of the recommended links. E-learning makes it easier for the teachers to collect, evaluate and classify students' individual assignments. Students are encouraged to critical thinking, use of more resources and implementing their own route planning experience.

4 Conclusion and Discussion

This paper approached the problem of how to increase the efficiency of teaching-learning process in orientation and navigation, by means of blended learning. The assumption corresponded to other researches [16], that it is possible to develop teaching-learning strategies to improve spatial competences by means of educational applications.

Landscape interpretation requires understanding the relations between the map, the represented space, and oneself, which is not an easy task. The findings of this study are consistent with other researches [10]. The students' abilities and skills concerning the work with a map in practice were found to be low, specifically in terms of students' ability to use maps, their ability to understand maps, and the cognitive complexity of a map use. As discussed in the literature review, a shift to the virtual environment has brought the teachers the opportunity to make the learning process more efficient and attractive. It is assumed that implementation of smart information technologies in navigation and orientation with appropriate methods and instructions in the learning process can help to improve students' orientation skills.

The suggested methods are convenient for tourism management students and tourist guides' practice. An increased level of acquisition of basic orientation techniques should increase self-estimation and reduce spatial anxiety. Tendency to underestimate oneself can be a limiting factor in the work of a tourist guide. Below-average level of self-estimation was indicated in the results of the pilot study. Women had lower self-estimation compared to men, however, searching for the detailed reasons was not a subject of this study. This might be related to a Central European cultural environment, where it is quite a common public opinion that "women cannot orientate themselves". Reducing spatial anxiety should increase self-estimation and lead to precise and smooth navigation.

The results should be treated as preliminary, pending a more rigorous controlled experimental setting. The usability and applicability of the designed blended learning model of orientation and navigation is to be verified in the on-going research. The model will be applied in the lessons of the methods of tourist guiding, included in the study curriculum in the three year bachelor study of Tourism Management. The subsequent validation is to be carried on from the academic year 2019–2020, in a continuous assessment, until the participants pass their state final exams.

References

1. Černá, M., Borkovcová, A.: Blended learning concept in selected tourism management e-Courses with focus on content development including recommender system. In: Cheung, S. K.S., Kwok, L.-f., Kubota, K., Lee, L.-K., Tokito, J. (eds.) ICBL 2018. LNCS, vol. 10949, pp. 175–187. Springer, Cham (2018). https://doi.org/10.1007/978-3-319-94505-7_14
2. Steyn, R., Millard, S., Jordaan, J.: The use of a learning management system to facilitate student-driven content design: an experiment. In: Huang, T.-C., Lau, R., Huang, Y.-M., Spaniol, M., Yuen, C.-H. (eds.) SETE 2017. LNCS, vol. 10676, pp. 75–94. Springer, Cham (2017). https://doi.org/10.1007/978-3-319-71084-6_10
3. Hu, L.: Blended learning: beyond technology to pedagogical structure design. In: Cheung, S. K.S., Kwok, L.-f., Shang, J., Wang, A., Kwan, R. (eds.) ICBL 2016. LNCS, vol. 9757, pp. 221–232. Springer, Cham (2016). https://doi.org/10.1007/978-3-319-41165-1_20
4. Pollatou, E., Gerodimos, V., Zissi, V., Zervanou, D., Karadimou, K.: Spatial orientation ability in boys and girls toddlers. Sci. J. Orienteer. **17**(1), 40–46 (2009)
5. Coluccia, E., Louse, G.: Gender differences in spatial orientation: a review. J. Environ. Psychol. **24**, 329–340 (2004)
6. Ishikawa, T., Fujiwara, H., Imai, O., Okabe, A.: Wayfinding with a GPS-based mobile navigation system: a comparison with maps and direct experience. J. Environ. Psychol. **28** (1), 74–82 (2008)

7. Pietropaolo, S., Crusio, W.E.: Learning spatial orientation. In: Seel, N.M. (ed.) Encyclopedia of the Sciences of Learning. Springer, Boston (2012). https://doi.org/10.1007/978-1-4419-1428-6
8. National Research Council [NRC]. Learning to Think Spatially. Committee on Support for Thinking Spatially: The Incorporation of Geographic Information Science across the K-12 Curriculum. National Academy Press, Washington DC (2006)
9. Kimura, D.: Sex and Cognition, 1st edn. MIT Press, Cambridge (1999)
10. Bednarz, S.W., Acheson, G., Bednarz, R.S.: Maps and map learning. Soc. Stud. Soc. Educ. **70**(7), 398–404 (2006)
11. Ormand, C.J., Manduca, C.A., Shipley, T.F., et al.: Evaluating geoscience students' spatial thinking skills in a multi-institutional classroom study. J. Geosci. Educ. **62**(1), 146–154 (2014)
12. Newcombe, N.S., Stieff, M.: Six myths about spatial thinking. Int. J. Sci. Educ. **34**, 955–997 (2012)
13. de Goede, M.: Gender differences in spatial cognition. Utrecht University (2009). ISBN: 978-90-393-5005-8
14. Eals, M., Silverman, I.: The hunter-gatherer theory of spatial sex differences: proximate factors mediating the female advantage in recall of object arrays. Ethol. Sociobiol. **15**, 95–105 (1994)
15. Voyer, D., Postma, A., Brake, B., et al.: Gender differences in object location memory: a meta-analysis. Psychon. Bull. Rev. **14**(1), 23–38 (2007)
16. Carrera, C.C., Asensio, B., Luis, A.: Landscape interpretation with augmented reality and maps to improve spatial orientation skill. J. Geogr. High. Educ. **41**(1), 119–133 (2017)
17. Schmitz, S.: Gender differences in acquisition of environmental knowledge related to wayfinding behavior, spatial anxiety and self-estimated environmental competencies. Sex Roles **41**, 71–93 (1999)
18. Radoczky, V.: How to design a pedestrian navigation system for indoor and outdoor environments. In: Gartner, G., Cartwright, W., Peterson, M.P. (eds.) Location Based Services and TeleCartography, pp. 301–316. Lecture Notes in Geoinformation and Cartography. Springer, Heidelberg (2007). https://doi.org/10.1007/978-3-540-36728-4_23
19. Huang, H., Schmidt, M., Gartner, G.: Spatial knowledge acquisition with mobile maps, augmented reality and voice in the context of GPS-based pedestrian navigation: results from a field test. Cartogr. Geogr. Inf. Sci. **39**, 107–116 (2013)
20. Jia, J., Chen, Z.: Blending smart phones into regular classroom learning. In: Cheung, S.K.S., Kwok, L.-f., Shang, J., Wang, A., Kwan, R. (eds.) ICBL 2016. LNCS, vol. 9757, pp. 337–347. Springer, Cham (2016). https://doi.org/10.1007/978-3-319-41165-1_30
21. Stockwell, G.: Using mobile phones for vocabulary activities: examining the effect of the platform. Lang. Learn. Technol. **14**(2), 95–110 (2010)
22. Hegarty, M., Waller, D.: A dissociation between mental rotation and perspective-taking spatial abilities. Intelligence **32**(2), 175–191 (2004)

Juniorstudium – Study Digital While Going to School

Pia Drews and Alke Martens(✉)

Institute of Computer Science, University of Rostock, Albert-Einstein-Str. 22, 18059 Rostock, Germany
{pia.drews, alke.martens}@uni-rostock.de

Abstract. After leaving school, many students in Germany are not sure which discipline they should take, when they decided to study at a university. As support in this orientation phase, quite a lot of universities in Germany offer "Juniorstudy" programs. Here, students can get deeper insight into universities and into the topics they are interested in. Most of these offers are difficult for students to realize, since there are classroom sessions at the university. The University of Rostock can look back on a more than ten year long experience in offering a digital Juniorstudy program. Accompanied by advanced student mentors, they work with digital material to look deeper into their courses. By participating in presence phases, they can also get a feeling for our university. In this paper, insights from this program are sketched – both on the computer science and on the learning psychological level.

Keywords: Online study · Digital study · Junior study program

1 Introduction

Juniorstudy programs (in German: Juniorstudium), also sometimes called orientation study programs [1], have been developed based on two main ideas. Firstly, there are always several students at schools, which are highly gifted or extraordinary gifted. Schools often have problems to offer additional material for these students, so universities used this gap and offer additional courses for these school students. For the universities, it is a win-win-situation, as they in most cases are able to relate to the highly gifted students as future university students. Secondly, it has been observed [2] that quite a lot of school students finish school without knowing exactly which study direction to take. Often, reasons for students changing their topics or study direction after the first try are related to disillusion about their decision, wrong ideas about the content to cover and sometimes underestimation the demands of certain topics (e.g. mathematics in the study program computer science or chemistry in the study program medicine). In this paper, the development and structure of Juniorstudy programs, especially Rostock's Juniorstudium will be shown. Furthermore, the first results of a learner type evaluation according to Kolb will be presented.

The invention of Juniorstudy program was a side effect of the meeting of three persons in 1968: as one of her summercamp students, the 8th grader Joe L. Bates, has shown a lot of talent in Mathematics, Informatics and Physics, Mrs. D.K. Lidtke spoke

M. A. Herzog et al. (Eds.): ICWL 2019, LNCS 11841, pp. 303–311, 2019.
https://doi.org/10.1007/978-3-030-35758-0_29

to Prof. J.C. Stanley and asked him, whether he would allow Joe to participate on different university courses. Joe got the allowance to addend courses at the university at the age of 13 in the year 1969 and finished with a master at the age of 17. Jonathan Middleton Ewards, who successfully finished College courses at the age of 13, was the second one of these students. These both early starters prepared the ground for establishing the Juniorstudy program at the John Hopkins University (they now call it Undergraduate Admissions). The first class started in 1971 with 20 students from the 8th and 9th grade, which have been allowed to look into mathematics courses at the university. As the program has been a success, it has been expanded over the years [3].

In Germany, the University of Cologne has been the first to establish an "Early study program" (Frühstudium) in fall term 2000/01. Their goal was also to support highly gifted students. In the last years, there was another aspect added to this first idea. A surprisingly high number of University students quits their first course of study in the first two to three semesters [2] – in the bachelor phase, this are about 29% of all starters. These students either change their topic or even leave the university to take up an apprenticeship. An investigation of this group, mentioned in [2], told the interviewers that the proficiency level at the chosen direction was too high (30%), that the university education was too theoretical for their taste (15%) or that they were not really motivated to study (17%). Most of them did not mention financial problems.

These observations lead to the guess that Universities in Germany have a potential to improve the dropout quote by offering an orientation phase at the university. Orientation studies and Juniorstudy programs were born – with the goal to inform, to orient, and to support highly gifted and "normal" students before enroll them as full-time students. In 2011 there were 52 Juniorstudy programs in Germany [1] – Gröbe, Müller and Kuhn [4] counted only 50 universities with so-called Orientation study programs. On the one hand, there are so called Juniorstudy programs, usually starting for school students from the 10^{s} grade onwards. On the other hand, there are so called Orientation study programs offered to students after finishing school as an orientation phase before beginning of the official university enrollment. However, often the terms are used interchanged. In the remainder of the paper, the focus will be on Juniorstudy programs. Our target group and thus the target of our investigation are school students between the 10th and the 12th grade (in German the Sekundarstufe II).

In summary, Juniorstudy programs have the following tasks:

1. Support of highly gifted students.
2. Orientation in the choice of their preferred study direction.
3. Offering courses that help to fill knowledge gaps, which exists directly before enrolling at a study direction at the university.

Most of the Juniorstudy programs are designed for highly gifted students. In the program of our University of Rostock, we had all the three aspects in mind and over the last 10 years had a proven success in all three fields. Especially the third field is currently growing towards a very important aspect of digitally supported learning in our pre-study phase. This will be sketched in the following.

2 Presence Versus Online

In Germany, there are two types of Juniorstudy programs: presence and online programs. In most cases, presence programs are realized. Condition for participating in these programs is to be at least gifted, if not highly gifted, because students have to participate in real life at university lectures [5]. Most times these lie in parallel to their school education time. Only gifted learners are able to compensate the missing school material and to additionally cope with the university material.

In 2018 only three universities in Germany offer Online Juniorstudy programs. The FernUniversity Hagen, the Technical University of Kaiserslautern and the University of Rostock offer programs for school students [4], which are mainly online. Our research has revealed that only the University of Rostock has a multi-topic program open for all school students – the University of Kaiserslautern offers programs for Mathematics, Computer Science and Physics. The FernUniversity Hagen allows students to participate (under certain conditions) at their regular distance education programs. Therefore, it seems like there is no special offer for these students.

The Juniorstudy program at the University of Rostock, which has started as a digital course program with presence phases in fall term 2008/09, has following structure:

1. It is a full online study program. Lectures of the university courses of the first and second semester are recorded (life in the real lecture) and prepared for online studies. The courses are available for the enrolled "Schüdents" (school students from the German term Schüler for student) at a special university platform (StudIP).
2. The courses are partly enriched by quizzes and interactive parts [6].
3. University student mentors accompany the students in their selected courses. A mentor is a senor student of a direction which is related to the Juniorstudy direction chosen by the student. Usually, a mentor has a group of one to 25 Schüdents. The mentors meet their Schüdents at presence phases twice to three times in a term.

Thus, our approach can also be called a blended-learning course, however we perceive it as a primarily digital study program.

3 Structure of Rostock's Juniorstudy Model

The Schüdents in Rostock's Juniorstudy Program have the possibility to enroll in certain modules. Each module is accompanied by a tutor – which is a senior University student in this topic (master phase). During the first days of the term, a presence day in Rostock is taking place, where the Schüdents get the first information, visit the University of Rostock real campus and meet their tutors and colleague Schüdents. The tutors are responsible for their group of Schüdents in their module for one semester. As most recorded lectures require knowledge which is mediated at school (and usually in higher classes), most of the Schüdents have knowledge gaps. The tutors support the students in detecting and filling these gaps. Also, the tutors post online tests and exercises, which give an insight in the requirement of the study course. For each interactive part, the tutors are responsible to give detailed feedback and support.

Additionally to these re-occurring test and interaction phases, each recorded lecture is accompanied by practical phases and tasks, which are comparable to exercises at a University. These might be realized as small talks or presentations which have to be prepared by the Schüdents, and which are controlled and evaluated by the tutors.

Our experience with the tutors have shown that Schüdents have very different levels of knowledge regarding text analysis and comprehension of text, with deeper investigations of topics, and with writing text. This insight surprised us – but we learned that our support of the Schüdents leads them to better grades in their real first University year, as they have understood some aspects of being a student on a deeper basis.

At Rostock, we currently have an amount of 313 students in fall term 2018/19 and 210 students in spring term 2019 enrolled as Schüdents in the Juniorstudy program. 73% are living in the region of Mecklenburg-Western Pomerania, the others are from other federal states or even live in other countries. We have an average of ten different study directions with a currently available amount of 18 courses. At the moment, the most popular direction is medicine (54.6% of all enrollments since fall term 2015/16). Currently, students get a video (with the length of 90 min) once a week. The video is available for them until the end of their time as a Schüdent.

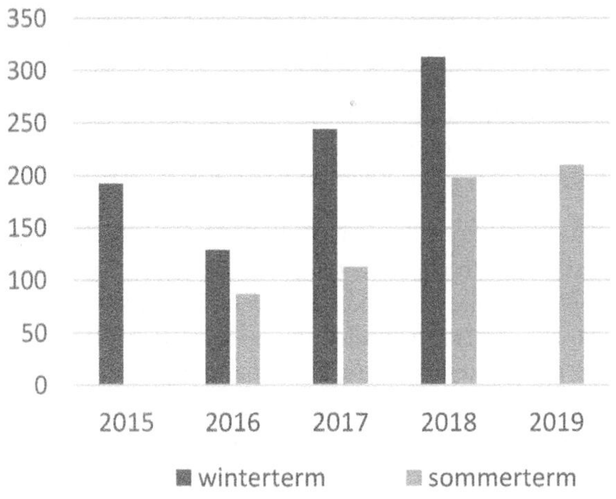

Fig. 1. Number of participants since fall term 2015/16

In contrast to other Juniorstudy programs, the program at the University of Rostock is not restricted to highly gifted student but is open for all. Thus, we were able to offer enrollment without test procedure or application procedure.

As we interact with many schools in Germany, sometimes teacher take the responsibility for enrolling their students. Sometimes, the students enroll themselves, ideally with support of their family. In these cases, the school has to be informed about the student's initiative so that the teachers are aware of the additional tasks and interest of the student. Especially the age distribution for the Schüdents in medicine is a bit different than in the other study directions, which is shown in Fig. 2. This seems to be caused by the age-restriction of anatomy courses (due to ethical limitation these Schüdents have to be at least 16 years old) on the one hand, on the other hand, there are many persons which didn't get a place at the University for medicine, so they use the time to prepare a prospective study.

On the first sight, this seems to be a bit strange to offer a great variety of Medicine courses, as the topic usually has no lack of students like for example the STEM group

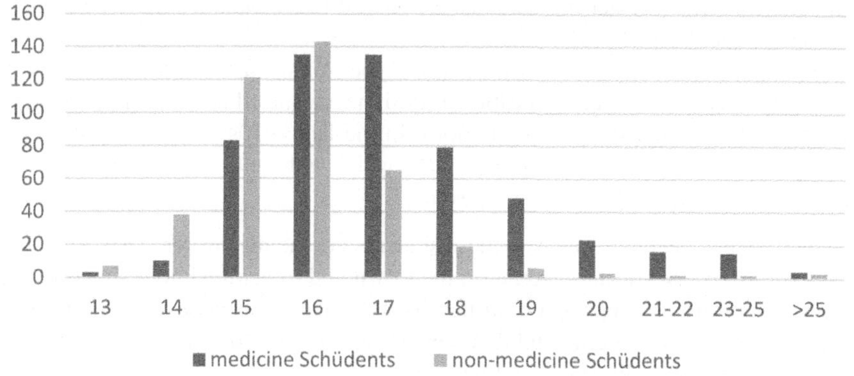

Fig. 2. Age distribution of the Schüdents from fall term 2015/16 to spring term 2019

(STEM = Science, Technology, Engineering, Mathematics). On the second sight, it seems more reasonable, looking at our (non empirical) observation at school: most of the students want to study something they seemingly know. A study from the spring term 2019 shows, that 69.9% of 70 Medicine students had a memorable occasion, which helped their decision to study Medicine. Only a few have a parent working in the medical sector (31% the mother and 22.5% the father) who could give a better insight in the job as a physician. This is not the best momentum of taking up a study direction, which requires knowledge about chemistry, human biology, and much more. We also learned that students starting their university career in Medicine often have severe problems with the chemistry part in the beginning of their study. Thus, we have developed a special course, where Schüdents and beginner students get the same material. We are currently evaluating the program, but it seems that a so-called "bridge course" in chemistry is a big advantage if absolved before enrollment at the university. It is still a big advantage if absolved immediately before the starting of the lectures, but the time pressure is quite bigger then. Generally, bridge-course students performed significantly better than the ones who have not prepared before the beginning of the lectures. However, this evaluation is content of another publication.

4 Learner Types of Schüdents

Currently, we have finished another evaluation with our students. Generally speaking, we had the impression, that the Schüdents are in most cases a certain type of learner. In contrast to the above mentioned programs for highly gifted students, our students are not selected based on criteria for this target group. However, they seem to have a quite similar learning behavior, if they are successful in our courses. As we are not developing a certain learning style as part of our courses, it must be something they bring from school education or which is related to their personality. Our Schüdents come from all over Germany, so even different kinds of school education cannot be the reason for the following insight. In the last semester, we have been able to investigate our target group with a questionnaire and some additional interviews. Based on [7] we wanted to find our whether our students are related to a certain learner type regarding the learner types of Kolb [8].

The knowledge about the students learner types, or at least a vague idea about this, helps the teachers in their educational design (meant: didactics in Germany or instruction in the English speaking region). In the late 1970s and in the 1980s, Kolb developed a model of learner types [8, 10], which is based on four main types and mixtures of these types. The main types are:

1. The diverger (feel and watch) – these students are the discoverer. They love to ask questions, to investigate material on their own and to learn without support. These advantages are accompanied with the disadvantages, that these learners need time for acquiring new material and that they are not quick in deciding thing. They love in most cases visually supported learning.
2. The assimilators (think and watch) are good in (reflected) observing and developmenting abstract knowledge items, so they can grasp the meaning of abstract models quickly. Their weak point is how to compensate emotional situations and to cope with situations, which cannot be structured systematically.
3. The convergers (think and do) are the decision makers. They are best in learning based on abstract knowledge models combined with active experimentation. Their main goal is to put theory into practice. They love to work in teams and have sometimes motivational problems when working alone.
4. The accommodators (feels and do) can also be called the practitioner. They learn mainly by experimentation and concrete insight. They strive towards putting plans to life and to facts. In contrast to the other learner types, they take more risks of failure, and thus, the trial and error style can often be observed in this group. They try to avoid abstract theories.

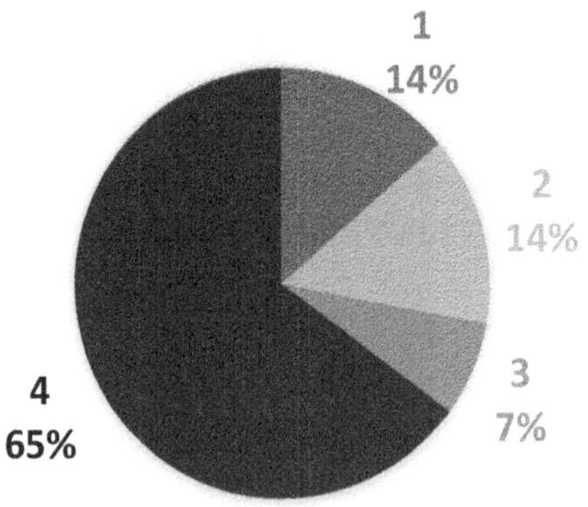

Fig. 3. Distribution of learner types set with n = 137 over all subjects in a semester; 1 - accommodators, 2 - assimilators, 3 - diverger, 4 - converger

Kolb has embedded two continuums in this type representation: one continuum is the processing continuum, which shows how a task is approached. The other one is the perception continuum, which shows how thoughts and feelings are about a task. More information can be found for example in [11]. The axes and the types are combined to a matrix, which shall not be sketched here but can exemplarily found on the mentioned website.

Based on Kolb's test [12], we have analyzed our students. We have been surprised by an amount of students being a converger (Fig. 3 with the complete spring term 2019 with n = 137 students). We have separated our set into the amount of STEM students, which have been n = 15, and the amount of medical students with n = 122. The main difference in these groups was that there are close to no divergers in the STEM student groups, whereas in both groups, the convergers showed to be the overwhelming amount of our Schüdents, to be seen in Fig. 4(A and B). At this early phase of investigation, we have abstracted from the gender aspects and just looked at the complete group. However, one additional question arose as we have evaluated the results of our study: Some of our students become Juniorstudy Schüdents, as the schools, which they visit, offer so-called "Wahlpflicht" (wp) courses. This means that the students can cover a complete school topic by selecting one of our offered courses. The school thus supports these extra courses by giving grades and allowing the students to collect points. Regarding the learning psychological background, this would be extrinsic motivation and our question has been whether the wp courses are types. This separation of groups leads us to the results shown also in Fig. 4 (C and D).

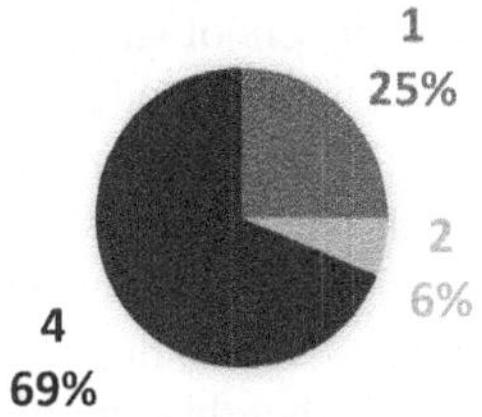

A - Subset of n = 15 non-medical students

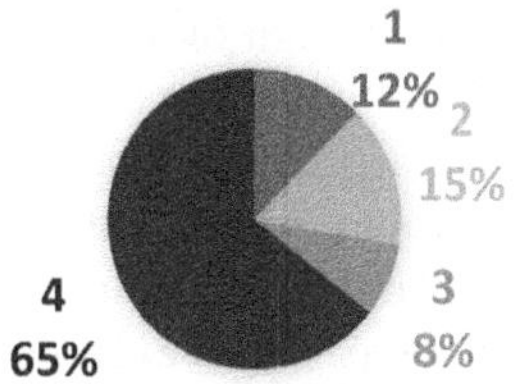

B - Subset of n = 122 medical students

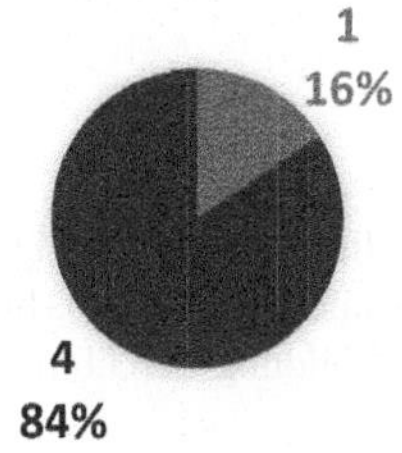

C - Subset of n = 18 WP students

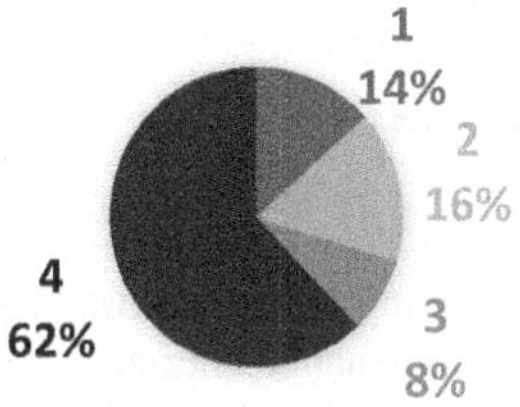

D - Subset of n = 119 non-WP students

Fig. 4. 1 - accommodators, 2 - assimilators, 3 - diverger, 4 - converger

There were n = 18 wp students in spring term 2019, which got the credits additionally from their school. Surprisingly, in this group were no assimilators and no divergers. However, as the number of students is rather small, this cannot be rated too high. In the non-wp students, which was an amount of n = 119, we found again the convergers. This leads to the insight, that most of our students are convergers, independently of the situation they have brought them to the Juniorstudy program.

5 Conclusion and Outlook

The study sketched in this paper was the first study related to the learner types in our Juniorstudy program. We started this investigation to find out, which way of distance education program is best suited for school students on their way to the university. We wanted to find our which learner types selected the Juniorstudy program with the idea to develop formats which are best suited for each learner type (e.g. described in [9]). Our idea was to develop more flexibility in our pre-study distance education program to support our Schüdents when they start their time at our university. Primarily, we wanted to find out if the combination of recorded courses, tutors and tasks to fulfill over the semester is a good combination, or whether it would be better to develop additional presence offers at least for the students who live close to Rostock.

The first insights of our study really came as a surprise. Most of our students have shown to be convergers. In the following semesters, this evaluation will be repeated and deepened, and also accompanied with an analysis of the first semester students in the different topics and the student in a later semester. Here, we want to find out whether the learner types change over time in a student life. The study will also be repeated to develop a real empirical insight and to draw more detailed conclusions regarding the design of a distance education program for school students who are not highly gifted but are nonetheless interested in starting an early study program.

Another aspect that should be investigated is the effect of a Juniorstudy program to the dropout rate, which will be a long-team study with recently questioned students.

A planned step is also to exclusively examine the highly gifted students in terms to their learner types. However, the number of highly gifted students in our program is not big enough – and in most cases, we don't even know whether they are highly gifted or not. Thus, we are looking for partners to expand our investigation.

References

1. Deutsche Telekom Stiftung: Frühstudium Telekom Stiftung, Bonn (2011)
2. Bundesministerium für Bildung und Forschung. Pressemeldung (2017). https://www.bmbf.de/de/studienabbrecher-beginnen-haeufig-eine-berufsausbildung-4283.html. Accessed 26 June 2019
3. Stanley, J.C.: In the beginning: the study of mathematically precocious youth. In: Benbow, C.P., Lubinski, D. (eds.) Intellectual Talent: Psychometric and Social Issues, pp. 225–235. Johns Hopkins University Press, Baltimore (1996)
4. Gröber, S., Müller, T., Kuhn, J.: The early entrance physics program FiPS. Physik und Didaktik in Schule und Hochschule, pp. 1–12 (2018)
5. Deutsche Telekom Stiftung, Solzbacher, C.: Frühstudium - Schüler an die Universität. Osnabrück (2008)
6. Waßmann, I., Müller, M., Tavangarian, D.: Adaptive Lehrvideos. In: DeLFI, 13. E-Learning Fachtagung Informatik, GI Edition, Bonn, pp. 131–144 (2015)
7. Möller, H.: Die Lernstilanalyse nach Kolb und ihre Konsequenzen für die Hochschul- und Schuldidaktik und die berufliche Aus- und Weiterbildung. In: 1. Innsbrucker Bildungstage, pp. 88–94. Univ. Press Insbruck (2006)
8. Kolb, D.A.: Learning styles and disciplinary differences. In: The modern American College, pp. 232–255. Jossey-Bass, San Francisco (1981)
9. Waßmann, I.: Dharma - dynamic, heuristic & adaptive peer recommendation in social learning environments. In: International Technology, Education and Development (INTED) Conference Proceedings, pp. 3515–3525 (2018)

10. McLeod, S.A.: Kolb - learning styles. https://www.simplypsychology.org/learning-kolb.html. Accessed 11 Aug 2019
11. McLeod, S.: https://www.simplypsychology.org/learning-kolb.html. Accessed 01 July 2019
12. Fatzer, G.: Ganzheitliches Lernen. Humanistische Pädagogik und Pädagogik und Organisationsentwicklung, Junfermann-Verlag, Paderborn (1987)

An Overview of Learning Design and Analytics in Mobile and Ubiquitous Learning

Gerti Pishtari(✉), María Jesús Rodríguez-Triana, Edna Milena Sarmiento-Márquez, Jaanus Terasmaa, Külli Kori, Mihkel Kangur, Oleksandr Cherednychenko, Terje Väljataga, and Liisa Puusepp

Tallinn University, Narva maantee 25, 10120 Tallinn, Estonia
{gpishtar,mjrt,msm,pootsman,kyllikor,mihkelk,olcher,terjev,liisa}@tlu.ee

Abstract. Mobile and ubiquitous learning models have been widely adopted in technology-enhanced learning (TEL) practices. Apart from potential benefits, these models introduce additional complexity in designing, monitoring and evaluating learning activities, as learning happens across different spaces. In recent years, literature on learning design (LD) and learning analytics (LA) has started to address these issues. This paper presents a systematic review on how LD and LA communities understand mobile and ubiquitous learning, as well as their respective contributions in these fields. The search included seven main academic databases in TEL, resulting in 1722 papers, from which 54 papers were included in the final analysis. Results point out the lack of common definitions for mobile and ubiquitous learning, raises research trends and (unexploited) synergies between LD and LA communities, and identifies areas that require further attention from these communities.

Keywords: Mobile learning · Ubiquitous learning · Learning design · Learning analytics · Systematic literature review

1 Introduction

There has been a growing research interest in mobile learning (m-learning) and ubiquitous learning (u-learning). Nevertheless, there is no consensus yet in the academic and professional communities about their meanings [19]. Indeed, both terms are often used interchangeably in literature [3]. Nevertheless, authors seem too agree on what m-learning and u-learning promote, highlighting among other aspects: accessibility, interactivity, self-regulated and situational learning, continuity and connectivity among contexts [3,19]. Despite these potential benefits, m-learning/u-learning pose additional complexity for designing, monitoring and evaluating learning scenarios. For example, in these settings, learning usually happens across multiple spaces. Designing in these situations typically involves the usage of different authoring tools, specific for each particular space (see for

M. A. Herzog et al. (Eds.): ICWL 2019, LNCS 11841, pp. 312–319, 2019.
https://doi.org/10.1007/978-3-030-35758-0_30

instance Smartzoos, for the design of learning activities in geo-located physical spaces [18], or PyramidApp in a digital space [9]), as well as requires gathering data from different spaces in order to achieve a global view of the learning process [14].

In the last 15 years, the communities of LD and LA have contributed with various proposals to address these issues in m-learning/u-learning. In general, the community of LD has been focused on the importance of facilitating practitioners in sharing, modifying and reusing their pedagogical plans. On the other hand, research in LA has aimed to investigate techniques of handling learners data to support decision making of different actors involved at different stages in the learning process [16]. There is also a growing community of researchers interested in the synergy between LD and LA. [2,10]. Locker et al. [8] claim that research in LD should take advantage and harness the results of the field of LA. The state of the art in LA for LD is still in its early days but preliminary research has shown the potential and has shown both the potential and challenges of aligning LA and LD [13]. Looking at mobile and ubiquitous learning contexts, few LD and LA research studies are found. Indeed, in a systematic review about research in LA for LD, Mangaroska and Giannakos [10] identified only 1 work (out of 43 reviewed), connected to m-learning/u-learning. While, existing systematic reviews in m-learning/u-learning have focused on: research trends [20], identifying open research issues [5], specific educational settings (e.g., m-learning in higher education [17]), or specific learning models such as collaborative learning [1]. Some of these reviews reflect on LD aspects (e.g., [1]), while none of them has focused on the role of LA in m-learning/u-learning.

Thus, in order to better understand the role that the LD and LA communities may play in m-learning/u-learning, and how they could enrich each other, we carry out a systematic review. Concretely, our research questions are:

- **RQ1:** What are the definitions and aspects of m-learning/u-learning which have been considered by the LD and LA communities?
- **RQ2:** How were the learning contexts where LD and/or LA supported m-learning/u-learning?
- **RQ3:** How have LD and LA supported m-learning/u-learning (type of contributions)?

2 Methodology

To carry out the systematic review we followed the guidelines proposed by Kitchenham and Chartrs [6]. We used seven main databases in TEL: ACM Digital Library, AISEL, IEEE XPLORE, SpringerLink, ScienceDirect, Scopus and Wiley. In addition, Google Scholar was included in order to detect potentially relevant grey literature. To perform the search, we broke down the question into the learning settings (m-learning, or u-learning) and the research field where the proposal was framed (LA, or LD). The resulting search string was ("learning design" OR "learning analytics") AND ("mobile learning" OR "ubiquitous learning"). Using this query, we obtained 1622 papers. In addition, we added the first 100 results from Google Scholar. The search was conducted on April, 4th 2019 and since then new papers might have appeared. To standardize the search (since different databases have different filtering criteria), we accepted papers where the query was satisfied in the core parts of the it (title, abstract, or keywords), resulting in 209 papers. Furthermore, each paper was reviewed by at least two researchers, discarding those that were out of scope, not in English, or less than 4-pages long. Doubtful papers were discussed among all researchers, resulting in 54 papers[1] which were considered for the in-depth review.

3 Results

This section provides an overview of existing LD and LA proposals in m-learning and u-learning. We analyzed the definitions of m-learning and u-learning that were covered in the proposals (Subsect. 3.1), the learning contexts where these proposals were framed (Subsect. 3.2), and the type of contributions (Subsect. 3.3). Table 1 provides a summary of the main results per research question.

Table 1. Main findings per research topic.

Research topic	Findings	
Core aspects of m-learning/u-learning which have been considered by the LD and LA communities	m-learning	Learning with mobile technologies (15)
		Learning anytime anywhere (13)
		User mobility (7)
		Context-aware learning (5)
		Learning across spaces (2)
	u-learning	Learning anytime, anywhere (7)
		Context-aware learning (6)
		Learning with ubiquitous computing technologies (4)
		learning across spaces (3)
Learning contexts where LD and/or LA supported m-learning/u-learning	Scenarios	Formal: university (24) + K-12 (8)
		Informal: open to all users (8) + children (1)
	Spaces	Across physical and digital spaces (39) + several digital spaces (4) + singe digital space (2) + several physical spaces (1)
		Physical spaces: indoor (11) + outdoor (7) + both (22)
	Target users	Teachers (37)
		Learners (22)
LD and LA contributions for m-learning/u-learning	LD	Theoretical: models (17), guidelines (6) and frameworks (6)
		Practical: tools used mainly before (10) and during (11) learning activities
	LA	Theoretical: data analysis (8), models (8), and guidelines/good practices (8)
		Practical: tools used during (16) and after (10) learning activities

[1] Reviewed papers: https://gitlab.com/gertipishtari/list-of-papers.

Out of 54 reviewed papers, 28 (51.9%) were about LD, 23 (42.6%) about LA, and 3 (5.6%) referred both LD and LA. Thirty (55.5%) papers referred m-learning, 15 (27.7%) to u-learning, while 9 (16.7%) referred to both terms.

3.1 Definitions of m-Learning and u-Learning

In order to answer RQ1, we analyzed thematically the definitions (separately for m-learning and u-learning) that were used by the communities of LD and LA, in order to identify common core aspects. We started by identifying the parts of the definitions that referred to specific aspects of m-learning/u-learning (e.g., learning with mobile technologies). These were later on clustered together and coded with a specific keyword, or phrase. Similar keywords were further grouped together to form the core aspects.

From papers related to m-learning, 14 provided their own definition, 13 referred to other authors, while 19 took the definition for granted. It should be emphasized that papers that were referring to other authors, mentioned in total more than 10 different publications. Despite the multitude of definitions, several core aspects related to the definition of m-learning that were mentioned across the papers surged from the thematic analysis, such as: learning with mobile technologies (15); learning anytime anywhere (13); and user mobility (7), and context-aware learning (5). In the case of u-learning, 6 papers provided their own definition, 6 referred to other authors, while 15 took the definition for granted. The core aspects that were mentioned in this case included: learning anytime, anywhere (7); context-aware learning (6); and learning with ubiquitous computing technologies (4). Core aspects of m-learning and u-learning do not change significantly, when we filter the results based on LD, or LA contributions.

The communities of LD and LA attribute similar aspects to both terms of m-learning and u-learning, such as learning anytime anywhere, or context-aware learning. In relation to this, one of the cited papers from u-learning, Hwang et al. [4], while discussing the similarities between m-learning and u-learning, proposes the term context-aware u-learning to distinguish u-learning from m-learning. As it can be seen from the results, m-learning tends to be more technocratic with attributes such as mobile technologies and user mobility, but these attributes mainly appear in older publications and they can be explained with the focus on technology that m-learning had in the beginning. Since then m-learning has undergone a transformation and it is not seen anymore as exclusively related to learning with mobile technologies, or user mobility. In fact Traxler [19], the most cited author from the m-learning papers under review (although not massively cited), analyses the evolution of the definition and of m-learning from its technocratic beginnings, into a more mature moment when the research field was trying to understand the meaning of m-learning in an age that is characterized by a fast evolution of technologies and when the focus passed from the technology to the learners and the learning process.

3.2 Learning Context

To answer RQ2, we grouped the papers based on learning scenarios, educational levels, spaces, and target users.

Learning Scenarios. From 54 papers, 26 (48.2%) targeted formal learning, 8 (14.8%) informal learning (together with non-formal learning), 2 (3.7%) both formal and informal learning, while 18 (33.3%) did not specify it. From the papers addressing formal learning, 24 were about university settings and 8 about K-12. In the case of papers addressing informal learning, 4 focused on university level, 3 papers were open to all users, 1 was explicitly for children, and 2 did not specify it. Both communities of LD and LA have principally focused on formal learning with 13 and 16 papers, respectively. It should be also noticed that most of the cases where the type of learning went unspecified belong to LD, concretely 14 papers.

Learning Spaces. We grouped papers based on the typology of the space where learning occurred. The most common typology of learning spaces was across physical and digital spaces (39), followed by in several digital spaces (4), in a singe digital space (2), several physical spaces (1), and not specified (8). From the papers that described a learning activity, 11 papers referred to learning activities that happened indoor (most of them in a classroom), 7 papers referred to learning activities outdoor (e.g., in thematic parks, or in the city), while in 22 papers learning activities happened both indoor and outdoor. In general, the community of LD has focused more on indoor learning activities (5) and activities in both settings (16), while papers related to LA had an even distribution between indoor (6), outdoor (7), and in both settings (8). As an example, Muñoz-Cristóbal et al. [15] propose GLUEPS-AR, a system that helps teachers to deploy and enact LDs across physical and digital spaces, both indoor and outdoor. In another paper, Melero et al. [11] present QuestINsitu, a tool that supports the design and monitoring of geo-localized learning activities outdoor, where the learning activity happens across digital and physical spaces. Lkhagvasuren et al. [7] propose the Learning Log Analytics Dashboard (L2D), which tracks, analyzes and visualizes data about learning activities that happen in a digital space that supports language learning.

Target Users. Various target users were mentioned in the papers such as teachers, instructional designers, learners, researchers and developers. When considering both communities of LD and LA, teachers in 37 out of 54 papers (68.5%) and learners in 22 (40.7%) were the main target users. The community of LD has focused mostly on teachers (25) and instructional designers (15), while the community of LA has focused more on learners (15) and teachers (15).

Traditionally, the community of LA has focused on analyzing students' data to inform teachers. On the contrary, in m-learning and u-learning there is also a large focus on supporting directly learners. This facet can be related to the self-regulated nature of learning in m-learning/u-learning, where the role of the student is central. Thus, we could expect contributions moving their focus from teachers to learners in the coming years.

3.3 Types of Contributions

To answer RQ3 we grouped the contributions based on the research field (LD, LA) and the type of contribution (theoretical, practical). Theoretical contributions were further clustered into architectures, theoretical models, indicators, frameworks, data analysis, guidelines/good practices. Practical contributions were grouped into functionalities that were expected to be used before, during, or after the learning activity. We also labeled the papers under review based on the purpose of the LD/LA functionalities that they described (e.g., support the design of learning activities, provide personalized feedback, etc.).

The revised papers were evenly distributed among LD (28), LA (23), while 3 papers referred to both LD and LA. Papers mentioning LD were found to include more theoretical (25) than practical contributions (11), while LA papers had a balanced distribution between theoretical contributions (19) and practical ones (17). The 3 papers related to both LD and LA offered practical contributions. Theoretical contributions in LD have been mostly models (17), guidelines (6) and frameworks (6), while theoretical contributions in LA have been mostly data analysis (8), models (8), and guidelines/good practices (8). Practical contributions from the community of LD (e.g., QuestInSitu [11]) were used mainly during (11) and before the learning activity (10). In the case of LA papers, practical contributions (e.g., SCROLL [7]) were expected to be used during (16) and after learning activities (10).

LD functionalities were mainly aimed to support the design of learning activities (29), while LA functionalities focused on providing personalized feedback (17), and supporting the reflection about the learning activities (10). Papers including contributions in LA for LD also emphasized other aspects such as raising awareness about LD practices and support the evidence-based decision making.

As it can be seen from the results, there is a low number of practical implementations benefiting from the synergies between both LD and LA. From these, two papers were LA for LD [11,14], while third case used to both LD and LA independently, without aligning them [12]. It should be mentioned that there were no contributions on LD for LA.

4 Conclusion and Future Work

Despite the lack of widely accepted definitions for both m-learning and u-learning, this review shows that both communities emphasize similar core aspects of m-learning and u-learning. The communities of LD and LA attribute similar shared aspects to both terms. M-learning tends to be more technocratic, but these technical attributes are found mainly in older publications, when the field of m-learning was focusing more on the technological aspect.

Regarding the learning context, a significant finding is about target users. LA papers in m-learning/u-learning emphasize the importance of informing learners, which can be related to the self-regulated nature of learning in these settings.

This could imply that more LA effort could be devoted to further support self-regulated learners in m-learning/u-learning. In a similar way as in other reviews about LD and LA, most of the papers have been focused on university settings. This is to be expected due to the fact that university environments are easier to access by researchers. Therefore, there is still a need to explore the benefits of LD and LA in m-learning/u-learning in K-12 contexts and in non-formal settings.

While responding to the RQ3, about the type of contributions, we identified possible points of synergies between the communities of LD and LA that may lead to a joined research agenda in m-learning/u-learning. We noticed a low number of papers that include aspects from both LD and LA (3). Two of these papers were about LA for LD, while none referred to LD for LA. There is a low number of implementations benefiting from the synergies between LD and LA. These two communities can complement each other. As identified from the analysis, LD can support participants before the learning activity, while LA can do it during and after the activity. Moreover, as mentioned in recent literature [2, 10], both communities can further collaborate and close the loop. Specifically, LD can guide and give a context to data analysis, by making them more meaningful for involved stakeholders, while LA can inform design decisions and support the process evaluating LDs (as emphasized also from the papers under review that had a contribution related to LA for LD).

Relevant limitations of the current review have to do with the keywords that constitute the query and the method that was used to filter the paper (respectively searching with the query in the title, abstract and keywords). Important contributions that did not comply with the search criteria might have been left out of the review. Also, other learning contexts such as seamless learning, or hybrid learning, as well as related terminology for LD (e.g., scripting), or LA (e.g., educational data mining) were not included in the query and could have left out complementary contributions to the list of works under review.

Future work will aim to extend further the review by: analyzing in detail aspects about the learning context; identifying important aspects that need to be designed or monitored in m-learning/u-learning; evaluating the maturity of the contributions; identifying the main challenges that should be addressed by the communities of LD and LA; as well as identifying potential synergies of both communities in these learning contexts.

Acknowledgments. This research has been partially funded by the European Union in the context of CEITER (Horizon 2020 Research and Innovation Programme, grant agreement no. 669074).

References

1. Fu, Q.K., Hwang, G.J.: Trends in mobile technology-supported collaborative learning: a systematic review of journal publications from 2007 to 2016. Comput. Educ. **119**, 129–143 (2018)
2. Hernández-Leo, D., Martinez-Maldonado, R., Pardo, A., Muñoz-Cristóbal, J.A., Rodríguez-Triana, M.J.: Analytics for learning design: a layered framework and tools. Br. J. Educ. Technol. **50**(1), 139–152 (2019)

3. Hwang, G.J., Tsai, C.C.: Research trends in mobile and ubiquitous learning: a review of publications in selected journals from 2001 to 2010. Br. J. Educ. Technol. **42**(4), E65–E70 (2011)
4. Hwang, G.J., Tsai, C.C., Yang, S.J.: Criteria, strategies and research issues of context-aware ubiquitous learning. J. Educ. Technol. Soc. **11**(2), 81–91 (2008)
5. Hwang, G.J., Wu, P.H.: Applications, impacts and trends of mobile technology-enhanced learning: a review of 2008–2012 publications in selected ssci journals. Int. J. Mob. Learn. Organ. **8**(2), 83–95 (2014)
6. Kitchenham, B., Charters, S.: Guidelines for performing systematic literature reviews in software engineering (2007)
7. Lkhagvasuren, E., Matsuura, K., Mouri, K., Ogata, H.: Dashboard for analyzing ubiquitous learning log. Int. J. Distance Educ. Technol. (IJDET) **14**(3), 1–20 (2016)
8. Lockyer, L., Heathcote, E., Dawson, S.: Informing pedagogical action: aligning learning analytics with learning design. Am. Behav. Sci. **57**(10), 1439–1459 (2013)
9. Manathunga, K., Hernández-Leo, D.: Authoring and enactment of mobile pyramid-based collaborative learning activities. Br. J. Educ. Technol. **49**(2), 262–275 (2018)
10. Mangaroska, K., Giannakos, M.N.: Learning analytics for learning design: asystematic literature review of analytics-driven design to enhance learning. IEEE Trans. Learn. Technol. (2018)
11. Melero, J., Hernández-Leo, D., Sun, J., Santos, P., Blat, J.: How was the activity? A visualization support for a case of location-based learning design. Br. J. Educ. Technol. **46**(2), 317–329 (2015)
12. Mikroyannidis, A., Gómez-Goiri, A., Smith, A., Domingue, J.: Pt anywhere: a mobile environment for practical learning of network engineering. Interact. Learn. Environ. pp. 1–15 (2018)
13. Mor, Y., Ferguson, R., Wasson, B.: Learning design, teacher inquiry into student learning and learning analytics: a call for action. Br. J. Educ. Technol. **46**(2), 221–229 (2015)
14. Muñoz-Cristóbal, J.A., Rodríguez-Triana, M.J., Gallego-Lema, V., Arribas-Cubero, H.F., Asensio-Pérez, J.I., Martínez-Monés, A.: Monitoring for awareness and reflection in ubiquitous learning environments. Int. J. Hum.-Comput. Interact. **34**(2), 146–165 (2018)
15. Muñoz-Cristóbal, J.A., Martínez-Monés, A., Asensio-Pérez, J.I., Villagrá-Sobrino, S., Hoyos-Torio, J.E., Dimitriadis, Y.A.: City ads: embedding virtual worlds and augmented reality in everyday educational practice. J. UCS **20**(12), 1670–1689 (2014)
16. Persico, D., Pozzi, F.: Informing learning design with learning analytics to improve teacher inquiry. Br. J. Educ. Technol. **46**(2), 230–248 (2015)
17. Pimmer, C., Mateescu, M., Gröhbiel, U.: Mobile and ubiquitous learning in higher education settings. a systematic review of empirical studies. Comput. Hum. Behav. **63**, 490–501 (2016)
18. Pishtari, G., Väljataga, T., Tammets, P., Savitski, P., Rodríguez-Triana, M.J., Ley, T.: SmartZoos: modular open educational resources for location-based games. In: Lavoué, É., Drachsler, H., Verbert, K., Broisin, J., Pérez-Sanagustín, M. (eds.) EC-TEL 2017. LNCS, vol. 10474, pp. 513–516. Springer, Cham (2017). https://doi.org/10.1007/978-3-319-66610-5_52
19. Traxler, J.: Learning in a mobile age. Int. J. Mob. Blended Learn. (IJMBL) **1**(1), 1–12 (2009)
20. Wu, W.H., Wu, Y.C.J., Chen, C.Y., Kao, H.Y., Lin, C.H., Huang, S.H.: Review of trends from mobile learning studies: a meta-analysis. Comput. Educ. **59**(2), 817–827 (2012)

Poster Papers

Evaluating Image Training Systems for Medical Students

Reza Sobhannejad, Liam Rourke, and Osmar R. Zaiane(✉)

University of Alberta, Edmonton, Canada
{sobhanne,lrourke,zaiane}@ualberta.ca

Abstract. Skin cancer is one of the common and most fatal cancers. In most cases, the similarity between benign (healthy) and malignant (harmful) makes it so difficult to diagnose the lesion correctly. Moreover, there are two levels of categorization for skin lesions. In addition to benign vs malignant (basic level), each skin lesion can also be categorized as one of the sub-types of benign or malignant (subordinate level). In most medical schools the distinction between skin lesions is taught to students in just four sessions and at the basic level - i.e. benign vs malignant.

In this research, we designed a learning system which can assist students in learning skin lesions effectively in only a few sessions through an application using skin lesion images. We also compared these two levels, basic level and subordinate level, and found that indeed learning skin lesions at the basic level is more effective at distinguishing harmful cases than at the subordinate level as it could be hypothesized.

1 Introduction

When one finds a lesion on their skin, they visit a doctor who might refer them to a dermatologist if the lesion seems harmful. In Canada it can take up to six months to see a dermatologist. This fact creates a good deal of anxiety for the patient and this shows how important it is for the patient to have their lesions diagnosed correctly in the first step, but this is not an easy task for family doctors. The problem is that they have not seen many harmful skin lesions in their office, even though they see many skin lesions. Most of the cases they see are harmless. Seeing more harmful skin lesions can help them categorize new skin lesions more accurately.

1.1 Skin Lesion Categories

Skin lesions are separated into two groups of benign (harmless) and malignant (harmful), but not all malignant lesions are similar. The same is also true for benign lesions. That is why specialists created four subgroups for each of these groups so that lesions from the same subgroup are somehow similar. The subgroups of benign are Lentigo, Blue Nevi, Seb Ker and Acquired Melanocytic

M. A. Herzog et al. (Eds.): ICWL 2019, LNCS 11841, pp. 323–326, 2019.
https://doi.org/10.1007/978-3-030-35758-0_31

Nevi and the subgroups of malignant are Lentigo Maligna Melanoma, Acral Lentiginous, Nodular Melanoma and Superficial Spreading Melanoma. These are the most common types of skin lesions. Each lesion belongs to one of the two groups (malignant or benign) and only one of the eight subgroups. The first categorization is called *Basic Level* and the second categorization is called *Subordinate Level.* In other terms, classifying lesions as 'benign' versus 'malignant' is a "basic-level" categorization; determining which of the four sub-types they are is a "subordinate-level" categorization (Fig. 1).

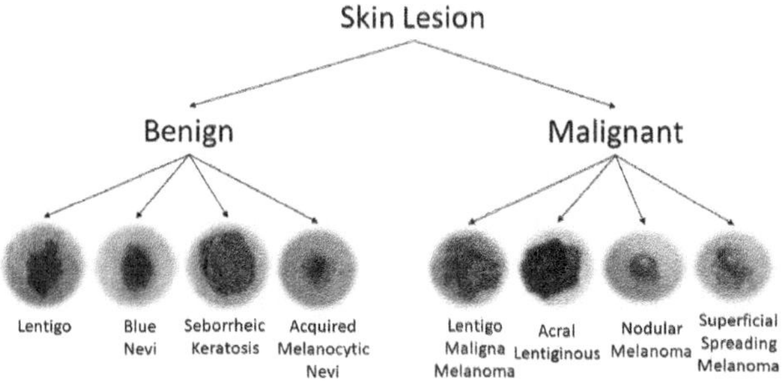

Fig. 1. Categorization of skin lesions.

2 Related Work

We know for a fact that visual category learning connects specific perceptual experience with abstract conceptual knowledge [5]. It is also argued that providing better labels alongside images in a visual category learning task can lead to a better performance [3]. In this section we review two studies related to different learning levels in visual learning subjects.

In 2006, a team of researchers compared basic level learning and subordinate level learning in distinguishing between birds [6]. In their research, two different types of birds were chosen, and the experiment focused on only these two types: Owls and wading birds. Each of these types can be further divided into sub-types just like skin lesions. In their experiment, they separated participants into two groups. One studied owls in basic level and wading birds in the subordinate level and the second group studied wading birds in basic level and owls in subordinate level. For each level, the use was provided with a sequence of bird photos with a label in the corresponding level. Before starting the experiment a pretest is performed in order to make sure that none of the participants had prior knowledge about bird types. This pretest also helped measuring the participants' performance after the experiment. The post-test included birds from three different groups of trained species/trained exemplars, trained species/untrained exemplars and untrained species which reveals the generalization ability of users.

The results show that each group has a better generalization in the type of bird that they studied at the subordinate level. This suggests that learning birds at the subordinate level is more effective than learning birds at the basic level.

In 2017, a team of researchers designed an experiment to compare basic level and subordinate level learning in recognizing rocks [4]. They introduced the "family-resemblance principle" first which states: "members of the same category share bundles of characteristic features that are not shared by members of contrasting categories". Then they defined two types of structure: compact structure which reflects the classic assumption of family-resemblance principle and dispersed structure which is exactly the opposite. The authors chose 30 rocks from three different types of rocks and asked the participants to rate the similarity between each pair. Using these pairwise similarities, they put the rocks in an M-Dimensional space which proved that rocks have a dispersed structure, because the members of a certain type of rocks were not really close. The classic research shows that when learning a new categorization in subordinate level the users end up having a better classification accuracy [2,6]. However, it was not necessarily clear for subjects with a dispersed structure. To investigate, they chose two groups of rocks (nine sub-types - three from each type) in a way that one had a compact and the other had a dispersed structured. For each structure, they had two groups of participants learning these rocks in basic/subordinate level. The results show that subordinate level learning is more effective in the compact structure while in the dispersed structure the basic level learning leads to a better performance. More importantly, learning rocks in subordinate level in conjunction with basic level is more effective than each of them alone.

3 Proposed Method

Going through hundreds of skin lesion images in a class makes students tired and they might not be able to concentrate on the images after a while [7]. Moreover, research shows that making mistakes while learning actually helps the learning better [1] and when passively showing images, as it is currently done, students would not have the opportunity to categorize lesions and make mistakes.

We designed a system for improving the speed of learning process of skin lesions; an on-line tutoring system with a large enough skin lesion database. We built an application for the iOS and Android that lets dermatologists take pictures of the patient's lesion and send the photograph and a dermoscopy picture along with the description of the lesion and the consent of the patient to use the data for research and teaching purposes, to our database server remotely. We also developed an Android application for pre-test and post-test which is a basic level test on 24 images selected from all 8 subgroups.

For the main learning process, we developed an Android app which lets a medical student learn skin lesions through different sessions, in basic/subordinate level using images of both harmless and harmful lesions. Each session lasts 15 to 20 min. In each session the user is presented with (1) skin lesion images and labels in the relative level and (2) some tests along the process asking for the correct label of a skin lesion. We used only 3 subtypes of each skin lesion type and kept the 4th subtype for measuring generalization in the post-test. In the benign sub session, we are trying to teach the difference between one benign sub-type versus other benign sub-types. In the malignant sub session, the students learn the difference between one malignant sub-type and other malignant sub-types. The Target audience of our app are medical students and we want them to be the best they can in basic level so they can refer all and only harmful lesions to dermatologists. That is why our pretest and post-tests are in basic level.

We performed an experience for comparing basic level learning and subordinate level learning with 5 participants. One of the participants scored 83% in the pretest and was removed due to previous knowledge. The other 4 participants were divided into two groups; one learning in basic level and the other in subordinate level. Table 1 shows the results of their pretest and post-test.

Table 1. Improvement after training

Participants	Pre-test	Post-test
Basic Level Participant #1	58%	92%
Basic Level Participant #2	62%	96%
Subordinate Level Participant #1	58%	71%
Subordinate Level Participant #2	58%	75%

There were some skin lesion images in the pretest which are obviously malignant and it makes sense when the pretest results are slightly higher than chance. The results show that the participants of the basic level were more successful in generalizing their knowledge and had an average of 34% improvement in the process, while the participants of the subordinate level had and average of only 15% improvement. This suggests that learning skin lesions in basic level is more effective than learning skin lesions in subordinate level.

References

1. Huelser, B.J., Metcalfe, J.: Making related errors facilitates learning, but learners do not know it. Mem. Cogn. **40**(4), 514–527 (2012)
2. Lassaline, M.E., Wisniewski, E.J., Medin, D.L.: 9 basic levels in artificial and natural categories: are all basic levels created equal? Adv. Psychol. **93**, 327–378 (1992)
3. Miyatsu, T., Gouravajhala, R., Nosofsky, R.M., McDaniel, M.A.: Feature highlighting enhances learning of a complex natural-science category. J. Exp. Psychol. Learn. Mem. Cogn. **45**(1), 1 (2019)
4. Nosofsky, R.M., Sanders, C.A., Gerdom, A., Douglas, B.J., McDaniel, M.A.: On learning natural-science categories that violate the family-resemblance principle. Psychol. Sci. **28**(1), 104–114 (2017)
5. Richler, J., Palmeri, T.: Visual category learning. WIREs Cogn. Sci. **5**(1), 75–94 (2014)
6. Scott, L.S., Tanaka, J.W., Sheinberg, D.L., Curran, T.: A reevaluation of the electrophysiological correlates of expert object processing. J. Cogn. Neurosci. **18**(9), 1453–1465 (2006)
7. Stuart, J., Rutherford, R.: Medical student concentration during lectures. Lancet **312**(8088), 514–516 (1978)

Domain-Specific Extensions for an E-Assessment System

Sebastian Pobel and Michael Striewe(✉)

University of Duisburg-Essen, Essen, Germany
{sebastian.pobel,michael.striewe}@paluno.uni-due.de

Abstract. E-assessment systems that provide automated feedback are a well-known part of modern education. Extensibility of e-assessment system with respect to domain-specific features is an import aspect of system design. This paper reports on two successful cases in which an existing e-assessment system was extended with domain-specific features.

Keywords: E-Assessment systems · Extensibility · System design · Case study

1 Introduction

Modern education uses a wide range of digital learning systems for learning management (LMS), intelligent tutoring (ITS), e-assessment, and other purposes. A particular feature of those systems is to provide feedback on exercise or exam solutions. A closer analysis reveals a distinction between generic e-assessment systems and domain-specific systems. While the former primarily offer generic features, the latter offer features that are required only in one particular domain or discipline. A typical example for a generic feature is an item type with input fields where the input is checked to be exactly the same as some sample solution. A typical domain-specific variant of that is to equip the input field with a formula editor to allow for input in mathematical notation and to check the input for equality by value with respect to the sample solution.

Extending an e-assessment system with domain-specific features has implications on the system design: First, the system architecture must be modular so that additional components can be added at all. Second, the internal data handling must be flexible so that domain-specific data formats or input representations can be processed. Third, the overall understanding of key concepts (such as "What characterized a correct solution?") must be universal so that domain-specific considerations do not contradict the system behaviour.

This paper reports on experiences that were made while we extended an existing e-assessment system with domain-specific capabilities for the domains of Chemistry (Sect. 2) and English as a foreign language (Sect. 3).

M. A. Herzog et al. (Eds.): ICWL 2019, LNCS 11841, pp. 327–331, 2019.
https://doi.org/10.1007/978-3-030-35758-0_32

1.1 Related Work

In recent decades, learning systems transformed from monolithic blocks via modular systems to service oriented frameworks [1]. While that targets the general extensibility or interoperability of systems, domains-specific extensions to e-assessment system require some specific considerations. One way of realizing such extensions is to plug-in self-contained modules that realize domain-specific item types. This is the way chosen for example by the JSME plug-in for MOODLE [2]. These modules provide extensions to the user interface as well as all necessary program code for evaluating user input and producing feedback. A different way of realizing such extensions is to connect additional modules for user interface, evaluation and alike as separate modules. This is the way it is done for example with computer-algebra-systems and domain reasoners in ACTIVEMATH [3].

1.2 The Existing System JACK

The e-assessment system named JACK is a modular system implemented in Java. It offers different item types with synchronous and asynchronous grading and allows to run modules for the latter distributed over several servers [4].

The workflow and component interaction for items with synchronous grading is as follows: A student requests an exercise via the web-frontend that in turn invokes the business logic. Exercise authors may include parameters into exercises and attach a set of expressions in an expression language to define values for them. If parameters are used, the business logic invokes an evaluator component to evaluate the respective expressions. When a student makes a submission to an exercise, the business logic is invoked again. It stores the submission in a plain serialized representation and forwards the submission to a synchronous checker for the particular item type. The rules for checking the submission for correctness may again include expressions in the expression language. The web-interface of JACK includes a formula editor based on the MATHDOX editor[1] and thus able to serialize the input into an OPENMATH XML string[2].

2 Extension Case 1: Chemistry

Handling molecular formulas and reaction equations required three extensions to JACK: The formula editor must allow notations for atom counts, charges, and alike. The underlying data format must represent molecular formulas correctly. Finally, the evaluator required new functions to compare molecular formulas and reaction equations based on specific chemical properties.

Molecular formulas look somewhat similar to mathematical formulas, but include some subtle differences: (1) Subscripts and superscripts are used for atom counts or charges and thus cannot be stacked and only allow positive integer numbers or specific combinations of characters; (2) Main elements are

[1] http://mathdox.org/formulaeditor/.

[2] https://www.openmath.org/.

atoms consisting of one upper case letter and potentially another lower case letter, while no spaces or dots are used to separate them within one molecule; (3) Positive integer numbers as main elements can only occur at the beginning of a molecule; (4) No parentheses are possible to change binding precedences.

All these features were implemented by creating a variant of the existing formula editor. The internal structure of the editor caused a significant problem in that endeavour: The editor is loaded as a JavaScript file in addition to the HTML page. Loading both variants on the same page for exercises that contain both mathematical and chemical input caused conflicts between the two variants due to duplicate definitions of classes or objects. In an ideal solution the editor will be modularized in such a way that common parts are only included once per page, while multiple domain-specific parts can be included in a single page as needed. Since this solution requires to re-implement larger parts of the editor the problem remains unsolved at the time of writing this paper.

As there are differences between mathematical and chemical formulas, they cannot be represented by the same serialization. However, the differences between them are not that large that a completely new form of data representation needs to be invented. In fact, there is already an existing XML representation of chemical formulas with the ChemML format[3]. The format is similar to MathML[4] that in turn has some relevant disadvantages in contrast to OpenMath. Consequently, we decided to create a new format called OpenChem to represent chemical formulas within the system JACK. Integrating the new format for data representation into JACK was as easy as expected. As the input editor was modified anyway, using the new data format was an integral part of that modification. The general data structures of the system JACK needed not to be changed, since any domain-specific knowledge on the data format is encapsulated within the formula editor and the evaluator component.

Two different additions were required in the context of expression evaluation: First, new functions were added to perform domain-specific operations. For example, a function named "compareNumberOfAtoms" takes two combinations of molecules as parameters and returns true if both parameters contain the same amounts of all occurring atoms. Adding new functions was possible without problems. Second, existing functions got new meanings. For example, a function named "contains" formerly checked whether a list or set contains a specific element. It now also checks whether a combination of molecules contains a specific molecule. These addition of new meanings to some functions required additional effort: Exercise authors must be able to define which domain must be used to evaluate expressions when a function is available in both domains. Hence the input format for exercises needed to be extended to allow proper settings both for the whole exercise and for individual expressions.

[3] http://www.xml-cml.org/.

[4] https://www.w3.org/Math/.

3 Extension Case 2: Language Training

The second case is to offer automated item generation in the domain of language training. The generated exercise should ask students to compare several simple sentences and to decide which of them have similar properties such as the same tense. The requirements in that case are entirely different than in the previous case: Data representation is not an issue, as generated sentences can be represented as plain strings. User input is also not an issue, as students just need to tick checkboxes to mark matching sentences. Instead, evaluator functions for generating sentences are the harder problem. Automated generation of natural language sentences in different tenses requires the use of some expert module. Adding such a module also requires to add appropriate functions to the evaluator component to invoke the extra module properly.

After some comparison of different expert modules for natural language generation, SimpleNLG[5] was selected to be used. As it is a Java library, it can be directly included in the evaluator component as dependency. The library offers a lot more complexity than actually required and hence a wrapper class was created to provide simplified access when implementing the evaluator functions.

The minimal requirement was to provide one single function that takes two nouns, one verb and a tense as input and returns a generated sentence using these words and the desired tense. However, sentence generation can only work properly for words that are included in the internal dictionary of SimpleNLG. Hence an additional function was added that filters a list of words to remove those that are not included in the dictionary.

4 Conclusions

The contribution of the paper is twofold: First, it shows that the integration of domain-specific capabilities into e-assessment systems is possible with relatively low effort if the systems provide a sufficiently modular architecture. Second, it shows the benefits of delegating specific data processing to specialized components as much as possible. Although we only considered only two small cases, we already could observe two strategies for delegation. One is to use standard formats like XML where the domain-specific knowledge can be encapsulated in schemas, while the other is to use third-party libraries encapsulated by wrapper functions to ensure a maximum of modularity.

Acknowledgements. Research for this paper was partially funded by the Federal Ministry of Education and Research under grant number 01PL16075.

[5] https://github.com/simplenlg/simplenlg.

References

1. Dagger, D., O'Connor, A., Lawless, S., Walsh, E., Wade, V.P.: Service-oriented e-learning platforms: from monolithic systems to flexible services. IEEE Internet Comput. **11**(3), 28–35 (2007)
2. Vedrine, J.M.: Javascript Molecular Editor question type for Moodle. https://github.com/jmvedrine/moodle-qtype_jme
3. Goguadze, G.: Active Math - Generation and Reuse of Interactive Exercises using Domain Reasoners and Automated Tutorial Strategies. Ph.D. thesis, Universitädes Saarlandes (5 2011)
4. Striewe, M.: An architecture for modular grading and feedback generation for complex exercises. Sci. Comput. Program. **129**, 35–47 (2016)

Designing a Mobile-Assisted English Reading Class for College Students

Nana Jin[1], Zili Chen[2], and Jin Wang[1](✉)

[1] School of Foreign Languages, Shenzhen University, Shenzhen, China
nanajin7@163.com, szuwangjin@163.com
[2] Division of Languages and Communication, CPCE,
The Hong Kong Polytechnic University, Hong Kong, China
val.chen@cpce-polyu.edu.hk

Abstract. Traditional classroom teaching is changing with modern technologies. A mobile-assisted classroom teaching is designed in the study and is proved an efficient teaching mode. The most popular mobile App WeChat in China is used as a course platform which could be easily tailored for any course exclusively. At the same time, several English learning mobile Apps are introduced to assist the English Reading class for college students, for example Xiao Huasheng App, Liuli Reading App, Ximalaya App. In the WeChat course platform, we integrate these mobile Apps at different times in classroom teaching and motivate students to participate in the course learning in class and after class. Mobile technologies plus linguistic knowledge and a well-planned teaching design are three key factors for a successful course teaching. Furthermore, this WeChat course platform is easy to build and makes a mobile-assisted language teaching accessible to every language teacher who may have a limited knowledge about technology.

Keywords: Mobile-assisted language teaching · Course design · WeChat · English Reading class

1 Introduction

With a fast and wide spread of modern educational technologies in language leaning and research [1], traditional in-class teaching mode is fading away. Since MOOC courses and many free mobile Apps are accessible to everyone, in-class teaching mode is changing and yielding to various multimodal technologies [2]. However, there is no clear rule about the balance of how much modern technology should be applied into an in-class teaching. Besides, there are other factors which will also influence the balance keeping, such as course types, students' motivations and teachers' abilities in applying educational technologies. An effective college English Reading class relies on in-time and clear instructions from the teacher and a monitored and guided self-reading after class by students.

This paper depicts the design and teaching procedure of an English Reading class for college students, which combines in-class teaching with a mobile Apps-based

M. A. Herzog et al. (Eds.): ICWL 2019, LNCS 11841, pp. 332–338, 2019.
https://doi.org/10.1007/978-3-030-35758-0_33

platform. In-class and after-class teaching are included in the study with the aid of mobile Apps to achieve an effective learning.

The mobile App WeChat helps grouping students together, and maintains the in-time interaction between a teacher and students. Meanwhile, WeChat is widely used in China and it is the most frequently used social software. WeChat helps teaching in many ways, such as students' attendance quick check, giving and reminding homework, giving answers, and in-time Q&A, etc. [3].

2 Methodology

One mobile social software and three English learning Apps are particularly integrated into the English Reading class—WeChat, Liuli Reading App, Ximalaya App, Xiao Huasheng App.

WeChat is a platform to keep interaction between a teacher and students in class and after class, the other three Apps are used to assist students to learn English after class. These Apps are believed to assist college students to achieve the aims of English Reading course: arouse reading interests, extend reading areas, and strengthen reading fluency. A WeChat-based course design with student performance records is illustrated in Table 1.

It is not wise to require students to read the same books after class, since they have their individual reading abilities and interests. And to achieve reading fluency and satisfaction, it is suggested to let students read easy materials. Suppose 'i' refers to an individual student's reading ability index, the difficulty index of the after class English reading should be 'i − 1' [4, 5]. Liuli Reading App and Xiao Huasheng App are used for students to choose after-class reading materials with suitable lexicon and grammar challenges.

Ximalaya App is audio corpus-based, which could be used to give students an audio input of those reading materials that they have read. The cognition effect of a reading material is believed more significant with multimodal inputs than singular input.

3 Class Design and Teaching Procedure

3.1 Before Class Preparation: A Survey on Students' English Reading Habits

There are 56 students participated in the survey [6], and the results show that most of the students read few English books after class. As for their English textbooks, the students focused on lexicon and grammar learning instead of achieving English reading joy. Some of them had tried to read English novels recommended by their high school teachers, such as *Pride and Prejudice*, *Jane Eyre*, *Great Expectations*. But they couldn't finish reading one whole novel at all, not even 50 pages of one book. It is therefore necessary to grade students' reading ability and recommend corresponding reading materials. Xiao Huasheng App offers an access to test one's reading ability and all reading materials offered in the App are marked with different reading grades.

Table 1. A WeChat Platform-based course design with student performance records.

WeChat Platform	Pre-class icebreaking-quotations sharing	Presentation team building	Text translation sharing	In-class interaction	Summary writing sharing	After-class reading monitor	After-class interaction
Student 1	*No one can give you brightness except yourself*	Topic 1	Text 1 Para 4–6	• quick response to questions • explain exercises • words' learning & translation • homework check • dictation • multi-modal instruction • giving answers	√ (omitted)	*Who is Elizabeth II?* …	• supplementary words • prefixes list • fast reading assignments • reminding homework • Q & A • peers learning • team building
Student 2	*I am thinking, therefore I am*	Topic 3	Text 1 Para 7–8		√ (omitted)	*The Giver* …	
Student 3	*Success is not final, failure is not fatal*	Topic 3	Text 1 Para 9–11		×	*The Mysteries from A–Z* …	
Student 4	*Life was like a box of chocolates*	Topic 2	Text 1 Para 12–14		√ (omitted)	*The Little Prince* …	
Student 5	*Tomorrow will be better*	Topic 2	Text 1 Para 15		√ (omitted)	*Matilda* …	
Student 6	*After all, tomorrow is another day*	Topic 5	Text 2 Para 4–5		√ (omitted)	*What was the WWII?* …	
Student 7	*Water, a desert blessing, an ocean curse*	Topic 1	Text 2 Para 6–8		√ (omitted)	*Who was Da vinci?* …	
Student 8	*Love all, trust a few, harm nobody*	Topic 1	Text 2 Para 9–10		√ (omitted)	*Charlotte's Web* …	
…	…	…	…	…	…	…	…

3.2 Before Class Preparation: A Survey on English Reading Textbooks

There are two major parts for English reading course: in-class textbook learning and after-class self-reading. As mentioned in the previous section, after-class reading materials should be tailored for each individual with the aid of mobile Apps Xiao Huasheng. As for in-class textbook, it is the compulsory one for all students no matter how different their language proficiencies are.

Textbook language is different from that of novels and stories. It is much more formal and grammatically well-organized. Bernstein [7] noticed the phenomenon and classified the language in textbooks and for teaching as vertical language, while the language used in daily life and acquired at home is classified as horizontal language. For learners of English as a second language (ESL), English horizontal language couldn't be acquired during one's childhood. Most Chinese students are exposed to English vertical language first at school, which is grammar-oriented and translation-oriented. Thus English horizontal language input is far less enough for ESL students. Since English textbooks are full of vertical language, the input of English horizontal language could be supplemented after class only.

Taking into account the two facts: students with various reading abilities, and English textbooks lacking horizontal language input, this study claims two basic principles for an exact and comprehensive choice of reading materials for students after class: difficulty = i − 1, and horizontal language oriented.

3.3 In-Class Teaching and Learning: Mobile-Assisted Instructions

In the first class of the English Reading course, an exclusive course WeChat group should be built on spot. Students and the teacher are united here. WeChat group building works like an icebreaking. It is time-limited in class, the course WeChat group can help saving time in attendance checking and encourage the whole class discuss and express themselves at the same time. For example, instead of asking students to introduce themselves to us one by one in person, each of them is asked to type their favorite sentence in the course WeChat group platform. Within two minutes, about 30 sentences will appear in the platform, and they are clearly shown to everyone in class (compared with the traditional classroom icebreaking, speaking in public is sometimes not clear and couldn't be understood due to difficult words or bad grammar). ESL students usually read better and faster than they listen. With a quick glance at the favorite sentences sent in the WeChat group platform, the similar minds go together and feel accompanied, even though they don't know each other in face. Compared with introducing your name, your hometown to your classmates, this quotes sharing in the platform (partly shown in Table 1 Column 2) goes deep in one's soul, and it is more efficient. Thus a nice and comfortable class environment is built with the aid of the mobile App WeChat. And everyone who participates in it leaves a record for class participation and performance.

For the English Reading textbook, the texts are usually longer and more difficult than the texts from *Comprehensive English* course. The texts usually cross over various topics, ranging from football industries to bioengineering, from religions to tax collection systems. To finish learning a text within 4 teaching hours - with about 1200 words in each text and the text difficulty is above one's reading ability- is very challenging both to students and the teacher. The unfamiliar topics of the texts and the mountains of new words are two major obstacles for the text understanding.

Lead-in is usually the first step in text learning, and we suggest that reading motivation come ahead of new words understanding. To arouse all students' reading motivations toward those difficult texts is not easy, but it's always worth trying. Students are required to make related presentations about each text in turns, either about the background information, or the introduction of the persons and places appearing in the text. Every text topic will be presented by 4–5 students at most from different angles. We prefer to give them enough time to think about it, and let them sign up for the presentation in the course WeChat group platform after class. All of this is done efficiently out of class with the aid of the course platform. While the presentation team is working on a presentation preparation, the course teacher can send a list of frequently used words on the topic in the WeChat group platform to keep other students connected to and immersed into the topic.

3.4 In-Class Teaching and Learning: Mobile-Assisted Learning and Sharing

The learning of each text is supposed to be finished within 4 teaching hours (2 h in each week) according to the syllabus. The first 2 teaching hours are usually for students' presentation on the text topic, a quick check on the glossary of the text, and the teacher's explanation and interpretation of the beginning part of the text. The rest 2 teaching hours in the following week will focus on the reading comprehension of the text, exercises and worksheets.

In the first 2 teaching hours, with the student presentation in class and the glossary check in WeChat group platform, the backgrounding and study environment for a text are created. Most students are ready for the further study of the text. They are encouraged to discuss with their peer classmates about the meaning skeleton of the text and then type the main idea in the WeChat group platform. Students can quickly learn from peers by reading each other's main idea writing on spot. It doesn't matter whether the main ideas written by students are accurately correct or not. The key point is to encourage students to participate in the text study and to be critical to different ideas about the text. They may find thoughts alike in the WeChat group platform and these positive mutual recognitions will greatly encourage students to dig the text deep. For those who might find they hold different ideas with others in the platform, their ideas are valued too, and they may challenge others with their logic. This is a good chance to let everyone have a second thought about the main idea before they go further into the text learning. No matter they agree with each other in the WeChat group platform or not, the most important thing is that almost everyone in classroom is activated and participates in the text learning activity.

In the second and last 2 teaching hours, students are mainly guided to understand the detailed information of the text with the main idea drawn in the previous class. When the text learning is finished in class, students will be given a worksheet of the text, which looks basically like a mind map of the text. Students are required to finish the blanks of the worksheet. Two students co-work with one worksheet, in order to encourage them to discuss, to co-operate, to compare their understandings and to persuade each other. This task might take 10 min and it is useful to keep everyone being participative. When they finish the worksheet filling blanks, they can take a photo of it and send it to the WeChat group platform to share with each other. And the teacher may also publish his answer of the worksheet in the platform, which is efficient and crystal clear to each one. Finally, every one of the students will have one worksheet at hand and they are required to briefly retell the whole text based on the worksheet within 5 min. This works as the last step of the text learning: General (main idea drawing) – Details (paragraph translating) – General (worksheet and retelling).

This is a complete pattern of an English Reading class for 4 teaching hours within 2 weeks. When students are familiar with the procedure, they can follow it quite well and sometimes they read the whole textbook beforehand and tell the teacher that they are very interested in some topics and would like to make presentations on those topics. And some students would like to create the worksheet of a text according to his/her understanding, which turned out quite correct and well-organized. Students are more active and self-motivated in the mobile-assisted English Reading class.

3.5 After-Class Guiding and Learning: Mobile-Assisted Learning and Sharing

There are 6 days between the first 2 and the second 2 teaching hours. To keep students being active and participative in the text learning, WeChat group platform is used to guide students to study individually after class. Students are required to translate the paragraphs after class with the aid of Google Translate or Baidu Translate. Each paragraph goes to one student and the students take turns to do this. All the translation is required to be sent in the WeChat group platform within two days after class, so that all students can self-study the text after class with the sharing of text translation.

Students are encouraged to use different translation software to finish their homework. They will compare the different translations and make a final version based on them. This process helps students save time in simple translation and requires them to put more effort in advanced translation, such as logical relations between clauses, and translation concordance with the main idea of the text, which are hard for machine translation.

Another major part of after-class learning task is extra reading materials. There are two kinds of materials: one is for reading fluency and joy, and the other is for reading accuracy in a limited time. To read for fluency and joy, students are encouraged to use mobile Apps such as Xiao Huasheng and Liuli Reading to search for their reading materials with interests. Our survey showed that for ESL Chinese college learners, English novels, such as *Pride and Prejudice*, *Great Expectations*, are not appropriate for students to achieve reading fluency and joy. Students are supposed to read something less difficult than the textbook in their after-class time. All these mobile Apps offer a broad range of books from fables, detective stories all the way to best sellers for teenagers. These "easy" reading materials serve as necessary reading gap fillings for the Chinese students, since they lack the English horizontal language acquisition in China. When they began to learn English, they learnt it at school and all they've been learning are from English textbooks, which belong to English vertical language. Furthermore, when they finish reading the interesting books, students are encouraged to listen to those books from the Ximalaya App, which is audio corpus based. With the two modes of input for one book - reading and listening, students will have a good language input and be expected to have good output: retelling and writing.

To read for accuracy in a limited time is always a must in every kind of language test and it is an important index to indicate one's reading ability. This exercise could be done by themselves after class and monitored by the teacher in the WeChat group platform.

4 Conclusion

A mobile-assisted college English Reading Class design is introduced in detail in this study. Since a WeChat group platform could be easily tailored and built exclusively for a course, it is efficient to communicate with everyone in class and after class. Students' performance could be monitored and guided on the platform. Students themselves also feel connected in the course WeChat group platform. This reading class design presents a new and holistic approach to not only improving an English learner's proficiency on reading, speaking, writing, speaking, translation, multiliteracy synthesizing relying on emerging technology, but also motivating students autonomous learning.

It is noted that the efficiency of monitoring the on-going posts is handicapped by the display of posts on WeChat when there is an influx of posts on the group platform, for example, during the in-class dictation or Q&A session. While WeChat as an educational platform is credited for its instant interaction, users' stickiness, and multiliteracy interface, further discussion on refining its user interface for a teacher to monitor an inrush of posts is suggested.

References

1. Chen, X., Hao, J., Chen, J., Hua, S., Hao, T.: A bibliometric analysis of the research status of the technology enhanced language learning. In: Hao, T., Chen, W., Xie, H., Nadee, W., Lau, R. (eds.) SETE 2018. LNCS, vol. 11284, pp. 169–179. Springer, Cham (2018). https://doi.org/10.1007/978-3-030-03580-8_18
2. Tian, L., Mu, Y., Yang, W.: Designing a platform-facilitated and corpus-assisted translation class. In: Hao, T., Chen, W., Xie, H., Nadee, W., Lau, R. (eds.) SETE 2018. LNCS, vol. 11284, pp. 208–217. Springer, Cham (2018). https://doi.org/10.1007/978-3-030-03580-8_22
3. Jin, N.: Mobile-assisted language learning: using WeChat in an English Reading class. In: Huang, T.-C., Lau, R., Huang, Y.-M., Spaniol, M., Yuen, C.-H. (eds.) SETE 2017. LNCS, vol. 10676, pp. 500–506. Springer, Cham (2017). https://doi.org/10.1007/978-3-319-71084-6_59
4. Anderson, N.J., Nunan, D. (eds.): Practical English Language Teaching: Reading, p. 79. Tsinghua University Press Ltd, Beijing (2013)
5. Krashen, S.: The Input Hypothesis: Issues and Implications. Longman, London (1985)
6. Yao, H.: A study on the English horizontal discourse of second language learners based on legitimation code theory. Unpublished degree thesis. Shenzhen University (2019)
7. Bernstein, B.: Vertical and horizontal discourse: an essay. Br. J. Sociol. Educ. **20**(2), 157–173 (1999)

Design of MicroLearning Course of Dynamic Web Pages' Basics in LMS with Interactive Code Testing Units

Radim Polasek(✉)

Department of Information and Communication Technologies, Faculty of Education, University of Ostrava, Dvorakova 7, 701 03 Ostrava, Czech Republic
radim.polasek@osu.cz

Abstract. MicroLearning (ML) was identified as one of the trends that can profile e-Learning now or in the near future. The author already conducted two experiments, where he tested newly created MicroLearning courses in comparison with "classic" e-Learning courses and got promising results [10]. The paper describes the creation of MicroLearning course "Creation of webpages". The author focuses on design of newly created course taking into account subject matter and concepts of creation of individual ML units using among others step by step instructional design. Mentioned is the way ML learning units for this course were created, also making use of video tutorials enriched with interactions and quizzes. LMS Moodle was chosen for ML course creation with added support for interactive multimedia. This was extended with interactive code exercises "Try, Alter and Execute" (TAE) with pre-prepared HTML codes. The course aims to support more active engagement of students as they try code alterations within LMS and offer benefits of numerous quizzes.

Keywords: MicroLearning · e-Learning · Web pages · HTML · PHP · LMS · Interactivity · Code testing

1 Introduction

Today's world is changing quite fast and educational institutions have a duty to react and keep pace. Society and mainly technologies (services) are changing fast and influence students. For younger generations, Web and social networks are services that they use on an everyday basis. In this world, classic study materials have to compete with interesting, in small doses available information that is almost always more appealing or interesting.

The classic approach to e-Learning is nowadays many times not following up-to-date trends. Already some time ago Nielsen defined "microcontent" [7] and this trend was later followed by the success of social networks – Twitter.com even explicitly restrict the maximum length of posts (at first limited to 140 characters, later extended to 280). Poe [9] speaks about the fact that short is what is connected with the Internet.

M. A. Herzog et al. (Eds.): ICWL 2019, LNCS 11841, pp. 339–343, 2019.
https://doi.org/10.1007/978-3-030-35758-0_34

2 From Microblogging to Creation of MicroLearning Course in an e-Learning Way

Nielsen [7] with term "microcontent" meant headings (describing macrocontent) not main content itself. Hug [4] later connected short texts with term MicroLearning and defined its main attributes. Lindner [5] used the term "microcontent" and finally connected it with short pieces of content. If we look at microcontent as a part of a subject matter, connection with learning objects [6] is obvious. The difference is that microcontent, in connection with ML, is called microcontent unit (MCU), aims to be focused on rather small parts of subject matter and comprise ML course.

Most approaches to ML are mobile-based ML [1, 2, 8]. Because of the use of LMS Moodle as the main e-Learning platform at our University, we decided to create the ML course in this LMS environment with mobile devices support. LMS Moodle with well-chosen template is responsive, so can be used on mobile devices. Unfortunately, because of mature of e.g. interactive videos they are not best viewed on devices with too small (narrow) screens. Only solution is to use mobile device in landscape mode.

In addition to Hug's [4] parameters, we added emphasis on interactivity, multimediality and integrated quiz questions. Capabilities of Moodle in the use of interactive content are quite limited, so we made use of H5P (www.h5p.org) that adds several interactive educational content types. We mostly used "Course presentation", "Interactive video" and "Quiz". We set limit, that one MCU should be around 5–7 min long and the number of terms should not exceed 5–7 per MCU.

2.1 Structure of MicroLearning Course of Dynamic Web Pages' Basics and Use of MCUs

The course consists of eleven topics that cover a creation of dynamic webpages (Introduction to web pages, HTML, CSS, CSS positioning, JavaScript, Basics of PHP, Forms, PHP and MySQL, Saving Form data to DB, PHP Functions, Form Validation). Each topic consists of compulsory parts set by the university's regulation, among them are learning outcomes, keywords, study materials, (optionally) examples, summary, control questions for students' self-evaluation and test. Units look like a classic Moodle-like course, the difference lies in used smallest parts – MCUs. They were placed in the course study materials section.

Our already finished research results showed students' better results in factual knowledge test [10] if they used an ML course. Taking this into account we decided to utilize gained experience and create similarly based ML course for subject dynamic web pages' basics. Each unit consists of mostly MCUs (in average 10 per unit) – besides summaries of e.g. protocol commands, etc. – and at the end of unit of summary quiz. For the creation of MCUs we employed below mentioned H5P content types.

Interactive Videos

Videos are suitable to be used as an introduction into a given topic, with a combination of images, animations or diagrams. These videos are turned into interactive by enriching it with various interactive elements. One of the basic are bookmarks, that give students the opportunity to skip parts, get to a certain point that student finds important, etc. We found good to mark beginnings of main parts of a video and enable viewers to navigate within them. Bookmarks virtually chop videos into even shorter parts, that covers only one specific detail. We also inserted into videos short texts, that points out key topic of a give part, important fact or give headings to video parts. Within interactive videos can be used also other types of H5P objects, mainly various quiz questions and tasks. Suitable are multiple-choice questions, drag the words or fill the blanks tasks. We placed them at the ends of particular parts to reinforce key facts or at the end of a video for summary revision.

Course Presentation with Interactive Content
Interactive course presentation was used as the main content type for MCUs. Simple use can be as follows – a linearly connected chain of slides with text. The approach we chose is to create this MCU with a limited number of slides (approx. 3–4, excluding title slide), without links, or when consisting of more slides (5 or more) interconnecting appropriate parts (slide with connected quiz questions).

Supported content for course presentation MCUs are besides text and again various quiz questions also videos, images, audios even interactive videos.

Try, Alter and Execute (TAE) Exercises
These exercises are meant to be supportive for students to see HTML (CSS, PHP) code, and have a possibility to experiment with it. TAEs consists of two windows where first shows code and the second is used for code rendering after pressing the button "Run code". TAE exercises have set task(s) that students should try and debug with given code. They are focused on altering prepared code in a different context and after that, with Moodle Assignment they must hand in completed task to the teacher.

2.2 Creation and Design of a MicroLearning Units (MCUs)

Each MCU was created in similar design, just with differences according to used H5P content type (interactive videos, interactive course presentations, Question sets). For purpose of creating MCU, we always took unit's content and from the beginning to end started to divide it by restraint of the number of possibly used terms for one MCU, but also taking into account logical groups within a given unit. If the size of a logical group would produce too long MCU, we created two instead.

Creating interactive videos was a bit different. The first and usually most important quality of a video that we searched for (besides content), was its length in minutes. We set a limit to approx. 7 min for introductory videos and approx. 12 to 20 min for coding examples. Next were marked main parts by Bookmarks and added labels where needed throughout a video. Lastly were added quiz questions and at the end short quiz for revision.

Application of Quiz Questions within MCUs
Some findings show that post-instruction testing improves delayed retention learning [3, 11], so we employed a similar approach with the use of MCUs. Not to limit students in a way they are going to use quiz questions in MCUs, we inserted links that are connecting "theoretical slides" with corresponding quiz questions at the end of

MCU. Also, backlinks were set. Within interactive videos we were not mostly inserting links as a screen of videos is usually occupied by text, graphic elements, text labels, test buttons and subtitles and yet another element could make it too chaotic.

3 Conclusion

The main reason for the creation of new ML e-Learning course was to offer to students (undergraduate IT teachers) more active way to study (for some) not very interesting subject. We see benefits of ML that by creating small chunks, it offers a way for students to create their study path and makes it easier for them to grasp particular parts of the whole. Important is to carefully prepare learning path by chaining MCUs as step by step parts that – though are self-contained – create the image of a whole.

Our approach to ML course is closer to the traditional e-Learning course, which is a little bit different from most approaches to ML. Use of LMS kept division into topic and activities. Because the creation of a new learning environment is time demanding and costly, we find the use of classic LMS as the best way. We hope that connection of attractive form of subject matter presentation with the possibility to test code snippets (TAE) directly within LMS opens the way for the improvement of students' motivation and higher rate of interest. Hopefully, also higher rate of gained factual knowledge and learning satisfaction will be met. ML is by many nowadays seen as a possible trend and we hope that makes use of ML in connection with LMS brings prospects of improvements of learning.

References

1. Cates, S., et al.: MobiLearn go: mobile microlearning as an active, location-aware game. In: MobileHCI 2017 Proceedings of the 19th International Conference on Human-Computer Interaction with Mobile Devices and Services, pp. 1–7. ACM Press, New York (2017). https://doi.org/10.1145/3098279.3122146
2. Göschlberger, B., Bruck, P.A.: Gamification in mobile and workplace integrated microlearning. In: iiWAS 2017 Proceedings of the 19th International Conference on Information Integration and Web-based Applications & Services, pp. 545–552 ACM Press, New York (2017). https://doi.org/10.1145/3151759.3151795
3. Haynie, W.J.: Effects of multiple-choice and short-answer tests on delayed retention learning. J. Technol. Educ. **6**(1), 32–44 (1994). https://doi.org/10.21061/jte.v6i1.a.3
4. Hug, T.: Micro Learning and Narration. Exploring possibilities of utilization of narrations and storytelling for the designing of "micro units" and didactical micro-learning arrangements. In: Online proceedings of the International Conference "Media in Transition 4: The Work of Stories." p. 13. MIT, Cambridge (2005)
5. Lindner, M.: What is microlearning? In: Micromedia and Corporate Learning. Proceedings of the 3rd Microlearning 2007 Conference, pp. 52–62 Innsbruck University Press, Innsbruck (2007)
6. McGreal, R.: Learning objects: a practical definition. IJITDL **2004**, 9 (2004)
7. Nielsen, J.: Microcontent: How to Write Headlines, Page Titles, and Subject Lines. http://www.useit.com/alertbox/980906.html

8. Nikou, S.A., Economides, A.A.: Mobile-based micro-learning and assessment: impact on learning performance and motivation of high school students. J. Comput. Assist. Learn. **34**(3), 269–278 (2018). https://doi.org/10.1111/jcal.12240
9. Poe, M.: A history of communications: media and society from the evolution of speech to the Internet. Cambridge University Press, Cambridge (2011)
10. Polasek, R., Javorcik, T.: Results of pilot study into the application of MicroLearning in teaching the subject Computer Architecture and Operating System Basics. In: Wang, F.L., et al. (eds.) 2019 International Symposium on Educational Technology, pp. 196–201. IEEE, Hradec Králové (2019)
11. Ramraje, S.: Comparison of the effect of post-instruction multiple-choice and short-answer tests on delayed retention learning. Australas. Med. J. **4**(6), 332–339 (2011). https://doi.org/10.4066/AMJ.2011.727

Design Considerations for a Mobile Sensor-Based Learning Companion

Haeseon Yun[1,2(✉)], Albrecht Fortenbacher[1], René Helbig[1], and Niels Pinkwart[2]

[1] HTW Berlin, Wilhelminenhofstraße 75A, 12459 Berlin, Germany
yun@htw-berlin.de
[2] Humboldt University Berlin, Rudower Chaussee 25, 12489 Berlin, Germany

Abstract. This paper presents the concept of a mobile learning companion which uses sensor data to support self-regulated learning. Based on design considerations derived from previous work, a prototype of a mobile learning companion (Charlie) was developed as a student project at HTW Berlin. A first qualitative study with 4 students aimed at validating Charlie's character as a friendly learning companion and its benefits and limitations for self-regulated learning. Future work will focus on improving Charlie to provide a positive learning support as a mobile learning companion.

Keywords: Mobile learning · Sensor-based learning · Learning companion · Self-regulated learning · Pedagogical agent

1 Introduction

Various research shows that self-regulated learning strategies can help students to cope with cognitively, emotionally and behaviourally challenging situations, and lead to academic achievements [14]. Corno [5] discussed that external support (by teachers or computers) can help learners to modify their cognitive, motivational and behavioural states. Even de-contextualized responses from a computer can support learners for positive learning achievements. Referring to various training programs and systems, Azevedo and Cromley [1] explored the advantages of a learning companion as a way to support self-regulated learning in an online-learning environment. In this paper, we present our conceptual work on using a mobile device with integrated sensors (e.g. camera, heart rate, proximity sensor, and microphone) for a context-aware self-regulated learning agent, named Charlie. Then we present a prototypical realisation of Charlie and report preliminary findings.

2 Sensor-Based Learning Companion for Self-regulated Learning

To be self-regulated learners, students should be aware of their responsibility to engage, learn and reflect on their learning, and they should be equipped

M. A. Herzog et al. (Eds.): ICWL 2019, LNCS 11841, pp. 344–347, 2019.
https://doi.org/10.1007/978-3-030-35758-0_35

with these core skills [11]. However, learners are limited in exerting their competency in self-regulation, because they cannot see the effects of self-regulation on their learning achievements, and because they are not convinced whether they could enact appropriate self-regulated strategies [14]. In addition, learners may lack motivation and interest in their learning tasks and feel no necessities to put self-regulation into action. Zimmerman and colleagues [14] suggested various methods to enforce and motivate learners' engagement in self-regulated learning. Operant views of self-regulated learning include external nudges (e.g. teachers' questions or alerts from a system) as methods to promote self-regulated learning, whereas phenomenological views of self-regulated learning emphasise the increase of self-awareness including planning, goal setting, monitoring, and evaluation of learners. Furthermore, not only the environmental and behavioural factors but also learners' cognitive and affective processes are advised under social cognitive views of self-regulated learning. Comprehensively, to support learners to be more self-regulated in their learning, both learner's internal (e.g. cognition, motivation, emotion) and external (e.g. environment and behaviours) conditions should be considered. In an informal learning environment, learning takes place in various locations (external condition), and the learning process and management are mainly controlled by learners (internal conditions). In this setting, a mobile device with integrated sensors is appropriate to support self-regulated learning phases and stages. Specifically, conditions of the learning environment (e.g. brightness, noise level) can be attained by sensors such as microphone and camera. In addition, GPS and WIFI can seamlessly locate learners' location [10]. This information can help learners critically evaluate their physical learning environment with respect to their learning goals and achievement.

3 Charlie, a Mobile Sensor-Based Learning Companion

Based on suggestions from [13], for the design of a sensor-based learning companion, a smartphone app (Charlie) was designed, and a first prototype of Charlie was implemented. Similar to [9], a neutral name was chosen, so Charlie can be seen both as a female and male character.

Designing a first prototype of Charlie, six design considerations were considered: (1) correspondence to learner's characteristics, (2) instructional advantages and encouragement, (3) initiation of dialogue ad engagement to reflect, (4) a simple and stylish visual with task and relation orientation, (5) a fellow learner and a real human, and (6) positive interaction and positive perception of overall learning experience. Charlie engages learners to set clear learning goals according to learning tasks of their choice by using the SMART goal model as proposed by [8]. Upon setting a goal, Charlie asks the learner to set a place and the expected time necessary to complete the goal. By setting a goal and the expected study duration, Charlie engages the learner to be aware of importance of specific goals which needs to be specific, measurable, attainable, realistic and time-bound. When a learner is ready to proceed learning, Charlie accompanies the learner by (1) showing the user-defined goal and place, (2) giving ambient information such as brightness and noise level, (3) informing about progress as time-lapse, (4) giving feedback and recommendations on demand.

To appear as a human-like peer, Charlie uses Emoji which has facial expression. Colours and messages were designed based on three design considerations of a learning companion: (1) a simple stylish visual [2,4], (2) encouragement-oriented and relation-oriented messages [12] and (3) fellow learner-human [6]. Empathetic feedback was supported by the use of affective colours [3]. For messages, three areas of volitional control strategies [7] (self-efficacy enhancement, stress reducing actions, negative based incentives) were adopted. Additionally, learning related humours and quotes have been chosen from online resources to improve human characteristics. In a student's project at HTW Berlin, a Charlie prototype was implemented as an Android app to gain learners' perception of a mobile sensor-based learning companion.

4 Results

Based on the first development of Charlie, four students at HTW Berlin volunteered to participate in interacting with Charlie and engage in open-ended interviews. When interacting with Charlie, learners expressed a positive impression toward the relation-oriented messages, in addition to being interested in the concept behind it. Yet, learners spoke up for more active involvement and clear indication of its extend of competence.

Overall, related to Charlie being a fellow learner/human, participants liked the default name, Charlie. In addition, participants stated that they had a personal feeling which was due to the look of Charlie. Regarding on a goal setting, learners felt **a bit forced** when writing their goals, because all the fields such as learning action, learning field, learning objective were mandatory. Interestingly, all participants claimed that they are well aware of how to set a goal, yet without assistance, goal setting was neither clear to them nor easy. Additionally, all participants liked the visualisation of their learning session and found the recommendations helpful. Regarding on the learning time, one participant was curious whether a companion will give him/her information when he/or she is **productive**.

5 Discussion and Outlook

Considering the availability of mobile devices like smartphones and their integrated sensor technology, the information that the device provides for learners can improve self-awareness of learning. The paper presents the theoretical background, idea, development and evaluation of Charlie as a mobile learning companion to support self-regulated learning. The learners' comments were analysed by conducting a qualitative research to reflect their impression when interacting with Charlie as a learning companion. Due to the low sample size, the results can not be generalised, yet comments from actual learners who have interacted with Charlie allowed us to reflect on future steps to improve a mobile sensor based learning companion.

References

1. Azevedo, R., Cromley, J.G.: Does training on self-regulated learning facilitate students' learning with hypermedia? J. Educ. Psychol. **96**(3), 523 (2004)
2. Bartneck, C., Reichenbach, J., Van Breemen, A.: In your face, robot! the influence of a characters embodiment on how users perceive its emotional expressions. In: Proceedings of the Design and Emotion, pp. 32–51. Ankara Turkey (2004)
3. Bartram, L., Patra, A., Stone, M.: Affective color in visualization. In: Proceedings of the 2017 CHI Conference on Human Factors in Computing Systems, pp. 1364–1374. ACM (2017)
4. Cercone, K.: Characteristics of adult learners with implications for online learning design. AACE J. **16**(2), 137–159 (2008)
5. Corno, L.: Self-regulated learning: a volitional analysis. In: Zimmerman, B.J., Schunk, D.H. (eds.) Self-Regulated Learning and Academic Achievement, pp. 111–141. Springer, New York (1989). https://doi.org/10.1007/978-1-4612-3618-4_5
6. Gulz, A., Haake, M.: Virtual pedagogical agents-design guidelines regarding visual appearance and pedagogical roles. Current Developments in Technology-Assisted Education, FORMATEX 2006 (2006)
7. McCann, E.J., Garcia, T.: Maintaining motivation and regulating emotion: measuring individual differences in academic volitional strategies. Learn. Individ. Differ. **11**(3), 259–279 (1999)
8. Robins, E.M.: An instructional approach to writing smart goals (2014)
9. Ryokai, K., Vaucelle, C., Cassell, J.: Virtual peers as partners in storytelling and literacy learning. J. Comput. Assist. Learn. **19**(2), 195–208 (2003)
10. Schmidt, A., Aidoo, K.A., Takaluoma, A., Tuomela, U., Van Laerhoven, K., Van de Velde, W.: Advanced interaction in context. In: Gellersen, H.-W. (ed.) HUC 1999. LNCS, vol. 1707, pp. 89–101. Springer, Heidelberg (1999). https://doi.org/10.1007/3-540-48157-5_10
11. Terras, M.M., Ramsay, J.: Massive open online courses (MOOCs): Insights and challenges from a psychological perspective. British J. Educ. Technol. **46**(3), 472–487 (2015)
12. Woolf, B.P.: Building Intelligent Interactive Tutors: Student-Centered Strategies for Revolutionizing e-learning. Morgan Kaufmann, San Francisco (2010)
13. Yun, H., Fortenbacher, A., Pinkwart, N.: Improving a mobile learning companion for self-regulated learning using sensors. In: CSEDU (1), pp. 531–536 (2017)
14. Zimmerman, B.J., Schunk, D.H.: Self-Regulated Learning and Academic Achievement: Theory, Research, and Practice. Springer Science & Business Media, New York (2012)

Exploring the Fully Online Learning Community Model: Comparing Digital Technology Competence and Observed Performance on PBL Tasks

Roland van Oostveen[1(✉)], Wendy Barber[1], Elizabeth Childs[2], Maurice DiGiuseppe[1], and Kristen Colquhoun[1]

[1] Ontario Tech U, Oshawa, ON L1G 0C5, Canada
roland.vanoostveen@uoit.ca
[2] Royal Roads University, Victoria, BC V9B 5Y2, Canada

Abstract. The Fully Online Learning Community (FOLC) model is intended to operate within a co-created Digital Space to (a) reduce transactional distance, and (b) incorporate newcomers into an established learning community. An operationalized version of the General Technology Competency and Use (GTCU) framework was used with a convenience sample of Ontario Tech University students to determine readiness to work in the Digital Space. Initial findings confirm the results of an earlier study, which found positive correlations between self-reported scores and overall performance quality at the high and low ends of the continuum. We suspect that while the GTCU aids in the identification of a threshold-based approach to identifying readiness to work in the Digital Space, the instrument is insufficiently granular to identify a precise readiness point. This led the team to continue to develop a more sophisticated version of the GTCU, the current Digital Competency Profiler (DCP), and its companion, the Fully Online Learning Community Survey (FOLCS).

Keywords: Readiness for online learning · Digital skills and competencies · Problem-based learning

1 Introduction

Currently, online learning is having profound effects on institutions of higher education. Seaman, Allen & Seaman [1] report that distance enrollments have increased for the 14th straight year and have grown over 5% between 2012 and 2016, with over 30% of higher education students in the United States having taken at least one online course. In Canada, "approximately 12% of college course enrolments are online, and 16% in universities" [2]. However, the online experience is highly variable, ranging from blended learning, where students complete in-class or at-home learning tasks using an Internet connection, to fully online courses, where students never physically come on campus but instead interact with each other using a variety of synchronous and asynchronous tools. As a result, the most common online courses have developed a reputation of leaving students feeling isolated, disconnected, and frustrated, resulting in

M. A. Herzog et al. (Eds.): ICWL 2019, LNCS 11841, pp. 348–351, 2019.
https://doi.org/10.1007/978-3-030-35758-0_36

retention and persistence issues [3]. Given the predicted trends in higher education, and the resulting needs of learners across sectors [4, 5], it is essential that educators in higher education begin to examine, and act upon, models of digital learning that facilitate the development of the skills and competences mentioned above.

The project being reported here is part of a larger set of studies which investigate various aspects of the Fully Online Learning Community (FOLC) model [6]. The overall intent of the larger set of studies is to better understand how FOLC's implementation may affect students' perceptions of inclusion, collaboration, and learning relevance, while simultaneously developing a wide range of competences that align with the outcomes and employability skills of agencies external to the university.

2 Literature Review

Models of online learning environments vary significantly, and include, but are not limited to synchronous, asynchronous, MOOCs, Wikis and hybrid courses. A common element of all online learning environments is the creation of a "democratic space" [7] wherein teachers and learners can ubiquitously integrate technology throughout learning. This is a central feature of the FOLC model, which also includes enabling all community members to contribute to the critical challenge of ideas and perspectives. In this way, a fully inclusive learning environment is created, where the roles of teacher and learner are redefined, and where individuals are required to be responsible for the quality of the overall learning community. Both challenge and support are essential elements of this approach, and the development of relationships results in decreased transactional distance between community members [8]. Along with a Problem-Based Learning (PBL) orientation, which has been well documented as an effective paradigm for co-designed open learning environments [9], the FOLC model currently serves as the basic modality for many of the courses in the fully online programs that employ a mix of synchronous and asynchronous affordances, offered by the Faculty of Education and Faculty of Health Sciences at Ontario Tech University.

3 Methodology

To determine readiness to work in the Digital Space, an operationalized version of the General Technology Competency and Use (GTCU) framework [10] was used for a convenience sample of Ontario Tech University students to complete randomly distributed Assessment and Performance Assignment Modules (APAMs), organized according to the four orders of competency in the GTCU framework. The assessment portion of the APAM captured individual participants' self-reported Frequency and Confidence Rating (FCR), using 5-point Likert-scale indicators, in relation to specific types of technology usage. The performance portion of the APAMs provide a "given" and "own" orientation [11] which enabled the study to examine the differential in what Savin-Baden [9] classifies as "Level 1 PBL" and "Level 5 PBL." In the process, the FCR questions are matched to a Performance Assignment (PA), which participants complete as a demonstration of their self-assigned FCR.

The performance tasks consisted of two parts. The first task was labelled a 10-minute Warm-up Activity. Following the characteristics of a given problem [11], the warm-up task was very specific in terms of the directions given and the type of product to be produced. In a second task, called a "30-minute Freestyle Activity, participants were asked to analyze a collage of graphics depicting various complex situations. with an instruction to "Examine the photos below, reflect on them, and identify an issue or problem that comes to mind, then address this issue in some thoughtful and creative way using the technologies available to you".

Sixteen student volunteers from faculties across Ontario Tech University responded to the invitation to participate by completing the FCR survey prior to their arrival in the EILab. For the performance portion of the APAM, the volunteers were seated at an EILab workstation and given an overview and basic instructions. The tasks were provided visually through a large monitor that was placed directly in front of the participant. Workstation set up included: 4 video feeds synchronized with each other; a camera (Face) placed on a tripod below the large monitor, trained on the participant face for use with FaceReader; a camera (Top) suspended above the workstation to allow all desktop surface movements to be recorded; a camera (Body) suspended in the corner of the room trained on the individual to record body movement; and a feed coming from the laptop (Device) used by the participant to allow for the recording of all inputs into the device.

4 Preliminary Findings and Conclusions

Detailed analysis of survey results and video recordings is ongoing. Participant videos (three video files per participant, e.g., top, device, and face) are currently being analysed. The analysis required the development of a multi-level coding strategy. Level 1: The analysis of the device and top video illustrating the work process engaged in by each participant, identifying specific events. Level 2: The analysis of facial expressions using Noldus FaceReader to detect 7 different emotional states. We link these emotional states to a determination of skill versus challenge. Level 3: The analysis of body language of the participant from the face video. These analyses will be scored against the determination of readiness provided by the self-assessed FCR. One participant has been analysed using this strategy and these results will be presented in the poster session.

Preliminary analysis of the data leads EILab researchers to believe that the findings will corroborate the major conclusions of the Blayone [12] study, indicating that there are general correlations between self-reported competences and the observed performances of the two groups. Those who claimed to be highly competent in the self-report instrument—typically individuals who owned or had constant access to a variety of digital technologies—were able to demonstrate their ability to complete both tasks to a high standard. The other group—typically including individuals claiming not to be digitally competent—generally presented with numerous difficulties in both tasks, and frequently became quite frustrated with their inability to complete the tasks.

The determination of a measurable index and reliable readiness threshold for online learning continues to be an elusive concept. The EILab researchers are well aware of the diverse and challenging sociocultural and economic issues that impact accessibility, availability, and opportunity for online learning. As EILab researchers, we are optimistic that a significant measure of readiness for online learning will emerge from this research and are hopeful that this work will stimulate further research on a local and global scale—research that may result in improved digital learning both domestically and internationally.

References

1. Seaman, J.E., Allen, I.E., Seaman, J.: Grade increase: tracking distance education in the United States. The Babson Survey Research Group, Wellesley (2018)
2. Bates, T.: New enrolment data for online learning in Canadian universities and colleges (2018). https://www.tonybates.ca/2018/11/09/new-enrolment-data-for-online-learning-in-canadian-universities-and-colleges/
3. Lehman, R.M., Conceição, S.C.O.: Concerns and opportunities for online student retention. In: Lehman, R.M., Conceição, S.C.O. (eds.) Motivating and Retaining Online Students: Research-Based Strategies That Work. Wiley, San Francisco (2014)
4. Bates, T.: What are the key online learning markets over the next few years (2019). https://www.tonybates.ca/2019/05/19/what-are-the-key-online-learning-markets-over-the-next-few-years/
5. Bates, T.: Rethinking the purpose of online learning for developing skills for a digital society (2019). https://www.tonybates.ca/2019/04/30/rethinking-the-purpose-of-online-learning-4-developing-skills-for-a-digital-society/
6. Childs, E., Van Oostveen, R., Flynn, K., Clarkson, J.: Community building in online PBL courses: instigating criticality. In: Higher Education in Transformation Conference, Dublin, Ireland, pp. 499–508 (2015). https://arrow.dit.ie/st6/3/
7. Blayone, T., van Oostveen, R., Barber, W., DiGiuseppe, M., Childs, E.: Democratizing digital learning: theorizing the fully online learning community model. Int. J. Educ. Technol. High. Educ. **14**(1), 13 (2017). https://doi.org/10.1186/s41239-017-0051-4
8. Moore, M.G.: Theory of transactional distance. In: Keegan, D. (ed.) Theoretical Principles of Distance Education. Routledge, New York (1993)
9. Savin-Baden, M.: A Practical Guide to Problem-Based Learning Online. Routledge, New York (2007)
10. Desjardins, F.: Les représentations des enseignants quant à leurs profils de compétences relatives à l'ordinateur: vers une théorie des TIC en éducation. Can. J. Learn. Technol./La revue canadienne de l'apprentissage et de la technologie, **31**(1) (2005)
11. Watts, M.: The Science of Problem- Solving: A Practical Guide for Science Teachers. Heinemann Education Books, Portsmouth (1991)
12. Blayone, T.: Readiness for digital learning: examining self-reported and observed mobile competencies as steps toward more effective learner readiness assessment. Unpublished thesis (2017)

On the Development of a Model to Prevent Failures, Built from Interactions with Moodle

Bruno Cabral(✉) and Álvaro Figueira(✉)

CRACS/INESCTEC, University of Porto, Rua do Campo Alegre 1021/55, Porto, Portugal
bruno.m.cabral@inesctec.pt, arf@dcc.fc.up.pt

Abstract. In this article we propose an automatic system that informs students of abnormal deviations of a virtual learning path that leads to the best grades in the course. Our motivation is based on the fact that by obtaining this information earlier in the semester, may provide students and educators an opportunity to resolve an eventual problem regarding the student's current online actions towards the course. Our goal is therefore to prevent situations that have a significant probability to lead to a pour grade and, eventually, to failing. Our methodology can be applied to online courses that integrate the use of an online platform that stores user actions in a log file, and that has access to other student's evaluations. The system is based on a data mining process on the log files and on a self-feedback machine learning algorithm that works paired with the Moodle LMS. Our results shown that it is possible to predict grade levels by only taking interaction patterns in consideration.

Keywords: Data mining · e-Learning · Grade prediction · Student learning path

1 Introduction

Nowadays, students are increasingly being evaluated using online platform. As such, educators had to change their teaching methods by making the transition from paper to digital media. The use of a diverse set of questions, ranging from questionnaires to open questions, is common in most college courses. In many courses today, the assessment methodology also promotes student participation in forums, downloading and uploading modified files, or even participation in group activities.

In the major learning management systems currently available, the interaction between the students and the system itself is stored in log files in the form of registers that mark beginning of actions performed by the user. Using the logged information, and new one computed by our system, such as the time each student spends on an activity, the number and order of resources used, the amount of interaction with other student's by means of messaging/posting forum answers/questions, and particularly, the access versus time of access to all proposed activities, to build a table that a machine learning algorithm can learn from, using already human assigned grades. Using patterns of access to resources we equipped the system with features to prevent a cold-star, and make predictions on a student's final grade by analyzing his behavior.

M. A. Herzog et al. (Eds.): ICWL 2019, LNCS 11841, pp. 352–356, 2019.
https://doi.org/10.1007/978-3-030-35758-0_37

Data was collected from the course DPI1001, also known as Technical Communication, of a bachelor's degree course in Computer Science. The main objective is to prepare students for "technical communication", especially in the areas of writing and evaluating articles, creating presentations and conducting oral presentations.

It heavily relies on Moodle as an intermediary between the students and the teacher. This platform was used to facilitate access to lectures files, work assignments, quizzes, templates and forums, where the students were able to discuss amongst themselves about lectured material, all under the watchful eye of the teacher. It also provided a centralized tool, for assignments/article submission and evaluations.

Students were evaluated in five stages. The first three stages were exams done via Moodle. The next stage, consisted of group work, where groups of 4 or 5 students made a set of slides regrading a given subject. The last stage was done individually and was the creation of an article, submissions were all done via Moodle.

The population consisted of the registered students who used Moodle, to access resources or participate in activities related to Technical Communication course. The collected data has registered data regarding, 90416 interactions between 522 students and the online platform, between the years 2015 and 2018.

2 Related Work

Moodle represents a modular object-oriented dynamic learning environment. This platform constitutes a Learning Management System (LMS). It's very easy to setup and use, with the advantage of being Open-Source, meaning that the community can help improve the platform without direct intervention of the developers. Most of these types of platforms are capable of keeping a recollection of every action performed.

Figueira [2] in 2016 tried to establish a relation between the usage of an LMS with the results in a course. More recently in 2019, Nam Liao et al. [3], presented a study describing a student alert system that used data collected by a clicker and a Support Vector Machine to alert student about their academic behavior which will lead to a failing grade. Conijn et al. [1], uses multiple courses to gather information to be used in the dataset. However, this creates a problem; as it cannot be ensured that the multiple courses, being studied, have the same approach and assign the same significance to the LMS in the learning process. Naturally, we can assume that different teachers have different methods of lecturing, using online environments, and evaluation methodologies. Therefore, it can be concluded that by analyzing data collected from various classes, all diverging from each other, is impossible to maintain a small degree of variation in the environment in which the data was collected. Moreover, the referred study also concluded that the portability of the predictive model between different courses is not reliable, there was too much variation in usage, dependency and importance, each class gave to the LMS. On the other hand, the studies concluded that this type of models can still be successfully applied to a single course. It is concluded that the smaller the variation in course structure the more accurate the predictions of a grade.

3 Predictive Modelling

To determine patterns that can lead to a specific grade we used a set of derived features. Activity Time (AT), which counts the number of minutes to access the group choice and registration for oral presentation activities after being made available. Before Test (BT), sub-divided in to BT1, BT2 and BT3. Each indicates the number of days, between the first access to the Lecture's, and the day of the respective quiz. The. Forum count's the number of entries related with the use of Forum. Time In/Out the Danger Zone (TIDZ and TODZ), represents the number of times submissions occur near the "danger zone", which was defined as being 10 min before the end of a deadline. Total Time Online (TTO), counts the number of minutes spent on the platform. Finally, SUM represents the similarity between one student's academic path and the closest resembling student whose grade is higher than 17.

To achieve this similarity factor, we used a process of Run-length encoding (RLE), which is a simple form of data compression, where "runs" (consecutive data elements) are replaced by the number of occurrences and the respective data value. Instead of the number of occurrences we used the time spent in that activity, in minutes.

Our approach relies on a transformation of all the sequences of activities, done by a student in a single day, into strings consisting of numbers and letters. So being that a single day of activities is represented by a single string. This process generates 103 strings per student, as each semester consists of 103 days.

Once a new format is obtained, we determined the similarities between the academic paths of two students, using the Euclidean distance to determine a match. When a match was found, we tracked the amount of different activities a student visited and how much time, in minutes, he spent in every activity when compared to the match. The final value is divided, by the number of seconds in an hour.

Applying this formula for each day and by adding all the values we obtain the final value of SUM, which indicates the similarity between the current student and the ideal high achieving match.

4 Results

After obtaining the features we, applied a decision tree algorithm. In which the target variables are four classes (using a 0 to 20 grade scale): class a, grades from 0 to 9, class b from 10 to 14, class c from 15 to 17 and finally class d grades 18 through 20.

The original dataset is divided in to two datasets, the train (70%), and test (30%). The train dataset is used to instruct the model on how to obtain a correct prediction, the algorithm analyses the features and determines the resulting class. Using the test dataset, the algorithm analyses the feature and makes prediction of what the class values should be. A comparison is then established between the predicted target variable obtained by the algorithm and the actual values, generating the results in Fig. 1.

Class	F Score	Accuracy Rate	Misclassification Rate	Precision	Recall	Data Size
a	0,461	0,903	0,097	0,667	0,353	51
b	0,831	0,737	0,263	0,746	0,94	300
c	0,373	0,845	0,154	0,69	0,256	78
d	0	0,988	0,012	0	0	5

Fig. 1. Class summary

By analyzing the obtained values, we can observe that the model is not able of identifying students that constitute class d, this is explained by the reduce number of case studies, only 5, which is not enough to allow the model to make prediction.

The results clearly show that despite class d, being unidentifiable by the tree, we can still identify the remaining classes with a high precision rate, in part due to the high data size associated with class a, b and c. We can verify the low misclassification rate and the high accuracy rate. It's concluded that given the right amount of data the model, can make a reliable prediction on the final grade of the students, providing that those grades are all grouped in predefined sets (grade-zone).

5 Conclusion and Future Work

In this paper we described a methodology that is capable of analyzing students' interactions with the online platform and extract relevant features from those interactions. Consequently, we used those features to create a machine learning model, in this case a decision tree. Ultimately, the automatically built decision-tree has be able to predict (by classification) what potentially will be the final grade-zone obtained by a given student. By ensuring that the lectures from which the data is collected, are similar, leads to better predictions to be made by the model. The lectures should have the same structure, follow the same evaluation methods and integrate the online platform in similar ways. New tests are also being executed, including new features, the correct identification of class d and improve the detection of the remaining classes.

Future work consists in the integration of new features and the use of balanced training sets. These new additions will increase the precision rate of the model and at the same time reduce the misclassification rate, making the model more relevant and able of classifying a bigger set of entries.

Acknowledgements. This work is financed by National Funds through the Portuguese funding agency, FCT – "Fundação para a Ciência e a Tecnologia", within the project: UID/EEA/50014/2019.

References

1. Conijn, R., Snijders, C., Kleingeld, A., Matzat, U.: Predicting student performance from LMS data: a comparison of 17 blended courses using moodle LMS. IEEE Trans. Learn. Technol. **10**(1), 17–29 (2017)

2. Figueira, Á.: Predicting grades by principal component analysis a data mining approach to learning analytics. In: IEEE 16th International Conference on Advanced Learning Technologies (ICALT), pp. 465–467. IEEE, Austin (2016)
3. Nam Liao, S., Zingaro, D., Thai, K., Alvarado, C., Griswold, W.G., Porter, L.: A robust machine learning technique to predict low-performing students. ACM Trans. Comput. Educ. (TOCE) **19**(3), 18:1–18:19 (2019)

Correction to: Does Group Size Affect Students' Inquiry and Collaboration in Using Computer-Based Asymmetric Collaborative Simulations?

Meeli Rannastu, Leo Aleksander Siiman, Mario Mäeots,
Margus Pedaste, and Äli Leijen

Correction to:
Chapter "Does Group Size Affect Students' Inquiry and Collaboration in Using Computer-Based Asymmetric Collaborative Simulations?" in: M. A. Herzog et al. (Eds.): *Advances in Web-Based Learning – ICWL 2019*, LNCS 11841, https://doi.org/10.1007/978-3-030-35758-0_14

The original version of the chapter 14 was previously published non-open access. It has now been changed to open access under a CC BY 4.0 license and the copyright holder has been updated to 'The Author(s).' The book has also been updated with the change.

The updated version of this chapter can be found at
https://doi.org/10.1007/978-3-030-35758-0_14

M. A. Herzog et al. (Eds.): ICWL 2019, LNCS 11841, p. C1, 2020.
https://doi.org/10.1007/978-3-030-35758-0_38

Author Index

The manufacturer's authorised representative in the EU is Springer
Nature Customer Service Centre GmbH, Europaplatz 3, 69115 Heidelberg,
Germany. If you have any concerns regarding our products, please
contact ProductSafety@springernature.com

Printed and bound by CPI Group (UK) Ltd, Croydon, CR0 4YY
30/09/2026
02225195-0018